PAYING for
contribution

PAYING for contribution

contribution

real performance-related pay strategies

Duncan BROWN

MICHAEL ARMSTRONG

KOGAN PAGE

Apart from any fair dealing for the purposes of research or private study, or criticism or review, as permitted under the Copyright, Designs and Patents Act 1988, this publication may only be reproduced, stored or transmitted, in any form or by any means, with the prior permission in writing of the publishers, or in the case of reprographic reproduction in accordance with the terms and licences issued by the CLA. Enquiries concerning reproduction outside these terms should be sent to the publishers at the undermentioned addresses:

Kogan Page Limited
120 Pentonville Road
London N1 9JN, UK

Kogan Page (US) Limited
163 Central Avenue, Suite 4
Dover NH 03820, USA

British Library Cataloguing in Publication Data

A CIP record for this book is available from the British Library.
ISBN 0 7494 2899 6

Typeset by Saxon Graphics Ltd, Derby
Printed and bound in Great Britain by Biddles Ltd, Guildford and King's Lynn

Contents

Acknowledgements

We are indebted and grateful to many people who helped us with this book.

First, to colleagues and clients who provided us with ideas and inspiration, and particularly to all those organizations and the people at them who contributed case material for us. These included Amanda Stainton, Robert Nuttall, Brian Dive, Chris Pryke, Steve Kear, Martin Ferber, Bill Shirra, Martin Neville, Peter Timmins, Phil Hooper, David Watson and Tim Wilson.

Second, to our publishers, Kogan Page, and to the journals and organizations who let us use their material in support of our findings, in particular Industrial Relations Services.

Third, a very special thanks to Helen Nagle who typed all the text, somehow alongside and on top of her day job. And finally to our families, for their support and understanding.

Thank you all.

Preface

THE EVOLUTION TO PAYING FOR CONTRIBUTION

During the 1980s individual performance-related pay had been one of the most well-supported and visible symbols of the seismic changes occurring in the political, economic and employment landscape in the United Kingdom. The 1970s' rigidities of fixed, negotiated general increases, incremental pay drift and flat rate 'bonuses' and supplements were rapidly supplanted by an advancing tide of new performance-related base pay increase and annual bonus schemes.

Personnel Management magazine bade 'Farewell to internal equity as companies reward merit'. The driving forces included globalization and increasing international competition, the Conservative Party's ideology of free-market individualism, and the spread of US Human Resource Management ideas.

Margaret Thatcher's government extended this private sector trend into the public sphere, with the break-up of national bargaining units and the Treasury's insistence on individual performance-related pay as a condition of pay budget funding for Departments.

There can be no doubt that the philosophy and growing application of performance-related pay played an important part in the shift in the United

Kingdom from passive, reactive pay administration to active, strategic reward management. It helped transform pay and benefits from being an isolated technical specialism into a strategic lever used in our larger organizations to support the achievement of business goals.

Yet by the mid-1990s the whole individual performance-driven pay edifice had apparently come crashing down. Academics, journalists and conference speakers everywhere appeared to have written off performance-related pay as a demonstrated and universal failure, a 1980s' aberration from the 'greed is good' decade, out of place in the faster-moving, more complex, team-oriented and 'softer' 1990s.

A string of research studies revealed the damage created by performance-related pay schemes. It was demotivating; it was badly managed; it bore no relation to organization performance, and was actually detrimental to it, with damaging effects on teamwork and quality; and in times of low inflation it failed even to differentiate effectively. There were some well-publicized withdrawals of schemes, and the 1997 Barclays Bank dispute, apparently, confirmed the difficulties. Reward writers have increasingly championed alternative approaches: team rewards, skill and competency-related pay, wholly market-driven systems, and so on.

Yet what we have found in our research for this book, and in our consulting work, is that individual performance-related pay is far from being in its death throes. Its advance is less rapid, but it continues to be a prime and extending feature of the pay landscape for the majority of UK and US employees and it is increasingly in evidence in continental Europe as well. More competency-related, team-based and market-driven pay approaches are being applied in addition to, and in conjunction with, individual performance-related pay, not instead of it.

Indeed, we argue in the book that many employers have no choice in the new millennium but to pay for performance in some way. Ever more intense international competition, cost pressures and technological change, in our increasingly service sector-oriented economies, make effective use of an employer's pay bill and its link to company performance and funding inescapable. And in principle at least, surely people who perform well and are more skilled and competent than the average employee should be paid more?

PAYING FOR CONTRIBUTION

However, the performance-related pay methods of the late 1990s are in many instances very different from the predominant model of the 1980s, indeed the whole approach is often distinct (see Table 0.1). The lessons of applying a relatively homogeneous, rigid, formulaic and top-down approach to our increasingly complex, empowered and rapidly changing organizations have apparently been learned. Indeed, while we could probably have summarized the main types of merit and performance pay schemes 1980s' style in a single chapter, a whole book now presents a challenge in trying to characterize this increasingly diverse and complex field.

These late 1990s' variants have evolved so far from their 1980s' forebears that we regard them as a different species. We have christened the contemporary approach as paying for contribution, a nomenclature, which as you will see from the examples described in later chapters, is becoming increasingly common amongst UK organizations, rather than performance-related pay. Our aim is to demonstrate that this is not just performance-pay 'old wine in new bottles', but a manifestly distinct approach, characterized in particular by:

- paying for *how* results are achieved, as well as the results themselves, paying for competence as well as performance;
- paying for those skills and behaviours supporting the future success of the individual and the organization, not just immediate past results;
- rewarding a combination of organization, team and individual performance, rather than concentrating wholly on the latter;
- the use of a broad variety of reward vehicles;
- a long-term evolutionary approach, incorporating a variety of HR systems and processes, rather than attempting a pay 'quick fix';
- addressing all aspects of reward strategy: the objectives and goals, the design and systems, and the implementation and operation, rather than just focusing on the design mechanics.

AN INTEGRATED, STRATEGIC REWARD APPROACH

Paying for contribution, in our view, should form part of an integrated and strategic approach to reward. This needs to flow from, and support, the business strategy; be related to the needs of all key stakeholders; and use an appropriate mix of total rewards. Although this book very much concentrates on pay, this does not mean that we underestimate the importance of non-financial rewards as a means of motivating and recognizing high contribution in your organization. This may be through the opportunity to use and develop skills, the scope for personal growth, increases in responsibility, a collegiate

Table 0.1 *Comparison of 1980s style pay for performance approaches with pay for contribution*

	Pay for Performance	Paying for Contribution
Organizing Philosophy	formulas, systems	processes
HR approach	instrumentalist, people as costs	commitment, people as assets
Measurement	pay for results, the 'whats', achieving individual objectives	multi-dimensional, pay for results and 'how' results are achieved
Measures	financial goals cost efficiency	broad variety of strategic goals: financial, service, operating etc added value
Focus of measurement	individual	multi-level: business, team, individual
Design	uniform merit pay and/or individual bonus approach throughout the organization	diverse approaches using wide variety of reward methods, to suit the needs of different areas/staff groups
Time-scales	immediate past performance	past performance, and contribution to future strategic goals
Performance management	past review and ratings focus top down quantitative	mix of past review and future development 360° quantitative and qualitative
Pay linkage	fixed formula, matrix	looser, more flexible linkages, pay 'pots'
Administration	controlled by HR	owned/operated by line/users
Communication and involvement	top down, written	face-to-face, open, high involvement
Evaluation of effectiveness	act of faith	regular review and monitoring against clearly defined success criteria
Changes over time	regarded as failure; all or nothing	regular incremental modification

sense of belonging and contributing to something important and successful, and non-financial forms of recognition. Alongside paying for contribution, these are powerful motivators and should play an important part in an integrated system of total rewards management.

PLAN OF THE BOOK

The first section of the book sets out our case for the continuing relevance and application, but also the evolution of individual performance-related pay (PeRP). In Chapter 1 we give a more in-depth consideration to the paradoxes of PeRP and also provide a framework of definitions and the terminology we use. The book is very much aimed at practising managers and while it hopefully avoids some of the academic, turgid, theoretical debates and hair-splitting evident in this area, a clear understanding of terms such as performance, competence and contribution is essential.

In Chapter 2 we consider what is really happening with PeRP in the UK and internationally. We review the data demonstrating its continued spread and relevance, consider the evidence as to its effectiveness, describe common problems highlighted by research studies, and chart the evolution into paying for contribution.

We devote the rest of the book to drawing out the major trends and threads in paying for contribution. A key feature of paying for contribution is that it is at least as much about pay processes as about designs or systems. US compensation expert Ed Lawler[1] identifies three elements in any reward system:

- the policy goals (Why are we doing this? How does it support business objectives?);
- the design mechanics (Is merit pay right for us? What about team bonuses?);
- the reality of operation (Does it work in practice? How well will we implement changes?).

As shown in Chapter 2, many of the research studies on performance-related pay found that the problems were largely in the first and third categories, not the design one. The goals of the schemes were often not clear, agreed nor accepted (nor even performance-related in some cases), and even more critically, the schemes did not operate in practice as intended. They were often badly managed and communicated, having been implemented in a top-down and inflexible manner.

Paying for contribution is not just a new set of pay scheme designs or delivery vehicles, but a broader approach to performance pay in which companies are addressing these strategic and process failings.

The second section of the book considers that initial, critical component in Lawler's reward model: the strategy, the why. Chapter 3 looks at this concept of reward strategy in detail. It demonstrates that individual performance-related pay has become a lower priority. It shows how companies are working more holistically to improve the links between their organization's strategic goals and performance, and the work, contribution and results of their employees, through a wide variety of more effective and truly performance-related pay and reward schemes.

The third section considers the 'What', the design mechanics of the next generation of performance pay schemes, resulting from these new reward strategies. It also reviews how competency-related base pay schemes and bonus plans are evolving so as to ensure pay is effectively related to past and future performance.

Chapter 4 reviews developments in the area of competency-related pay. We review the strengths and weaknesses of the approach and demonstrate that it is rarely used in a pure form, but is generally being introduced in conjunction with, rather than as an alternative to, pay for performance. One of the key components of paying for contribution is paying for future as well as past performance, and paying for the 'how' as well as the 'what'.

Chapter 5 looks at changes to systems of individual performance-related base pay increase, often referred to as merit pay schemes, and shows how companies are trying to introduce greater variability and flexibility. Chapter 6 considers variable pay and bonus schemes, and how these are increasingly focusing on rewarding team and multi-level and dimensional performance. We show that in some instances, the traditional divide between base pay and bonus schemes related to performance is breaking down.

The fourth section of the book moves on to look at the 'Hows' of paying for contribution, the process improvements to pay for performance. Chapter 7 considers trends and examples in performance management, the linchpin of any effective pay-for-performance scheme. Significant developments here in terms of the purpose and balance in performance management processes, the criteria reviewed, and even the identity of reviewers, have all supported the shift towards contribution pay.

Chapter 8 reviews the important role of communications and involvement. Paying for contribution involves employees themselves making a major input and having a significant stake. We consider not only the forms of communications and involvement, but also the broader employment relationship in which the pay system operates. We demonstrate that effective pay for contribution depends on an open and trusting employment climate.

Chapter 9 considers the management of pay. It profiles the shift away from uniform, formula-driven performance pay schemes, centrally controlled by the HR function, to devolved ones operated at the local level by line managers. It considers how to achieve an effective balance between locally flexible and diverse, and centrally co-ordinated and controlled schemes.

The book is particularly aimed at these responsible for performance pay systems, whether in terms of introducing them, or experiencing and managing some of the difficulties we document. Each chapter contains plenty of case material and examples, while Chapter 10 gives a more detailed, practical guide to auditing, introducing and reforming performance pay schemes in your own organization.

In the concluding section, Chapter 11 summarizes the key reward strategy, design and process trends we have identified. It argues that we need to adopt a broader and more holistic view of reward strategy, as well as performance-related pay, to produce truly effective and contributing pay schemes.

AIMS

The real rub of paying for contribution, and the importance we believe of this book, is at this strategic level. In the new millennium, employee contribution will be recognized as, genuinely, the only long-term sustainable source of competitive advantage across virtually all sectors of the economy. As a Utility Chief Executive put it, very simply, during our research 'to be a world-class company we have to have the most competent, the most committed people'.

Paradoxically, the whole role and existence of the HR function, the supposed specialists in pay and people management, appear to be being called increasingly into question in the late 1990s. As Thomas Stewart[2] put it recently in *Fortune Magazine*, 'They don't add anything... nuke them.' In response to such accusations, Bruce Ellig, Head of Human Resources and reward management expert at Pfizer,[3] has defined three ways in which the HR function must contribute if it is to develop and thrive in the future. Its policies, he writes, must contribute to:

- aligning employee behaviour with strategic goals through appropriately designed HR policies and practices;
- higher levels of cost effectiveness through appropriately servicing internal customers;
- defining and supporting the appropriate culture and values.

We regard paying for contribution as a key means by which the HR function can demonstrate its own essential purpose and contribution, with an impact on all three areas. Perhaps most importantly of all, it is also a means by which organizations can fully develop and exploit the talents of their employees, with reward systems which reinforce business and cost goals, yet are part of a genuinely humanistic and supportive people strategy. This book is dedicated to HR professionals and practitioners out there who are striving themselves, every day, to improve their own contribution in this way.

NOTES

1. Lawler III, EE (1994) Effective reward systems, in A Howard (ed)*Diagnosis for Organizational Change: Methods and models*, Guilford Press, New York
2. Stewart, TA (1996) Taking on the last bureaucracy, *Fortune Magazine,* 15 January
3. Ellig, BR (1996) Don't write off the HR function, *Compensation and Benefits Review*, September/October

1

The performance-related pay paradox

Financial rewards are one of the most complex areas of managing. We preach equity and fairness, yet most reward systems are unfair. We preach transparency yet have persistent anomalies.

(Professor John Hunt)[1]

Charles Handy called this 'The Age of Paradox', and explaining and addressing the paradox of individual performance-related pay is the mission of this book which we authors, and indeed many employers, face. How is it that when the pressures to relate pay to performance in our organizations have never been greater, and when the majority of UK employees are subject to systems which claim the relationship, we face such an overwhelming and apparently unanimous barrage of criticism of such systems: from academia, research institutes, conference platforms and the press? We need to do it, we are doing it but individual performance-related pay, apparently, simply does not work.

In this chapter we consider this paradox in more detail and demonstrate just how intractable a dilemma it appears to be, which is perhaps not surprising given the controversy over the motivational theory on which performance-related pay (PeRP) rests. We describe the continuing importance of paying for performance, and the spread of pay schemes in the 1980s, followed by the critical reaction in the 1990s. We demonstrate the contradictory attitudes many of us hold towards PeRP.

Our mission is not with the theory but the practice, however, and so we set out towards the end of this chapter the key practical questions and issues that we attempt to address and answer in the rest of the book. We also, necessarily, define the main remuneration terms and types of scheme which we refer to in the area, so as to avoid at least one common source of confusion.

THE IMPORTANCE OF PeRP

Looking at the most publicized UK pay developments in a single month (May 1998) vividly demonstrates the essential requirement in our ever more global and rapidly changing economies to establish a close relationship between an organization's performance and its pay costs.

- Chancellor Gordon Brown saw the UK private sector earnings growth of 5.6 per cent as giving 'serious cause for concern',[2] threatening the competitiveness of the UK economy and the maintenance of price stability; in June the Bank of England cited wage increases outstripping productivity growth as the prime justification for an increase in interest rates and Employment and Education Secretary David Blunkett said that rising wages could, 'destroy the enormous prize of economic growth and stability'.
- Management consultancy McKinsey published a study demonstrating that despite the improvements of the 1980s, and despite lower unit labour costs, UK productivity across virtually all economic sectors was some 20 per cent behind Germany and 40 per cent behind prevailing US levels.[3]
- Vauxhall Motors[4] followed its sister company Opel in introducing a long-term pay deal incorporating radical changes in pay and working practices, designed to improve flexibility, productivity and cost effectiveness. This included a link between the level of overall pay increase and the strength of sterling, so employees share some of the risks of the global economy faced by shareholders. At the same time managing director Nick Reilly voluntarily reduced his own base pay level.

The motor industry presents a good example of the competitive pressures which have forced similar changes in pay and working practices across many sectors. The threat in a ruthlessly competitive European market from Far East manufacturers, and the opportunities for an increasingly concentrated set of globally organized companies to shift production to lower cost locations (VW in Eastern Europe), or closer to new markets (Mercedes and BMW in the United States), means that the European firms simply cannot afford to have uncompetitive wage costs which are out of line with the productivity and performance of alternative locations. BMW has instigated a series of changes in working and pay practices at Rover in the United Kingdom to close the 30 per cent productivity gap between their manufacturing plants in the two countries. Between 5 per cent and 10 per cent of the wages of BMW's employees in Germany are now linked to the achievement of business unit targets.

In a Towers Perrin research study of privatized utilities[5] in the United Kingdom, the Operations Director of a water company explained the major cultural changes involved with the 'substantial increase in performance standards we require: changing our working methods, our traditions and attitudes, to focus on the customer and our financial goals'. In his view, reforming their hierarchical, complex and service-based pay systems represented 'the most important but also the most difficult set of changes we face' in making this transformation. Over 90 per cent of companies in that study had introduced performance pay schemes for managers since privatization, and 80 per cent had plans to extend it to professional and administrative staff. A number of the companies have since been taken over by US utilities, who have speeded up the process of introducing and extending individual performance-related pay systems.

Similarly, at international food and drinks company Cadbury, Personnel Director Keith Dennis' view is that the biggest change in Personnel over the last decade has been the need to support 'corporate performance transformation driven by the realization that competition was global'. He identifies the most significant policy change at Cadbury in support of this as 'a reward system realigned to individual performance'.[6]

With the expanding service and knowledge-based industries now employing more staff than manufacturing, these pressures have become even more intense. Staff can represent over 70 per cent of total costs in these sectors, and the professional and staff groups which predominate here, as we shall see, are those in which the growth of individual PeRP schemes has been most apparent. Thus in retailing, major blue-chip employers such as Marks and Spencer and Boots extended individual merit pay schemes right the way down to sales assistants on the shop floor.

For these reasons, Adair Turner, Director General of the CBI called in 1995 for members to operate more flexible and performance-based pay schemes, 'to control UK unit labour costs, keep UK economic growth on track and secure jobs'.[7] John Monks of the TUC agreed that, 'there is a relationship between pay, productivity and inflation' and said at the 1998 TUC conference that a central problem in the UK economy has been that pay rises have always run ahead of productivity increases.[8]

THE 1980s' SPREAD OF PeRP

IN THE PRIVATE SECTOR

Individual performance-related pay is of course as old as the industrial revolution itself in this country, and piecework systems for manual workers persist in a number of sectors. However, it was with the intensification of these competitive pressures following the recession of the early 1980s that individual performance-related pay systems began to spread rapidly for white-collar, professional and managerial staff in the United Kingdom.

Table 1.1 presents data from a variety of research studies[9] in the late 1980s and early 1990s indicating that between 50 per cent and 60 per cent of UK companies operated individual performance-related base pay systems by that time. A London School of Economics study, for example,[10] found that the proportion of companies using merit pay increased every year between 1986 and 1990, while the Policy Studies Institute found that 37 per cent of participants had been linking pay more closely to individual performance in the previous two years. Similarly, in respect of individually oriented management bonus plans, Figure 1.1 demonstrates the steady increase in their use by Financial Times Top 100 companies on Towers Perrin's survey database, peaking out when over 90 per cent of companies operated them in 1990.

Although individual performance pay is seen as being more well established in the United States, these figures are consistent with the data from the other side of the Atlantic. One study of Fortune 1000 companies between 1987 and 1993, for example,[11] found that the

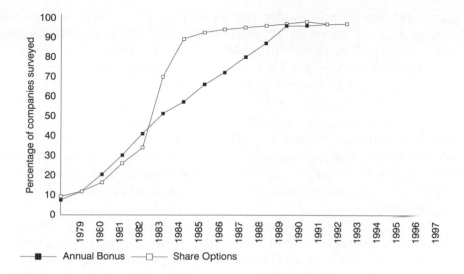

Figure 1.1 *Growth of executive annual bonus and share option schemes in the United Kingdom.*

Table 1.1 *Survey evidence on the use of individual-based performance pay in the United Kingdom in the early 1990s*

Study	Sample size	Percentage of organizations withPeRP	Sectors covered
EOC/IRS (1991)	150	62	private
Mercers (1990)	73	60	private
PSI (1990)	164	42	all sectors
IPM/IRS (1991)	204	30	all sectors
LACSAB (1989)	272	23	local government
IPM/NEDO (1992)	390	47	all sectors
IPM/IMS (1991)	860	54	all sectors
Poke (IPM) (1990)	186	61	private

Source: Mark Thompson

proportion using individual performance pay for more than 20 per cent of their workforce had increased from 38 per cent to 50 per cent.

However, it is important to stress that this movement was very much a white-collar phenomenon. The breakdown of incidence by occupational grouping in these surveys shows considerable variations, and only between 7 per cent and 15 per cent of organizations applied individual, appraisal-based performance pay to their manual workers. Table 1.2 shows the variations in application of different performance pay schemes by staff group amongst 638 companies in 1991.

Blinder[12] observes 'the tides of interest in performance pay plans have more to do with social, political and economic fashions than with any scientific evidence on how well they work'. Two other sets of factors, along with the economic, were important drivers of the UK expansion in performance pay. The first was the extended period of Conservative Party government throughout the 1980s with their ideology of free market individualism, and succession of legislative measures designed to weaken the collective power of the trade union movement.

Chancellor of the Exchequer Ken Clarke formally declared himself in favour of pay-for-performance and against the evils of job evaluation, grading structures and closed-shop bargaining. The rose-tinted language of the CBI's 1988 booklet *Managing People* gave clear expression to this individualistic philosophy, recommending pay systems 'focused on the needs and performance of individuals'. Its vision for the year 2000 was a world of 'open-ended contracts, where individuals are free to decide where and how they work and be rewarded for their performance'.

Kessler and Purcell's study[13] of performance pay in five organizations found evidence for these goals of 'stimulating cultural change',

Table 1.2 *Various types of performance pay by staff group*

Occupation	Profit sharing %	Appraisal- based individual merit pay %	Individual bonus %	Team bonus %	Share schemes %
Senior managers	41	54	36	6	36
Other managers	28	44	28	9	12
Other white collar workers	22	31	20	11	8
Manual workers	18	7	24	27	7

Note: IMS/IPM Survey 1991
N = 638)

'providing scope for the exercise of managerial control', and 'the individualisation of the employment relationship'.

IN THE PUBLIC SECTOR

Public sector corporations privatized during this era rapidly adopted what they saw as leading-edge and prevailing private sector practice, with 93 per cent of those in the Towers Perrin utilities study[14] introducing individual performance pay for management staff. However, the Conservative government helped to ensure that the spread of performance-related pay also extended into the public sector.

The Megaw Committee report of 1982 had supported the operation of performance-based systems, but the dismantling of national pay structures and bargaining arrangements in the Civil Service and local government under the 'Next Steps' initiative, and to a lesser extent through the NHS reforms, opened the way for a rapid uptake of individual performance pay. According to the Department of Trade and Industry, 'Public sector pay should be linked to performance, so that those who contribute most get the greatest share.' National Pay Review bodies were encouraged to apply such schemes, and a series of budget freezes and pay limits ensured that productivity and performance became the main drivers of public sector pay increases.

By the early 1990s the Treasury was making the introduction of individual performance pay schemes a condition of pay budget funding. By then government departments such as Customs and Excise and the Inland Revenue, public corporations such as the BBC and Nuclear Electric, local authorities such as Westminster and Surrey Councils, even the Royal Household, were all operating merit pay schemes. Some 70 per cent of NHS Trusts operated performance pay for senior managers by 1996. According to Hudson and Brown's research study, the rapidity of the take up demonstrated that these organizations 'behaved like lemmings'.[15]

The shifts in the ideology and identity of personnel management and the adoption of US-inspired Human Resources Management (HRM) ideas in the 1980s also gave ideological support to the performance pay trend, representing the third important driver. The emphasis placed on business-driven and aligned rather than employee-oriented personnel policies, and as Guest[16] observes, the individualist and unitarist focus of its values, all gave theoretical underpinning and reinforcement to the trend. So did the emphasis phased by US academics such as Beer on reward as an important policy change 'lever' within HRM.

Storey's[17] research demonstrated the widespread uptake of individual performance pay amongst a sample of companies regarded as being at the forefront of implementing HRM. For example, Mike Goodswen, then deputy general-manager of HR at National Westminster Bank, emphasized the important role which the implementation of individual performance pay in 1989 had played in reinforcing business planning and the achievement of business goals.

Whatever the sources and drivers therefore, the spread of individual merit pay was as Industrial Relations Services puts it, 'without doubt the big idea of late 1980s remuneration',[18] presented according to one leading authority on reward as, 'the single answer to motivating people and developing performance-related pay arrangements'.[19] Detailed job evaluation schemes, cost-of-living pay awards, fixed job rates and service-related increments were, it was claimed, being rapidly replaced by market-related base pay ranges and individual progression through them on the basis of personal performance. Of the 90 companies in Thompson's Institute of Employment Studies research,[20] 66 per cent had introduced PeRP in order to link pay to productivity and to control pay costs, while 50 per cent regarded it as more motivating to employees. But 17 per cent admitted their main motivation to be the example set by other companies.

THE 1990s' REACTION

The wisdom of Blinder's observation on the shifting tides of HR and reward practices appears to have been borne out by the 1990s' experience of individual performance-related pay. Given the expansion just described, there has been a remarkable reversal in commentaries on the practice, until we have reached the stage where the criticisms are so vehement and the lack of effectiveness so widely accepted, that it is hardly seen as an issue worth debating. According to Helen Hague, in the late 1990s it is, 'The end for merit pay': 'Far from rewarding performance it is demotivating staff and is inappropriate for professionals, damaging to teamwork and often applied unfairly... irrelevant to helping individuals and organisations in meeting their objectives'.[21]

Bill Callaghan, Chief Economist of the Trade Union Congress contrasted, at a 1996 Towers Perrin conference, the withdrawal of wholly quota-based payment systems for manual work as being detrimental to quality, teamwork and skills development, with the continued application of 'white-collar piecework'.

A variety of recent research studies and individual examples appear to bolster their case. An in-depth, longitudinal study of individual performance-related base pay at the Inland Revenue, updated in 1997, concluded that it 'reduces civil servants' motivation and makes them less willing to co-operate with colleagues and managers'.[22] Some 80 per cent of staff felt it had not improved the quality nor the quantity of their work. Similarly, the conclusions of a more wide-ranging study by the Industrial Society were that 'PeRP, hailed as one of the great drivers of productivity, has caused disruption and disappointment in many organizations'.[23]

Research in 1997 on performance management systems by the Institute of Personnel and Development[24] found that those linked directly to pay through performance rating were regarded as far less effective by staff than systems in those companies which did not link them to pay (see Chapter 7). A client study by Towers Perrin in a large IT company in the United Kingdom found that two-thirds of managers felt that their individual performance-based bonus scheme had no influence on their actions or performance, while a trade union study[25] of BT managers revealed that only 6 per cent felt PeRP had motivated performance improvement, compared to 70 per cent who felt it had not. Kessler and Purcell's research[26] demonstrated the gulf between the intentions and aims of performance pay, and the practical realities, in five organizations.

This lack of attractiveness for senior management and the economy was apparently confirmed by the absence of any relationship found between corporate performance and the use of PeRP in Thompson's research.[27] Indeed, a number of studies suggested that PeRP actually increased costs and that overall pay increases were consistently higher in organizations with all-merit as opposed to general/cost of living awards. Incomes Data Services[28] found that all-merit pay awards between 1992 and 1997, covering over 700,000 employees, were at least half a percentage point ahead of those in companies making flat rate general pay awards. In 1996 for example, the average general award was 3.2 per cent, the average all-merit review 4.1 per cent.

Certain individual and well-publicized cases in the press appear to back up these findings. Barclays Bank experienced the longest industrial dispute in UK financial services sector history in late 1997 and 1998 as they attempted to introduce a system of individual merit pay for branch staff. Yorkshire Bank experienced similar difficulties, while BT suspended the operation of its merit pay system for managerial and professional staff due to a lack of adequate funding.

Kerrygold and Glory Mill Papers went one step further and withdrew their systems altogether. Withdrawal has been most apparent in the public sector, where councils such as Lewisham, Sheffield, Kent and Coventry, and NHS trusts such as Southend and Portsmouth, have abandoned the approach.

Even in the United States, where according to *The Economist*, 'PeRP has been an article of faith for many years',[29] the reaction and criticisms have been increasingly evident. As Matthew Budman puts it, 'Your managers hate it, your employees hate it... nobody believes that traditional merit pay systems motivate people'.[30] Professor Jeffrey Pfeffer concurred: 'Individual performance pay in reality undermines teamwork, encourages a short-term focus and leads to compensation being linked to political skills and personality rather than performance'.[31]

In his view, 'Most merit-based systems share two attributes: they absorb vast amounts of management time, and they make everybody unhappy.' US Quality experts such as Edward Deming strongly opposed the use of such systems for providing incentives to cut quality, and as detrimental to team working.

Again, a variety of recent US studies and cases appear to lend support to the receding tide of PeRP. One longitudinal study into the introduction of merit pay schemes in 20 social security offices found that it had no demonstrable effect whatsoever on office productivity.[32] Meanwhile, Hatcher and Ross's study[33] in a US exhaust systems manufacturer demonstrated the improvements in productivity, quality and job satisfaction resulting from the shift from an individual to a team-based performance pay scheme.

Indeed, on both sides of the Atlantic, alternatives to individual performance-related pay, such as team-based and competency-related rewards, are increasingly being championed. Towers Perrin's 1997 study of recent and planned reward changes in 303 European organizations[34] found that paying for individual performance had been replaced as a top five reward priority by aims such as paying for competence, and rewarding teamwork. Some 70 per cent of the participants were planning to establish or reinforce the link between the development of essential skills, competencies and pay over the next three years, which Mike Redhouse, then of Guinness, described as 'the way tomorrow's organizations will pay'. 30 per cent of the participants were planning new or modified team-based reward schemes over the next three years.

A survey later in that year by Industrial Relations Services[35] of 240 UK organizations found very similar results. The number of participants using competency-related pay methods had increased over the past 12 months from 10 per cent to almost one in five. A further 18 per cent planned to introduce it in 1998, which represented the most frequently cited area of planned change in reward methods.

So, individual performance-related pay appears to be at the point of being intellectually and practically bankrupt: it has no positive effect on organization performance, and actually damages teamwork and quality; it doesn't motivate staff to high individual performance; and it is apparently on the point of being overtaken by other, more enlightened approaches. It is a remnant of the 'greed is good' decade, destined for the same fate as Milliken and Boesky and their paper-based investment vehicles, or the 'flash' entrepreneurs and their over-diverse conglomerates, fated to go the same way as Ratners, Blue Arrow and Coloroll.

THE PARADOX OF THE PRINCIPLE AND THE PRACTICE

Yet the final twist in this paradox of individual performance-related pay is that many of us still appear to support it. In the Towers Perrin European reward study, 96 per cent of HR Directors regarded individual performance as the number one factor that should influence pay increases (see Figure 1.2), ahead of other important issues such as competitive market position and external rates of increase. The Industrial Society's research[36] similarly found that 'three quarters of managers think that a desire to reward individual performance is the key factor driving the introduction of new reward strategies'.

Professor Laurence Handy of Ashridge concludes that there is 'a clear mismatch between organizational and individual belief in the value of PeRP'. We might say we are not influenced by it, but we believe our organizations should apply it. 'There was much soul-searching in the personnel department about performance-related pay and its effect on the motivation of staff' at the Abbey National, according to Human Resources Director John King, 'but it made no sense to have a system (of general increases) which did not underpin the business objectives, especially when you are attempting to change attitudes.'

And this contradiction extends well beyond the realms of HR Managers. An international water company's 1996 attitude study found that a majority of its staff supported the principal of PeRP and felt it had led to improved objective-setting and performance feedback. But only 10 per cent felt it had affected their own behaviour, and only 9 per cent said their system did actually reward superior performance. In a situation of comparatively low inflation and average awards of 3–4 per cent, the additional 2–3 per cent for exceptional performance was not seen as enough of an incentive for high performance.

Exactly the same pattern emerged from Towers Perrin's US Workplace Index, a biannual study of employee attitudes to a range of employment and reward issues among 1,200 staff in large US corporations.[37] Those employees who believe outstanding performance in their organizations is rewarded are more motivated to help their company succeed, and have a better understanding of the factors driving business success (see Figure 1.3). Yet only a minority, under 40 per cent of them, actually feel superior performance is rewarded by their organizations, while the number who feel they share in the success of their company declined over the prior two years.

Even in the public sector, where according to the critics the culture of public service and the relative absence of hard, financial performance measures had made PeRP so difficult to apply, this pattern is repeated. Some 76 per cent of Inland Revenue staff were not motivated in practice by PeRP, but 57 per cent agreed with the concept,[38] and a majority of those in French and Marsden's research felt that it had improved goal-setting. Similarly, an Institute of Health Service

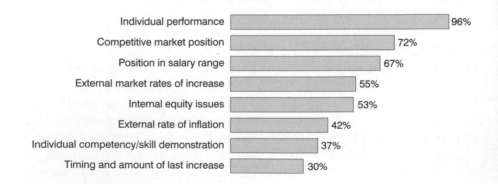

Figure 1.2 *Factors which European HR directors feel should influence the pay increases of their staff.*
Source: Towers Perrin

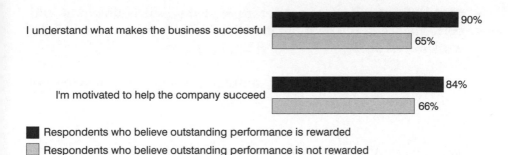

Figure 1.3 *Impact of performance pay schemes on employee motivation in the United States.*
Source: Towers Perrin

Management survey of 1,600 NHS managers found a majority in favour of PeRP in theory,[39] but opposed to their experience of it.

PERFORMANCE-RELATED PAY: THE QUESTIONS

In this chapter we have highlighted the paradoxes of performance-related pay: the apparently rapid shift from ideological championing and widespread adoption to the current position of apparent demotivation, failure and removal; and the contrast between the theory and the practice. The key questions our analysis has raised, which we aim to address in the remainder of this book are the following:

- To what extent are performance-related pay schemes actually being withdrawn in practice?
- Do PeRP schemes really motivate people and do they have any effect on individual and organizational performance?
- If they are failing, why are they failing?
- If individual performance-related pay is not appropriate, what should we be introducing instead?
- What is the relationship between individual PeRP and competency, team and other pay methods? Are the latter coming in to replace PeRP?
- Is there any one best system or approach to relating performance and pay, or is it totally dependent on the environment in which it operates?

- Should I introduce and operate systems which link pay and performance in my own organization? If so, how do I make them work in practice?

We return in the final chapter to summarize some of the answers we have discovered.

DEFINITIONS AND TERMINOLOGY

The debate and confusion over performance-related pay have often not been helped by the variations in the terminology employed. There are many different types of performance pay schemes and the Institute of Employment Studies makes a useful classification of them illustrated in Table 1.3.

Below we list our working definitions of the pay and performance terminology used in this book.

- *Performance pay*: The process of providing a financial or financially measurable reward to employees linked directly to individual, team or organizational performance, whether it be in the form of base pay or cash bonus payments.

Table 1.3 *Different types of performance-related pay*

| | | Organization level | | |
		Individual	Team	Organization
	Base pay adjustment	• merit pay • pay at risk	• team adjustment to base pay funding	• varying pay budget according to organization performance
Reward vehicle	Variable pay and bonuses	• executive bonus • individual bonus • piecework • sales commission	• team bonuses • project bonuses • gainsharing • location bonus	• profit sharing • gainsharing
	Other forms of reward	• individual non-cash recognition eg holidays • learning opportunities • executive share options	• team non-cash recognition	• corporate events • all employee share options

Source: Institute of Employment Studies

- *Individual performance-related pay (PeRP):* Any pay scheme which relates the award of a base pay increase or an individual cash bonus to the results achieved by that individual.
- *Merit pay:* A common name for schemes which relate individual base pay increases to the results delivered by each individual, most commonly through an individual appraisal of performance and award of a performance rating.
- *Competency-related pay:* Defined and considered in more detail in Chapter 4. Most typically these systems relate the base pay level and increase of a person to their demonstrated level of competence in doing their job, that is the required skills, behaviours and attributes which they need to display in order to perform highly. It therefore relates pay to how well someone does their job, as well as in some cases, the development and improvement in their personal level of competence.
- *Pay for contribution:* As defined in the introduction, a diverse, comprehensive, high involvement and flexible approach to pay, which employs a variety of tailored vehicles to reward the achievement of significant business, team and personal goals, and how those goals have been achieved.
- *Bonuses/variable pay:* Non-recurring cash lump sums related to the performance achieved by the individual, team and/or organization. Considered in more detail in Chapter 6.
- *Pay at risk:* Considered in Chapter 5. These schemes, in theory, involve employees giving up a proportion of their fixed base pay or base pay increase, in return for the opportunity to achieve higher pay levels according to the performance of their business. Correspondingly, if performance targets are not achieved, their base pay is actually reduced.
- *Profit sharing schemes:* Schemes which share a proportion of a company's profit with employees, typically on a common basis.
- *Approved profit related pay (PRP) schemes:* An Inland Revenue approved and tax-effective means of sharing the profits of a business with employees. In order to qualify for the tax relief, schemes have to comply with a detailed set of criteria. The tax relief on these schemes will be removed by year 2000.
- *Gainsharing schemes:* Bonus schemes which share a set proportion of any performance gains made above an agreed level, for example in the labour productivity of a factory, directly with employees. The higher the level of performance, the greater the gain for both the company and employees.

SUMMARY

- At the national, economic level, establishing effective links between pay, performance and productivity is regarded as increasingly important in our ever-more global and competitive world.
- In the late 1980s and early 1990s, schemes to establish linkages between pay and individual performance expanded rapidly in the United Kingdom. Between 50 and 60 per cent of companies introduced and operated such schemes. Conservative party ideology and the influence of US Human Resource management ideas encouraged the growth in incidence, in both private and public sectors.
- Yet by the late 1990s, individual performance-related pay is being strongly criticized by many commentators for being inflationary, demotivating and either having no effect, or a detrimental impact on company performance. A variety of well-publicized research studies and practical cases of companies having difficulty introducing merit pay have given weight to these criticisms. Other pay approaches such as team and competency-related pay are increasingly being advocated instead.
- This stark reversal of attitudes is not the only aspect of the performance pay paradox. Another is that managers and many employees still seem to support the principle of performance-related pay even if they argue that, in practice, it is either not rewarding high performers appropriately, or proving damaging to collective performance.
- This book attempts to provide some answers to this paradoxical situation.

NOTES

1. Hunt. JW (1998) A salary can't buy happiness, *The Financial Times*, 13 May
2. Adams, R (1998) Earnings rise rewakens inflation fears, *The Financial Times*, 13 May
3. Chote, R (1998) Poor management blamed for low output, *The Financial Times*, 15 May
4. Industrial Relations Services (1998) Vauxhall Motors, *Pay and Benefits Bulletin,* **448**, May
5. Towers Perrin (1994) *Improving Performance Through People: HR issues in the utility industry*, Towers Perrin Research Report, December 1994, available from Towers Perrin, London.
6. Dennis, K (1998) Under the microscope, *Centre Forward* (in-house magazine of Centrefile Ltd), Spring, London
7. Performance pay welcomed, *The Financial Times*, 4 October 1995
8. Taylor, R (1998) Monks new unionism, *The Financial Times*, 18 September 1998

9. All cited in Thompson, M (1992) *Pay and Performance: The employer's experience,* IMS Report No 218
10. Wood, S (1996) High commitment management and pay systems, *Journal of Management Studies,* January
11. Ledford, G (1996) Designing nimble reward systems, *Compensation and Benefits Review,* March/April
12. Blinder, AS (1989/90) Pay, participation and productivity, *The Brookings Review,* Winter
13. Kessler, I and Purcell, J (1992) Performance-related pay: objectives and application, *Human Resource Management Journal,* **2** (3), Spring
14. Towers Perrin Research Report, op. cit.
15. Reported in Jane Pickard (1997) Experts greet moves to collectivism, *People Management,* 24 July
16. Guest, D (1989) HRM's implications for industrial relations, in *New Perspectives on Human Resources Management,* ed J Storey, Routledge, London
17. Storey, J (1992) HRM in action, *Personnel Management,* April
18. Industrial Relations Services (1998) There is merit in merit pay, *Pay and Benefits Bulletin,* 445, April
19. Armstrong, M (1996) *Employee Reward,* IPD, London
20. Thompson, op. cit.
21. Hague, H (1996) The end for merit pay, *Personnel Today,* 4 August
22. Marsden, D and French, S (1998) *What a Performance: Performance-related pay in the public services,* London School of Economics Centre for Economic Performance, London
23. Donkin, R (1996) Performance pay criticised, *The Financial Times,* 11 March
24. Armstrong, M and Baron, A (1998) *Performance Management: The new realities,* Institute of Personnel and Development, London
25. Rewarding in secret, *The STE Review,* July 1991.
26. Kessler and Purcell, op. cit.
27. Thompson, op. cit.
28. Incomes Data Services (1997) General awards: fact and fiction, *Management Pay Review,* July
29. Just deserts, *The Economist,* 29 January 1994
30. Budman, M (1997) Is there merit in merit pay?, *Across the Board,* June
31. Pfeffer, J (1998) Six dangerous myths about performance pay, *The Harvard Business Review,* May/June
32. Referenced in Pfeffer, op. cit.
33. Ross, H (1991) From individual to organisational gainsharing, *Journal of Organisational Behaviour,* March
34. Towers Perrin (1997) *Learning from the Past, Changing for the Future,* research report from Towers Perrin, London, March
35. Industrial Relations Services (1997) Pay prospects for 1998, *Pay and Benefits Bulletin,* November
36. The Industrial Society (1996) *Rewarding Performance: Managing best practice,* Report No. 20, London
37. The 1997 Towers Perrin Workplace Index, available from Towers Perrin, London.
38. Inland Revenue Staff Association (1991) *Does Performance Pay Motivate?,* HMSO. London
39. Institute of Health Service Management (1991) *Individual Performance Review in the NHS,* research report, Institute of Health Service Management, London

2

Performance-related pay today: what's really happening?

Contrary to the popular belief that organizations are becoming disillusioned with it, the results strongly suggest that the use of all forms of PeRP are growing.

(IPD Research 1998)[1]

The performance-related pay movement was based on a false assumption: that organisations can be administered scientifically, that inequities and emotions can be squeezed out by applying a common, objective system.

(Professor John Hunt)[2]

In this chapter, we demonstrate quite clearly that performance-related pay is neither dead nor dying, but is continuing to be applied and grow. The prophets of doom quoted in the previous chapter have seen, to quote Aldous Huxley, 'a beautiful theory destroyed by a nasty little fact': performance pay continues to spread.

The research to support its effectiveness remains contradictory rather than uniformly negative, reflecting partly on the difficulty of isolating the practice from underlying motivational theories and its political and social context. However, the spread in incidence has undoubtedly slowed and the practical problems in implementation and operation are increasingly well recognized and documented. Performance-related pay is not dying, but it is changing.

CONTINUING APPLICATION AND GROWTH

IN THE UNITED KINGDOM

Surveying the late 1990s' UK reward environment, Judith Oliver's conclusion expressed in *Management Today* was that, 'UK companies continue to put their faith in pay for performance',[3] with between a half and two-thirds of organizations operating such systems for at least some groups of staff. A wide variety of research studies support her conclusion.

The largest contemporary survey of 1,158 organizations covering 1.5 million employees, was undertaken by the Institute of Personnel and Development, published in 1998:[4] 40 per cent of the participants operated merit pay systems, although over half of the private sector companies did so (see Figure 2.1). It remains considerably more popular than the alternative reward strategies we saw advocated in the previous chapter, and the study clearly demonstrates that practices such as team and competency-related pay are growing *alongside*, not instead of, individual performance pay. The annual cessation rate of the practice was less than 3 per cent, and fewer than 10 per cent of companies had plans to abandon it, while 59 per cent of operating schemes had been introduced within the last five years. Finally, the proportion of the workforce covered by individual performance pay in these companies had increased to a median of 70–80 per cent, which was also much higher than for team or competency-related pay.

Other studies support these conclusions and suggest a higher general incidence. A survey by *Personnel Today*[5] found that 67 per cent of participants operated merit pay schemes, which were, 'still the most widely-used pay adjustment mechanisms by UK companies, and are generally seen as an effective performance motivator' (see Figure 2.2).

A larger study in late 1997 of 240 organizations by Industrial Relations Services[6] showed individual merit pay systems to be over-

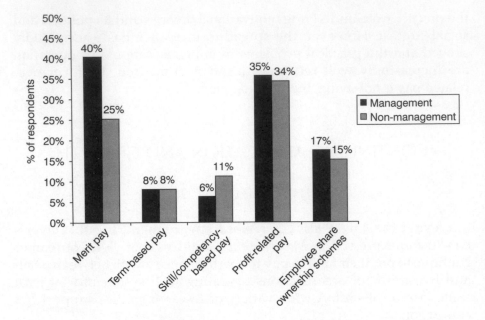

Figure 2.1 *Incidence of performance pay schemes in the United Kingdom, 1997*
Source: IPD

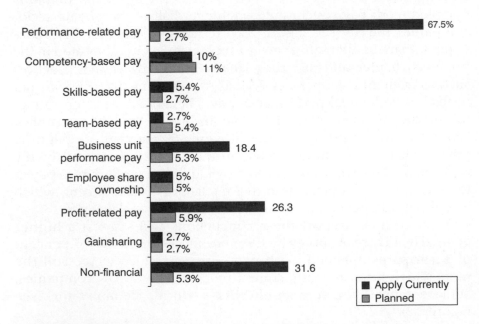

Figure 2.2 *Incidence of various performance pay delivery vehicles*
Source: Personnel Today

whelmingly the most common component of companies' reward strategies. They were employed by 70 per cent of them (see Table 2.1) compared to 63 per cent two years previously. Thus, 100 per cent of financial sector organizations, 73 per cent of engineering and 62 per cent of other service sector organizations applied it, while across the whole sample, 13 per cent had plans to introduce or extend it over the next twelve months. According to an earlier study which IRS carried out,[7] 87 per cent of managers, 57 per cent of professionals and 41 per cent of clerical staff were covered, although the expansion had not affected manual workers, whose pay was performance- based in only 9 per cent of cases.

Continued growth but varied incidence by sector and employee group is confirmed by Incomes Data Services research.[8] Looking at 400 UK organizations they found that the proportion of all-merit pay awards in the United Kingdom had continued to slowly expand up to 1996, but that there was a marked shift to this pay adjustment method in the service sectors, and particularly in financial services, where the proportion had more than doubled since 1990 (see Figure 2.3).

Another *Personnel Today* study[9] in 1998 found a majority of organizations using merit pay, but the incidence by sector varied from 41 per cent in government to 72 per cent in financial services. Incidence also related

Table 2.1 *Current and planned incidence of various reward strategy components*

Reward strategy	Current strategies % of all respondents	Planned changes % of all respondents
Merit pay	70.0	12.9
Market-based pay	47.9	6.7
Inland Revenue-registered profit-related pay	41.3	3.3
Broadbanding	31.7	14.6
Incentive pay/bonuses	30.0	7.5
Competency-based pay	18.8	18.3
Profit sharing	18.3	6.3
Skills-based pay	14.2	7.9
Team reward	8.8	12.1
Gainsharing	2.9	2.5

Source: Industrial Relations Services
Note: Sample size = 240

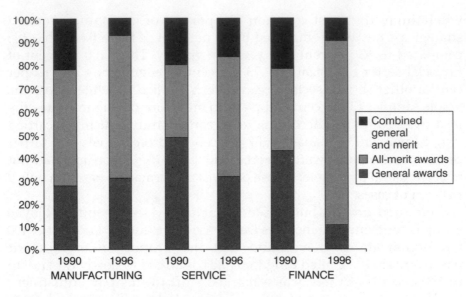

Figure 2.3 *Managerial pay awards by sector, 1990–96*

to company size, increasing from 55 per cent amongst organizations with less than 500 employees, to 81 per cent for those with over 5,000.

INTERNATIONAL

Towers Perrin's research[10] amongst 303 mostly multinational organizations confirmed the trend in the United Kingdom and found performance-related pay becoming increasingly common in continental Europe as well. Individual performance was found to be the most important factor affecting executive and managerial pay increases, and was becoming increasingly significant for non-management staff (see Table 2.2). Only in Germany and Spain did the majority of non-management employees now receive wholly general, across-the-board, flat-rate base pay increases.

One-third of these organizations in Europe had moved towards broader pay bands, most commonly in order to produce more scope for individual, performance-based differentiation. European companies such as ABN Amro, Moulinex and Fiat have all moved to adopt the so called 'Anglo-Saxon' model of individual performance pay. Further afield, large Japanese corporations such as Honda and Toyota have adopted performance pay for all staff in their UK-based manufacturing sites, while companies such as Seiko-Epson, Sanwa Bank and

Table 2.2   *Incidence of the different methods of adjusting the base pay for staff in Europe*

	Managers/ Professionals	Non-management
Merit/individual performance-based	68%	51%
Across the board/ general increases	8%	25%
Service-based	2%	7%
Skill/competency-based	4%	8%

Source: Towers Perrin (1997) *'Reward Challenges and Changes' Study of 303 European Organizations*

Matsushita have also moved to performance-related base pay progression in Japan, instead of or alongside their traditional service-based approaches. According to Hutton, in Japan, 'performance-related pay is replacing annual increases and jobs for life', as 'egalitarianism is gradually breaking down'.[11]

THE RATIONALE

The problems with hierarchical and service-based pay systems, as well as the necessity of being continually more competitive in global markets, and ever more cost-efficient in the public sector, helps to illustrate why there has been no significant move away from individual performance pay. According to Jack Welch, the well-respected CEO of General Electric, 'You can preach all you want about a learning organization but from our experience, reinforcing appraisal and compensation systems are the critical enablers that must be in place if the rhetoric is to become reality.'

Or perhaps less positively, as Helen Murlis put it at a recent IQPC conference, in respect of merit pay in the public sector, 'It may not be working very well, but what's the alternative?' A power station manager told us recently that there may be problems with the merit pay scheme in his company, but at least now there was some relationship between pay and performance. In the past, just about everything – temperature, hours of work, time of work, etc – except performance had influenced his pay costs.

SOME EXAMPLES

Looking beneath the research figures, there are plenty of practical case examples of organizations introducing and extending individual performance-related pay schemes to illustrate the growth trend. For every Barclays cited in the press (who have now successfully implemented their scheme, in keeping with all of their major competitors), there has been a Royal Sun Alliance, who contemporaneously, quietly, and with staff and union agreement, introduced a very similar set of merit-based pay arrangements in their branches. Companies such as Pfizer in the private sector, partnerships such as lawyers Edge and Ellison, privatized companies such as Nuclear Electric and National Grid, charities such as Remploy, and public sector bodies such as the Health and Safety Executive and Babergh District Council (with full union and staff support) have all introduced schemes in the last two years, which relate individual pay more directly to performance.

Birmingham law firm, Edge and Ellison, for example, intended to create a 'real meritocracy', with the Senior Partner saying that 'any scheme which does not measure achievement and commitment is just a lock-step arrangement which we can no longer afford'.[12] Similarly, the charity Remploy saw the introduction of merit pay and bonuses in 1996 as essential in supporting moves towards becoming a more commercial and efficient organization. The replacement of annual increments saw the costs of salary drift fall from 2.2 per cent to 0.3 per cent of payroll.

Just this week, a leaflet dropped through the letter box seeking shop staff at retailer Waitrose, promising as a primary benefit of working for them, 'performance-related pay, with each individual's contribution to the success of the branch assessed and rewarded accordingly'. As described in our case study, at Yorkshire Water Services individual performance pay was 'not a threat but a fact of life', a 'vital step in moving YWS forward', when, 'our customers demand it..., our shareholders expect us to be effective, (and) our cost effectiveness is a critical factor for the Regulator'.

While these studies and examples demonstrate that the picture of the death of performance-related pay presented by much of the media has been a total misrepresentation, they do, however, indicate that the growth rate has slowed considerably. The conclusion of IRS's 1997 research[13] was that, 'most of the workplaces suited to individual performance-related pay already have it in place', and as can be seen from the data in Table 2.1, other reward approaches were forecast to grow more rapidly. Almost 13 per cent were planning to introduce or extend merit pay, compared to 27 per cent in the same survey two years earlier. In the *Personnel Today*[14] study, only 3 per cent of organizations had plans to introduce or extend merit pay, compared to 11 per cent for skills and competency pay, a figure replicated exactly in a 1996 Hay/CBI survey.

THE RESEARCH: IS IT WORKING?

As we saw in the previous chapter, considerable publicity has been given to a number of performance-related pay studies which indicate the difficulties and the failings of schemes. The question of their effectiveness relates to two main issues:

1. Does individual performance pay have any impact on organization performance?
2. Does it motivate staff and have any effect on individual performance?

This book is concerned more with the practice of performance pay than in-depth academic debate, but clearly we have to address the issue of 'does it work' as well as the practical steps required to make it work better.

We have researched the academic literature and research in some depth, going back as far as the 1920s, and the main conclusions we draw from this are twofold:

1. It is an extremely difficult area in which to carry out research, given the difficulty of isolating variables and identifying and attributing causation, and due to the broader political and social philosophies and debates which invariably interfere with objective research.
2. There are at least as many research studies suggesting that performance-related pay can reinforce and support high organizational and individual performance as there are suggesting that it doesn't.

THE RESEARCH DIFFICULTIES

Part of the problem with investigating this issue is that it gets to the root of people's political affiliations and their core beliefs on human motivation. Therefore, it is very difficult to conduct truly objective research. Can it be just coincidence, for example, that the prevailing negative views of the UK press and academics come from sectors in which individual performance-related pay has been (often badly) applied over the last decade, representing an aspect of the government's removal of lifetime tenure for university posts in the latter case, and one symbol of the assault on collectivism in the newspaper industry, alongside Wapping and the like for the former?

Performance-related pay has become so strongly associated with the right-wing politics of the 1980s that judgement on it, in some cases, appears to have become a matter of political faith. Will Hutton, for example, in his influential best seller, *The State We're In*,[15] documents the rise of US-style income differentials and fragmented pay bargaining in the United Kingdom as 'the Thatcherite programme was imposed at colossal social cost,... putting the axe to the root of organised labour'. This extreme free market economics was, he describes, 'personified in the obsessive linkage of pay with performance', which in his opinion universally creates, 'low morale, weakens worker's commitment and leads to higher labour turnover'.

The fact that other, older forms of performance-related pay such as profit and gainsharing were championed by left-wing politicians and writers such as Robert Tressel appears to be ignored, and a number of New Labour ministers have expressed support. Jack Cunningham, for example, wrote, 'Labour supports the view that good performance should merit good rewards.'[16] And David Blunkett has supported the concept of relating pay to performance for teachers. Conversely, a number of Conservative-controlled councils and health authorities appeared to put in individual performance-pay largely as a matter of political faith, with little thought as to the cultural fit or support systems required to make it work.

Perhaps more significantly for those of us with weaker political affiliations, performance-related pay is inextricably intertwined with theories of motivation and the critical question of the importance and influence of money. Writers such as Kohn[17] cite countless studies showing that staff regard money very much as a secondary motivator, and that the use of money as an incentive to perform actually weakens the more important intrinsic motivators such as responsibility, work interest and social belonging.

A powerful thread of motivational theory and research from Maslow and Herzberg onwards underpins these ideas, and helps to explain the contradictory views of many HR managers, as revealed in the previous section. Like us, you probably feel that you are not personally strongly influenced by high financial rewards, just as you agree with all the psychologists who tell us that we should not use excessive positive or negative reinforcement with our children, or the builders on our extension. Yet the reality, we all know, is that is exactly what we do – offer bribes of sweets, make threats of refusing treats or payments – even if only as part of an overall motivation strategy. The same is true in organizations. As Gupta and Shaw put it, 'Methods for motivating people to do their best must be developed against the reality, not against idealised fantasies. We must confront the fact that many jobs are dull and boring, and most of us are motivated by money – some more so than others.'[18]

In addition, as Hunt writes,[19] 'On salary, Herzburg's neatness lets us down. It is not just a contextual factor. It also establishes our place in the scheme of things, affecting our sense of personal worth and self-esteem... it crosses the barrier from hygiene to motivator needs.'

This very complexity also of course makes it almost impossible to isolate the effects of money on performance. There is a strong line of research in goal theory, for example, supporting the role of objective-setting,[20] a key element of most performance-pay schemes, as a powerful motivator in its own right. Clear, participative objective-setting has been shown to correlate with improved motivation and performance in situations as diverse as Canadian forests and London building sites. Goal setting helps to direct attention, mobilize effort and increase persistence and a number of research studies, such as French and Marsden's, demonstrate how performance-related pay can be associated with improved goal setting. Who is to say whether a pay scheme influences effort and behaviour because of the money on offer, or because of the objectives and target achievements which have to be satisfied?

This overlap of motivational and other contextual variables also makes effective research studies very difficult to conduct, particularly in respect of individual performance pay schemes. If the artificiality of laboratory studies using children and students are to be avoided, in real company situations, generally a whole range of factors are changing at the same time as the pay scheme – the business strategy, the organization and job structure, performance management processes, and so on. So isolating the effects of the performance pay scheme is very difficult. It is surely no coincidence that the research on team and collective reward schemes, is generally more positive than for individual schemes (see Chapter 6), when the results of these schemes, for example in a gainsharing plan, where the payment directly relates to the value of gain to the organization, are much easier to measure.

The famous Hawthorne experiments in the Western Electric company in Chicago in the 1920s are often used to demonstrate the importance of non-financial motivators, such as social needs. Yet a recent book[21] accuses Elton Mayo of playing down the influence of performance-related pay in this work. According to Western's personnel manager at the time, 'Economic and financial factors are of considerable importance in the test room: the employees are anxious for high earnings.'

THE CONFLICTING FINDINGS

None the less, Hunt's conclusions, like ours, from a thorough review of the research on performance pay is that, 'today, no one would argue that salary is not a motivator'.[22] Or perhaps you would prefer Judith Oliver's slightly less positive conclusion that 'No one can prove performance-related pay improves performance, but then, no one can prove that it doesn't either.'[23] Thus, for every negative piece of research such as those presented by Thompson's IMS study or Kohn, there is a corresponding and usually less well-publicized piece of research demonstrating the opposite positive effects.

A lot of studies quoted by both 'sides' are weakened by their reliance on the views of the respondents taking part in the survey research. Thus, a fairly typical example would be the findings from the IPD's study of over 1,000 UK organizations (see Table 2.3). Nearly three-quarters of respondents felt individual performance pay had a positive effect on individual and organization performance, while on the downside, effects on team working and on perceptions of fairness were the only significant negative ratings. Researcher Ray Richardson's conclusion was that, 'merit pay is generating useful if not startling gains... it seems to be giving value for money.'[24] *Personnel Today's* study[25] found a somewhat closer 36 per cent reporting predominantly positive gains and 24 per cent negative, while the IRS study[26] found 76 per cent of participants claiming a positive effect on individual performance and 54 per cent on organizational.

More rigorous and in-depth studies, often restricted to small samples, produce similar contradictions, displayed even from studies carried out by the same researchers. We mentioned Thompson's well-known study for the Institute of Manpower Studies, which revealed the in-depth problems with individual performance pay experienced by three employers, and found no correlation between its use and organizational performance across a much larger sample.

Table 2.3 *Self-rated effectiveness of merit pay schemes in the IPD's research.*

Q: What effect do you think your system of individual performance-related pay has on the following:

	Improves	No change	Worsens
Employee performance	74%	26%	0%
Delivering a clear message about the importance of organizational performance	59%	27%	4%
Rewarding employees in a way they think is fair	57%	29%	14%
Your ability to identify and get rid of poor performers	52%	46%	2%
Facilitating change in your organization	41%	54%	5%
Employee commitment/loyalty	41%	53%	6%
Encouraging employees to suggest improvements and innovation	28%	68%	5%
Effective team working	28%	59%	13%
Curbing union influence on pay decisions	14%	84%	3%

Source: Institute of Personnel and Development (1998)

Yet the same Marc Thompson, now research fellow at Templeton College, Oxford, more recently carried out a study amongst 400 companies in the aerospace sector, publishing the results in 1998.[27] This produced a fairly sophisticated measure of added value per employee in each company which was then correlated with the application of various HR practices. The high value added and low value added companies were clearly differentiated in terms of their pay practices, with virtually double the number of high value added companies applying individual performance-related pay schemes to more than two-thirds of their staff, and a similar differentiation evident for those using broadbanded pay approaches (see Figure 2.4).

Research into the psychological contract by the IPD, and the results of the 1998 Workforce Employee Relations Survey, described in Chapter 8, also reveal correlations between productivity, employee satisfaction and the use of a basket of 'progressive' HR practices, including schemes which link performance and pay.

In the United States, Huselid[28] drew similar conclusions from a study of 3,400 companies. He found a correlation between high performance

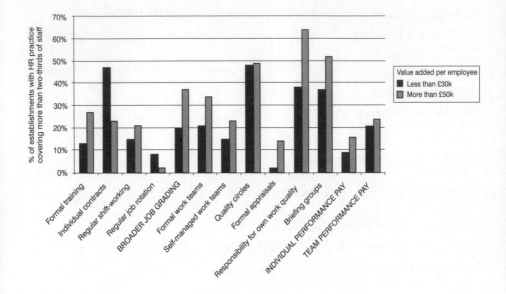

Figure 2.4 *Thompson's Templeton College research showing differences in the HR practices used between high and low values-added companies in the aerospace sector*

work practices, including close links between appraisal and pay, and the use of profit and gainsharing schemes, and the financial performance of these organizations. A one standard deviation increase in the use of these practices yielded a $27,000 increase in sales and a $3,800 increase in profits (see Figure 2.5). Lawler, Mohrman and Ledford found that the extensive users of high performance work practices averaged a return on equity of 22.8 per cent, compared to 16.6 per cent amongst low users. These practices included sharing information, redistributing power, developing knowledge and rewarding performance.

Professional sport, according to the Professor Keith Bradley of the Open University reflects the payment methods which more and more organizations will have to pursue in a knowledge-driven economy with increasing skill shortages, in which key individuals have a major impact on organizational performance. (Witness the changes in Newcastle United's share price on the day after Alan Shearer was signed, and then the day after he broke his ankle.) It again illustrates the research contradictions, as well as the difficulties of defining 'effectiveness'.

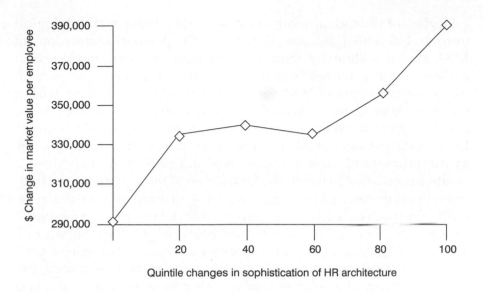

Figure 2.5 *US research findings on the effects of HR practices including performance-related pay on company performance.*

Towers Perrin carried out unpublished research into the relationships between baseball players' pay and performance during the 1994 dispute between owners and players. They found virtually no correlation between any of the numerous statistics on individual performance in the current season and contractual earnings. However, there was a strong correlation with historic performance, both a strength and weakness of individual performance pay in these rapidly changing times which we shall consider in later chapters. Presumably this is partly because a rookie player has an exceptional season and then negotiates a longer-term, multi-million dollar contract, the bulk of which is guaranteed.

On the UK side of the Atlantic, Sue Fernie and David Metcalfe of the London School of Economics, no fans themselves of HRM theory and ideas, produced an interesting study in horse racing on jockey's pay.[29] Jockeys are generally paid a low flat rate fee per race, and then receive the bulk of earnings as a commission on winnings. Perhaps not surprisingly, this produced a high correlation in their study between the earnings of the jockey and the number of races won, although the direction of causation and the driver of the high performance (rider versus horse) is still open to question.

Studies of individual motivation face even more methodological hurdles, but here again, for every list of the personal motivations of MBA students showing money down near the bottom, there is a contrary finding. Katzell[30] researched amongst knowledge workers in the pharmaceutical and IT sectors in the United States, a group who, it has been claimed, are particularly strongly motivated by work interest and opportunity, rather than money. Gupta and Singhal, for example, list a trusting environment and non financial recognition, 'not money as the prime motivators for scientists'. Katzell found a significant positive correlation between the motivation of these workers and individual performance pay systems, which scored highly in comparison with alternatives such as common pay levels or service-based progression. Peter Le Blanc and Paul Mulvey [31] similarly found in a survey of 1,500 American workers across a range of industries a preference for fixed base pay and individual performance-related pay increases, rather than team rewards. Their conclusion was 'Employers ignoring individual pay for performance could be making a big mistake.'

More comprehensive meta-analyses of a series of separate research studies on the subject again can be used to argue on either side. Gupta and Shaw[32] found 39 research studies on the effects of financial incentives on performance. They revealed a .34 correlation between the use of these incentives and performance quantity, but no strong correlation with performance quality. However, they could only find six studies which actually separately measured the effect on performance quality. If it tells us anything, this review of the research literature supports a point we make throughout this book, which is that the success criteria and objectives for performance pay schemes need to be set out clearly in advance, and their level of achievement regularly reviewed in operation. How can we ever assess if any pay scheme is a success if, as Mike Langley found when he examined sales incentive plans in 20 UK companies, 'only one company had made any attempt to evaluate whether or not their scheme made one iota of difference to performance, and they could find no clear evidence either way'?[33]

LEARNING POINTS

You might conclude from this lengthy analysis of the academic research that we have made little progress in addressing the practical dilemmas and issues which HR and line managers face with performance-related pay: should we or shouldn't we, and what is the best way of doing it? However, we would extract two useful conclusions from what one researcher called this 'quagmire' of a debate.

First, *performance-related pay cannot be endorsed or rejected universally, out-of-hand, as a principle.* It appears to work in some situations and not in others. One of our favourite pieces of research on the subject, by Ryan, Mims and Koestner,[34] illustrates this superbly. They were examining the issue of whether or not financial incentives do decrease intrinsic motivation (work interest etc) in a variety of companies. Their findings were that it did do so in a what they measured to be a high-control organizational culture, but that in the organizations with the opposite high communications cultures, both intrinsic and extrinsic motivation was enhanced by monetary incentives.

We will return to the importance of communications and involvement in supporting effective pay-for-performance relationships in Chapter 8, but the key point for now is that these situational variables, rather than just the type of pay scheme design, are vitally important determinants of success or failure. Similarly, Canadian research by Cameron and Pierce[35] found that financial rewards can lead to increased performance and work interest, but only when those rewards are given for meeting clear performance standards and contingent on performance quality.

Second, *no type of performance-pay scheme is universally successful or unsuccessful.* All have their strength and weaknesses, and the key issue for practising managers is not only to pick the appropriate pay scheme for their own situation, but also to work to maximize the potential advantages and minimize the potential disadvantages. Bowey et al.[36] research clearly demonstrated this in a study which found that the performance pay scheme design bore no correlation with successful outcomes. This was far more dependent on associated actions in communications and support systems, which could help to render any design as more or less successful. The naïvety of the common 1980s' assumption that PeRP was, in itself, a major lever for organizational and behavioural change, was thereby exposed.

The research and sharp-end experience of the majority of UK companies who have now travelled down the performance pay route have clearly revealed the weaknesses and problems with some of the predominant approaches and schemes that were adopted. Many did assume, at least tacitly, an over-simplistic and monolithic view of money-oriented human motivation, ignoring difference in circumstances, situations and motivations. Money can be a motivator in relation to performance, but as Kohn correctly points out, rarely in a crude, behaviouralist, Pavlov's dog-type way. As expectancy theories of motivation suggest, and goal-setting research has demonstrated, employees not only have to value the performance-related rewards on offer, but also to see clear links between their performance goals, their efforts and the rewards.

In addition, employees are generally not operating in isolation and as equity theories of motivation suggest, their efforts relative to those of their internal colleagues and external comparators also enters into this complex equation. Perceptions of the relative as well as the absolute adequacy of performance-related rewards, as most of us have found from our experience, play an important part in motivation.

It is with a better understanding of these problems, and a more realistic appraisal of the strengths and weaknesses that companies have been revisiting, revising and changing their performance-related pay schemes, evolving them into what we see now to be a fundamentally different and contribution-based approach.

THE PROBLEMS WITH PERFORMANCE-RELATED PAY

As Hunt acutely observes in our opening quotation, many organizations implementing performance pay in the 1980s initially developed a highly formulaic approach. This was based on the annual setting of measurable, individual objectives and targets, the level of achievement of which drove either the size of the base pay increase, or possibly a cash bonus. The higher the rated achievement of objectives, the higher the base pay increase or bonus award. The approach owed a lot to the original ideas of management by objectives by Humble and others, and attempted to make the process as defined and objective as possible.

Then as the pressures to introduce performance related pay more widely came about, as Flannery, Hofrichter and Platten[37] observe, 'many organizations began to expand the use of PeRP by simply pushing this traditional executive approach deeper into the organization', often without a great deal of thought for the different jobs, work organization, circumstances and motivations of staff to whom this system was then applied. The failure of communications and lack of preparation for merit pay were illustrated in one financial services organization in the early 1990s. There we found examples of managers who had mixed up the rating scales for their staff under this new appraisal system, and so rated their highest performers at the lowest level.

For base pay purposes, many organizations, in addition, related the size of the annual pay increase to the level of the individual's current salary versus the market, often through the operation of a matrix. Thus at a given level of performance, someone higher in their pay range and versus the market would receive a lower level of increase, reflecting on their already high level of pay. Someone low down the range and requiring to be moved up to market rate, with a high level of performance would receive a correspondingly larger increase. And someone high in the range whose performance declines would, over time, fall back, relatively, within their range. Table 2.4 shows as an example the actual 1997 pay increase matrix at financial services organization the Alliance and Leicester. In the public sector this is generally known as an equity shares approach.

Another control device applied in many, particular public sector, organizations was to 'force fit' the distribution of performance ratings in order to support a consistent and equitable approach to rating performance, and to ensure that the total pay budget was not exceeded by managers giving their staff too many high ratings. So the pattern of ratings awarded by departmental or unit heads for their staff would have to be normally distributed. The National Health Service, for example, introduced this type of quota system for its senior managers.

The problems with this predominant and uniform approach to individual performance-related and merit pay are now well documented and recognized, and with hindsight, hardly surprising. A particularly honest and insightful summary of the major problems was provided by the 25 per cent of companies in Towers Perrin's European research who admitted problems with their pay schemes,[38] which are illustrated in

Table 2.4 *1997 merit pay increase matrix at the Alliance and Leicester*

| Performance rating | Position in the salary range | | | |
	Less than 85%	85%–99.99%	100%–114.99%	More than 114.00%
1. Outstanding	7.0%	6.0%	5.0%	5.0%
2. Excellent	5.5%	4.75%	4.5%	4.5%
3. Good	4.5%	4.0%	4.0%	4.0%
4. Satisfactory	3.75%	3.5%	3.25%	3.25%
5. Below standard	2.0%	1.5%	1.0%	1.0%
6. Major improvement required	0%	0%	0%	0%

Figure 2.6. These difficulties can be considered in terms of the strategy and objectives for performance pay, the scheme design, and most importantly the implementation and operating processes.

PROBLEMS: THE STRATEGY

Many organizations who as Income Data Services described it, 'followed the herd' into individual performance-related pay did so without a clear set of objectives, and did not implement it as part of an integrated HR strategy, with associated changes in related HR areas. Not only did this mean that the criteria against which to judge scheme success were never clearly outlined, but also that managers and staff were often unclear as to the rationale for the change, and what it was designed to achieve. This clarity and communication of scheme objectives, generally linked to business strategy and goals, were found to be a key differentiator between successful and unsuccessful performance pay schemes in Bowey's research,[39] as illustrated in Figure 2.7. Similarly, Thompson[40] found that lack of clear objectives and poor communication and implementation largely explained the failure of schemes, rather than any inherent, philosophical or design weakness.

In the public sector, Brown and Hudson[41] suggest that in many cases performance pay schemes were never intended, in practice, to link pay and individual performance effectively, but were often just adopted as a tactic to achieve more flexibility in base pay levels, so as to be able to respond to external market pressures and skill shortages. Kessler and Purcell's research[42] demonstrated retention via more market-related pay rates to be an important goal of PeRP schemes. There were central guidelines in a number of the cases they studied to allocate 'performance' pay budgets to those experiencing the strongest labour market pressures.

The General Secretary of the National Association of Head Teachers advocated performance pay for teachers on this basis in 1998 as 'good graduates are voting with their feet and seeking jobs where salaries are more attractive'.[43] Thus, 17 per cent of those in the Industrial Relations Services study[44] listed retention problems as a key reason for introducing performance pay, while 12 per cent saw it as a lever to reduce the scope of collective bargaining.

Hence, little effort often actually went into trying to make PeRP schemes work effectively on the ground, and as Peter McGrath of the Clydesdale Bank puts it, 'PeRP schemes don't just happen: they require

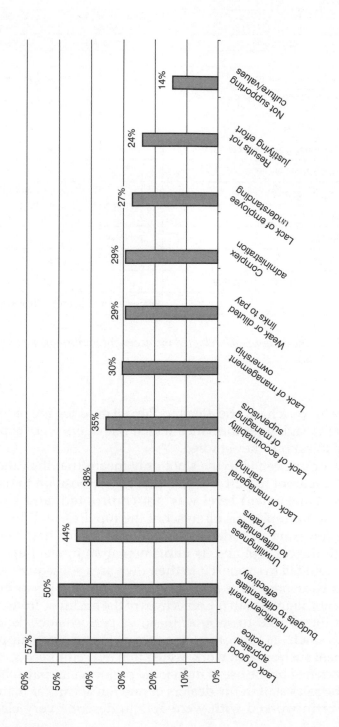

Figure 2.6 *Difficulties with pay review and performance management systems*
Source: Towers Perrin

Approach	Unsuccessful Plans Companies					Successful Plans Companies				
	A	B	C	D	E	F	G	H	I	J
Senior management support	✔					✔	✔	✔	✔	✔
Clear and available performance measurement system				✔		✔	✔	✔	✔	✔
Clear plan objectives				✔		✔	✔	✔	✔	✔
Strategic business goals reflected in bonus						✔		✔		✔
Performance appraisal		✔				✔	✔	✔	✔	✔
Clarity of organization structure						✔	✔	✔	✔	✔
Quality Initiatives						✔		✔		✔
Team building		✔					✔		✔	✔
Quaility circles	✔					✔	✔			✔
Strong emphasis on communications		✔				✔	✔	✔	✔	✔
	Piecemeal Approach					Total Approach				

Figure 2.7 *Strategic approach adopted in successful performance pay plans in the United Kingdom.*

managers to work hard.' Kessler and Purcell describe the practical diffi-culties in managing performance which managers were experiencing in the organizations they studied.

Lack of, or unclear, objectives not only meant that the rationale was often not apparent to staff, but also that any opposition to the concept at senior management level was not confronted, and so a lack of support and example was often set at the top. Research in the Inland Revenue for example,[45] demonstrated that senior managers would agree with the concept and its implementation in meetings, but then rubbish it and fail to support it in their own area subsequently.

Lack of clear objectives also may mean that the performance pay scheme is not aligned with the objectives of the business. Ironically, while generally introduced to support business performance, key business objectives such as customer service, or values to support their achievement such as team work, were often not reinforced, and in some cases threatened by the use of individual performance pay schemes.

Thus the sales staff in the dealers of one European car manufacturer Towers Perrin worked with were able to describe very clearly their business strategy. It was to move up-market and to sell fewer, higher value cars, with a high customer retention rate, achieved through superlative customer service. They also saw the complete inconsistency of this goal and their current, highly-geared individual performance pay scheme, which rewarded them purely based on the profitability of sales they achieved. It was an incentive, as one salesperson put it, to 'screw the customer', who if they found out that they had been sold a highly priced financing package or set of accessories, 'probably won't come back'.

That individual performance pay, in a sense, was working too well and encouraging individual performance at the expense of broader corporate goals was also revealed by a University of Bath study. One manager told the researchers, 'We worship at the altar of team work and then destroy it with our (individually-based) pay system', and this was the most significant negative effect revealed by respondents in the Institute of Personnel and Development Survey.[46] According to Towers Perrin's data it also meant that 20 per cent of UK companies are planning to place a stronger emphasis on team work in their management incentive plans. So much for the argument that money doesn't motivate!

PROBLEMS: THE DESIGN

Compensation and HR managers have also not helped themselves in some cases by the design of their performance pay schemes, which in a sustained period of historically low inflation in many Western countries, and through the application of the uniform merit pay/equity share model, have seen very narrow base pay differentials available to reward performance. The common use of pay matrices operating with total pay budgets of 3–4 per cent have seen relatively small gains on offer to the highest performers. As Budman[47] put it, 'A difference of $10 a week, after all that effort, is unlikely to inspire the laggard to scale the heights of high performance.'

Thus, 74 per cent of those in the IPD research[48] felt that the amounts involved were too small to motivate effectively, with a mean pay difference between outstanding and average performers in 1997 of 4 per cent. BT suspended the operation of its merit pay scheme in 1994 because there was, 'not enough money to make PeRP a sensible way of deciding pay rises',[49] while Komatsu dropped its individual performance pay scheme for all employees altogether in 1997, due to similar budget restrictions. Thames Water in the same year abandoned its individual performance/position in range matrix to try to address employees' perceptions of the lack of sufficient performance-related differentiation.

These budget restrictions were of course even more severe in the public sector during the 1990s, with a succession of imposed maximum pay awards and freezes. In the Industrial Society research,[50] only 43 per cent of public and voluntary sector respondents regarded monetary incentives as an effective means of motivating employees, compared to 82 per cent of those in the services sector. Secretary of the Civil Service Unions Charles Cochrane believes that the Cabinet Office's review of public sector pay schemes, to be completed by April 1999, will result in 'something that retains the link to performance-related pay but moves away from the dogmatic adherence to equity shares'.

Other design failings evident, as Cochrane suggests, often revolve around a failure to take account of the culture in which the scheme operates. In a culture of service increments, James Richards at National Power observed to us that, 'PeRP just became another increment, which was only stopped when an employee did something outrageous.' A South East county council found this out when it tried to control incremental increases with a series of performance bars. Effective performers could only progress up to the range mid-point, high performers to the 75 percentile and only outstanding performers up to the range maxima. A normal distribution of rating assessments was also imposed on departmental managers to ensure budgets were controlled. Our research showed that the response of line managers was to reserve all of their 'quota' of outstanding performance ratings for those already in the high portion of the range. As one told us, giving an outstanding rating to someone below mid-point was 'a waste', as they could progress anyway with just an effective rating. Highly motivating to the newer, high performing staff!

We even found one retailer where a proportion of the store manager's annual bonus was based upon their success in beating their store's staffing budget. Hardly surprisingly, we found the vast majority of sales assistants to be in the lowest 10 per cent of their broad and supposedly performance-related pay range.

Perhaps the key design failure, as Flannery, Hofrichter and Platten[51] observe, however, has been the application of the already referred to uniform, management-derived merit pay model in such a wide variety of situations and circumstances. Given this diversity, it is perhaps not surprising that in trying to address such a variety of circumstances and needs, individual merit pay schemes often ended up satisfying nobody.

Kunkel's research[52] with employees in product development clearly demonstrated this requirement. He concluded that 'compensation systems must be tailored to the culture of the organization and to ensure management commitment to the process', as well as being 'continually reviewed and refined in a rapidly changing environment'.

PROBLEMS: THE PROCESSES

These cultural issues, however, highlight what is perhaps the key area of difficulties and problems with performance related pay which are the 'soft' process aspects. As Judith Oliver put it, 'performance pay is beautiful in theory but difficult in practice'.[53] In the Industrial Society's study,[54] 51 per cent of managers agreed that pay should be linked to appraisal, but a majority felt that the link was not currently operating effectively. Similarly, in the public sector, half of the line managers studied by the London School of Economics believed that performance-related pay had improved goal setting and productivity, but staff were deeply hostile to the way performance-related pay was managed and administered.[55]

Virtually all of the research studies we have considered, such as Thompson's, Kessler and Purcell's and Bowey and Thorpes', reveal that performance pay failures are rooted in implementation and operating processes. These failings are typically evident in two areas in particular: performance management and communication and involvement. This is clearly demonstrated by the findings of the Towers Perrin study[56] (see Figure 2.6). Virtually all of the problems highlighted by participants in this study, apart from limited individual pay differentiation referred to earlier, can be grouped under these two headings.

Thus, 70 per cent of the respondents in the IPD survey[57] were not satisfied with line managers' use of their appraisal systems, on the basis of which performance-related pay increases are most commonly based. Culturally, performance management has a long history of failure in the UK environment, as we review in Chapter 7. An employee in one of the IPD's researched companies told us, 'Our manager seems uncomfortable in the appraisal meetings, like it's a relief to get it over with for another year.'

In some cases appraisal schemes are rigid, formulaic and points based. As the Woolwich concluded (see Case Study 4.1), these can become something of an annual ritual for managers and staff to go through with low credibility, little relevance to either individual or organizational 'real life' performance, and very little impact on pay. Similarly, for Pfizer's UK salesforce, the strong central control of the pay increase matrix by HR meant that line managers and staff felt they had little influence on the pay process, and therefore did not 'buy in' to its outcomes. A majority of their employees felt that their performance did not strongly influence their pay, despite the use of a merit pay scheme and a 20 per cent target performance bonus.

Perhaps more common is the perception of excessive subjectivity of performance ratings, which Allied Domecq identified as the major problem with their scheme[58] and which often lies at the heart of trade union opposition to PeRP. Thus Robert Taylor observed that, 'even the Society of Telecom Engineers wants to see BT continue with some form of PeRP'[59] but their major concern was with the fairness and consistency of performance ratings. Staff were not told their assessment scores and nearly a third raised grievances over this. Kessler and Purcell[60] found common problems to be 'the lack of support systems, the lack of management training and the highly subjective nature of assessments'. The difficulties were 'greatest at the performance assessment and rating stage', with managers often 'taking the easy option and allowing ratings to drift up', and employees suffering from 'the demotivating effects of not being labelled a high flier', and being told 'you are just satisfactory'. We review performance management processes in more detail in Chapter 7.

Similarly, at the Clydesdale Bank, which experienced industrial action after the attempted introduction of their merit pay scheme, Head of HR Peter McGrath observes that performance pay schemes 'are often not sufficiently transparent, and staff don't understand the measurement system'. Being further removed than the senior management of the organization from business results make this transparency more difficult to achieve, for as Flannery, Hofrichter and Platten observe, 'if the link is so tangential or vague then the chances of the programme succeeding are greatly diminished'.[61]

But the lack of transparency is also generally a sign of lack of employee involvement and communication in the design and operation of performance pay systems. A wide variety of research studies, some of which are summarized in Table 2.5, reveal that the extent of staff communications and involvement correlates more strongly with performance pay scheme success than any other design or environmental variable. Communications and involvement is the means by which staff come to understand how and why a scheme operates, and how their performance does impact on the organization and their pay.

And as expectancy theories of motivation illustrate, it all depends on the perceptions of these vital linkages, rather than how the system, in theory, is supposed to operate.

Table 2.5 *Summary of factors which related to the success of performance pay, demonstrated in research studies*

Study	Factors correlating with success of performance pay	Factors where no correlation found
Bullock & Tubbs (1990) n = 330	• Formal plan involvement structure • Staff involvement in plan design • Employee favourability • Participative management style • Controllability of targets* • Productivity rather than profit orientation* • Shorter payout periods*	• Size of organization/plan membership • Union presence • Industry • Technology

Bowey & Thorpe (1982) n = 63	• Extent of consultation
	  – involvement
	  – amount of communication
	• Supervisory skills/spans of control
	• Market/sales growth
	• Shorter payout periods*
	• Smaller size of membership*
		• Plan design in terms of:
		  – performance measures
		  – level of measurement
		  – type of staff covered

Towers Perrin (1990) n = 177	• Senior management commitment • Employee support/involvement • Emphasis on communications • Related HR activities eg. training • Performance measurement at levels below corporate • Shorter payout periods* • Operational or Blended rather than wholly financial measures*	• Organization size • Union presence • Age of plan • Industry
American Productivity Centre (1985) n = 10	• Management and supervisory support • Amount of communications • Clear and shared objectives	• Size of gain/potential payment • Direct design link to strategic goals • Association with quality circles
American Compensation Association (1992) n = 432	• Frequent comunications • Employee involvement in design/operation • Clear plan objectives and link to business goals • Higher labour costs • Frequent payments • Operational or blended measures	
Lawler (1990) – Research summation	• Communications • Employee and management attitudes • Supervisory skills • Predictable performance measures	

Note: *Weak correlation

43

Thompson's research[62] covering over 1,000 employees, concluded that scheme success depended on employee trust, and that the more involved staff were in design, the better the performance. 'Where there is trust, involvement and a commitment to fairness, the schemes work,' he concluded. Yet many employers have not built up, and often not even tried to develop this trust. Only 7 per cent of companies in Towers Perrin's research[63] had involved employees in the design of their performance pay schemes, while at the Inland Revenue,[64] 60 per cent of staff felt that individual targets were 'imposed by managers' rather than discussed. We review this issue in detail in Chapter 8.

THE CHANGE FROM PERFORMANCE- TO CONTRIBUTION-RELATED PAY

Lack of an articulated and effective HR and reward strategy; bad, often uniform and inflexible design; and most of all, poor processes and management appear to explain the difficulties which organizations have experienced with their performance-related pay systems in the 1990s. Yet as we have seen, they are not abandoning their schemes, but rather changing and adapting them to address these weaknesses and make them more relevant for the new millennium. As Judith Oliver puts it, 'Firms continue to tweak, tinker with and transform their performance pay systems.'[65]

Over 90 per cent of organizations in the Towers Perrin research[66] had changed their pay systems in the past two years and 96 per cent forecast further changes in the next two, with the greatest incidence in the areas of performance-related variable pay and pay progression (Figure 2.8). Some 40 per cent of the organizations in the IPD research[67] had changed their performance-related pay systems since 1995, with a third of them describing the changes as radical and 61 per cent antici-pated further changes in the next two years (with only 9 per cent of these anticipating withdrawal).

Thus there has been a marked shift in the type of performance pay schemes now being introduced and altered in UK organizations, with a much more holistic and business-integrated perspective being taken and a greater diversity of schemes emerging. The slowdown in the growth of applications, to our minds, indicates a much more realistic perception of the nature and requirements of performance-related pay, and that some of the earlier failings just described are being avoided. As

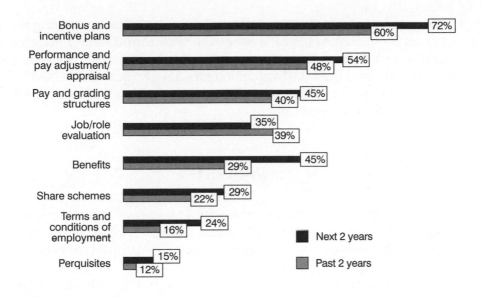

Figure 2.8 *The Significant level of changes in pay and reward policies in Europe*
Source: Towers Perrin

Industrial Relations Services put it in 'Merit moves on', 'Many employers in the first wave of merit payers in the 1980s are reflecting on their existing systems, refining and overhauling them, attempting to make them more applicable to business needs and those of their employees.'[68]

We have characterized this revised approach as paying for contribution (see Introduction, Table 0.1) and in the following chapters we describe its major features in respect of:

- its strategic components, philosophy and relationship to business and HR strategy; paying for contribution recognizes that individual, management-type financial objectives are often not the only, nor even the most important, performance goals which pay can be used to reinforce, and a much greater variety of reward scheme designs is therefore emerging;
- its design features; this variety of scheme designs is evident within as well as between organizations, with designs tailored to suit the needs of different groups and circumstances; companies are paying for how results are being achieved as well as the results, themselves; they are also working to increase the variable component of pay;

- the process aspects, the 'how' of paying for contribution; paying for contribution eschews PeRP's obsession with formulas and systems and is at least as much concerned with processes: how performance is managed and how staff and managers can get much more heavily involved in performance pay programmes, so that their objectives can be realized in practice.

SUMMARY

- Whatever the academic and press criticisms of performance-related pay in the late 1990s, there has been no widespread withdrawal from such schemes, with between a half and two-thirds of organizations continuing to operate them.
- The expansion in incidence has continued, particularly in the UK service sector, and spread across continental Europe, although it is generally a white-collar phenomenon, and the growth rate has slowed considerably.
- The necessity for organizations to relate pay costs to performance in some way, and the absence of practical alternatives, help to explain why there has been no wholesale reversion in practice.
- The research is actually ambiguous rather than uniformly negative in respect of the effectiveness of individual performance pay, although it is a notoriously difficult area to research objectively and independently. Studies by Thompson and Huselid, for example, show individual performance pay being used in conjunction with a number of other HR practices in high performance and high added value workplaces. Studies in the US have demonstrated correlations between the motivation of knowledge workers and individual performance pay.
- However, the research does show that the effectiveness of individual pay-for-performance is highly context- and situation-specific, and it has highlighted the practical problems which many companies have experienced with their schemes.
- Problems with individual performance-related pay often resulted from applying a uniform merit pay and objective-based appraisal system throughout the organization. These difficulties can be categorized into three areas. First, there is the lack of a strategic approach to performance pay, with unclear objectives and rationale, and a lack of related, supporting HR initiatives. Second, in the area

of design, differentials in a low inflation environment between high and low performers have often been very small, and systems have suffered from uniform and inflexible design. Third, shortcomings in the areas of performance management and communication have generally been major contributors to the failings of performance pay schemes, which were often characterized by low levels of management involvement and staff communications and understanding.

- These problems have led a majority of companies to revise their performance pay schemes and we define these newer approaches as *paying for contribution*, characterized by: clearer and broader, more strategic performance objectives and awareness; by greater variety and flexibility of design, and reward for the 'hows' as well as the 'whats' of performance; and much greater attention to the processes of communication and performance management.

CASE STUDY 2.1

Introducing merit pay at the BBC
BACKGROUND

The BBC employs 23,000 staff in the United Kingdom, and its total paybill in 1995 was nearly £700 million, representing a third of total operating costs. While it is not in the private sector, the radical changes in the broadcasting industry have helped to drive a significant shift in reward strategy that has been pursued through a series of modifications during the 1990s. Performance-related pay remains at the heart of that strategy.

Broadcasting has become a highly competitive, global business dominated by commercial priorities. With a flat licence fee in real terms, the BBC has instigated a wide range of initiatives to increase efficiency and flexibility, including the creation of distinct independent business directorates and the introduction of producer choice in programme making.

THE REWARD STRATEGY

Pay policies are seen as being a key reinforcer of these changes and the achievement of business goals. The objectives of the BBC's reward strategy have been 'a modern flexible pay system which helps to attract, retain and reward the best talent with the most competitive pay, and create a close link between pay and performance'. Initial changes in 1991 focused on the objectives of simplicity and flexibility as the number of grades were reduced from over 40 to 20, and pay allowances and 'add-ons' were simplified and removed. Then in 1995, 11 broader salary ranges were introduced in place of the 20 grades, and incremental pay steps were replaced by market-related starting rates and progression based on performance (see Table 2.6). Jobs are now placed in bands using a tailor-made, computerized, points factor job evaluation scheme. Staff and trade unions were closely involved in developing this scheme, and the measurement factors employed are designed to reflect key business and cultural requirements, and essential employee skills and competencies.

PERFORMANCE MANAGEMENT

In respect of performance, the broad principles of the BBC's personal performance review system are that, 'staff will be clear about their role and purpose, and how this fits into the overall objectives of their department and those of the BBC'. This is being achieved by:

- cascading objectives, linked to business strategies (for example, improving efficiency) down the organization, with managers agreeing staff objectives after they have agreed their own;
- agreeing objectives (for example, doing something more cheaply) on an annual basis, with managers discussing progress throughout the year

Table 2.6 *Salary ranges at the BBC as at 1 August 1998*

Grade	Job Example	National Min, £PA	National Max, £PA	London Min, £PA	London Max, £PA
1	Print operator	8,960	14,160	11,560	16,760
2	Administrative assistant, wardrobe assistant	10,120	16,010	12,720	18,610
3	Library assistant, secretary	11,500	18,200	14,100	20,800
4	Production assistant, schedules assistant	13,120	20,750	15,720	23,350
5	Researcher, subtitler	14,950	23,660	17,550	26,260
6	Engineer, production manager	17,060	27,000	19,660	29,600
7	Radio producer, personnel officer	19,430	30,740	22,030	33,340
8	Reporter, designer	22,120	35,000	24,720	37,600
9	TV producer, personnel manager	25,080	39,670	27,680	42,270
10	Correspondent, senior producer	28,030	44,350	30,630	46,950
11	Managing editor, executive producer	31,340	49,590	33,940	52,190

particularly when priorities change or achievement is threatened by external factors; and

- setting between four and six objectives for each individual to achieve during the year.

Appraisals contain:

- a review of performance against objectives;
- a review of the way in which objectives were achieved in the previous 12 months;
- a discussion of individual training and development needs and career plans; and
- a summary of performance to support recommendations about staff development, future work and recognition.

The process is intended to be very much two-way, and on-going. There is no rating or points scoring scheme to determine the link to pay, which was regarded as getting in the way of open, two-way discussion on performance.

THE LINK TO PAY

Each August, a 'standard' pay rise is negotiated with trade unions at the corporate level. Managers then recommend additional merit awards for high performers. In the 1995–6 year the standard increase was 3 per cent, and a 0.5 per cent merit pot of £3.5 million was used to reward the top 15–20 per cent of performers. In cases of unsatisfactory performance, since 1996 pay levels for individual employees can be frozen, and can actually be reduced by up to 4.5 per cent. Such a step would only be taken after a formal interview had been held following the identification of poor performance.

Managers may make salary adjustments at other times of the year, for example, to reward new skills and job growth, or to respond to external market pressures.

Although there is considerable local flexibility over the job evaluation and pay review process, in order to ensure consistency and equity in appraisal and pay management:

- the job evaluation scheme and pay awards are subject to a thorough equal value review process;

- information on the distribution of awards in business units is monitored centrally;
- recommendations for merit pay awards have to be signed off by two levels of senior managers.

The change process has led to concerns expressed by trade unions and staff, and short-term industrial action was taken in 1994. BECTU, for example, described the system of merit pay as 'inherently unfair and discriminatory'.

LEARNING POINTS

None the less the BBC's experiences help to demonstrate the important part which systems to relate pay to performance, even in the public sector, play in an increasingly rapidly changing business environment. They also demonstrate the importance of a long-term perspective and the BBC continues to evolve and improve its arrangements, and respond to external developments. Directorates are being given increasing freedoms in respect of reward areas, and a broader variety of methods of linking pay and performance, such as incentives and profit share schemes, are also being investigated.

CASE STUDY 2.2

The necessity of paying for contribution in Yorkshire Water Services

Yorkshire Water Services introduced what they have called pay for contribution in 1998, replacing across-the-board pay increases for all staff with performance-based, individual increases. Their experiences provide an excellent example of both the importance of a strategic reward approach, and the practical realities and challenges of implementation and operation.

THE TRADITIONAL APPROACH

The core water business of Yorkshire Water has changed out of all recognition since privatization in the mid-1980s, with staffing for example being reduced by two-thirds to approximately 3,000 today. It would be fair to say, however, that these changes were focused on operational and structural issues, and HR and reward policies and the whole employee relations climate in the organization were largely untouched.

Staff were paid within a nine grade structure, receiving an annually nego-tiated pay award and service-related pay increments. Over half of staff had more than ten years of service and were on the ceiling of their pay scale. Staff turnover was generally low, as was the awareness of reward practices and changes in other organizations. In a number of areas pay and benefit levels were significantly ahead of comparable private sector activities with, for example, 32 days holiday for longer-serving staff. It was an ethos of enti-tlement and claims rather than performance and contribution.

The internal culture was predominantly task and production, rather than customer service and performance-oriented, with a somewhat 'top-down' management approach, focused on assets rather than people, and a strongly collectivist employee mindset. Communications and performance management systems were generally under-developed in the business, and newer graduates and professional employees found the lack of performance information and feedback frustrating.

THE NEED FOR CHANGE

The well-publicized problems connected with the water shortages in 1995–6 led to major changes in the management of the organization. Karen Moir and Amanda Stainton joined the business from National and Provincial as HR Director and Reward Manager, respectively, while a new managing director took over the Water Services subsidiary in 1997.

In consultation with fellow directors Moir rapidly developed YWS's 'Approach to People', an HR strategy focused on, 'the needs of the business'. This coincided with the business commencing on a major culture change programme which is still continuing. At the core of the approach are competencies and rewarding contribution, although she regards the culture change as supporting a move 'from Theory X' to 'Theory Y' management in the organization.

The dozen core principles underpinning the approach and communi-cated to staff include:

- recruiting and selecting individuals based on their competence, ability to contribute and potential;
- enabling all individuals to develop their own competence and potential as they contribute to business strategy;
- rewarding individuals for their contribution to the business plan (both what is achieved and how);

- rewarding individuals for the development and application of competencies (appropriate to their role and business needs).

A 20-item competency framework, organized into personal, people, process, and professional skills groupings, was developed in the business, and this has been at the centre of improvements to all HR systems.

A key priority has been the development of a performance-based culture, and paying for individual contribution has been a major component of this. As was explained in a communication to all staff, the impending regulatory review in 2000 and the need to achieve even tighter customer service and efficiency standards mean that:

> YWS is having to change its approach to business, its strategic objectives and values. We now need new HR and reward policies to help the company achieve its goal... (for) it is better that we manage this change ourselves rather than have others do it to us.

As Amanda Stainton elaborates, 'Money is not the most important motivator in life, but it is a lever for change, a symbol, a way to change behaviour.' Without the pay linkage, she feels that the new performance management system would not have had the power and the priority required to really impact on management and behaviour in the organization: 'the history was of managers backing away from tough decisions'.

The new performance management system was applied to management employees in 1996 and then extended to all staff in 1997. All staff now have a defined role profile and the performance management process is designed to facilitate the development and application of their required competencies, and the related achievement of objectives and results (see Figure 2.9).

IMPLEMENTATION

The reward change agenda that was implemented in 1998 has four main components. First, it has involved moving all employees into a flatter structure of six broad bands, replacing the existing nine staff and five management grades. According to the employee briefing, this was designed:

- to remove the focus on hierarchical progression and provide greater potential for personal development (and) encourage movement across roles and teams;
- to support the simpler, flatter organization design;

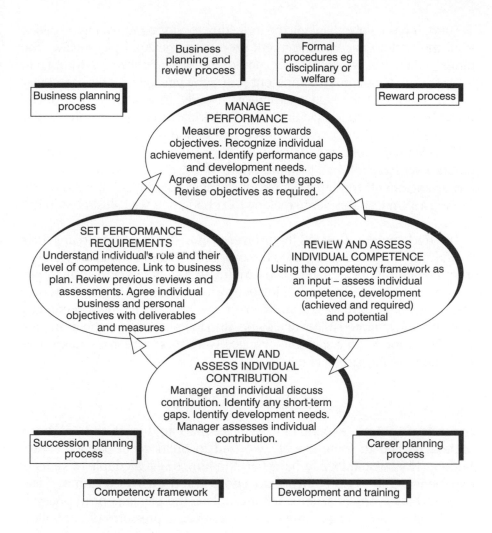

Figure 2.9 *Performance management process at Yorkshire Water Services*

- to provide greater flexibility to pay individuals according to their contribution and development of competence, to focus on achieving objectives that are critical to moving the company forward.

Second, there has been a downward revision of holiday entitlements, bringing the business more into line with external practice, and as part of a wider set of changes to achieve more flexibility in resourcing to match customer demands in a 24 hour, 365 days a year business.

Third, it has involved linking the individual performance ratings resulting from the performance management process to the April pay review. The range of increases was from 0 per cent for the worst performers, through to 3.5 per cent for the fully competent staff achieving all of their objectives, and 5.1 per cent for high contributors. Finally, to encourage the development of competence within roles, individuals may also receive a pay increase for significant personal development and growth in contribution.

This clearly represents a major change agenda and the performance pay paradox we have referred to in this book, of a traditional culture and set of pay arrangements requiring significant change, but that culture also representing a significant barrier to making the changes, is well illustrated in this case.

The trade unions declared themselves opposed in principle to any form of performance pay and opposed the proposals. Despite the offer of an upfront compensatory payment, two employee ballots saw a majority reject the new terms and conditions. However, after prolonged negotiations over the summer of 1998, and a number of revisions, including a secondary review of all staff rated as not achieving, and the phasing in of the reduction in holidays for existing staff, the changes were supported by a majority of staff and formally agreed in July.

LEARNING POINTS

Amanda Stainton recognizes that, 'we had to forget the textbook approach', and to some extent, 'we had to bulldoze in pay for contribution'. They would love to have had the time to get a couple of years of experience with performance management and their new communications and involvement systems before making the pay link, or to phase in the changes over a longer time scale. But business pressures did not allow this. She also is very much aware that 'we are at the start of a long journey'. Improvements in day-to-day performance management must continue, while more flexible approaches to working hours and benefits, and various forms of variable pay for all staff, are next on the agenda.

Yet YWS still, more than ever, regard the core tenets of their reward approach as essential, and a vital component of their cultural and business change programme, according to Stainton, 'a signal that things really were going to change this time'. Paying for contribution was not about implementing an alien ideology or cutting pay costs but recognizing that, 'we have to spend our pay budget in the right way, in the right places', and that people costs are only funded if regulatory and customer demands and standards are achieved. As evidence of the change in mindset, Stainton cites the payment of retention bonuses in IT. Formerly she felt these would have been delivered as a flat amount to all IT staff, whereas in practice today, they are being focused on the high contributing staff with the competencies that really are in demand in the business and in the market.

Karen Moir sums up the essential demands for, and nature of, pay for contribution in YWS as follows:

I believe the new approach to reward is a vital step in keeping YWS moving forward towards achieving the vision of becoming the best water company in the UK, and of working in an organisation which we are proud of. There is a compelling drive to get ourselves fit for business in a demanding public service environment. Our customers demand it, getting the maximum value for every pound they pay us. Our shareholders expect us to be effective... our cost effectiveness is a critical area with our Regulator and we are falling down the league table. This is not a threat but a fact of life... (and) we recognise that some of the changes are viewed as difficult.

We are convinced that the changes result in a reward system which is fairer to everyone, by taking into account individual contribution and competence. It is not fair that individuals who achieve their objectives receive no greater reward than those who simply 'tick over'. The changes also enable pay to reflect broader career development.

NOTES

1. Institute of Personnel and Development (1998) *1998 Performance Pay Survey, Executive Summary*, IPD, London
2. Hunt, JW (1998) A salary can't buy happiness, *The Financial Times*, 13 May
3. Oliver, J (1996) Cash on delivery, *Management Today*, August
4. Institute of Personnel and Development, op. cit.
5. Creelman, J (1995) Prime movers, *Personnel Today*, 14 February
6. Industrial Relations Services (1997) Pay prospects for 1998: a survey of the private sector, *Pay and Benefits Bulletin*, **435**, November
7. Industrial Relations Services (1994) Paying for performance: a survey of merit pay, *Pay and Benefits Bulletin*, **361**, October
8. Incomes Data Services (1997) General awards: fact and fiction, *Management Pay Review*, **197**, July
9. Daly, N (1998) Merit pay given another lashing, *Personnel Today*, 5 November
10. Towers Perrin (1997) *Learning from the Past: Changing for the future*, research report from Towers Perrin, London, March
11. Hutton, B (1998) Japan's career escalator slows to a halt, *The Financial Times*, 27 February
12. Verkaik, R (1998) Partnership makes pay bonus, *The Law Society Gazette*, May
13. Industrial Relations Services (1997), op. cit.
14. Creelman, op. cit.

15. Hutton, W (1996) *The State We're In,* Vintage, London
16. Quoted in Preston, R (1995) Labour calls for merit pay, *The Financial Times,* 8 June
17. Kohn, A (1993) *Punished by Rewards,* Houghton Mifflin, Boston
18. Gupta, N and Shaw, J (1998) Financial incentives are effective, *Compensation and Benefits Review,* March/April
19. Hunt, op. cit.
20. Locke, EA and Latham, GP (1979) Goal setting, a motivational technique that works, *Organisation Dynamics,* **8**
21. Wren, D and Greenwood, R (1998) *Management Innovators: People and ideas that have shaped modern business,* OUP, Oxford
22. Hunt, op. cit.
23. Oliver, op. cit.
24. Institute of Personnel and Development, op. cit.
25. Creelman, op. cit.
26. Industrial Relations Services (1994), op. cit.
27. Thompson, M (1998) HR and the bottom line, *People Management,* 16 April
28. Huselid, M (1995) The impact of HRM practices on turnover, productivity and corporate performance, *Academy of Management Journal,* June
29. Quoted in *The Economist* (1998) Riding high, 18 May
30. Katzell, ME (1993) Recognition, reward and resentment, *Research and Technology Management,* July
31. Le Blanc, P and Mulvey, P (1993) How American workers see the reward of work, *Compensation and Benefits Review,* January/February
32. Gupta and Shaw, op. cit.
33. Langley, M (1987) *Rewarding the Salesforce,* Institute of Personnel Management, London
34. Ryan, RM, Mims, V and Koestner, R (1983) The relation of reward contingency and interpersonal context to intrinsic motivation: a review and test using cognitive evaluation theory, *Journal of Personality and Social Psychology,* **45**, 4.
35. Cameron, J and Pierce, WD (1997) Rewards, interest and performance: an evaluation, *ACA Journal,* Winter
36. Bowey, A *et al.* (1982) *The Effects of Incentive Pay Systems,* Department of Employment Research Paper No 36, DOE, London
37. Flannery, TP, Hofrichter, DA and Platten, PA (1996) *People, Performance and Pay,* Free Press, New York
38. Towers Perrin research report, op. cit.
39. Bowey, op. cit.
40. Thompson, M (1992) *Pay and Performance: The employer experience,* Institute of Manpower Studies Report No 218, London
41. Brown, W and Hudson, M (1997) referred to in J Pickard, Experts greet move back to collectivism, *People Management,* 21 July
42. Kessler. I and Purcell, J (1992) Performance related pay: objectives and application, *Human Resource Management Journal,* 2 (3), Spring
43. Timmins, N (1998) Performance pay urged for teachers, *The Financial Times,* 2 June
44. Industrial Relations Services (1994), op. cit.
45. Marsden, D and Richardson, R (1994) Performing for pay?, *British Journal of Industrial Relations,* June
46. Institute of Personnel and Development, op. cit.
47. Budman, M (1997) Is there merit in merit pay?, *Across the Board,* June
48. Institute of Personnel and Development, op. cit.
49. Taylor, R (1994) Must try harder, *The Financial Times,* 2 February

50. The Industrial Society (1996) Rewarding Performance: Managing best practice, Report No 20, London
51. Flannery *et al.*, op. cit.
52. Kunkel, JG (1997) Rewarding product development success, *Research and Technology Management,* September
53. Oliver, op. cit.
54. The Industrial Society (1996) op. cit.
55. Marsden, D and French, S (1998) *What a Performance: Performance-Related Pay in the Public Services*, Research Paper, Centre for Economic Performance, London School of Economics, London
56. Towers Perrin, op. cit.
57. Institute of Personnel and Development, op. cit.
58. Incomes Data Services, op. cit.
59. Taylor, op. cit.
60. Kessler and Purcell, op. cit.
61. Flannery *et al.*, op. cit.
62. Thompson (1992), op. cit.
63. Towers Perrin, op. cit.
64. Marsden and Richardson, op. cit.
65. Oliver, op. cit.
66. Towers Perrin, op. cit.
67. Institute of Personnel and Development, op. cit.
68. Industrial Relations Services (1997) Merit moves on, *Pay and Benefits Bulletin*, **416**, January

3

Taking a strategic reward approach to paying for contribution

Rather than abandoning individual performance-related pay, organizations are adapting their schemes to improve the 'fit' between reward and the organization's business strategy.

(The Institute of Personnel and Development)[1]

The hard lessons from the UK experiment with performance pay may encourage managers to take a more strategic and reflective approach to pay in the future.

(Marc Thompson, Templeton College)[2]

We have already characterized paying for contribution as a more strategic, holistic and integrated approach to reward management than traditional performance-related pay. In this chapter we consider this whole issue of reward strategy in more detail:

- defining what a reward strategy is, and why organizations need to have them;

- describing the characteristics and changes taking place in contemporary reward strategies;
- assessing and illustrating the impact of these new strategies on approaches to paying for performance, and demonstrating the broader focus on contribution which is emerging.

In doing so we illustrate both the more comprehensive set of business and personal performance goals that pay and reward schemes are now being used to reinforce, and the much greater diversity of schemes and 'total reward' vehicles that is resulting. Finally, we show how international reward strategies are also illustrating this move towards contribution-related reward.

REWARD STRATEGY: ORIGINS AND IMPORTANCE

Ed Lawler was one of the first writers to champion the idea of reward strategy, which is now widely accepted in companies and HR departments. After all, how many of us today would recommend that our employer takes a non-strategic approach to reward? Rather than consisting of largely technical and administrative work, Lawler advocated that compensation and benefits staff, and their employers, should adopt, 'an integrated reward approach, linking company strategy, pay systems and employee behaviours'.[3] Figure 3.1 illustrates a simple model which we use building on these ideas, indicating how pay and reward policies need to reinforce the organization capabilities or critical success factors which will deliver strategic business goals.

Pay systems thus become an important means of communicating and reinforcing the achievement of the business goals of the organization, not just because pay represents an important cost for the business, but because pay systems can encourage and reward employees to pursue and achieve these goals and to develop and apply the essential capabilities supporting them.

US business strategy guru Michael Porter believes that, 'having the right rewards in place helps people to make the right choices to support your strategy', and so HR managers become 'the engineers of strategy implementation'.[4] London Business School professor Linda Grattan is critical of traditional UK personnel practices on this basis, in that, 'too often we see people management factors such as reward in

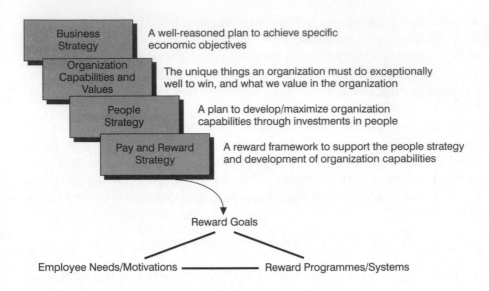

Figure 3.1 *A model for developing strategic reward practices*

isolation, in terms of tools and techniques, rather than strategic goals and values'.[5]

The most popular pay textbook in the UK has reflected the shift in emphasis as its title has changed in successive editions from passive *Pay Administration* to active *Reward Management*. Armstrong and Murlis under this latter title write of the necessity that, 'reward strategy and policies should be business-driven, responding to the needs of the business'.[6] The authors explain that while changing pay systems is always a sensitive process, alignment with business strategy is vital, rather than maintaining outdated practices, or just following fad or fashion.

As Grattan observes, however, the uptake and increasing significance of the concept of HR and reward strategy have been driven by senior managers, as well as by compensation and HR specialists seeking increasing organizational power and influence. 'To gain sustainable competitive advantage', she writes, 'we must operate effective HR strategies'.[7] Almost without exception, the key business strategy thinkers – Hamel and Prahalad, Collins and Porras, Gupta and Govindarajan – describe how economic and competitive trends mean that employees – the service they deliver, their commitment and motivation, their willingness to stay and develop – these are the factors that will drive successful organizations into the next millennium. As Collins and Porras explain, cost-effectiveness has now become merely a criterion to 'enter the competitive game', but 'the sources of sustainable competitive advantage have shifted from finance, to technology and now to human capital'.[8]

Increasing global competition, the growth of the information and service economy, and increasing skill shortages in the West have all meant that people really are an organization's most important asset, and an increasing number of research studies lend weight to these views. A longitudinal study carried out by Sheffield University for the IPD for example,[9] found that HR policies were a significant differentiator between high and low performing medium-sized companies. Similar research by Andrew Pettigrew at Warwick found that successful companies took a positive, asset-oriented approach to managing their employees.[10]

Research also demonstrates a correlation between particular business strategies and approaches to reward, supporting the practical existence of the concept. An Ashridge College study, for example, by Michael Goold and Andrew Campbell[11] demonstrated that performance bonus schemes were used more aggressively by larger, more diverse businesses with a 'financial control' management style, rather than more focused 'strategic controllers'. This confirmed the results of earlier research by Stephen Kerr and by Lorsh and Allen (see Table 3.1). Towers Perrin's utilities study[12] similarly found that individual performance pay schemes were used most often by those companies with a cost leadership strategy. Those with a greater emphasis on a business strategy of customer service enhancement used more team-based pay approaches and concentrated on achieving greater flexibility in employment conditions.

THE LACK OF FIT BETWEEN BUSINESS AND REWARD STRATEGY

The pressures for change in reward policies often brought about a move into individual performance pay as Chief Executives and HR Directors sought a greater return on their pay costs. Even if the methods were wrong, the motives were often right. Similar pressures are now hastening the moves for a rethink and moves into a contribution-based approach.

Table 3.1 *Relationship between remuneration and the business strategy of companies revealed in two research studies*

	Kerr[1]	Mixed	Gold & Campbell[2]		
			Strategic Planners	Financial Controllers	Strategic Controllers
Business Strategy	Vertical integration, constrained, diversifier, internal growth	Linked multi-businesses, unrelated, acquisitive growth	• Centralized • Internal growth eg BP, Cadbury, UB	• Decentralised • Acquisitive growth eg BTR, Hanson	• Mixture eg ICI, Courtaulds
Bonus		Mix			
• Payout	20–30%	40%	Average 14% Max 37%	22% 56%	22% 50%
• Measures	Corporate	Divisional	Corporate, often operational	Corporate and subsidiary, usually financial	Most often corporate & operational
• Targets	Subjective and qualitative	Objective and quantitative	Quantitative and qualitative, some *post facto* discretionary	Wholly quantitative, fixed hurdles	Quantitative and qualitative
Salary Increases	Tenure and performance	Performance			
Perks	Many	Few			
HR Philosophy	Hierarchy	Performance	Build on tradition, no reprisal, broad direction	Competition between subsidiaries, succeed or out, specific results	Mix of carrot and stick

Notes: 1. 1980s US PhD research (44 companies)   2. 1980s UK research (16 companies)

These pressures are perhaps most clearly evident in the practical examples of 'misfit' and misalignment between business strategy and reward, rather than in research studies. We have already described the misalignment in the example of the car salesmen in the previous chapter. They were encouraged to 'screw' their customers by their aggressive individual incentive scheme which purely rewarded sales margin, in contradiction to their service-oriented business strategy.

Table 3.2 illustrates the clear lack of fit between business goals and reward policies which Towers Perrin's work revealed in a large US oil company in the early 1990s. A major business strategy study had highlighted significant performance shortcomings. It produced a three-pronged focus for the future, centred on:

- reducing costs, given that it was the least efficient and productive of the major oil companies;
- growing more rapidly outside the United States;
- responding more quickly to potential overseas investment opportunities, addressing its laggardly performance in entering new markets in Eastern Europe and China.

The misalignment with reward was plain for all to see. A universal upper quartile pay stance in the oil market, itself a high paying sector, contributed to the lack of cost-effectiveness. A strongly US-oriented reward approach helped to stifle overseas initiatives and growth. Executives were awarded share options for example, even in countries

Table 3.2   *The business–reward lack of fit in a large oil company*

Business issue	Reward policies
The need to become a truly international organization	Worldwide US stock plan Wholly US Board One way expatriate policies
The need to reduce employee costs	Upper quartile market stance for all employees
The need to get fast and flexible	Worldwide US stock plan Top down and centralized annual planning, pay review and appraisal systems

where it was tax ineffective to do so. There was a rigid, top-down, objective setting and merit pay system, which saw remote overseas managers receiving their objectives late in the year, with no reflection of their more varied and risky conditions.

The same picture was evident in a large European gas company. There was no positive reward or reinforcement at all for the cultural values which the organization had recently expensively defined and promulgated, such as team work, innovation and performance focus (see Table 3.3). Here is a good example to support Lawler's contention that 'strategic thrust has been absent from most pay systems'.[13]

Similarly, the Operations Director of a privatized utility in Scotland told us, 'pay represents the most important set of changes we have to make', in order to help ' instill commercial, risk-taking attitudes, stimulating and accommodating change, in people who joined us for a quiet, orderly life in an engineering-driven culture'. The misalignment demonstrated between the new business and cultural requirements and their existing pay systems in his organization is illustrated in Figure 3.2.

Table 3.3 *Current misalignment in reward and recognition policies in a large gas company*

Business requirement	Current reward and recognition policies
• Performance: achieving superior business results	• Little differentiation in base pay levels within a grade • Limited differentiation in base pay increases according to performance • Hierarchical pay and benefits structure, recognizing position not performance • Limited variability in management bonus schemes
• Productivity improvements, increased RoA	• 'Cost of living' pay mentality prevails in many countries • Lack of variable pay and gainshare-type programmes below management levels • Little reward/recognition for bulk of employees for substantial 1995 improvements
• Behaviours consistent with our core values, to close the capability gaps: 　• innovation 　• customer focus 　• leadership 　• teamwork	• Lack of reward for such behaviours and teamwork • Evaluation and grading focuses on job content and size, not development/display of such behaviours • Very weak on non-pay recognition of valued behaviours

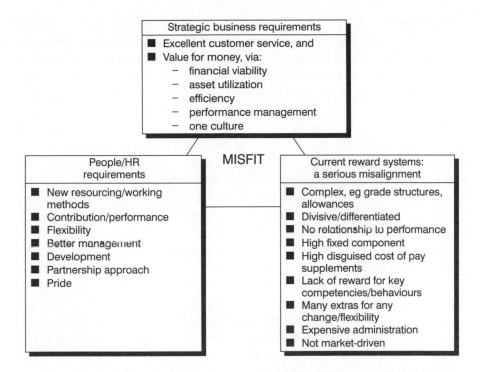

Figure 3.2 *Misalignment between reward and business/HR needs in a Scottish utility*

Their new commercial environment, with demanding financial and customer service targets, led to them placing a strong emphasis on efficiency and service in their business strategy. The HR requirements and values illustrated were researched and then promoted in the organization in support of this.

But the existing reward systems, inherited from their local authority past, directly conflicted with many of these aims. They were complex, expensive to operate and difficult to maintain, with no collective or individual reinforcement for any of the behaviours or results required to achieve the strategic goals.

Less than a quarter of executives in Towers Perrin's study[14] of this utility and fourteen other privatized companies thought that HR and reward policies were 'well integrated with our business goals and aid competitiveness'. With an ever-quickening pace of market, technological, product and organizational changes in the modern world, the dangers of this type of misalignment occurring is becoming apparent in more and more companies.

Another important change objective which performance-driven reward strategies have often been designed to reinforce has been the issue of status and hierarchy. Over 90 per cent of organizations in the Towers Perrin's European reward survey[15] had undergone major restructuring in the past three years, most typically involving delayering and downsizing. Employers are seeking much more responsive and performance-focused behaviours from employees, yet in a number of well-known cases the existing reward systems, with their hierarchical grading structures, graduated benefits entitlements and limited pay for performance were the most visible symbol of the old culture. 'The association between reward, hierarchy and status has to be broken', one participant in the European study told us, 'this was a vital driver of the new reward strategy'.

This was also an important motive for the new reward strategy at the Woolwich (see Case Study 4.1) which was adopted as the building society prepared to transform itself from a mutual into a more commercial and entrepreneurial PLC during 1997. And in the UK National Health Service, Health Minister Alan Milburn[16] explained the move towards a more performance-related pay system for nurses in late 1998 in similar terms. The existing system, he said, involves 'dozens of hierarchical and segmented grades', 'arcane allowances', and 'increments that are paid, irrespective of changes in skills, responsibilities and performance'.

CHANGING REWARD STRATEGIES IN SEARCH OF BUSINESS ALIGNMENT

Recognizing this need for business alignment, 70 per cent of the 300 companies across Europe in Towers Perrin's research[17] had a defined and articulated reward strategy. But reflecting on the rapid pace of organizational and environmental change, half had been either developed or substantially revised in the last 12 months, and the agenda has been very much a business-driven one. Figure 3.3 illustrates the most commonly cited business priorities and issues which these companies told us were creating the need for these new reward strategies and practices. We consider the second of these, the need to enhance employee competence in Chapter 4, but the first of these priorities, focusing employees on customer needs, was very much

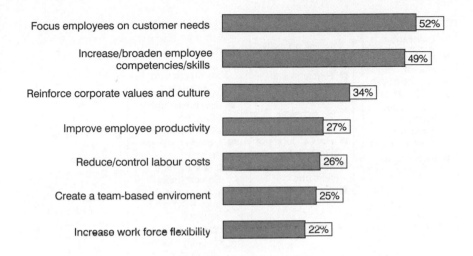

Figure 3.3 *Business priorities driving European reward strategies and changes*
Source: Towers Perrin

evident in the car company example we referred to earlier. This misalignment of business strategy and reward, and its subsequent redress in this case are illustrated in Figure 3.4. It also illustrates the dangers of a uniform and simplistic focus on individual and financial performance in performance-related pay schemes.

A CAR COMPANY EXAMPLE

With very low margins on new cars in the fiercely competitive UK market-place, and an aggressive individual commission-on-margin pay scheme (performance-related payments made up over three-quarters of total cash earnings), sales staff were directly and strongly encouraged to act in a way which conflicted with the company's business strategy. In this cut-throat market, the company's business strategy was to move to sell fewer more expensive models, achieved by excellent products and supported by teamwork and excellent customer service in the dealerships, as the basis for a long-term relationship-building process with customers. In practice, with the margins on new cars reduced substantially by the competition, sales staff were faced with having to make a decent living by competing with each other to get customers, and then going for a 'quick sale' on higher margin items such as financing. The most successful

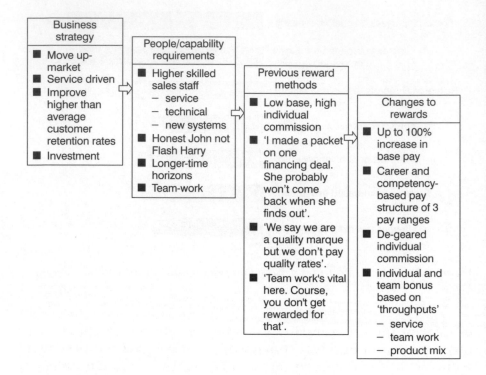

Figure 3.4 *Aligning reward systems with business strategy in the dealers of a European car company*

salesperson in doing this each year received a Rolex watch, just to reinforce the message!

The changes made to the sales staff pay schemes in 1996 illustrate some of the key trends evident in a more strategic and contribution-based approach. The level of individual performance pay in the form of monthly commission has been reduced. Base pay has been substantially increased from its former level of £6,500 and related to the essential skills and competencies required to build and maintain relationships with high net worth customers, which will fuel the future success of the organization. Finally, a new annual bonus scheme related to both team and individual contribution has been introduced. This incorporates measures of financial performance such as total sales and profitability in the dealership, but also reflects the critical customer service performance levels, as measured by a survey of all new customers, and statistics on repurchase rates.

GENERAL UK CHANGES TOWARDS PAY FOR CONTRIBUTION

These changes are symptomatic of the trends which UK and European-based organizations predict will be evident in the objectives and characteristics of their reward schemes over the next three years. The Towers Perrin European study[18] revealed a general and marked shift in reward strategy objectives:

- away from a strong internal equity focus, towards more externally market-driven pay;
- away from wholly job-based systems, towards more person-based approaches;
- away from a purely individual focus in pay, towards more varied individual, team and organization-based rewards;
- away from predominantly fixed pay, towards greater variable rewards;
- away from a total focus on financial outputs, towards considerations of competence, quality and service;
- away from boss and HR-driven reward systems, towards line manager and employee-driven approaches.

These objectives really specify the agenda for contribution-based reward which we describe in the rest of this book. They demonstrate the shift away from a narrow, near obsessive focus on individual performance-related pay, as the change in the overall ranking of top five reward objectives most frequently cited by these companies makes clear (see Table 3.4). In terms of the changes made to reward schemes in the last three years, pay for individual performance was rated as the third most important overall objective, yet it drops well

Table 3.4 *Changing emphasis in reward strategy: the top five reward objectives*

	Now	Future
Reward/retain best performers	1	1
Achieve/maintain market competitiveness	2	3
Pay for individual performance	3	–
Link pay to organization's key success factors	4	2
Control fixed pay costs	5	–
Pay for competence	–	4
Reward high levels of productivity, quality and customer satisfaction	–	5

Source: Towers Perrin

down the ranking for the future. So, interestingly, does a high focus on pay cost control.

Yet this is not to say that performance-related pay is being rejected as inappropriate for the future. Retaining high individual performers remains the number one priority in the future. But motivating the whole workforce to support the organization's key strategic success factors, such as quality and service, supported by high levels of employee competence, are seen as being much more important objectives for future reward strategies.

A much more sophisticated, diverse and tailored set of reward schemes than just individual merit pay is essential to deliver on this agenda. In the rest of this chapter we consider how in practice a much broader set of performance goals are being linked to reward, and how total reward strategies, encompassing the full diversity of reward schemes, are being used to reinforce them.

CHANGES IN THE PERFORMANCE MEASURES: FROM FINANCIAL PERFORMANCE TO CONTRIBUTION

In an economic sense, contribution is the difference between the cost of goods and services bought into an organization, and the value of those it delivers to its customers. The investment which the organization makes – in capital, technology, systems and employees – clearly has a major impact on the value which it can add and the contribution its employees make. Ultimately, the value added does reflect in high financial performance and returns to the shareholders, who provide the investment financing in the private sector. But short-term measures of financial performance and shareholder returns may not always be accurate indicators of how best to maximize the value-added in the longer term.

Hence, Prahalad and Hamel satirized the prevailing British attitudes to management in manufacturing industry at the start of the 1990s: 'by the end of the decade the one remaining employee in UK industry will be the most productive son-of-a-gun on the planet'.[19] Performance in terms of customer service, quality, innovation and growth also need to be accounted for. By contribution-related pay, we mean using pay to relate to this full range of performance factors, through which the contribution of employees to the business can be measured and promoted.

THE SPREAD OF STAKEHOLDER IDEAS

The broadening of the definitions and measures of performance in UK organizations reflects not just trends in business strategy thinking, but also social and political ideas during the 1990s, which have given a considerable boost to the concept of stakeholding. As expressed by writers such as Etzioni, Handy and Pfeffer, these ideas emphasize that a business is not just responsible to its owners, its shareholders, but to a much broader range of audiences. As Handy puts it, 'The premise of Anglo-Saxon capitalism, that the people who provide the money own the company, will not hold up in the new world'.[20] It is according to Freeman, 'radically outdated', in a society of 'globalisation and instant information where everyone's business is everyone else's business', and where, 'managers simply have to pay attention to customers, suppliers, employees, financiers and communities'.[21]

The business goals of organizations have increasingly come to recognize the importance of these ideas, and to set specific goals and objectives, and specify and record performance measures across a much broader terrain. Environmental and employee reports are now common additions to annual financial reports in public companies.

The business case for this broader agenda has been clearly highlighted in research studies. Pfeffer's research[22] demonstrated that the highest performing companies in terms of shareholder returns in the United States between 1972 and 1992 had been those which placed a major emphasis on their customers and employees: Nordstrom, Hewlett Packard and South West Airlines.

In the United Kingdom Professor Peter Doyle[23] reported on Warwick University research showing the significant costs to UK companies of being 'too narrowly focused on short-term financial returns', which led to them becoming 'hollowed-out companies, with uncompetitive products in declining markets'. Their study demonstrated that poor customer service was costing the average UK business £267 million in profits over a five-year period. A Surrey University study[24] similarly showed that amongst 225 mechanical engineering companies, those with a focus on quality standards who had been awarded ISO 9000 achieved significantly above average performance in terms of profitability and return on equity.

In the United States, Jack Welch of General Electric has stated that the most important measures in a business are not profit or financial returns to shareholders but 'customer satisfaction, employee satisfaction and cash flow'. Indeed, it has now reached the stage where the Divisional Vice-President of Mobil's US downstream marketing division could express pleasure with his business's first quarter 1995 performance, despite the fact that a warm winter saw a worsening of financial results. But he felt they had 'moved the needle in all the areas we could control in the right direction', such as market share, controllable operating expenses and employee satisfaction.

REWARDING CUSTOMER SERVICE

Not surprisingly, therefore, pay and reward schemes have also been used to reinforce this more diverse set of performance goals and objectives. Customer service measurement is the area where the trend is most apparent, and a significant and growing minority of executive and employee performance pay schemes now reflect these criteria. Thus, 50 per cent of the bonus of IBM's sales staff, for example, now reflects the customers' views of the salesperson, and IBM has calculated the significant profit value which favourable customer attitudes add to their business. Similarly, the bonus scheme of Anglian Water's executives is affected not just by financial performance, but also by measures of the regulatory service standards achieved by the company, a relationship strongly advocated by the UK's Labour government.

Looking at 23 of the management incentive plans on Towers Perrin's database of executive remuneration in UK plcs, only four now rely purely on measures of corporate financial performance. The annual bonus of Richard Eyre, Chief Executive of ITV, relates to a variety of targets, including viewing figures. At Railtrack, executive bonuses depend not just on the financial and operating performance of the company, but also of the train operating companies that use its tracks. 'It's no good us saying we are doing well if the performance of the train companies does not match up,' according to one executive. In 1998 the company committed to the rail regulator to reduce delays by 75 per cent and between 10 and 30 per cent of the directors' bonuses, which range from a maximum of 35–45 per cent of earnings, is dependent on operating performance.

In a UK drinks company, the base pay increases of all managers now depend on the achievement of customer service, as well as the financial objectives of his/her area. Consideration is also given to the assessed competence of the manager in areas such as relationship building and communications. Figure 3.5 illustrates the performance review form used. The actual and required level of performance against these competencies is compared, and the results, as well as the achievement of personal financial objectives, determine the size of the increase. We review this type of change to merit pay plans in Chapter 5.

Telephone-based employees in the mushrooming number of call centres in UK businesses (over 2 per cent of the employed workforce will work in them by 2005) are often remunerated in this way. This is normally delivered in one of two ways. In some cases an assessment of behavioural and customer service skills is related to the base pay increase of individuals, as at banks First Direct and Barclays. In others it works through the operation of a bonus scheme which incorporates customer service measures, as at the Prudential Bank and Lloyds/TSB.

At Rank Xerox, there are many different ways in which customer service is reflected in the reward package. The total base pay increase

Name:	Date:	
Objectives	**Results achieved**	**Final rating**
1. Achieve financial targets	1 2 3 [4] 5	4
2. Achieve customer service targets	1 2 3 [4] 5	4
Key competencies	**Levels**	**Final rating**
1. Teamworking	1 [A 2] [R 3] 4 5	3
1. Communications	1 2 3 [RA 4] 5	4
1. Innovation	1 2 [3 A] 4 [5 R]	3
Overall performance summary	[R=Required A=Actual]	**Overall rating** 4

Figure 3.5 *Relating pay increases to competencies and results in a UK drinks company*

'pot' of UK employees is adjusted, up or down, each year by an index of customer service performance. This comprises a mixture of 'hard' operational measures, such as product returns, and 'softer' attitudinal surveys of a sample of customers. British Steel similarly uses performance pay schemes which now vary in each business unit but reflect this broader agenda, replacing the traditional productivity-based bonus schemes. In Strip Products, for example, a monthly bonus plan now operates which, as well as productivity, also rewards product quality and customer delivery performance. Indeed, according to the CBI's data, 24 per cent of collective bonus plans now contain measures of work quality and 32 per cent incorporate measures of customer satisfaction. We consider contribution-related bonus schemes in Chapter 6.

USING THE BALANCED SCORECARD

Perhaps the best operationalization of these ideas of stakeholder-driven business strategies, which considers the full range of contributions made by the organization, has been the balanced business scorecard. Originally developed by Kaplan and Norton,[25] the scorecard essentially provides a framework for organizations to use to define and assess their performance in respect of each of their main stakeholder groups. Thus in their original scorecard they illustrate:

- the financial perspective in terms of traditional measures of profit and returns for shareholders;
- the internal business perspective, including measures of operational efficiency such as asset utilization;
- measures of learning and innovation, as an indication of future strategic prospects;
- the customer perspective in respect of measures of service and market stance.

According to a Business Intelligence Survey,[26] 48 per cent of the organizations attempting to better align compensation practices with their business strategy are now using a balanced scorecard, and 13 per cent some type of added value methodology such as EVA. The Boards of some very well-known UK companies, such as BA and BT, have adopted these ideas and use them to guide performance measurement and targeting throughout their organization. A number also use the scorecard in their performance pay systems. According to Norton, 'compensation should be one of several elements linked to the scorecard... serving as a reinforcer.' The actual measures and weighting on them obviously vary according to the function, level and job being considered, but the balanced scorecard provides a common organizing framework for performance across the organization.

So, the Board of BT's annual bonus is now affected by selected measures of performance for their employee and customer stake-holders, as well as their shareholders. Bass Brewers is re-designing its management and all-employee bonus schemes on a similar basis (see Case Study 4.2). Sears, the retailing group, has a three-point business strategy of making its business a compelling place to invest, by making it a compelling place to shop and a compelling place to work. Its research indicates that a five-point improvement in employee atti-tudes correlates with a 1.3 point increase in customer satisfaction, and a 0.5 per cent increase in revenue growth. The long-term incentives of its 200 senior managers are therefore based one-third on investor returns, one-third on customer satisfaction and one-third on employee attitudes.

Similarly, in 1995 British Gas Transco adopted its Group Performance Reward Scheme. Under this scheme the base pay budget increase for all employees was modified by four measures of company performance which are contained within its scorecard: financial performance, transport system utilization, customer satisfaction and customer service standards.

The variety of stakeholders and measures also makes this scorecard approach particularly useful for non-profit-making organizations, where the absence of the profit motive and strong financial measures undoubtedly limited the effectiveness of the early performance pay schemes that were introduced. Indeed, often they were perceived in care-based organizations simply as a crude incentive to support management cost-cutting initiatives, as part of a 'jobs for pay' trade-off. Balanced scorecard-type principles are being employed by public sector organizations such as the Post Office (who relate it to their variable pay scheme), Ofgas, and the Funding Agency for Schools.

Indeed, one of the best definitions of a contribution-based reward approach we have seen came from recent guidance issued by the Cabinet Office to many of the Governmental organizations and bodies who have taken on delegated pay responsibilities. The, 'you must have individual performance pay' rhetoric of earlier years has been replaced by a more strategic perspective. It advises them to review not just 'the effectiveness of performance pay', but also consider 'the interaction of pay with other HR issues and the extent to which pay systems meet government objectives, including cross-boundary working and equal pay'. The guidelines elaborate 'the emphasis on the link between performance and pay remains, but there are a range of options for reward systems being introduced – greater use of competency, team-based systems, bonus schemes, etc. The evaluation of (existing schemes) provides an opportunity to consider being more innovative and forward-looking with reward strategy.'[27] The UK government's 1999 proposals for performance pay for teachers seem to reflect similar broad principles and measures.

An example of the impact of the scorecard on the way in which this broader concept of performance is rewarded in a UK bank is shown in Figure 3.6. This example illustrates the pay methods recently introduced for Client Relationship Managers, who lead cross-functional teams of staff, and are responsible for managing the bank's relationships with its largest clients. The 'hard' financial performance of the client team in achieving income targets through its customer base, and measurable customer performance in terms of their perceptions of service levels, and the number who are placed in the highest net worth category, affect the annual bonus of the individual CRM.

However, the two other categories of the scorecard are not regarded from a pay stance just as 'nice-to-have'. The most measurable is not necessarily the most important. The internal efficiency of the CRM and their team, his or her management style as applied to their team members, and the broader contribution they make to other colleagues in the bank, for example in producing new business leads and referrals,

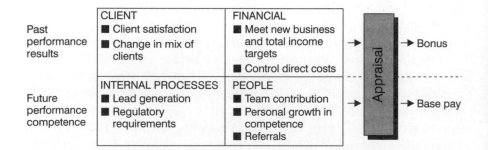

Figure 3.6 *Paying for contribution using a balanced scorecard in a UK bank for Client Relationship Managers*

are all used to influence their annual base pay increase, which is totally contribution-based. The bank also argues that though this means it is rewarding both immediate past performance in the bonus, and the basis for its future success and performance through the base pay vehicle.

CHANGES IN THE PAY SCHEMES: FROM MERIT PAY TO TOTAL REWARDS

This last example illustrates another key aspect of paying for contribution, which is the growing diversity of reward vehicles now being used to encourage and reward higher contribution, and tailored to the specific needs of each organization. As we noted in the last chapter a key problem with merit pay has often been uniformity and inflexibility. As *IDS Focus* put it, 'conventional wisdom is that merit pay recognizes people are different. In practice it has treated everyone the same.'[28] Today, however, as *The Economist* notes, 'Firms are abandoning the rigid formulas (and wholly merit pay) of the 1980s in favour of varied and tailor-made schemes.'[29]

Thus, 48 per cent of companies in the Towers Perrin European study[30] now had two or more different performance pay plans in place. Through this increasing diversity, organizations are better able to reflect the specific needs, goals and motivations of different parts of their business, rather than assuming that often distant financial goals of senior management will motivate everyone. Indeed, it has perhaps reached the stage in some organizations that there is such a plethora of different pay schemes that the overall strategic direction of the organization is in danger of being lost, and a potential conflict between different schemes produced. We have certainly found this to be an issue amongst staff in certain retailing distributors. The range of schemes on offer, from the employer and from manufacturers, often leaves sales staff either confused, or not focusing on their employer's strategic priorities as they chase the highest earnings.

This is where the use of a strategic framework and clear reward goals are so vital. Figure 3.7 illustrates how a financial services organization communicated its new reward strategy to its employees. On the left-hand side of the figure the interlocking aspects of company performance, supported by team and individual performance are

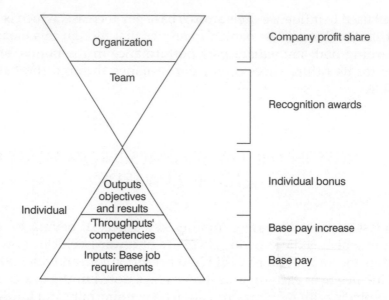

Figure 3.7 *A strategic approach to rewarding contribution in a UK company*

illustrated. Individual performance in the triangle relates to the tasks and responsibilities of the job, and the application of employees' skills and competencies to achieve the desired individual results.

Different facets of the reward strategy are used to reinforce these different levels of performance in this company. Base pay increases relate to the broad, individual competence and contribution of each employee, while the narrower achievement of the key personal targets drives an individual bonus. To reinforce collective performance and avoid any damaging effects on team work (which we saw in the previous chapter, has been a danger with more narrowly focused performance pay plans in the past), the company also now has a very active series of 'spot' and league-table based recognition awards. It also operates a company-wide profit sharing scheme to reinforce inter-team, cross-company performance and give everyone a share in the success of the business.

Pearl Assurance has similarly mapped out how the essential staff competencies it needs to develop and apply for future strategic success are all reinforced by different components of their total rewards package (see Figure 3.8). Again a very broad range of reward vehicles is being used.

Some companies achieve similar goals by operating multi-tiered or combination pay schemes which reflect a number of these different

COMPETENCIES	REWARD REINFORCERS
■ Customer service orientation ■ Problem identification	■ 360° assessment for pay increase ■ Customer satisfaction results for bonus ■ Non-cash awards/recognition
■ Initiative ■ Tolerance for stress	■ Market rates of pay ■ Flexibility of package ■ Broadbanding
■ Communication ■ Work standards	■ Open/simple reward system ■ Employee assistance programme ■ Pay equity/monitoring
■ Teamwork/co-operation ■ Planning and organization	■ Team/individual bonuses ■ Celebrate success
■ Maximizing performance ■ Decision-making	■ High variable pay element ■ New performance management system ■ Bonus availability at all levels
■ Leadership ■ Delegation and follow up	■ Even higher variable pay ■ Open communication of results ■ Catch people doing it right

Figure 3.8 *How essential competencies are reinforced by the reward and recognition strategy at Pearl Assurance.*

levels and aspects of performance. Such schemes were the fastest growing and most highly rated type of performance bonus scheme in Towers Perrin's research,[31] and we consider these in more detail in Chapter 6. However, there can be the danger of these schemes becoming overly complex and difficult to understand and this helps to explain why British Gas Transco reformed its GPRS scheme in 1998.

Linking each aspect of performance to a defined reward policy goal or mechanism, as at the Pearl, can be an extremely powerful communications vehicle for employees. It can also help to address some of the unclear and often overly-optimistic expectations which were placed on 1980s style performance-related pay schemes.

Figure 3.9 illustrates the results of an analysis which we carried out with a UK utility company which wanted to strengthen the relationship between pay and performance in its new, more competitive and commercial business environment. We got the board to list out their reward objectives, which included both providing a direct individual incentive and focus on important personal goals, but also a broader desire to reinforce the culture change process underway in the business and reward collective success.

Type of scheme	Direct incentive to improve performance unlock performance barriers	General recognition thank you	Cultural changes and team work identification	Changing business cost structure	Ease/cost of implementation	Tax effectiveness
Profit sharing	✗✗	✓✓	✓	✗✗	✓✓	✓✓
Gainsharing	✓	✓	✓	✓	✓	✓
Small group bonus	✓	✓	✗	✓	✗	✗✗
Individual performance bonus	✓✓	✓	✗✗	✓	✗✗	✗✗
Individual base pay movement	✓✓	✓	✗✗	✗✗	✗✗	✗✗

Key

✓✓ Strongly contributes to this objective
✓
✗
✗✗ Does not meet this objective

Figure 3.9 *Analysing the different reward options in a UK company.*

The analysis demonstrated that these aims were not necessarily contradictory, but that their reward strategy needed to prioritize them, and develop specific schemes to address each. No single performance pay scheme could achieve all of these objectives. Profit sharing schemes for example, remain tax-effective in the UK and although this benefit is being withdrawn, there is research evidence demonstrating that they are positively associated with long-term company success, and with favourable employee attitudes and lower employee turnover.[32] Yet they do not motivate individuals to achieve short-term personal goals in the way that an individual incentive may. This company therefore adopted a variety of performance pay schemes at different levels in the organization, to fully reward and reinforce the range of contributions required from its employees.

TOTAL REWARDS

Employers therefore need to consider the total rewards environment in the organization and what, beyond pay, can be used to attract, motivate and retain high performing and contributing staff in the longer term. As we have seen from a variety of the motivation studies reviewed in Chapter 2, many factors beyond the purely monetary motivate people.

In Figure 3.10, we present a simple model of four different aspects of total rewards. In an increasingly complex, heterogeneous and fast-changing world, HR and reward issues – just as in medicine and social services disciplines – increasingly demand interdisciplinary solutions. The financial rewards in the upper quadrants of this model represent transactional rewards which are necessary to recruit and retain employees. But as Bloom and Milkovich[33] observe, financial rewards alone cannot extract those employee behaviours that really add value, which create the mindset required for an employee to voluntarily commit to fully contribute to competitive success. They can also generally be easily copied or exceeded by competitors.

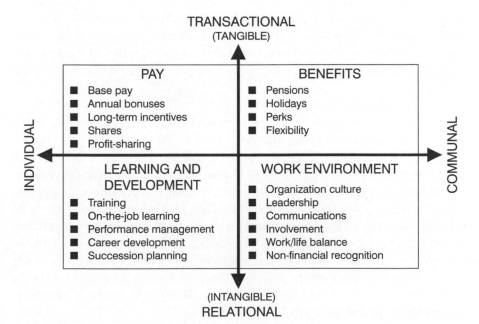

Figure 3.10   *Model of total rewards*

Relational rewards, on the other hand, produced by the lower quadrants of learning and development and work environment in the model, are essential to enhance the value of the upper quadrants. A variety of research studies indicate that a combination of transactional and relational rewards creates a broad and flexible employment relationship, in which employees are committed to common goals, values and long-term success. As Bloom,[34] and Gerhart and Milkovich[35] demonstrate, a broad 'bundle' of valued rewards must be offered in exchange for a 'cluster' of employee contributions.

Performance-related pay schemes do not inherently conflict with this relationship but as we saw in the previous chapter, they interact with the other rewards and motivations such as goal achievement. This research also demonstrates that the ability of performance pay schemes to motivate a high level of contribution by employees depends on factors in the other quadrants, such as employees' sense of security, their autonomy to affect results, and their degree of trust in the organization – all aspects of the work environment (see, for example, Huselid[36] and Bloom and Milkovich[37]).

UK accountants Saffrey Champness introduced performance pay primarily to help in breaking down their old hierarchical and status-based culture. According to their HR Director, it works because, 'people recognise their pay operates in a co-operative, supportive environment', illustrating these interactions in the total rewards 'bundle'. Similarly, the total rewards approach, including performance pay, at clothing company Lands End is, 'concerned with the entire workplace'.[38]

Actions and initiatives in respect of the broad environment which the employer provides – the level of communications and involvement, learning and development processes, and so on – are today therefore an integral part of an effective reward strategy. They are often, in our experience, under-leveraged. This is particularly so in cash-restrained public sector organizations, who often cannot offer more money, but can offer employees considerable benefits and opportunities such as flexible working, and a stimulating environment. Generally we tend to be very limited in our concepts of reward and ignore many of these potential motivators. A list of the wide range of potential rewards for Research and Development staff is shown in Figure 3.11. We return to this subject of the broad reward environment and a trusting employment relationship in Chapter 8.

Research on the motivations of Generation 'X', the technologically literate generation born between the mid-1960s and mid-1970s, and

Recognition

PRAISE
- Feedback
- Private praise
- Not taking scientists for granted
- Enthusiasm and support from top management
- Appreciation
- Company praise
- Public praise

MORE RESPONSIBILITY AND AUTHORITY
- Freedom to develop solutions to solve problems
- Freedom of action
- Responsibility
- Authority to carry out responsibilities
- Budget control
- Expense account
- New position

PROFESSIONAL RECOGNITION
- Authorship on papers
- Association awards
- Fellows programme
- Honours dinner
- Plaque/trophy
- Title
- Certificate

WORK SITUATION
- Meeting personal goals
- Sense of accomplishment
- Challenging research
- Interesting/meaningful research
- Setting joint objectives
- Team membership
- Dual ladder
- Personal interaction with upper management
- Special parking

Rewards

INCOME
- Salary increase
- Equity position
- Profit sharing
- Promotion
- Pay-for-performance
- Bonus
- Patent royalties
- Gainsharing
- Merit salary
- Percent of savings
- Restricted stock purchase plan
- Bonus for patents
- Stock options
- Cash awards
- Incentive award
- Cost-of-living salary adjustment

IMPROVED WORKING CONDITIONS
- Satisfying scientists' needs
- Flexible schedule
- Adequate resources to run projects
- Earned time off
- Personalized office redecorating

PROFESSIONAL DEVELOPMENT
- Trip to meeting
- Membership in professional association
- Paid education

BENEFITS
- Fringe benefits
- Retirement plan
- Stock purchase plan
- Membership in country club

Figure 3.11 *Listing of different forms of recognition and rewards in R&D*
Source: LW Ellis (1992) Reward Strategies in R&D, *Research and Technology Management*, March/April

from whom the next generation of senior management will be drawn, demonstrates the importance of these factors to their motivation.[39] Contrary to popular perceptions, this group is not averse to monetary rewards and are extremely hardworking on jobs that interest them. Recognition of their performance in a financial and non-financial sense is important. But they are also seeking interesting and varied jobs, project work, an attractive work environment and constant learning and development. If their employers fail to provide it, they will move on. Towers Perrin's Workplace Index research amongst large US companies found these employees generally seeking a broader range of rewards, such as skills development and scope for career movement, as well as a financial share in the success of their company.

A number of major employers, such as Unilever, are recognizing the long-term potential contribution of high performing individuals in this category by providing them with detailed career planning assistance, and funding learning opportunities on an on- and off-the-job basis. This structured career planning and development seems to be becoming more, not less, important in our turbulent times and appears to have a high appeal to graduate recruits.

In the IT Department of a recently merged UK-based insurance company, attitude studies showed that bonuses were not the key to retaining highly prized systems development specialists. They wanted competitive pay, recognition for their contribution and certainly not service or hierarchical-based rewards. But what really kept them and motivated them was the complexity and interest of the work, and the learning they were receiving on the massive projects which the company had underway. They also valued the open, non-controlling environment in which they worked, which meant they could contribute fully, yet be flexible and work from home, if required and if it suited them. Both parties valued this type of contractual relationship based on 'employability', which we describe in more detail in Chapter 8.

A US telecomms provider similarly needed to look at total rewards in response to the requirements of its increasingly international business operating across seven countries. The business strategy focused on corporate customers and demanded a uniformly high level of service worldwide. Current problems were found, in part, to relate to inconsistent HR and reward programmes and messages in their different locations. A variety of changes were initiated, including improved career development, better communication on HR issues and practices, an all-employee bonus scheme focused on customer service performance, and a flexible benefits programme.

RECOGNITION SCHEMES

Recognition schemes and non-cash awards can play a vital part in the total rewards package in reinforcing the business priorities and supporting values in an organization. In the United Kingdom at present these are where some of the most creative and probably highest value-added work is going on in the reward field. Over 50 per cent of companies use these types of scheme and they have a very high rate of assessed effectiveness relative to other performance rewards.[40] The average number of staff receiving such awards in the organizations surveyed by Towers Perrin is 4 per cent pa, although in some sectors such as healthcare the numbers average 8–9 per cent. These rewards may be in the form of gifts, vouchers, holidays, perks such as use of a car or holiday home, or maybe recognition in the form of dinners, awards and ceremonies. They are particularly prevalent in knowledge and technology-based industries, as well as sales and service functions. Of course, many recognition schemes have been in place for years, but two key trends are evident in their late 1990s' evolution.

First, there is much clearer focus on key strategic business goals and values, such as team work, customer service or business improvement. Land Rover's revamped suggestion scheme, introduced as a support for its new culture of empowerment and involvement, has produced annual savings of over £5 million pa since its launch. It is an important component of Rover's 'new deal' and employment relationship with its staff (this, incidentally, also saw the removal of narrow, productivity-focused bonus schemes). Similarly, South West Airlines in the United States is not the highest paying airline company but makes extensive use of these types of awards, to reinforce its customer and employee-focused ethos. As its Chief Executive observes 'you can't provide greater customer service if your people are miserable', and there is a strong 'fun' element to many of the generally low value recognition devices it uses.

Second, as South West Airlines also demonstrates, there has been a shift to a much more inclusive philosophy of recognizing as many winners as possible, rather than simply rewarding an elite of high performing superstars. As the IPD's research on performance pay found, many performance-related reward schemes are designed to motivate the small group of already high performing individuals, and therefore ignore the bulk of an organization's employees. While the majority of respondents in that survey felt that their merit pay scheme affected the behaviour of high performers, only 4 per cent felt it had a significant impact on average performers. In many sectors it is the contribution of all employees, not just a few superstars, which will really ramp up the organization to world-class performance standards.

Thus many organizations have reformed and reformulated their recognition programmes. Pfizer UK has done so for its UK salesforce. It has made its elite, high performers 'club' a less grandiose and expensive scheme, and introduced in addition a wider diversity of recognition schemes. These are focused on the company's values and designed to reward the contribution of a wider population. The distribution of these awards is largely handled locally. In its Research division, staff representatives help make award nominations (see Case Study 5.1).

The strategic framework of different recognition schemes now operating in a public sector organization is illustrated in Figure 3.12. A small number of competitive schemes are designed to publicly recognize very high performance, but there is now a whole range of low cost ways of immediately recognizing good performance at the local level. Leyland is another company with a flat organization structure, who now use a variety of non-monetary techniques to recognize and reward people, including quality awards, team dinners and on-site learning centres.

Continental Airlines was performing poorly by industry standards in 1995. It introduced a series of cash and non-cash recognition awards for all staff, which were earned when the company was in the top five airlines for on-time departures in the United States. That year, they made the top five in nine of the 12 months. According to their then Vice President, the schemes helped 'get the entire organization wrapped around that goal'.

CONTRIBUTION-BASED APPROACHES TO INTERNATIONAL REWARD

This new, broader, contribution-based focus on total rewards is evident in current trends in international remuneration.[41] Many compensation professionals have now realized that spending hours on the latest pay

	Distribution	Frequency	Size	Currency	Purpose	Operation
PART C	To highest performers against key criteria	Annual	Significant, but with non-financial as well as financial recognition	Reasonable financial reward with high recognition attached	Reinforce importance of demonstrating core values and achieving key goals, illustrate highest performance, customer service award, etc	Organization-wide, centrally controlled
PART B ←			Intermediate			→
PART A	To as many as possible, so long as criteria met	Fast and as frequent as possible, so long as criteria met	Low value but still meaningful, eg letters, vouchers	As varied as possible to address individual motivations	Provide general broad-based recognition and thanks for good performance and significant efforts beyond the norm	Devolved as far as possible

Figure 3.12   *Recognition policy in a public sector organization*

'tweak' to their expatriate reward policies – the fanciest purchasing-power-parity calculation or whatever – is generating little return in providing multinational employers with the increasingly global and mobile workforce they require. As Percy Barnevik of ABB puts it, 'to be a global company we have to develop a global mindset', and the motivation and development of international staff are key to the realization of the increasingly global ambitions of many companies. Yet traditional, technically and expatriate-focused pay programmes are failing to deliver on this agenda. Lawton speaks of the 'fossilisation of current paradigms in international rewards',[42] while a US study found common criticisms of international remuneration policies for being inflexible, expensive and lacking in innovation.[43]

Three important trends emerging in response are: first, a greater focus on performance-related rewards, rather than simply cost add-ons; second, greater flexibility in the make up of the reward package; and third, more attention to the environmental and developmental aspects of the total rewards package. Some illustrative examples are described below.

In respect of performance, one UK-based industrial utility company now retains a premium for its expatriate employees but only so long as the sponsoring manager can justify the excess cost in terms of the greater contribution and value added by expatriates, as compared to local employees (see Figure 3.13). But that extra cost is no longer all paid as up-front, cost-of-living supplements and allowances. It is largely in the form of a project completion bonus, which is related to the successful delivery of key objectives and added value on the assignment. US company Placer Dome has similarly replaced a number of the traditional cost add-ons designed to 'bribe' people to go abroad with a long-term, capital accumulation programme for its international employees.

Another UK industrial company meanwhile retains a package of various payments and allowances, but allows employees to select from a mix of them. It also gives a choice in terms of where payments are made. Like many companies, they are also recognizing the importance of cultural and supporting environmental issues, as well as remuneration, in successful overseas postings. With over 50 per cent of expatriates now in dual career households, they have followed the example of multinationals such as Shell and introduced a comprehensive programme of preparation, cultural training and

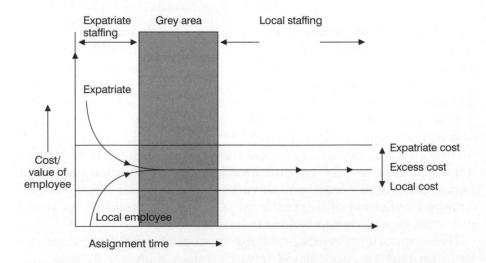

Figure 3.13 *Comparative value analysis in international reward management in an industrial company*

spouse assistance, in the form of training provision, and local advice and support. A number of research studies have found family problems to be an important cause of the high failure rates in expatriate postings.

Finally, reflecting on identified shortcomings in the development of its overseas staff, this industrial company has followed companies such as Shell and Unilever and has introduced mentoring programmes as part of a more structured approach to career planning and repatriation. It has also instituted a global recruitment programme aimed at creating a much more diverse and international expatriate workforce.

CONCLUSIONS ON CONTRIBUTION-RELATED REWARD STRATEGIES: BREADTH, DIVERSITY AND TRANSITION

So, employers are increasingly taking a more strategic perspective to performance pay, as a significant component of their new, business-focused reward strategies. Driven by business demands in an increasingly competitive and rapidly changing world, these strategies are characterized by a much broader definition of performance criteria and contribution, and by a greater diversity and flexibility of reward vehicles. We illustrate more fully the varied designs of reward schemes which are emerging in the next chapter.

Yet a final point to reflect on reward strategy is that strategies are much easier to define than to implement and operate. Working recently for a European manufacturing company, we researched the effects of a new performance-related bonus plan which had been introduced two years earlier. It had been designed so as to reward the achievement of seven performance targets, each related to one of the seven strategic goals of the company. The senior executives were delighted at the obvious level of business alignment. Yet our research found that around two-thirds of employees felt unable to exert any influence on the performance measures used in the plan, and over half would have preferred a return to their pre-existing pay arrangements. As one Personnel Director told us, the only reward strategy worth having is one that works!

Reward strategies are important and we would not advocate a return to the tactical, reactive and short-term practices of old. The 'knee-jerk responses to skill shortages' recently described by IDS in the growing use of retention bonuses for IT staff is not, in our opinion, a positive trend. But reward strategy has to take account not just of business strategies and philosophies, but also the reward mechanisms used to deliver that strategy, and most crucially of all, the implementation and operating processes which determine how employees perceive and are motivated to behave by them. As we saw in Chapter 2, some attempts to operate performance-related pay were destroyed by lack of preparation and over-hasty implementation, with low levels of employee involvement. A phased approach to introduction, as illustrated in the water company case study (Case Study 3.2), and considerable attention to implementation and operation, we believe, are often the key factors which determine whether a performance-related reward strategy succeeds or not. National Grid has displayed a similar approach in introducing a new merit pay schemes, under a three-year pay deal agreed in 1997. Individual's performance will not affect their pay in the first year, while performance management arrangements are finalized and tested. It will be related to pay increases in the second year, with a minimum 'floor' of increase to help develop confidence and trust in the process. Only in the third year will the fully variable linkage of pay and individual performance operate.

Contribution-based reward approaches are differentiated from traditional performance pay schemes by their focus on implementation and process, as well as by their links to business strategy.

SUMMARY

- The concept of reward strategy, of using reward to positively reinforce the achievement of business goals, has become widely accepted in the 1990s.
- Performance-driven reward strategies have often been adopted to address the lack of alignment between existing pay policies and future business goals. This may be because existing reward practices have reinforced status and hierarchy, or because they have focused narrowly on individual financial performance and have been detrimental to other important goals, such as customer service.
- Organizations are therefore introducing and modifying their reward strategies, focusing them more on the person than the job,

incorporating higher levels of variable pay, rewarding a broader agenda of collective and individual performance, and using a wider diversity of performance criteria, such as quality and service, rather than just financial results. These are some of the features of what we term contribution-based pay and reward strategies.

- The wide range of performance measures used in contribution-based approaches is illustrated by the number of organizations now linking aspects of pay to customer service results, and those employing a balanced scorecard of performance criteria to relate to various pay and reward outcomes. Organizations employing this methodology include BT and Bass.

- Other companies, such as Pearl Assurance, are using many different pay and reward schemes, each focusing on rewarding a specific aspect of their broad business performance agenda.

- Organizations are also recognizing that a truly effective performance-related reward strategy needs to consist of more than just pay schemes. The work environment and culture, and the approach to performance management, communications and staff development all influence employee's support, motivation and commitment to business goals. They also affect the effectiveness of pay plans designed to encourage and reward high contribution.

- Recognition schemes focused on business goals and core values, and recognizing the contribution of as many 'winners' as possible illustrate this total rewards approach which is increasingly in evidence.

- The area of international reward management demonstrates the increasing application of pay for contribution approaches, with a greater focus on performance-earned bonuses, more flexible packages and a broader mix of reward methods employed.

- However, the complexities and difficulties of implementing contribution-based reward strategies means that it can take many years to accomplish and generally requires a phased and transitional approach to managing the changes.

CASE STUDY 3.1

Taking a long-term, strategic approach to rewarding performance at Unilever

The experiences of Unilever with various forms of performance related pay for their 20,000 managers, over the last 30 years, demonstrates the importance of a long-term and flexible perspective, incorporating a holistic and integrated HR and rewards approach.

Since the 1960s, in line with many large multinationals, Unilever has had a reward strategy based on paying for responsibility, performance and potential. Jobs were placed in a grade using a global job evaluation system, and then managers received performance-related increments to progress through them, up to the top of their grade. Regular promotions led to them being upgraded, and then up the next incremental scale.

Over the years, this model experienced significant difficulties. High inflation in the 1970s eroded the impact of performance on pay, and high tax rates further reduced the size of take-home payments. Organizational delayering reduced the scope for administrative promotions, while the need for personal and business development accelerated.

Unilever's performance pay programme was launched and modified a number of times in the 1970s and early 1980s, but by the 1990s performance-related pay was still very restricted in its effectiveness. Pay scales in the relatively large number of grades overlapped significantly; there was still little differentiation for performance between the best and the rest (a base pay differential of less than 2 per cent across Unilever management, net of market movement); and young, high potential managers were being paid less on average than older, lower potential managers in the same grade.

In 1994, having analysed these trends, the Board met and debated the necessary response to this dilemma described in Chapter 2: do we change our policy or our practice; do we re-design performance pay or ditch it altogether? The Board decided that the policy principles were right but that the practice of performance pay had to be brought into line with the policy. In response, the company has spent the last four years developing and implementing a series of reward changes, as part of what is called its 'integrated approach' to people management, that is both integrating people management processes with business objectives, and performance and HR systems integrated with each other. As Brian Dive, Senior Vice President

Remuneration explains, 'this means our work in organization design, reward management, individual development and career planning is now driven by a common, underlying logic', rather than, 'being linked administratively but not conceptually integrated'.

The integrating logic for this approach has been the introduction of Work Levels. Dive, the chief architect of the Work Level approach in Unilever, conducted extensive empirical work across the company with David Billis from the London School of Economics. They fundamentally modified, refined and extended earlier work done by Billis and Rowbottom[44] and Elliott Jacques[45] to ensure it reflected responsibilities carried out in Unilever, whether on a national, regional or global context.

Work Levels is a system of responsibility and accountability definitions which has identified six levels of qualitatively different work in Unilever (see Table 3.5). It has been shown that only one value adding layer of hierarchy is necessary in each Work Level. This has major implications for organization design, individual development and career planning and reward. The organization and pay structures have been correspondingly delayered, with five levels below the board replacing the previous 17 job classes. A typical Level 1 job would be a supervisor, while the Chairman of a large national company would be a Level 5. National market data is used to establish pay ranges at each level, and in the higher grades there are two market-related pay points, each of which acts as the centre of its own pay range.

Five clusters of key competencies have been identified for every level, and each individual's personal development and display of them, as well as the results they achieve, now determines their pay progression. Jobs are paid in a range of 90–110 per cent around their pay point, with the top 25

Table 3.5 *The Works Levels model*

Work level	Nature of contribution	Management layer	Pay scale	Potential lists (*)
	Strategic			
6	↑	V		–
5		IV	£	6
4		III	$	5
3		II		4
2		I	Y	3
1	↓			2
	Operational			

Note: (*) The Potential lists identify people capable of reaching a higher Work Level within 5 years

per cent of performers able to enter a premium zone up to 125 per cent of the point (see Figure 3.14). The average merit increase of the high performing group has to be at least twice that of the average overall pay increase. Bonuses are paid in addition, related to the achievement of key business results, and an exercise is currently underway to improve the quality of the target-setting processes. Brian Dive anticipates a continuing increase in the level of variable pay in the future, and a greater emphasis on team rather than individual performance goals.

It has taken over three years to implement the Work Levels model across over 90 countries and 12 major Business Groups. The changes were

Pay scales are established through regular surveys of a select group of leading companies in each national market

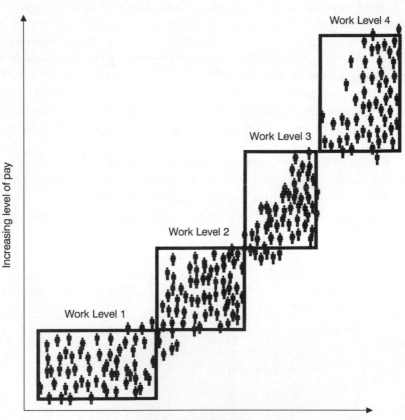

Figure 3.14 *Work levels and pay*

accompanied by a massive initial and ongoing communications and training exercise, involving workshops, management briefings and communication kits including brochures, videos and CD-ROMs. Brian Dive sees the up-front endorsement of the changes by senior executives as being particularly important.

Staff concerns, particularly in Europe, appeared to centre around the delayering involved and the apparent loss of grade-based promotion opportunities. According to Dive:

> It is an intriguing phenomenon that although frustrated and demotivated with straw jobs in over-layered and cluttered hierarchies, people fret about the removal of these so-called promotion opportunities. Part of the reason of course stems from the fact that grade drift in traditional HR systems has delivered more pay than performance-related increases, but it further distorts the organization structure and scope for genuine empowerment and the acquisition of further responsibility, ie a true promotion.

However, as the Work Level moves are now less frequent and more significant, the Company places an enormous amount of effort on its training and career management systems, maintaining for example various lists of managers on the basis of their predicted maximum potential. These lists are based on regular competency assessment. The competency definitions have been aligned to Work Levels and the promotion lists are expressed in Work Level terms (see Table 3.5).

In summary, therefore, Unilever regards the criticisms and problems of performance-related pay largely having stemmed from environmental factors. Dive feels that in increasingly global, competitive markets successfully implementing performance-related pay, including variable pay, will be one of the critical success factors for those companies setting out to lead the way into the 21st century.

CASE STUDY 3.2

The importance of a strategy of transition in a privatized water company

Privatization presents one of the most extreme examples of environmental transformation, requiring major changes in internal systems, culture and HR policies. Yet, as in this case, it can also produce a very significant gap between the need for the organization to change its HR and reward policies, and the actual ability of the organization to manage that change.

This particular water company recruited a new HR Director from outside of the sector. The core themes of the reward aspects of the new HR strategy they developed, post-privatization, were:

- flexibility and efficiency;
- fixed cost reduction;
- performance-relationship.

The arrangements, he felt, needed to match those of the most efficient and customer-oriented organizations in the private sector.

The first set of changes followed relatively quickly, and the 60 or so most senior managers in the new company were moved onto personal contracts, involving:

- placement into one of three, new, market-related pay bands;
- a merit pay system for determining future individual base pay adjustments;
- a management bonus scheme, rewarding both personal and business performance.

The changes were felt to have progressed fairly well and in the following year a similar agenda was adopted for over 1,000 middle, junior management and professional staff in the organization. Over less than 12 months these changes involved:

- the introduction of a new, well-known, points-factor job evaluation system;
- on the basis of evaluation points, jobs were placed in a new, flatter and harmonized pay structure, with market-related pay bands established for each new grade;
- the implementation of a fully performance-linked system of base pay adjustment, based on the ratings produced by an equally new performance appraisal system;
- finally, a new single table bargaining structure with which to negotiate over the outcomes of these changes.

With a much larger and geographically dispersed population, who were moving out of a set of nationally bargained industry arrangements, which meant that most employees were highly placed against the market and received an excellent service and grade related package of benefits, the proposed changes ran into severe difficulties. The job evaluation system placed almost one-third of jobs above their new grade maximum, and so their salaries were frozen. Meanwhile, almost 20 per cent of the population, concentrated in IT and commercial areas, were evaluated under their grade minimum. But the company could not afford to move them up to the minimum immediately.

Meanwhile, the appraisal system was introduced with little preparation and was perceived very much as a 'top-down' management imposition, with summary ratings awarded when employees had not agreed performance objectives or standards in advance. In response, the trade unions who had agreed to the need to change in principle, threatened industrial action. The variety of pay increases that would have resulted, meanwhile, created severe problems for the company's antiquated payroll department.

Within a month of the annual pay review, when the new pay structure and rates were due to be introduced, the Company agreed to revisit the proposals. It was recognized that the agenda had exceeded the company's capacity to manage it, given the raft of other business and organizational changes underway. The experience had shown up a lack of experience and competence in actually managing the new market and performance-related systems, and the 'buy-in' and commitment of staff clearly had not been achieved.

As a result, a three-year phasing of the new reward strategy was adopted, giving time to build up these vital three 'c's' of capacity, competence and commitment to change (see Figure 3.15). The pay adjustments were made without account taken of individual performance. The immediate changes introduced concentrated on getting job evaluations and new role profiles agreed, and jobs placed in a more market-related pay structure. The performance appraisal system was revised and relaunched, with objective- setting taking place early in the new year. Only twelve months later did it come to actually influence an individuals' pay increase. On this basis, the changes were agreed and successfully implemented.

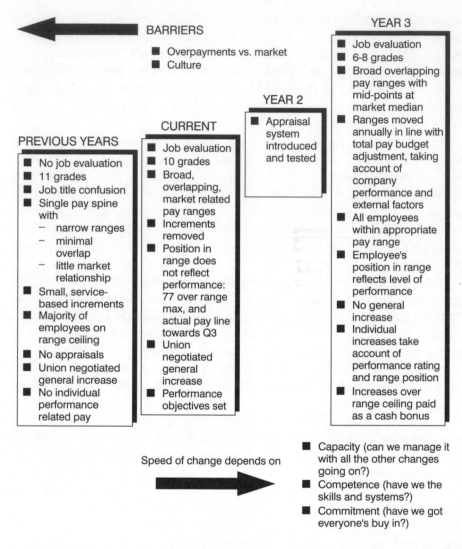

Figure 3.15 *A three-year plan for reward strategy implementation in a privatized utility*

NOTES

1. Reported in Industrial Relations Services (1998) There is merit in merit pay, *Pay and Benefits Bulletin*, **445**, April

2. Thompson, M (1998) Trust and reward' in *Trust, Motivation and Commitment: A reader*, eds S J Perkins and St John Sandringham, Strategic Remuneration Research Centre, Faringdon

3. Lawler III, E.E (1994) Effective reward systems, in *Diagnosis for Organizational Change: Methods and Models*, ed A. Howard, New York

4. Michael Porter, addressing the 1998 IPD Conference in Harrogate in his Business Strategy Master Class
5. Grattan, L (1998) *HR Strategies in Transforming Companies*, Oxford University Press, Oxford
6. Armstrong, M and Murlis, H (1997) *A Handbook of Reward Management*, 3rd edn, Kogan Page, London
7. Grattan, op. cit.
8. Collins, J and Porras, J (1998) *Built to Last*, Century, London
9. West, M, Patterson, M and Lawthorn, R (1997) *The Impact of People Management Practices on Business Performance*, IPD, London
10. Quoted in People are the most valuable asset, *People Management*, 19 March 1998
11. Goold, A and Campbell, M (1987) *Strategies and Styles*, Basil Blackwell, Oxford
12. Towers Perrin (1994) Improving performance through people, *HR Issues in the Utility Industry*, Research Report, London, December
13. E E Lawler III, speaking at an SRRC Master Class, 14 May 1996
14. Towers Perrin (1994), op. cit.
15. Towers Perrin (1997) *Learning from the Past: Changing for the future*, research report from Towers Perrin, London, March
16. Timmins, N (1998) NHS pay set for radical overhaul, *The Financial Times*, 18 December
17. Towers Perrin (1994), op. cit.
18. Towers Perrin (1994), op. cit.
19. Hamel, G and Prahalad, CK (1994) *Competing for the Future*, HBS Press, Mass
20. Handy, C (1996) The white stone: six choices, *Business Strategy Review*, Spring, London Business School
21. Edward Freeman, R (1979) 'Understanding stakeholder capitalism, *The Financial Times*, 19th July
22. Pfeffer, J (1994) *Competitive Advantage Through People*, HBS Press, Mass
23. Doyle, P (1996) The loss from profit, *The Financial Times*, 25 October
24. Donkin, R (1995) Quality shows a profit, *The Financial Times*, 26 July
25. Kaplan, R and Norton, D (1996) The balanced scorecard: measures that drive performance, *Harvard Business Review*, Jan/Feb
26. Business Intelligence Survey (1998) *Rethinking Pay and Performance*, London, Business Intelligence
27. Cabinet Office (1998) Personnel Management Division, *Pay and Grading Guidance*, April
28. Incomes Data Services (1991) Performance pay, *IDS Focus*, **61**, December
29. *The Economist*, Just deserts, 29 January 1994.
30. Towers Perrin (1997), op. cit.
31. Towers Perrin (1997), op. cit.
32. Wallace Bell, D and Hanson, C (1989) *Profit Sharing and Profitability*, Kogan Page, London
33. Bloom, M and Milkovich, G (1998) Rethinking international compensation, *Compensation and Benefits Review*, April
34. Bloom, M (1995) *The Bundle of Valued Returns: A psychological contract view of incentive pay*, Cornell University Center for Advanced Human Studies, Working Paper No 95–1
35. Gerhart, B and Milkovich, GT (1992) Employee compensation: research and practice, in MD Dunnette and LM Hough (eds), *Handbook of Industrial and Organizational Psychology*, Consulting Psychologists Press, Palo Alto, California
36. Huselid, M (1995) The impact of HRM practices on turnover, productivity and corporate performance, *Academy of Management Journal*, June

37. Bloom, M and Milkovich, G (1995) 'Managerial compensation and social contracts, *Trends in Organizational Behaviour*, **3**
38. Ashton, C (1999) *Strategic Compensation*, Business Intelligence Report, London
39. See, for example, B Tulgan (1997) *Generation X*, HRD Press, Minneapolis
40. Towers Perrin (1997), op. cit.
41. Described more fully in D Brown (1998) Current trends and issues in international reward, *Benefits and Compensation International*, November/December
42. Lawton, M (1997) Death of a paradigm?, *Benefits and Compensation International*, September
43. Sheridon, WR and Hansen, PT (1996) Linking international business and expatriate compensation strategies, *ACA Journal*, Spring
44. Rowbottom, R and Billis, D (1987) *Organizational Design*, Gower, Aldershot
45. Jacques, E (1996) *The Requisite Organization*, Cason Hall, US

4

Using competency-related pay to reward contribution

Traditional job and objective-based pay systems do not work well for knowledge workers, whose performance is often based on specialised, applied competence, and cannot easily be categorised into five or six neat objectives.

(Armstrong and Baron)[1]

54 per cent of employers say that the competency pay approach is better than the traditional performance pay based on appraisals (and)... popular with employees.

(The Industrial Society)[2]

THE CLAIMS AND THE CONTROVERSY

Performance-related pay rewards people for the results that they achieve. Competency-related pay, the subject of this chapter, rewards people for how those results are achieved. Pay for contribution, which appears, as we shall see, to be an approach which an increasing number of organizations are gravitating towards, rewards people for both.

Competencies can justifiably lay claim to being the HR movement of the 1990s, the concept that has incurred more HR Department resource and spawned more initiatives than any other. Pay has been one of the most recent, practical applications for competency ideas and frameworks.

Yet, increasingly extravagant claims have been made as to its effectiveness, and even its necessity in the new millennium: to enhance organizational effectiveness, in flexible, knowledge-based organizations; to increase employee satisfaction, development and contribution in tight labour markets; and most radically, as a replacement for the traditional pay concepts of paying for the job through job evaluation, and paying for performance through merit pay and results-based bonuses.

Hofrichter and Spencer describe competencies as 'one of the most powerful approaches at our disposal to enhance organizational performance',[3] while Mark Thompson of Telecom Eireann regards it as 'essential to reward people according to their skills and competencies'.[4] O'Neal describes it as, 'the way tomorrow's organizations will pay' as 'compensation objectives shift from paying for jobs to paying for competencies'.[5] And putting it at its simplest, the prime rationale for adopting competency-related pay expressed by one HR director we spoke to was that, 'anything is better than performance-related pay'.

Among the 300 companies in Towers Perrin's European reward study,[6] over the next three years relating pay to the skills and competence of employees was the single objective increasing most in importance compared to the prior three years, along with a desire to link pay to the organization's key success factors, such as customer service and quality (see Figure 4.1). Thus, 70 per cent of organizations were planning to reinforce the link. The importance of individual performance pay showed a major decline.

In concept, competency-related pay seems relatively straightforward and sensible: pay your employees more as they become more competent, and pay the most to the most competent. Yet the whole concept of relating competencies to pay, in any shape or form, is highly controversial and anathema to many HR and development specialists. Some organizations, such as Boots the Chemists, regard it as undesirable, compromising the fundamental developmental objectives of competencies, and focusing performance management wholly on the link to pay.

Objectives significantly increasing in importance over next 3 years	Objectives significantly decreasing in importance over next 3 years
• Paying for skills and competence • Ensuring workforce flexibility • Achieving an employee ownership mentality • Linking pay to organization's key success factors: quality, customer service, etc • Rewarding group/team results • Manage reward on a total remuneration basis	• Pay for individual performance • Controlling pay costs • Rewarding employees for staying with the organization • Ensuring internal equity • Pay based on total organization results

Figure 4.1 *Shifting emphasis in the objectives for making pay and reward changes in Europe over the next three years*
Source: Towers Perrin

Others regard it as impossible to achieve in practice, with Sparrow[7] for example pointing out the weaknesses and definitional confusion regarding competencies. 'We should avoid over-egging our ability to test, measure and reward competencies', he argues, citing the difficulties of measuring personal traits and behavioural competencies, and the lack of alignment between competency menus and business success.

Lawler similarly feels that it is 'a poor foundation for the new pay',[8] driven more by fad and fashion than organizational need. He points out the difficulties of measuring generic 'off-the-shelf' competencies which are not necessarily related to successful performance, as well as the dangers of linking personality traits, such as discrimination to pay. Courtaulds Textiles agree that the measurement of competencies is not precise enough for pay determination purposes, while the Automobile Association recently abandoned its pay adjustment approach using competencies as too complex and difficult to apply.

So what is the answer? Is competency-related pay the essential, future replacement for individual performance-related pay, or just the latest HR dream? In this chapter, we try to clarify the confusion and controversy. First ,we consider the evidence for its growth, and why companies are moving to introduce it in increasing numbers. Then we define what exactly competency pay is and review and illustrate the main methods by which competencies are being used to link to pay. We conclude by illustrating the spread of the 'mixed' model, demonstrating that competencies are generally being integrated with, rather than replacing, traditional performance pay approaches, to produce a diverse and potentially more effective approach, which we define as paying for contribution. In many ways, competencies are at the heart of this emerging approach.

GROWTH OF COMPETENCY-RELATED PAY

Controversial and confusing undoubtedly, yet despite the doubts, an increasing number of organizations throughout the Western world are investigating, developing and introducing schemes that link competencies and pay. The Industrial Society's survey[9] of 344 UK organizations showed that a third either have or plan to introduce in the next year a system of competency-related pay. Similarly, Industrial Relations Services[10] found that 18 per cent of their UK sample had some form of competency-related pay in place, while 18 per cent were planning its introduction, the most popular area of change in reward by a considerable margin.

Towers Perrin's 1997 European survey revealed that over 20 per cent of participants were already linking skills and competencies with pay for at least some of their staff, while 70 per cent of them were planning to create or reinforce this link. On the other side of the Atlantic, 17 per cent of the companies in a large American Compensation Association study[11] already had competency-related pay systems in operation, with a similar proportion planned or already under development.

Looking at individual examples, the list of companies already paying for competence includes many well-known names from a wide variety of sectors: ICL, Glaxo Wellcome and SmithKline Beecham in innovation and knowledge-based industries; National Westminster Bank, Bank of Scotland and the Prudential in the increasingly service-oriented and competitive financial services sector; and Corning Glass, Guinness Brewing and Scottish & Newcastle in more traditional industries.

THE RATIONALE

So why are they doing it? The reasoning appears highly diverse but can broadly be grouped into three categories: one business strategy focused, one more structural and the third concerned with performance pay.

DRIVING BUSINESS STRATEGY

The business drivers relate to the critical importance of the skills and competencies of staff to the implementation of more heavily customer service, quality and innovation-based business strategies. Looking at the most successful and enduring companies in this century as a key to survival in the next, Collins and Porras conclude that, 'the sources of sustainable competitive advantage have shifted from financial resources, to technology, and now to human capital'.[12] In other words, as the Managing Director of a UK water company put it to us, 'to be a world class company, you have to have the best, most competent workforce'. According to Reed, the vast majority of UK executives agree that their staff, their skills and actions and motivation, are now the key performance differentiator for their organization.[13] Companies such as Honda and General Electric have prospered by focusing on the development of their core competencies.

Some 45 per cent of the companies in the ACA study were aiming to 'raise the bar' of the competence of their employees through this pay approach, enabling them to thereby gain sustained competitive advantage. Rather than compromising the development of employee competencies with messy pay issues that interfere with development discussions, they regarded pay as a primary reinforcement of them. As Mike Westcott of Guinness Brewing explained, 'Although our competency work was always about contribution to the business, the link to reward has given an additional edge to it, as well as clarifying what the company really is paying for.[14]

DEVELOPMENT

Existing pay arrangements often do not provide incentives for employees, to develop and behave in line with company strategy. In Table 4.1, we show the results of an analysis we undertook with the HR staff in a train-operating company in Southern England. The business and HR strategy of the company emphasized revenue and value maximization with fewer, higher skilled employees delivering a flexible, high quality service to attract and retain increased numbers of passengers. In reality, their inherited British Rail, public sector pay structures promoted the reverse amongst on-train and station staff. Fixed rates and the lack of pay flexibility meant that employees saw no reward for growing their skills or improving their level of customer service. The low basic pay and large number of additional cash

Table 4.1 *Potential lack of fit between desired behaviour and reward systems at a train operating company*

Behaviours company might want from staff	Current structure/reward situation	Behaviours company may be getting	Implications
• Sales maximization • Commitment to a new, common, corporate identity	• Differentiated structures and pay arrangements • Inherited BR structure • No job evaluation	• Them and us 'why should I, what's in it for me?' • 'Why can't it be like the old days?' • Equal pay claims • Concern at loss of BR	• Harmonize terms and conditions with a distinct company identity • Establish evaluation system reflecting what you want to pay for
• Clear job accountabilities	• Unclear roles eg supervisor	• Lack of accountability for problems/performance	• Clear, communicated, understood structure and roles • New team leader role on management terms
• Taking on responsibility: focus on outcomes and performance, 'can do' attitude	• Hourly rates for some • Unclear performance goals and measures • Fixed job rates: no reward for extra contribution	• 'I'll stick to what I know' • 'I'm only doing my job' • Missed opportunities: frustration: waning enthusiasm/loyalty	• Harmonized, salaried terms • Pay related to performance and growth in skills/contribution
• Job flexibility, providing a 24-hour service	• Fixed job rates • Normal work day focus of conditions	• Pay me extra for working somewhere else/outside normal hours	• More flexible and possibly varied contracts and packages
• Cost effectiveness, short- and long-term	• Relatively low basic pay plus significant number/ value of 'add-ons'	• 'I'll maximize my earnings, irrespective of effects on the Company' • Administrative expense • Staff turnover/absenteeism	• Increase base pay and performance-related variable element • Simplify/remove add-ons
• Excellent service	• No reward for high service levels • Unclear links of service goals, what I do and how I'm rewarded	• Delivery of varied levels of service	• Structure which focuses on service delivery • Incentives for high service levels • Clarify and communicate strategy → structure → reward → behaviour links

payments and allowances encouraged employees to maximize their working hours, rather than their efficiency, and demand extra payments for any flexibility or job change.

Such behaviours do not, of course, change overnight. The research suggests that, as at Guinness, competency-related pay is not being introduced as a 'quick fix' or fad. Some 75 per cent of companies in the ACA survey[15] and 61 per cent of those in Towers Perrin's European study[16] already used competencies within their performance management and staff development systems before making any link to pay. On average, companies spent over a year developing the linkage before implementation. Mike Westcott, and many companies making the competency pay linkage, are aiming to provide more scope for people to develop and be rewarded in relation to their personal growth, rather than restrict them within a traditional, hierarchical, job-based organization and pay structure. This aspect of personal and job development is the second key driver of competency pay.

Ghoshal and Bartlett[17] explain how the re-engineering of core processes in many large organizations has shattered authority-based hierarchies, 'building competencies across the organization'. In these flatter, more flexible structures, writers such as Bridges have forecast the end of the traditional job. O'Neal foresees that, 'as the basic unit of work shifts from the job to the role', a more flexible definition of work is emerging, designed, 'to fit the strengths and limitations of the people who fill them'. Thus, 'compensation objectives will shift from paying for the job to paying for the person and their competence'.[18] Companies are increasingly wanting their staff to work outside their job description, to develop themselves as much as possible in ways that add value to the company.

Correspondingly pay structures are being flattened and broadened to provide greater scope to reward this development, and competence-related pay structures are often introduced in conjunction with broad-banding (in 45 per cent of cases in the Towers Perrin[19] study). Anglian Water, for example, introduced competency pay for 1,000 production employees to support a major programme of up- and multi-skilling, thereby improving efficiency and customer focus.

PERFORMANCE PAY

Addressing the problems of performance-related base pay progression systems is the third important driver of competency-related pay approaches. As described by participants in the Industrial Society study,[20] particularly for knowledge-based professional and front-line customer service workers, traditional objective-based, merit pay systems have often been difficult and unpopular to apply. Reviewing the level and application of essential technical skills and behaviours generally makes a lot more sense for a physiotherapist, a police officer, a research chemist or a software specialist. Thus, 36 per cent of those introducing competency-related pay in the ACA study[21] cited improvements in their method of relating pay to performance as a primary goal. As we shall see subsequently, however, very few companies are actually replacing performance pay with competency pay.

Often, of course, the rationale has been a combination of these factors, with Pilkington Optronics explaining their move to create 'a more focused workforce, that understands the pay system and can see opportunities to develop themselves in a way that provides the company with the necessary competitive advantage'. There is therefore a wide diversity of reasons for, and practice in, competency-related pay, which partly helps to explain the controversy and confusion on the subject.

It also demonstrates that competency-related pay, like performance-related pay, cannot be dismissed or endorsed universally. Its effectiveness, in our view, is totally contingent on the circumstances, in terms of how competencies are defined and related to pay, in each situation. As we shall see, in many situations, pure competency pay is not being used. So how can we define and categorize the plethora of different methods that are emerging?

DEFINING AND CATEGORIZING COMPETENCIES AND THEIR PAY-RELATED APPLICATIONS

DEFINITIONS

Defining, nay even spelling, competencies has proved a controversial task in itself, described by one academic as akin to walking through a minefield. No wonder organizations such as BOC and ICL avoid the term altogether and talk about capabilities, values and behaviours instead. Boyatzis originally defined the term competency very broadly as, 'a motive trait, skill, aspect of one's image or social role, or body of knowledge which he or she uses'.[22]

We can therefore define competence-related pay as paying employees for the development and application of essential skills, behaviours and actions which support high levels of individual, team and organizational performance. Contrary to popular misconceptions, it does not mean paying people for any skill or qualification they choose to obtain; nor paying people for behaving in a nice, friendly way; nor, as we shall see, is it the opposite of paying for performance.

The origins of competency-related pay are largely twofold. First, in the skills pay systems which originated in manufacturing industry, and were generally used to help multi-skill operating and craft employees to make them more flexible and efficient. Second, the technical pay ladders for research and development staff in companies such as ICI and BP have been used for many years to pay staff in relation to the personal growth and contribution. Typically they avoid or can run through the restrictions of hierarchical grade structures in the rest of the company. These are also areas where short-term, bonus-related objectives are often difficult to specify.

Boyatzis's broad definition emphasizes two points: first, usage and, second, breadth. Shakespeare wrote in *Henry IV, Part 2*, 'Skill is nothing, a mere hoard of gold 'til it is set to work', and companies are only interested in rewarding those skills and behaviours, as Woodruffe puts it, 'that affect job performance'.[23] A failure to recognize this has led to practical problems in applying the concept in some companies, such as pay cost escalation.

In terms of breadth, whereas skills-pay systems traditionally focused on technical, usually 'blue-collar' skills, competency-related pay typically involves consideration of a much broader combination of knowledge, skills and behaviours. Sparrow[24] asserts that only behavioural competencies are generally being used to relate to pay, but it is more typical to include technical skills, as well as considering job accountabilities and results when pay relationships are in operation. Indeed, this is why we prefer the term competency-related rather than competency-based pay. The latter implies a type of fixed, formulaic relationship solely based on competencies. Typically, the competency pay link is more flexible, and influenced by a wide range of factors, not just competencies.

This breadth of components, and Boyatzis's original definition, have encouraged both the diversity of competency-related pay and HR applications, but also the controversy concerning them. In particular, the inclusion of personality traits such as enthusiasm or reliability can cause enormous problems in relation to pay, creating scope for discriminatory and ill-founded decisions. It has also led some organizations into over-complexity. Thus one UK bank introduced competency pay with managers expected to select appropriate competencies and levels for their staff from a huge dictionary of over 50, with very little guidance.

So, a number of companies such as Glaxo Wellcome, NatWest Life and Scottish & Newcastle Retail only use part of their full competency menu when making the pay linkage. They reserve any traits and more developmentally oriented competencies, for example, developing self and others, for non-pay-related applications, such as career planning. The competency menu used at Glaxo Wellcome is shown in Figure 4.2. As you can see, personal qualities, and the competencies of team working and feedback are unidimensional, and not used to define pay grades.

Woodruffe[25] specifies a simple, twofold categorization of competencies that has received wide acceptance. This describes them first, as hard 'competences' (note the missing 'i'), the standards that people carrying out a job are expected to attain, what they have to be able to do. The second category is the softer competencies, the behaviours and dimensions that underpin competent performance, or more generally, as Thomas Cook define them, 'the way people go about their work', how they are expected to behave.

CLASSIFICATION

Woodruffe's twofold categorization is very useful for classifying the many different approaches to competency-related pay, as shown in Table 4.2.

Essentially, reward is being linked to competencies in two main ways: as a job-focused process that uses competencies as the criteria, wholly or partly, to evaluate jobs; and second, as a people-focused process that links pay levels and increases to the level of competence attained by individuals. In Towers Perrin's European Study (see Figure 4.3), 28 per cent of companies related individual pay reviews partly or wholly to competence and 22 per cent included competencies within their job evaluation systems, with both approaches growing rapidly. This compares with the ACA's US data in which of the 17 per cent of companies with competency-related pay applications, 42 per cent used competencies for salary increase determination and 15 per cent in job evaluation.

Profile of one grade

These competencies are unidimensional

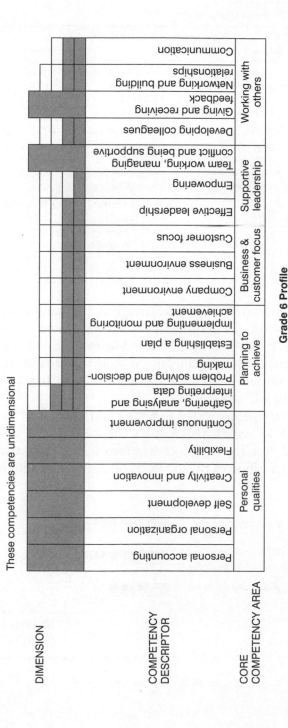

Figure 4.2 *How competency dimensions are used to grade jobs at Glaxo Wellcome*

Table 4.2   *Typology of competency-related pay*

		Focus of competency definition		
		Job	**Role**	**Person**
	Evaluation	• Point factor plans and grade structures eg Portsmouth Housing Trust	• Role classification systems into broader pay bands eg Motorola	• Person-based pay setting in very broad bands, eg SmithKline Beecham
Method of linkage	**Pay adjustment**	• Skill/competence pay steps in ranges and pacificorp • Formula-based increases, eg VWUK	• Pay increases based on assessment of results and competencies eg Woolwich	• Pay increases based wholly/largely on personal competence eg ICL
	Bonus and recognition		• Bonuses related to assessment of results and competencies, eg US computer company	• Recognition awards for personal behaviours in line with corporate values eg South West Airlines

In both cases, a much smaller percentage were using cash bonuses and recognition awards as another means to reinforce competencies. Organizations such as Asda and South West Airlines have focused these low cost, high excitement incentives and rewards on reinforcing core company competencies and values, such as team work and customer service (see Chapter 3).

But classifying competency pay is not as simple as just considering the reward method used. Moving to the horizontal axis of our framework (see Table 4.2), some organizations focus on a narrower and more traditional definition of the job and concentrate on relating pay to

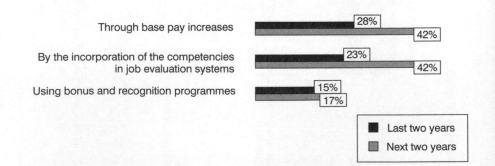

Figure 4.3   *Incidence of, and growth in, different means of linking pay and competency*
Source: Towers Perrin

'hard' and demonstrable competences. Others relate pay to a much wider and more flexible concept of the behavioural competencies displayed by the individual, which represents the most radical, and also most criticized, wing of the paying-for-competence movement. And as ever, the majority of organizations – 42 per cent in the ACA survey, and including UK companies such as Guinness and the Woolwich – use both main pay methods of linkage, and consider aspects both of the job content and the individual contribution.

LINKING PAY AND COMPETENCIES THROUGH JOB EVALUATION

Just as it has been portrayed as a replacement for performance pay, so competence-related pay has been described as a more forward-looking and flexible alternative to job evaluation. According to Emerson, the latter is 'out-of-date, inflexible and time consuming, rewarding rigidity and ignorance'.[26] The link to competencies on the other hand, 'rewards people for customer service, adaptability and market-related behaviour', the things that really support the organization's core capabilities and drive strategic success. Entrepreneurial firms such as telecomms company One-2-One therefore totally and deliberately avoided job evaluation in their early years.

In reality, the majority of large organizations (84 per cent in the Towers Perrin[27] European study) retain their job evaluation systems, with points factor methods still being the most popular. Yet almost half of these companies had modified their existing evaluation schemes in the previous three years, and 60 per cent were considering the incorporation of competencies into them. Companies are moving towards using simpler, less mechanistic evaluation schemes, which really do value the competencies that the company wants to grow, encourage and reward, and which really add value.

A traditional evaluation factor, for example, would assess management responsibilities in terms of numbers of staff reports or the size of a budget. But a newer, competency-related factor considers the managerial demands and requirements, and the skills that need to be displayed in addressing them. Manager X might have far fewer people to manage than Manager Z, but be responsible for a much more diverse and dispersed range of individuals, making the managerial skills required for planning, decision-making, influencing, and so on much greater. Such a behavioural and skill-based definition also addresses the 'empire building' syndrome which many traditional evaluation factors tacitly support, as well as redressing the over-emphasis in some schemes on job 'inputs', such as qualifications, which may not be related to added value in the organization.

A competency-related evaluation scheme was developed at Portsmouth Housing Trust in 1997. A joint management and union committee defined the organization's core competencies. These provide an integrating framework and serve as the basis for an evaluation factor plan that places all jobs within a flatter and broadbanded pay structure. The competencies also provide a basis for performance management and staff development processes. This type of integration of HR and reward methods can be a particularly valuable feature of a competence-related strategy.

Volkswagen UK and ICL have introduced analytical evaluation schemes based entirely on competencies, while companies such as Thomas Cook and Triplex Safety Glass employ hybrid schemes containing traditional accountability and newer, competence-related factors. The Educational Competencies Consortium, a group of over 100 UK universities and colleges, has developed a hybrid system over the past two years, in support of a move to single-status employment conditions and to address major equal value concerns. The system covers all jobs in these institutions from professor right the way through to domestic porter. The Consortium's computerized, point-factor system measures 14 elements. These are a mixture of traditional criteria such as knowledge and experience, and newer, competency-related considerations such as pastoral care, teaching, and communication skills.

Other UK organizations, such as One-2-One and Scottish & Newcastle Retail have gone for simpler, partly analytical evaluation schemes that allocate broadly based and generic role profiles to broad pay bands or job family levels with reference to competency-related definitions. Fewer, briefer role profiles, being placed in fewer, broader bands, reduces the requirement for very exact competency measurement, and shifts the emphasis from the detailed job content towards the contribution of the individual in the role.

At Glaxo Wellcome, East of Scotland Water and Guinness Brewing, broad pay bands are profiled in terms of the level of required competencies, which describe the typical or minimum requirements of the roles allocated to each band. Individual roles are then slotted into the appropriate band by comparing their profile with the band profiles.

Table 4.3 illustrates the band descriptions for the sales job family in a technology company. Again, we can see the mixed, contribution-based model at work, for the descriptions not only include the competency levels shown, but also give indications of the performance standards and accountabilities for individuals within each band.

In another example, the UK manufacturing subsidiary of a US pharmaceutical company reduced the number of separate jobs in its UK facility from over 200 to less than 50 broad multi-skilled roles, significantly increasing productivity and job satisfaction as a result. Roles are now slotted into six broad pay bands, described in terms of accountabilities and competency requirements. These replaced a heavily segmented and hierarchical structure of fixed job rates.

Competency-related evaluation suits organizations with a predominantly professional workforce and a non-hierarchical work structure. VW UK, for example, found their scheme to be popular with staff, and it largely removed traditional debates and disputes about job content and upgrades. These organizations seem well aware of the potential measurement problems raised by the critics. They are normally using internally researched and tested, rather than off-the-shelf competencies, and combination, contribution-based approaches incorporating traditional accountability and responsibility factors, as well as competencies, in their evaluation frameworks.[28]

COMPETENCY-RELATED BASE PAY ADJUSTMENT

Just as Armstrong and Baron[29] conclude that 'competence-related job evaluation processes are more likely to enhance traditional forms of job evaluation, rather than completely replace them', so the use of competencies for pay adjustment purposes does not represent the death-knell of performance and results-based pay. A small minority of companies, such as Thomas Cook Direct, have removed their merit pay system and implemented a wholly skill and competency based series of pay progression steps. The annual merit pay increases of shop staff in a large UK retailer are now totally dependent on their display of critical competencies: customer service, presentation and teamwork (see Figure 4.4). Those whose competence exceeds the required levels receive a larger pay increase.

Yet the vast majority continue to relate pay reviews to considerations of individual performance (70 per cent of those in IRS's study[30] of 144 UK

Table 4.3 *Competency-related evaluation system in a technology company*

Band	A	B	C	D
Primary focus of the role and key implications	To sell application-based solutions within a major account (or part of a major account) • assumes a strong base business • relationship management and building an understanding of the customer's business will be a key focus • relatively shorter selling cycle for solutions	To sell application-based solutions to a number of named accounts or market sector or through channels • knowledge of customer/market/channel business and internal capabilities • development of new business and accounts • complex interdependency with 3rd parties	To sell large-scale, often high risk application based solutions to new or existing customers • building high credibility through knowledge of customer's business and influence of external environment • high level customer relationship management • qualification process is critical wide scope and high criticality of interdependency • long selling cycle	To sell specific products to a number of existing and new customers requiring a technology solution to a defined business problem • strong technical input • short cycle, medium to high volume sales • sells to meet specific technology not necessarily business needs
Competencies: Level of contribution required in the role	Customer understanding 2 Market & competitor knowledge 2 3rd party capabs knowledge 1 Commercial awareness 2 Building relationships 4 Communicating & persuading 5 Opportunism & initiative 3 Evaluation & judgement 2 Leadership 2 Planning, monitoring & forecasting 3	Customer understanding 2 Market & competitor knowledge 3 3rd party capabs knowledge 2 Commercial awareness 2 Building relationships 3 Communicating & persuading 5 Opportunism & initiative 3 Evaluation & judgement 2 Leadership 2 Planning, monitoring & forecasting 2	Customer understanding 3 Market & competitor knowledge 3 3rd party capabs knowledge 2 Commercial awareness 2 Building relationships 5 Communicating & persuading 5 Opportunism & initiative 3 Evaluation & judgement 3 Leadership 3 Planning, monitoring & forecasting 3	Customer understanding 1 Market & competitor knowledge 2 3rd party capabs knowledge 2 Commercial awareness 1 Building relationships 3 Communicating & persuading 5 Opportunism & initiative 3 Evaluation & judgement 2 Leadership 1 Planning, monitoring & forecasting 1

	Exceed	Met	Fell Short
1. Customer Service			
■ Respond quickly,helpfully and willingly to all customers			
■ Listen carefully and make sure you understand what the customer needs			
■ Use knowledge and help customers so that all possible sales are made			
■ Suggest further products or services to increase sales			
■ Be polite and friendly to all customers and colleages			
Overall customer service			
2. Presentation			
■ Keeping stock filled up and pulled forward and positioned in linc with display pannels			
■ Count stock accurately and use correct company procedures for stock ordering			
■ Keep areas clean and tidy to ensure good appeerence and safety standards			
Overall presentation			
3. Working Within the Team			
■ Complete assigned tasks to agreed standards and within the time allocated			
■ Use initiative to assist supervisor or manager to ensure the smooth running of the store			
■ Support colleagues to improve store performance			
■ Contribute knowledge and skills to develop other team members			
■ Seek opportunities to keep skills and knowledege necessary to do the job well, up to date			
Overall teamwork			

Overall Summery of Assesment _____

Signed_____ Person Assessed _____ Date____
Signed_____ Assessor Manager/Supervisor _____ Date____
Signed_____ Reviewing Manager _____ Date____

Figure 4.4 *Competency assessment linked to base pay increases in a UK retailer*

organizations), and to external market pay levels (48 per cent of these companies). Competencies, the 'hows' of performance, are becoming an increasingly important influence on the levels and rates of increase in pay in UK organizations. But they are invariably used alongside of these other criteria, such as performance results achieved, job size and market worth, not instead of them. It is often therefore contribution-related, not competency-based pay, and it is generally rewarding a person's broad contribution and value to the organization, not just their level of skill and competence. This can be seen in the growing incidence of performance management systems reviewing both the 'whats' and the 'hows' of performance, as we describe in Chapter 7.

In considering how companies are linking competencies to base pay increases we briefly need to consider: whether they are measuring 'hard' competences or 'soft' competencies, to use Woodruffe's categorization, and the emphasis they place on paying for what people do, as well as how, and how well, they do it. We then describe the actual methods for making the pay linkage.

USING BEHAVIOURAL COMPETENCIES

Behavioural competencies are frequently used as the criteria for competency-related pay increases in the UK, for example by Abbey Life, Derby City General Hospital and Scottish Equitable. They all use the competencies themselves as the criteria for assessing pay increases. They may be core or generic competencies under general headings. At financial services company Colonial, for example, the competencies include 'Providing Leadership and Direction', 'Ensuring Achievement of Goals', and 'Maximizing Others' Contribution'. Or they may be expressed in terms of core values, as at BOC.

Three or four levels of each competency area are typically defined. For example, the three levels of a problem-solving competency in an industrial company are defined as follows:

1 *Level 1.* Uses data as an aid to put forward solutions and solve problems.
2 *Level 2.* Conducts systematic analysis and establishes causal links in data, drawing logical conclusions and putting forward a range of workable solutions.
3 *Level 3.* Sees issues at both macro and micro levels and cuts through data to the real issues. Combines innovation and creativity with strong critical assessment in producing solutions.

A target profile is then developed for all jobs, against each of the competencies, and individuals are assessed against their job profile, as illustrated in Figure 4.5. The individual's pay increase relates to their level of progress toward the desired levels of competence for the job, but progress beyond the required levels is not rewarded. As we shall see, however, some companies, such as Glaxo Wellcome, take a much more person-based approach and reward growth in any of the desired competencies.

This 'softer', behaviour-orientated competencies approach does appear to flow naturally from the construction of competency frameworks for recruitment, promotion and developmental purposes. Competency analysis therefore becomes an integrating process, as at Guinness Brewing and the Woolwich (see Case Study 4.1). However, some organizations believe that this raises the risk of the reward and the developmental aspects of competencies coming into conflict. Scottish & Newcastle Retail specifically made the decision to use competencies for job evaluation purposes, but to relate pay increases to performance and results, to avoid any conflict of this type. ICL's reforms to their competency pay system reflect their experiences of this problem (see Case Study 4.3).

There is also a risk of assessment being made on the basis of personality traits, as Lawler describes, so that competency pay schemes begin to look like the discredited merit-rating systems of the 1950s and 1960s.

Competency	Competency Level			
	1	2	3	4
Communicating				Required by the job
		Actual rating		
Influencing				
Teamwork				

Figure 4.5 *Personal assessment of competencies against a target job profile in a UK life assurance company*

Finally, concentrating on behaviours may give the impression that people will be rewarded for behaving nicely, irrespective of the degree to which that behaviour impacts on results. This was a common initial reaction to the concept of competency-related pay by line managers in many of the companies we have talked to. It also partly explains the changes made to their competency-related pay systems by Bass and ICL (see Case Studies 4.2 and 4.3), where there was felt to be an insufficient focus on results occurring.

USING RESULTS-FOCUSED COMPETENCES

ICL, Bank of Scotland and Land Registry are examples of UK organizations using a competence-focused approach. This contradicts Sparrow's contention[31] that only behavioural competencies are being used to link with pay. The approach is designed, at least partly, to avoid some of the potential difficulties just described.

Each competence heading used by these companies provides an answer to the question, 'What does a person in this job or role have to do to be regarded as fully competent in this area?' It also needs to address the secondary question, 'What evidence is available to measure what has been achieved?' Clearly, you can only relate pay increases to competence if you can measure it. Thus British Sugar defines the necessary performance standards required for employees to be credited as competent against each competence heading. Royal Bank of Scotland similarly aligns the competences people need to develop with specified business results.

These companies use evidence of what individuals have actually been doing and achieving in each area of competence, often gathered and discussed at regular appraisal meetings. Bass Brewers are moving to a system of quarterly reviews, and the approach suits many social services and charitable organizations, such as Portsmouth Housing Trust, where regular supervisory meetings are held with care staff. The aim is to avoid subjective judgements about behavioural and personal traits. Each competence heading is assessed against a fixed rating scale. A large UK retailer, for example, uses a three-point scale: fell short; met or exceed the required competence level (see Figure 4.4). Or the rating may be made against a percentage scale, as was formerly the case at the Woolwich (see Case Study 4.1). The bank set 80 per cent as a minimum (threshold) level of competence, 100 per cent as the expected level, and 120 per cent as the highest achievable level.

Separate assessments for each competence area are then generally summed or summarized in an overall assessment or rating which links to the pay increase. Thus at Bass, actual ratings are compared with the target or required level, and an overall competence rating produced on a five-point scale, ranging from unacceptable, through improvable and on-target, to superior.

A competence approach is concerned more with outputs than behaviours, with impact rather than input. Thus, the approach would appear to address the critics' claim that competencies have no relationship to organizational performance. It is saying that competence is about performance and that increases in competence are only rewarded when they lead to higher levels of contribution. However, a focus on the effective use of competences (essentially on delivered performance), rather than their acquisition, means that competence-related pay begins to look suspiciously like performance-related, merit pay schemes. It is therefore open to all of the criticisms we recorded earlier in this book. As Helen Murlis of Hay puts it, 'it all becomes smoke and mirrors', and the distinction may be lost on employees.

To avoid these problems, some UK organizations, such as the Bank of Scotland and ICL, incorporate a mixed model of both hard competences and softer behavioural competencies in their assessment framework, a combination that seems to work well for them in practice, although it may horrify the academics. Moloney, for example argues that 'getting them mixed up is dangerous',[32] yet it can help address the weaknesses of both categories of competency definition. At a UK pharmaceutical company, the four dimensions for the 'Establishing a Plan' competency, within the 'Planning to Achieve' cluster, are as follows:

- *Level 1.* Planning your own daily or weekly work, with the impact just on yourself.
- *Level 2.* Involved in team planning, impacting on the whole team plan.
- *Level 3.* Planning for a department or function.
- *Level 4.* Planning company-wide, which would affect everyone.

Note that these dimensions refer to work requirements and impact, mixing competencies and competences. They do not eliminate subjectivity but provide a framework for objective judgements to be made.

Scania Great Britain Limited recognized that it could not simply extend its results-based pay determination system for senior management down to cover other staff when it wished to move to a more performance-related approach in 1997. Now personal objectives and competency requirements are determined for each job, and discussed and assessed using their new Performance Appraisal and Development system, in order to determine individual pay increases. The system was trialled for a year before, being linked to pay.

In the Branch Banking business at Royal Bank of Scotland, managers are set targets both for competency development, such as problem assessment and work management, and key result areas, such as customer satisfaction and cost control. Every competency development target has to link to a key results area, to demonstrate that competency enhancement does result in improved outputs. This is at the heart of what we mean by paying for contribution: rewarding results achieved and how those results are achieved, linking past and future performance, in a mutually reinforcing relationship. So that is what is being assessed. But how does the link with pay actually work?

THE LINK TO BASE PAY INCREASES: WHERE PERFORMANCE AND COMPETENCE COME TOGETHER

STEPPED PAY INCREASES

The simplest way in which competency assessments and considerations are converted into pay increases mirrors the system of skills pay 'steps' used in manufacturing industry with fixed increases up a pay range awarded once a level of competence has been displayed and certified. Volkswagen UK, Reigate and Banstead Council, Pacificorp and First Direct are all examples of companies using this type of approach.

First Direct adopted competency-related pay because it was consistent with the organization's people development philosophy, and because performance-related merit pay was believed not to be working in a number of UK banks. Role profiles were defined through workshops with staff covering core tasks, behavioural competencies and required technical knowledge. Banking representatives and team leaders progress through defined pay points based on the acquisition and application of defined levels of skills and competencies. For example, for banking representatives the three competency-related pay levels in 1994 were: Banking Representative I £8,500; Banking Representative II £10,000; Banking Representative III £11,500. Using this approach, competency-based increases are awarded as and when staff become competent, and usually general, annual pay increases are provided as well. Other approaches integrate these two aspects of pay adjustment.

Relating fixed pay increases or increments to appraised performance or contribution ratings, with competence affecting the rating in some way, is another common method of making the link. At Scottish Equitable, for example, staff are rated against six core competencies. Each competency is rated on a five-point scale, ranging from 'not meeting requirements' through to 'consistently exceeds requirements'. A simple average is then calculated to produce a summary rating which determines the size of the pay increase.

These stepped, rating or points-based schemes appear very objective but have three primary dangers. They, first, imply a level of precision in competency measurement which may not exist. Second, when the bulk of employees reach the top 'step' of competence, there is often pressure to introduce other pay progression opportunities. First Direct, for example, operates a team bonus scheme but has also recently introduced a merit pay zone to reward high performers who are capped on the top of their scale. However, the most significant risk, as companies such as Motorola found with skills pay, is that stepped increases became semi-automatic and costs escalate.

Research by the Center for Effective Organizations in Los Angeles[33] amongst 50 US companies confirms that competency pay can be an expensive option. In 40 per cent of the companies they studied the systems were assessed to have failed, primarily because they underestimated the cost impact, and there was insufficient opportunity to generate a business return on the additional costs incurred. Wage costs rose by an average of 15–20 per cent and training costs by 25–30 per cent in the researched companies. In effect, these systems were failing, like some performance pay systems, because they were too successful: people acquired the skills at a rate which exceeded the organization's ability to use them to add value. Cummins Engines at Daventry recently took out its skill pay system and replaced it with a performance bonus for similar reasons.

Motorola found at some of its locations that employees progressed far faster than anticipated up the competence steps, and there was insufficient high value added work to utilize their additional skills. The training was therefore cut back and progression stopped, but of course, employee expectations and the credibility of the pay system were by then severely damaged. This is not of course the case in all, and perhaps an increasing number of situations. In one food manufacturer Wallace[34] studied, the additional pay costs of $94,000 were more than offset by the gains resulting from the higher quality and speed of work of the more competent workforce. These produced business gains of $390,000 in the first twelve months, a ratio of return of over 3 to 1.

FLEXIBLE, CONTRIBUTION-BASED INCREASES

However, to ensure that these returns are delivered and achieved, it is *the mixed model of paying for contribution*, that is paying for competence and paying for performance, that appears to be the predominant model that is emerging in the new millennium. Contribution captures the full scope of the things people do, the level of skill and competence they apply, and the results they achieve, which all contribute to the organization achieving its long-term goals. Contribution pay works by applying the mixed model of performance management: assessing inputs and outputs and coming to a conclusion on the level of pay appropriate for people in their roles and their work; both to the organization and in the market; considering both past performance and their future potential. It is the approach that increasing numbers of organizations who focus purely on rewarding results, and those such as ICL and Bass who moved to relate base pay almost wholly to competence, are now moving towards.

The actual ways in which this combination of competence and result affects pay takes many different forms. Probably the commonest way in which competencies have been introduced into the pay systems of organizations, as at National Westminster Bank and BOC, is to incorporate competencies into existing results-based, performance management and merit pay schemes. While ensuring that the organization is not paying for 'nice-to-have' competencies, this combination can help to avoid the common pitfalls of individual performance pay schemes, which we have considered in such detail, such as being purely backward-looking and encouraging an excessive focus on individual and short-term goals. It ensures that both results achieved and how they were achieved are rewarded.

Bass, for example, found that their existing merit pay system led to an over-concentration on individual targets and immediate past performance. The switch to competencies meant that they were now rewarding the basis for future success and developing the skills and behaviours needed to achieve it, although they are now moving to use a balance of both aspects to influence base pay awards.

Reigate and Banstead Borough Council similarly moved to paying for contribution largely due to the failings of their traditional merit pay system, and a desire to reflect the important, qualitative aspects of performance for a council, such as public service. All staff now have a performance agreement and a role profile, defining the key tasks and the behaviours required in the job, across 14 competency areas. Competencies are defined as 'those key behaviours which are essential to achieving and maintaining a quality performance'. A combination of task performance and display of competencies is used to arrive at an overall performance rating, on a three-point scale. Good performers receive the general pay award plus a salary increment of 2.5 per cent.

Increasingly, however, organizations such as National Westminster Bank, ICL, Bass and Zeneca are relating pay progression much more flexibly to an overall assessment of competence and contribution, with no fixed relationship between levels of competency, ratings and pay. At one of the brewing companies, for example, managers rate their staff on a 1–4 scale according to results achieved, competency levels displayed, and market worth. On this basis they agree individual increases within a range of 0–10 per cent. The only restrictions on flexibility are that managers cannot exceed the total pay budget.

ICL (see Case Study 4.3) also places considerable emphasis on managerial judgement and the market in structuring a very flexible relationship of competencies with pay, and actually emphasize the new salary paid, rather than the size of increase. Their recent changes emphasize the market even more strongly. This is partly designed to demonstrate that salaries are market competitive, and also that in a fast-changing business, competency developments and changes do not necessarily lead to a pay increase. Zeneca and Bristol Myers Squibb at Chester have eschewed ratings altogether, and we consider these developments in performance management in more detail in Chapter 7.

The accuracy and fairness with which any of these less structured methods are used depend on the quality of the initial competency development programme, the precision with which the dimensions and levels are defined, the validity and reliability of the evidence on which judgements are based and, importantly, the ability of managers to make justifiable and consistent judgements. These are tough although not impossible criteria, and usually apply with equal force to traditional merit pay systems. Two-thirds of the organizations in Towers Perrin's European research study[35] were taking steps to improve their performance assessment processes, for example by improving assessor training and introducing multi-rater appraisal systems. Involving managers and staff directly in the development of competency frameworks and these related processes for assessing and rewarding competence is, in our experience, a critical requirement for success.

In between these extremes of full flexibility and incremental fixed steps, pay decisions may be structured through a traditional pay matrix with competency assessments replacing or combined with performance results ratings, as illustrated in the example in Figure 4.6. High levels of results achievement and high competence displayed produce high pay increases. Position in the range or versus the market may also be taken into account so that rapidly developing staff who are low in their pay range and against the market, thereby, move through their range relatively swiftly. The base pay progression of highly competent individuals near the top of their range and paid fairly well against the market, correspondingly slows down, or as at Nat West Life, is rewarded with a larger cash bonus.

		Competence			
		a-Low	b	c	d-High
Results	A-Low	-	-	2%	3%
	B	-	3%	4%	5%
	C	2%	4%	6%	8%
	D-High	4%	6%	8%	10%

Note: Figures are annual percentage increases

Figure 4.6 *Contribution-based pay matrix from a UK life assurance company*

COMPANY EXAMPLES

A telephone banking operation we worked with moved to this more flexible, matrix approach from a simple stepped progression for their telephone associates in 1999, as illustrated in Figure 4.7. Staff increasingly felt that the existing competency pay steps were simply rewarding service, and high performing individuals were not being recognized sufficiently. They therefore moved to the concept of zones of contribution illustrated in the upper half of Figure 4.7.

Within fewer broader pay ranges, staff now move through a learning and developing, and then fully competent pay zones according to their pace of development. Once at the ceiling of the competent zone, they can only progress into the next zone on the basis of exceptional and sustained competence, or by taking on additional responsibilities such as coaching others. Both technical and behavioural skills such as team work, as well as results achieved (individual productivity and quality) affect the performance ratings of staff, who have monthly performance development reviews with their supervisors. On the basis of these assessments, staff progress up to the position in the range that matches their level of contribution. If their level of contribution declines, then relatively so does their pay level, through the operation of the pay

■ Pay range

	Pay Zones	Differential Skills	Expected Performance Standards
£13,000 Maximum	Exceptional		
£11,300 desired market position	Fully competent		
	Developing		
£9,650 Minimum	New		

■ Pay adjustment process

		Existing Pay Zone				
		New	Developing	Competent	Exceptional	
Level of Contribution	Outstanding	12	10	8	6	% of Basic pay increase
	Exceeds	10	8	6	4	
	Achieves	8	6	4	2	
	Unsatisfactory	0	0	0	0	

Figure 4.7 *Rewarding contribution through pay range progression in a telephone banking company*

matrix shown in the lower half of Figure 4.7. The pay ranges move by the budgeted amount, which a fully achieving and competent performer in the competent zone would also receive. But someone in the exceptional zone who only delivers an achieving level of contribution would receive an increase of less than the average and so move, relatively, back down the range.

A combination of fixed and flexible increases, and competency and performance considerations is used to try to achieve the best of both worlds by a UK water company. For a number of employee groups, pay progression from the 85 per cent minimum to the 100 per cent midpoint of the pay range occurs in defined steps, and wholly on the basis of the application of required competencies. Progression from 100 per cent to the 115 per cent maximum of each range is then wholly based on results achieved, and movement can be, relatively, down as well as up the range if a given level of performance is not sustained. In another organization we worked with, staff progress up to a fixed rate for a fully competent person, and thereafter receive cash bonuses according to the results they achieve.

At Nuclear Electric (see Case Study 5.2) staff are being moved into very broad, job-family-based pay ranges. Competency platforms define the bundle of competencies required by employees to progress to the next pay level, but they represent the ceilings of progression for staff with those skills, rather than immediate 'go to' points. Movement between platforms is in stages and depends on the assessed contribution and results achieved by the team member.

The relative emphasis on past results achieved and competence displayed, the basis for future success, will obviously vary between organizations and jobs. The Birmingham and Midshires Building Society introduced such a combination approach, with the emphasis initially on the objectives and results aspects of performance. But with greater experience and confidence in their competency framework, concerns over cost escalation were addressed and the weighting is now reversed. At the Woolwich the balance varies according to job function and level. Area Managers have a higher weighting on results achieved than competencies displayed in comparison with branch staff.

Bass moved to wholly competency-related increases five years ago to address the problems of merit pay. But they are now moving to an equal balance between results achieved and level of competence displayed in determining the rate of base pay increase. Staff perceive there to be an insufficiently strong relationship between pay and performance.

As well as annual pay increases, a number of UK organizations are now using competencies to help define developmental pay increases, which may occur at any appropriate time in the year. These are, in a sense, the replacement for promotional increases in a flatter pay structure. At the BBC, for example, each year a developmental pay increase 'pot' is agreed separately in each department. So it might be larger in a department with a lot of relatively new, rapidly developing staff.

A significant 'vertical' or 'lateral' growth in competencies is rewarded at Nortel and the Clydesdale Bank by a specific pay increase, which has to be at or above a specified minimum percentage. At Bristol Myers Squibb at Moreton the performance management systems consist of two distinct, if linked, processes. Performance Review focuses on setting objectives, assessing results and linking to the annual pay increase. Performance Partnerships is concerned with medium and long-term employee growth development. Market-related pay increases, if required in particular functions meanwhile, are made at different times in the year. Addressing developmental and market pay issues separately from individual performance can help reduce the burden of demands and expectations on the annual pay review process, which has served to defeat the effectiveness of many merit pay plans.

BASE PAY AND BONUS LINKAGES

Another way of combining these considerations of levels of competency and results achieved in determining pay awards, employed by organizations such as Eagle Star, Bass (see Case Study 4.2), Nat West Life and ICL, is to relate base pay increases wholly to increasing competence, and to reward results achieved in the form of cash bonuses. The model formerly used at ICL is shown in Figure 4.8.

This approach is now widely used for sales staff in a number of sectors such as insurance and computers, and has a number of advantages. It has a great deal of logical sense and support. Skills and competency development, which enhances future value and ongoing worth to the organization, is reflected in base pay. The results employees achieve may be much more variable from year to year, and so a variable bonus is an appropriate vehicle to reward them.

It is also a simple approach which is easy to communicate, and separate processes for determining pay increases and bonus awards

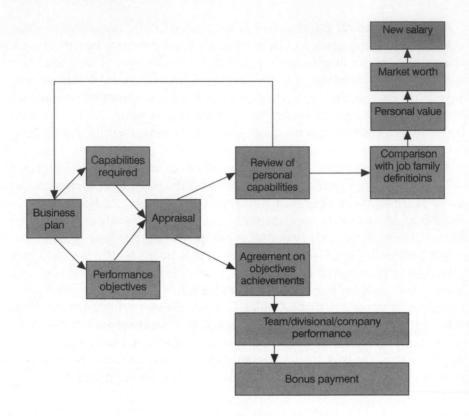

Figure 4.8 *Pay for contribution approach at ICL*

can operate, avoiding any conflict between the two. Somebody could well merit a high bonus for individual results achieved that year, but not have developed themselves, or supported their colleagues and so receive no base pay increase.

Sales people in various life insurance, IT and car distribution companies were traditionally paid very low guaranteed salaries with the bulk of their earnings paid as commission, a straight percentage of the value of the products they sold. In insurance, criticisms and regulatory fines as a result of pensions mis-selling helped encourage these companies to place a much higher emphasis on the quality of customer service and of their sales staff. As Prudential Chief Executive, Sir Peter Davis explained, 'It is essential that high quality, objective advice is not seen to be adversely influenced by remuneration systems.[36] This, in turn, required an increase in the calibre and base pay level of sales people. Car companies aiming to succeed on the basis of customer service excellence and retention have reacted similarly, increasing the competence and base pay of their sales forces.

As well as reducing the proportion of commission earnings, a majority of IT and life insurance sales staff are now paid using a combination of three pay schemes – base pay, bonus and commission. An example of the same contribution-based model now used in the dealers of a car company in the United Kingdom, is shown in Figure 4.9. Base pay reflects the essential knowledge and 'inputs' the salesperson brings and develops in their job: their product knowledge, their selling and service skills, their record of performance. Commission on sales remains as a smaller component (around one-third of the total pay package), rewarding the revenues and margins achieved.

But the new third element is a bonus scheme, used to reward the competencies or 'throughputs' that most directly lead to the individual converting their skills and knowledge into results. Teamwork, customer service and quality standards, and for car sales people, sheer effort and activity rates, these are rewarded with a salary-related bonus of up to 20 per cent of their basic pay p.a. for the most competent staff. In insurance, the Prudential is moving to this type of more bonus-orientated approach, with factors such as customer retention, policy lapse rates, and portfolio growth also influencing variable earnings.

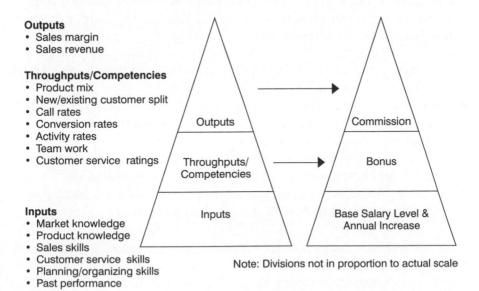

Figure 4.9 *Linking contribution to the different elements of pay for sales staff in a car company*

PURE COMPETENCY AND PERSON-BASED PAY

A few organizations have taken the ideas of the importance of personal competence and the death of the job to its logical extreme and moved to paying people very largely on the basis of their individual competence, irrespective of the immediate results they achieve or the specific tasks they are carrying out at any particular moment.

The obvious problem with applying any form of person-based pay is how to define, structure and assess the skills, behaviours and contribution that is required from each individual. The fear of most organizations is that it would result in pay anarchy, with no control on costs, inequitable pay judgements, and the money directed to those who shout loudest.

THE LIFE CYCLE MODEL

A person-based approach to structuring these decisions, which has been used successfully by a small number of companies is a model of life cycle stages. This was developed through research by a number of US academics, including Dalton, Driver and Boyatzis. The model posits that we all have the potential capability during our career to pass through four stages of development:

- a learning stage, of learning how to do work and developing up to the required standard;
- an applying stage, when we apply and further develop our skills in our own specific area of expertise, sometimes to a very high standard;
- a guiding stage, when we apply our expertise more broadly to benefit our organization, and develop and coach others; and
- a shaping stage, when we come to provide strategic leadership and promote the development of the whole organization.

Dalton's research suggested that around 60 per cent of people in an organization are in the first two stages, 30 per cent in the guiding stage, and 10 per cent in the shaping stage. The competencies required obviously vary in each stage, with a focus on technical and operational skills in the first two stages, relationship and business competencies in the third stage, and conceptual and strategic competencies in the fourth.

Lex Vehicle Services, Coventry Building Society, solicitors Mills and Reeve and SmithKline Beecham have all used this model in parts of their organization to manage pay in relation to personal competence. Required competencies are defined at each of the four career stages. For example, the communication and persuasiveness competency from one organization is shown in Figure 4.10, with levels defined at each of the four career stages.

Pay ranges are then developed, normally by benchmarking the competencies of a typical individual at each career level in the external market. A major challenge represented by any system of competency-related pay is in fact the ability to obtain accurate market data, when pay surveys still largely provide data on a job basis. In a UK service company, these market-related ranges are set in relation to broad work functions, to help ensure competitiveness and avoid pay drift (see Figure 4.11). But individual progression nonetheless is very strongly based on displayed personal competencies within and between each life cycle stage.

Learning	Applying	Guiding	Shaping
■Communicates key information to others	■Liaises with others, actively seeking out and passing on information	■Identifies the need to know and ensures all are kept up-to-date	■Plays a key role in industry networks to ensure the organization is abreast of key developments; cascades information
■Uses standard set of guidelines to convey or collect written/oral information	■Discusses options and influences others to see the merits of own suggestions	■Anticipates issues and concerns and structures communication accordingly; helps others to see all sides of the picture	■Communicates at both a strategic/ conceptual level and an operational/ detailed level according to need
■Voices own thoughts and needs	■Shows confidence in communication on own subject in varied situations	■Helps others to consider the impact of their message and to convey information in the most effective way	■Communicates in a way that fires others' enthusiasm and wins commitment

Figure 4.10 *Communication and persuasiveness competency applied to career life cycle stages*

133

Professional

	Minimum	Mid-Point	Maximum
Developing	£10,000	£12,500	£15,000
Delivering	£14,000	£18,000	£22,000
Guiding	£19,000	£24,000	£29,000
Shaping	£24,000	£29,500	£35,000

Office-based sales

	Minimum	Mid-Point	Maximum
Developing	£11,500	£13,750	£16,000
Delivering	£12,500	£16,000	£19,500
Guiding	£17,000	£22,000	£27,000
Shaping	£25,000	£32,875	£40,750

Field sales

	Minimum	Mid-Point	Maximum
Developing	£18,000	£21,000	£25,000
Delivering	£22,000	£26,000	£30,000
Guiding	£26,000	£31,000	£36,000
Shaping	£34,000	£39,000	£44,000

Figure 4.11 *Pay ranges applied across three job families using the life cycle model by a UK service organization*

PERSON-BASED PAY AT MILLS AND REEVE

Norwich-based solicitors Mills and Reeve are moving in the direction of a personal pay model, as explained by Chris Ashton in his report, *Strategic Compensation*.[37] In the past, solicitors were measured and paid largely on results achieved, in terms of chargeable hours. But as Head of Personnel Charlotte Points explains, nowadays 'valuing their contribution is difficult... they are expected to market, train new staff, win new business', and a whole host of other activities.

Now, therefore, individual development and performance are reviewed on a six-monthly basis by team leaders using a career stages model, and with the emphasis on self-assessment. Reward packages are flexible and pay levels within very broad pay bands are based on individual skill levels and contribution. As Charlotte Points explains, 'different rates are paid for different skills' and different levels of competence and contribution. She can foresee a move 'to completely individualized contracts and tailored packages, depending on a person's motivations, skill and performance... each individual will negotiate their rewards each year and the contribution they make in return... the emphasis will be on "let's do a deal".'

PERSON-BASED PAY IN A PHARMACEUTICAL COMPANY

The life cycle approach was applied in the technology division of an American pharmaceutical company in the United Kingdom and the United States. The division had a record of poor performance and a sequence of downsizing had left it with 400 employees, and the threat of complete closure. Radical measures were called for.

The staff moved therefore to a totally flexible, team-based work approach, with no job titles. They developed seven core competencies to underpin their strategic survival and success, including Innovation, Use of Resources, Technical Ability, Team Work and Customer Satisfaction. Critical incident interviews helped to define the levels of these competencies displayed at each of the life cycle model stages.

Base pay is now managed on a single continuum split into the four stages, originally running in the United Kingdom from £17,000 up to £85,000. New entrants are slotted in by matching their initial competency and skills assessment to an appropriate market rate, and compared to similar staff internally. Thereafter, pay progression is wholly dependent on the development, in breadth and depth, of their personal level against the seven core competencies, and irrespective of their short-term work function. Increases are obviously constrained, however, by the size of the pay budget, and ceilings in pay ranges do apply, related to market rates for a sample of benchmark roles. Administrative staff are excluded from the structure.

Competencies are assessed through a quarterly performance management process, incorporating 360° feedback and the input of customers. Even in this setting, however, performance results are rewarded, in the form of a bonus, related to a mixture of division, team and individual performance. The organization has survived and prospered using this approach, with markedly increased levels of customer satisfaction, declining cycle times, and more projects carried out by fewer staff.

PAYING FOR CONTRIBUTION: AN INTERIM CONCLUSION

This last case was clearly an extreme case, in a do-or-die situation and with a high proportion of knowledge workers. Yet the emphasis now in many of our slimmed-down organizations is on developing and deploying the ability of our staff to the full. Getting underneath the jargon and the fancy life cycle model, rewarding people rather than jobs is a logical extension of the pay changes that many of us have been making in our organizations in recent years. Lawler pointed out more than ten years ago that, 'if an organization's key assets are its human resources, a reward system that focuses on people rather than jobs is a better fit'.[38] Too many HR and reward systems are still focused entirely on controlling pay costs, rather than maximizing the added value of employees. As Michael Bichard, Permanent Secretary at the Department of Employment and Education, put it recently, management practices in the UK Civil Services have sought 'to control the brainpower of their organization, not to maximize it'.[39]

We recently interviewed a director of an auctioneering house, who had started there with virtually no qualifications as a clerk. Her competence, her contribution and presumably her pay level had been maximized to the full. The organizations which survive through the next millennium will almost certainly be those which are able to develop people in this way, and manage their pay accordingly. Bill Gates probably never had his job defined or evaluated, nor his results assessed on a five-point scale. As Moss Kanter describes it, economic, industrial and organizational shifts are 'rattling the cages'[40] of traditional pay administration and control systems, and the competency-related pay movement we have been considering is gradually edging the reward practices of UK companies very much in this direction.

The competence-related emphasis in pay decisions is particularly appropriate in sectors where employee skills and behaviours are recognized as the key to competitive success, as in pharmaceutical research, computer software, and management consulting companies. Applications are particularly evident for the knowledge workers and professional staff who predominate in these sectors, and for whom conventional performance-related pay schemes often do not work effectively. These organizations are also generally characterized by flat and flexible structures and by lateral and continuous employee development and broad banded pay structures. In organizations with a strategy based more on cost leadership with many lower skilled employees, then a competence-related pay approach may well not be appropriate at all.

Paying wholly for personal competence, and indeed any form of competence-related pay is not a simple, risk-free approach, and hence the criticisms and the controversy. Escalating pay costs, overly subjective appraisals and pay-increase decisions, over-competent employees, and paying for 'nice-to-have' behaviours are all risks.

Yet the organizations we have cited seem well aware of these potential problems, and are generally combatting them by combining considerations of competence and competency with more traditional market and results-based influences on pay. Both Bass and ICL have recently moved away from a base pay process very strongly based on competence to a more balanced approach. As they illustrate, companies are paying attention to the criticisms of overly complex and subjective systems, unrelated to business success, and carefully developing systems to avoid them and meet their own objectives.

Given the direction of economic development in the new millennium, with an increasingly global information and service-based economy, the incorporation of and increasing emphasis on personal competence is becoming ever more appropriate for more and more organizations. The use of competencies can, in particular, help to address the failings of traditional merit pay schemes, for example in their application to professional staff, as evident in voluntary organizations and local government in the United Kingdom.

But as we have seen, competence-related pay is not replacing traditional performance pay schemes in the main, nor traditional job evaluation schemes, but rather fusing with them. Paying for contribution is the way more and more organizations are paying, developing unique, hybrid and tailored pay solutions, to suit their own business and HR priorities. Rather than a unitary focus on past individual results within a standard merit pay scheme, a complex variety of different approaches have emerged. But we can simply summarize the increasing diversity of schemes within the paying for contribution approach in a formula, as follows:

Paying for Past Performance + Paying for Future Success = Paying for Contribution
↑   ↑
Results   Competence

SUMMARY

- Paying for competence is a controversial subject. Proponents regard it as an essential method for rewarding the growing numbers of professional staff in organizations whose competitive success depends on the core competencies of their employees. Critics argue it damages the developmental objectives of competencies and is impossible to manage in practice.

- Competency-related pay applications in the United Kingdom and United States are growing rapidly, although on average they take at least a year to develop and implement. There appear to be three categories of reasoning for its spread: 1) the importance of employee competence as the basis for competitive success; 2) organizational restructuring and the emphasis on individual and lateral growth and development; 3) to address the failings of traditional merit pay schemes.

- Competencies are generally being linked to pay through two vehicles: 1) a job-focused process that uses competencies as the criteria wholly or partly to evaluate jobs; 2) a more people-focused process that links pay levels and increases to the level of competence attained by individuals.

- Both 'hard' results-focused competences and 'softer' behavioural competencies are being used and assessed in establishing these pay relationships.

- The problems of competency-related pay can include over-complexity, measurement difficulties, and rewarding personal traits and 'nice-to-have' behaviours which do not relate to the success of the business or the organization.

- While some companies, often in extreme situations, have moved to pay wholly on the basis of personal competence, many are combining competency considerations with more traditional job and results-focused systems, in what we have termed a paying for contribution approach.

- Paying for contribution can ensure that the organization is paying for results and how those results are achieved, for past and future performance, avoiding the measurement problems of pure competency-based pay, and the excessive focus on individual results which performance pay can engender.

- The pay vehicles for rewarding contribution vary considerably. Some companies use pay steps related to increases in certified skills and competence. Others combine considerations of levels of competence and results achieved to arrive at a performance rating and then make a base pay increase decision. Others relate base pay increases wholly to the development of required competencies, and reward results achieved with a bonus.

CASE STUDY 4.1

Paying for contribution, 'The Woolwich way'

BACKGROUND

The Woolwich was ahead of many equivalent UK financial sector organizations in the 1980s when it moved away from time-served, incremental pay progression and introduced merit pay. Since 1990 it has related the pay increases of employees to their contribution, in respect of the achievement of personal objectives and levels of competence displayed. Yet in keeping with their significant levels of business and organizational change, notably the conversion from mutual status to becoming a plc in 1997, and associated formation of independent business units, the Woolwich is continuing to evolve the most appropriate reward systems and performance-delivering HR approach.

Between 1990 and 1997 the 7,000 staff of the Woolwich were rewarded within a pay structure of 12 grades. Pay progression depended on assessed performance using a highly structured appraisal system. Each member of staff was awarded an annual points score according to their achievement of both a series of defined business goals, such as sales and service levels, and demonstrated competence against a detailed, corporate competency framework. Thus 50 per cent of the points of a Branch Service Adviser was based on their personal competence, and 50 per cent on the achievement of results.

The system was seen as having contributed to a stronger focus on results and how these results were achieved in the Society. However, investigations during 1996 revealed a number of problems with the pay/performance relationship:

- the merit pay system was seen as producing too little differentiation for the considerable efforts involved;
- the appraisal system had limited local management and staff ownership, and was generally regarded as a once a year, bureaucratic, points-scoring exercise;
- the pay structure with differentiated, grade-related benefits was felt to reinforce a traditional, status-based organization rather than a true meritocracy;

- the general staff bonus scheme, paying out a common amount to all staff was seen as providing no incentive, nor did it reflect market rates of increase or variable pay in a number of specialist functions such as Treasury.

These pay issues are being addressed as part of a much wider HR agenda. Initially in 1996 the 'Impact' project was established, with the objective of making the HR function and HR policies much more business-driven and value-adding. More broadly, this was aligned with other changes supporting the new shareholder and values-focus in the organization: the Woolwich Way. This is providing a framework for managing the business and driving a whole series of initiatives around organization, structure, management style, development and reward.

A crucial aspect of both developments has been re-engineering the HR function, placing HR managers in the operating businesses and giving each business much greater freedom and accountability for their own HR policies, including reward. There are few areas where the operating business have not been given autonomy – pay review strategy and share schemes are two examples in the reward area.

PAY CHANGES

The framework for this devolvement and 'freeing up' of reward has involved the following:

- briefer and more flexible role profiles for all staff; in the branch network for example there are now just eight roles;
- moving all staff into a new, flatter pay structure of six broader bands, with market-related pay ranges;
- placing staff into these bands on the basis of defined accountabilities and competencies at each level of the organization, with descriptions covering managerial and technical roles (see Figure 4.12).

These aspects of the process were carried out and implemented in 1997 by 40 trained line managers, to emphasize its business-driven nature.

In respect of the base pay review process:

- the performance management system and competency framework have been considerably simplified, with the number of competencies reduced to those which really make a contribution to the business (see Table 4.4), and the mechanical points scoring and weighting system

Band 4	Band 5	Band 6
Accountabilities	**Accountabilities**	**Accountabilities**
Leader	■ Responsible for carrying out a wider variety of generally routine and non-routine tasks with responsibility for organizing and carrying out own work.	■ Carries out a range of largely repetitive activities.
■ Supervises and co-ordinates a small team engaged in generally routine/processing work, planning and allocating work, coaching, ensuring performance standards are achieved.	■ Work unsupervised to achieve prescribed standards, for example of customer service, and may advise/guide less experienced staff on basis of knowledge/experience.	■ Generally works within well-defined guidelines, adhering to clear procedures and performing to set standards, often under relatively close supervision.
■ Works within guidelines to meet agreed performance standards, but required to act without reference to senior colleagues in addressing issues, exploring opportunities, making routine decisions, and suggesting improvements.	■ Deals independently with own work, often addressing more difficult tasks/customer queries, requiring ability to assimilate and interpret information, spot opportunities, build rapport, and select best alternative action.	■ May be required to adapt work in response to changing circumstances, but refers non-standard/complex tasks to supervisor.
Specialist	■ Required to work as an effective team member, communicate clearly, supporting colleagues and influencing performance.	■ Generally works within a team, exchanging information and providing efficient customer service, possibly in a support capacity to colleagues.
■ Specializes in providing a restricted range of technical or product advice to a team, supporting more senior and coaching more junior colleagues.	■ Typically requires a period of directly relevant experience, as well as working knowledge of products/systems and GCSE level education.	■ Basic working knowledge of procedures/systems and education to GCSE level normally required.
■ Requires ability to research, analyse and write reports, with limited scope for innovation.	■ Able to provide a basic level of technical advice to customers and colleagues and may be starting to progress towards a relevant professional qualification.	
■ Specific responsibilities for management information or sales objectives may be involved.		
■ Typically requires a period of experience in the specialism and education to at least A level standard. May be working towards further technical/professional qualification.		

Band 4			Band 5	Band 6
Competence indicators	Level Team Leader	Team Specialist		
■ Planning to achieve	B	A	■ Planning to achieve A	■ Planning to achieve A
■ Improvement through change	B	B	■ Improvement through change B	■ Improvement through change A
■ Self development	B	B	■ Self development A	■ Self development A
■ Effective Communication	A	B	■ Effective Communication A	■ Effective Communication A
■ Influencing others	B	A	■ Influencing others B	■ Influencing others A
■ Helping others to achieve	B	A	■ Helping others to achieve A/B	■ Helping others to achieve A
■ Managing performance	B	A	■ Managing performance A	■ Managing performance A
■ Making decisions	A	B	■ Making decisions A	■ Making decisions A
■ Specialist knowledge	B	B	■ Specialist knowledge B	■ Specialist knowledge A

Figure 4.12 *Role evaluation framework at the Woolwich*

removed; the emphasis is now much more strongly on achieving two-way communication between manager and employees and establishing an effective objective setting, coaching and mentoring process;

- from 1999, a flexible matrix will be used to determine pay increases in each business, with positioning in range and level of performance affecting the size of the base pay increase.

The most significant shift, however, has been in the area of variable pay. All branch staff now have the opportunity to earn an annual bonus of up to 25 per cent of base pay. A common framework of performance criteria operates, covering revenues, costs, customer satisfaction and employee satisfaction. But the actual individual measures and payments are determined in each business.

In addition, specific market and performance-related bonus schemes have been established in the different businesses and functions: an IT scheme focused on Year 2000 issues; a Treasury scheme reflecting the predominant schemes in that market place; a surveyors' bonus plan, and so on. The terms and conditions for Area Managers, a key line role in the branch network, have been substantially revised, with performance bonuses of up to 100 per cent now introduced.

A sharesave scheme reinforces the importance of shareholder returns and performance, and acts as a 'glue' to reinforce co-operation across the organization. In addition, a share option scheme has been introduced for 400 managers.

The central HR function's agenda is now very much driven by the needs of each business and providing support systems to help them manage their own pay and performance issues: access to quality market data, advice on operating the new pay review process, help in improving objective setting, improvements to the systems for providing HR and performance information.

The reward agenda is moving on, in search of greater flexibility in terms and conditions to deliver improved service and efficiency. New and promoted staff are already on more flexible contracts, and flexibility of choice in the benefits package is just around the corner. Although a lot of effort has been already put into communicating pay changes, Compensation Manager Chris Pryke sees this as something that will continually need to be improved and reinforced.

Table 4.4 *Example from the Woolwich's competency menu*

Competence	Level 1	Level 2	Level 3	Level 4
Planning to achieve: Ability to organize work to ensure successful achievement of business goals	• Plans and prioritizes workload • Able to work within agreed schedule • Seeks clarification on priorities when conflicts arise	• Prepares clear work plans for specific work activities • Estimates time scales and resources necessary • Identifies links between own plan and overall operational plan	• Develops effective overall plans to meet business goals • Builds in flexibility and contingency plans to accommodate changes • Involves stakeholders in planning processes	• Develops corporate vision • Translates vision into strategic plan • Forecasts future resource requirements to achieve long-term business goals
Improvement through change: Using change methodology to develop innovative solutions to improve business performance	• Identifies and develops more effective ways of working on daily tasks • Identifies needs of internal and external customers • Takes an active and cooperative role when change is required and identifies benefits	• Creates new and innovative practices and processes to meet needs of team and customers • Takes initiative to develop ways of maintaining effectiveness and minimizing risk when implementing change.	• Actively seeks new ideas and opportunities to challenge status quo, generating new solutions to improve business unit performance and customer service • Finds ways to capitalize on unexpected changes, looking for potential benefits • Helps others to adapt and implement change effectively	• Designs change to match organizational need • Uses network to develop ideas for future direction and strategy • Identifies opportunities to make radical change to benefit the business • Engages and enthuses others to implement change

LEARNING POINTS

The Woolwich's experiences offer a number of important learning points for those progressing down what we have characterized as the contribution-related pay route. The early introduction of competency-related pay was no more a 'magic' technical solution to pay issues than a uniform merit pay approach. But share schemes and particularly a greater emphasis on variable pay have been used to deliver a stronger pay for performance message.

The Woolwich approach has become more genuinely strategic: focusing on the real business and organizational drivers; re-engineering the HR function to support the new organization structure; providing links between pay and performance through a variety of tailored vehicles; addressing a whole variety of HR and cultural issues; and supporting the operating and performance management processes at the sharp end, where the real pay for performance relationship has to happen. 'We didn't really have a total reward strategy,' explains David Smith, Head of Human Resources, and accepts that a number of the changes were not fully thought through as part of an overall business strategy. Only recently has a formal people strategy document been drafted, linked to business strategy.

But Smith sees this as having had a number of advantages, in that the line managers in the businesses would almost certainly have seen an obvious grand strategy paraded in advance, as simply a cloak for continued central control. Instead, the changes have had to run in line 'with the grain of the business' and really address local issues. 'Managers were being told to run their own business so it was logical to say manage your pay budget too,' says Smith. Now they have experienced for themselves the value of the competency-related pay matrix and bonus schemes and are coming to HR asking for help to make them work more effectively.

Incremental changes also meant that people were prepared to work on and help with the process, whereas Smith feels that if people had seen the whole agenda in advance, they might have reacted against the scale of the transformation involved. Rather than rolling out mandatory performance management and competency training programmes, which would have made the exercise a 'nine day wonder', the business needs for these tools are now obvious. A broader leadership development process is being designed to improve the underlying quality of managers' use of these approaches, and to help make paying for contribution a practical reality.

The process has not been without its hiccups and problems. Staff concerns at the lack of pensionability of bonus have led to the introduction of a pensionable bonus waiver, so people can use part of their bonus to boost their pension contributions. And Smith considers that the changes have worked best where the operational HR managers have really contributed to the local business.

It is still early days to assess the effects of the changes, but a MORI poll in early 1998 found Woolwich staff to have very high relative scores in terms of commitment to servicing their customers and recognizing the need for change, a mutually reinforcing combination.

CASE STUDY 4.2

An evolutionary approach to the alignment of performance, competence and pay at Bass Brewers

Bass Brewers employs approximately 4,000 staff in six breweries and at its Head Office in Burton. It has been linking competencies to pay since 1993, but 1999 will mark a significant shift in its approach, which illustrates many of the points regarding the nature of paying for contribution.

THE ORIGINAL 1993 LINKAGE

Competencies had already been established in the Company's HR policies, employed for graduate development and recruitment purposes, using a tailored version of the menu designed by its PLC parent. But the original move to link competencies to pay had two main drivers:

- First, the complete re-structuring of the brewing industry in the UK and Bass's response to this; following the divestment of its tied pubs arm, this focused on delivering major efficiency gains by reorganizing on a work process rather than a functional basis; competencies were seen as a powerful tool to underpin the behavioural changes necessary to deliver these planned efficiencies.
- Second, dissatisfaction with the company's existing pay management systems.

Bass had a fairly traditional approach to pay, with 10 management and 37 clerical grades. Pay progression for these non-negotiated staff was managed with a standard merit pay grid, relating increases to the level of performance achieved against up to six annual objectives. A detailed

145

review by the HR Department revealed an over-concentration on the achievement of individual financial targets, the lack of any incentive for supporting the changes necessary to succeed in the future, and a lack of pay flexibility in response to the market.

The company therefore introduced a more flexible, flatter structure of four management and four clerical staff pay bands in 1993. Pay progression within these bands was related wholly to the level of competence achieved, while performance results were rewarded with cash bonuses. The competence assessment for all staff was originally made against the seven core competencies of the company, each rated on a three-point scale as superior, met or improvable. Bass defines competencies as 'the displayed behaviours or attitudes identified as the key to the success of a business and which are shared by everyone'. In 1994, four management competencies and up to two technical competencies were added to the menu, to relate it more specifically to the needs of different groups of staff.

On the basis of these criteria, staff receive an overall competence rating (see Figure 4.13). This rating helps to determine the individual's pay increase, although line managers have a lot of freedom, within their overall budget, to allocate individual awards, and also to relate them to external rates of market increase.

The original concept of the bonus was to link it to company, team and individual performance, but this was felt to be too complex to design and operate. So a single company scheme was introduced, with the bonus related wholly to company profits, although the maximum payment opportunities were differentiated by level, ranging from 5 per cent to 25 per cent of base pay.

THE 1999 SHIFT

Minor changes have been made since then, including the introduction of a more focused senior management bonus in 1996, and the addition of a sales volume target to the company bonus. But significant modifications to both the base pay and bonus approaches have resulted from a similar combination of business strategy drivers and HR policy reviews.

A major exercise, the Business Alignment Project, has been underway during 1998, with the aim of getting a much better understanding throughout the company of the strategic goals, in order that staff can really make the brand strategy happen, and deliver a further step-change improvement in performance in the future. The company's traditional reticence about communicating performance information has been set aside.

CORE COMPETENCIES	TARGET RATING	ACTUAL RATING
Putting the customer first		
teamwork		
Dedication to quality		
Bias to action		
Commercial focus		
Fairness and decency		
Communications		
MANAGERIAL COMPETENCIES		
Problem solving		
Focus on results		
Interpersonal skills		
Managing people		
TECHNICAL COMPETENCIES		

OVERALL COMPETENCE RATING

Overall Competence Rating: ⬜

Please give an overall rating of current competence in this job using **only** the following levels:

1	Too early to rate	2	Unacceptable
3	Improvable	3.5	Improvable+
4	On target	4.5	On target
5	Superior		

PERSONAL BUSINESS OBJECTIVES

	Y/N

Figure 4.13 *Bass Brewers' performance and development review form*

The five components of the company's mission, its values and its strategic intent, (which now include the goal of having empowered and motivated staff), are being communicated and cascaded down the business.

A balanced business scorecard is being used as the framework for this, both to set individual goals, and to measure progress towards those five strategic aims (see Figure 4.14). Ten overall measures are being used across these five categories, which include measures of customer, consumer and staff satisfaction.

A revamped performance management system is being used as a primary vehicle to cascade and manage this process of alignment, with pay changes playing a supporting role. The desire to extend performance management to cover negotiated staff, and apparent problems with the existing appraisal system, led the HR Department to carry out a detailed staff attitude survey in 1998, involving questionnaires and focus groups.

The survey validated initial perceptions that the appraisal system was not being given enough attention, that performance was not being actively managed, and that managers were failing to differentiate between staff on the basis of either their competence or their performance. Under-performing staff were not therefore having their development needs identified and addressed, while high performers were not being recognized and rewarded appropriately. Only a quarter of staff felt that there were effective linkages between pay and performance, and the company bonus scheme was seen as being too far removed to affect individual behaviour, even though it had paid out at the maximum level in the previous year.

The changes are focusing on the process aspects of performance management, as well as a simplification, focusing and sharpening of the competency pay approach. All staff will now undertake a commitment schedule (see Figure 4.15), consisting of up to five personal objectives, each of which has to relate back to one of the five strategic themes and balanced

Figure 4.14 *Balanced scoreboard categories at Bass Brewers*

scorecard categories. The breadth of performance criteria should avoid any excessive focus on short-term financial goals. Progress against the schedule will be monitored and discussed on a quarterly basis, as indeed will the company's overall progress against the scorecard, which will in future drive the company bonus scheme. All 1,100 managers have been put through a development workshop to explain the refocusing of the system, emphasize its importance, and practise the necessary appraisal skills.

Competencies will still play an important part in the performance management process, acting as the basis for individual development plans, and continuing to influence the base pay increases of staff. However, now only up to five competencies will be selected for each person, acting as the focus of their performance improvement efforts for each period, rather than rating every member of staff or against all of the company's menu. The range of competencies to select from will be broader, with less emphasis on the uniform menu, and more on job-specific skills and behaviours. The concept of job families, linking in to career ladders, has already been successfully piloted in the IT area and will be extended

From 1999 therefore the performance rating, which relates to the annual pay increase of staff, will be determined both by the level of performance against personal objectives, and against competence targets, the combination at the heart of the paying for contribution approach.

LEARNING POINTS

According to Human Resources Manager Steve Kear, the original HR and reward objectives have remained broadly consistent, but 'the pieces within

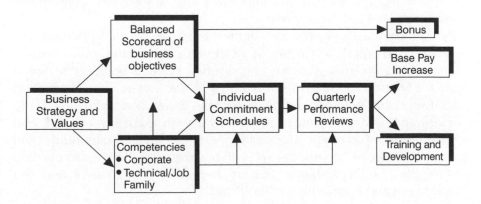

Figure 4.15 *New performance management process*

the jigsaw have needed to be shuffled', reflecting both on changes in emphasis in the business strategy, and the practical experience of competency pay. The requirement in 1993 was to get a common shift in process-focused behaviour, whereas now the complexity of the different criteria which will make the brand strategy happen are being accounted for, but still within a common and manageable framework of the balanced scorecard.

Indeed, practicality, workability, even pragmatism lie at the heart of the Bass approach. If you need an example of the necessity rather than the fad of competency pay then this must be it. Support in concept for team rewards was abandoned once the complexity and difficulty of doing it in practice became evident, an assessment which has also led to the idea of flexible benefits being parked for the time being.

But in terms of paying for both competence and results, whenever the principle and the practice has got out of alignment, the board has supported a reassertion of the principle and a modification of the practice. According to Kear, 'the original emphasis on competence in the pay decision was necessary to support the required behavioural shift'. He feels, 'It has taken five years to get competencies really understood and fully embedded in the day-to-day operation and language of the business.'

Now that this is the case, rebalancing the pay decision back towards results achieved makes sense, particularly as the balanced scorecard reflects the totality of the contribution that employees make in delivering on the strategy. He describes it as a more 'holistic', and ultimately more effective approach, with pay playing an important but, 'back-end reinforcement role' in the total performance management system. The tailoring of the competencies should also, according to Kear, give them even greater local meaning and impact, and improve their use for a full range of HR applications, not just the pay one.

And finally, Bass's experiences demonstrate the critical importance of process, particularly in terms of communications and performance management, to make pay for contribution really a reality. The initial launch communication and effort in 1993 was not really followed up effectively, contributing to the divorce of the theory and the reality of the performance management process. Now, with quarterly reviews and regular reporting on progress against the scorecard targets, communication is more 'built-in' to the process. As ever, however, its ultimate success rests not in the HR Department, but on the skills of managers and the involvement and contribution of their staff.

CASE STUDY 4.3

Rethinking competency-related pay at ICL[41]

Katherine Adams

ICL, the global systems company, with revenues of £2.5 billion and 19,000 employees worldwide, is one of a growing number of organizations that turned to competency-related pay (CRP) as a way of dealing with changing business realities. As with many other employers, it has used the idea of broadly defined job families as the launching pad for this approach. Yet ICL's experience demonstrates that CRP is far from an easy solution, and that too strong an emphasis on competencies can create problems.

WHY COMPETENCY PAY?

In the beginning, CRP was seen as an attractive alternative to the company's existing pay system. This employed a single, job-evaluated grading structure, with a hierarchy of 20 pay bands, each divided into a number of pay points. The system was seen as increasingly inappropriate, given the changing nature of the computer business. As with other computer firms, ICL was no longer a straightforward producer of computer hardware, but provided a much wider range of IT services. Increasingly, the company needed its employees to work in new ways, using new kinds of skills.

Tim Evans, Employee Development Manager, explains: 'The grading structure had become an end in itself, with people focusing on the rewards they would get as they moved up each point.'

It was also out of touch with differences in market rates. Evans says:

> We realized that some managers had to break the system in order to pay the right money to the right person. They had to over-promote some people so that they could get the market rate. Others were being forced to make the wrong decisions on pay because the single grading system could not accommodate the vast range of different jobs and market rates.

PROFESSIONAL COMMUNITIES

In 1996, with the help of external consultants from Towers Perrin, the company decided to move towards using CRP. The first step was to scrap the old grades and replace them with a system of job families. There were 25 job families in all, known as professional communities. Evans says:

> The organization was changing so fast that job descriptions were out of date by the time they were published. The speed of change was also a problem as the organization changed and divisions formed and reorganized; people become confused about their roles. Being in a community gives them a point of stability and reference, and a source of 'professional' information and training. Professional communities were designed to offer people a broader understanding of their roles.

With the help of human resources experts and line managers, teams of managers and employees in each community brainstormed questions about the business, roles within the community, and the capabilities (that is, the competencies) required for these roles. High-performing employees were also interviewed. Using this information, the company drew up a broad description of each community's purpose, and a definition of each role within the community, itemizing the responsibilities, technical skills and knowledge, competencies, entry criteria and key performance indicators. (This process is still continuing as all the roles are analysed and redefined.)

Because this work was carried out separately for each community, the competencies that resulted varied in content and structure (see Figure 4.16). For instance, some competencies included both positive and negative behavioural indicators, while others had only positive ones. Some defined competencies at four levels, others provided just one, general definition. Evans says: 'We had to choose between designing our competency analysis tools to the nth degree and running the risk that they would be out of date before we started, or just starting with some professional communities, and building from there. We couldn't afford to wait.'

COMPETENCY-RELATED PAY

The new CRP system was introduced on a voluntary basis. Staff who wanted to could join a suitable community of their choice. This meant having their annual appraisals and pay decisions run according to the new system. Those who did not choose to join stayed with the old grading system.

Every new role within each community was linked to pay-range guidance on market rates for competent, skilled performance. There were no rules about the maximum percentage increase an individual could

Competency matrix

Teamwork

Negotiation skills

Communication skills

Facts and data-information seeking

Analytical thinking

Qualifications

Typical previous roles

Recognition

IT literate

External contacts

Example: Communication skills

Level 1

■ communicates effectively with suppliers and internal customers:

■ develops and produces standard reports.

Level 2

■ develops good communications with all levels of suppliers and customers;

■ has demonstrated effectiveness in presenting to senior management.

Level 3

■ initiates and fosters good communications to a high standard;

■ is able to facilitate discussions between cross-company and cross-functional teams;

■ takes lead in communication with suppliers to achieve maximum benefit to ICL.

Level 4

■ able to handle extremely sensitive communications with all levels of suppliers and customers;

■ produces persuasive reports and presentations;

■ proven effective management of communication between cross-functional, senior management groups.

Figure 4.16 *Competencies for ICL's purchasing professional community*

receive. The pay range was directly linked to market rates by bench-marking roles to market practice. For roles that were applicable to more than one market sector, there was scope to make a link to more than one market pay range.

The professional communities and role descriptions were linked to ICL's Performance-Plus appraisal system. At annual appraisals and interim-performance or project reviews, staff and their managers assessed both the competencies required of the individual and his or her actual competencies. This resulted in a rating for each competency along the following five-point scale: A (aware), B (basic), C (competent), D (distinguished) and

E (expert). The individual was also assessed on his or her achievement of objectives and, together, these assessments were used to make an overall assessment of performance on the following four-point scale: B (below requirements), R (good, but requires improvement), G (good and improving) and E (excellent).

THE DRIFT BACK TO GRADES

The intention was never to make an exclusive link between competencies and pay. Evans says: 'It was intended to be a holistic judgement, looking at the person's capabilities, role, impact on the business and overall performance. It wasn't just a case of having the competencies, but of applying them and also taking into account the market worth of those competencies.'

He says that the system asked a lot from managers: 'They had to "think outside the box", rather than asking us what the percentage increase was that year. Some approached the review very scientifically, using spreadsheets to balance the basic pay decisions, others were less scientific.'

It became apparent that the managers using the new system were reverting to previous methods. Evans says: 'People felt the need for some structure, and it became clear that they were using competency levels, where they existed, and the four-point performance assessment to provide that structure. It became clear that we were slipping back to the old grading system.'

TOO MUCH EMPHASIS ON PAY

The introduction of competency pay also made people see the new professional communities primarily in terms of pay, when they had been intended as a way of encouraging career development, especially lateral job moves. Evans recounts: 'Suddenly, people weren't limited to their grade band, but were being assessed against the competencies for their role. If they got more pay as a result, they thought that going into a community was all about getting more money.' 'Red-circling' of existing salaries also meant that the new system had a negative impact on costs.

The company's Director of Employee Development, Jeremy Webster, believes that it was a mistake to allow staff to choose whether or not to join a community, and which community to join. He says: 'People were looking around for the best deal to improve their terms and conditions.' In addition, he says,

The new system was segmenting the organization as badly as the old grading structure. The communities were elitist, covering project managers and engineers, but excluding the non-graduates and secretaries. And there were lots of small engineering communities – different ones for systems engineers and help-desk engineers, for instance.

The system also worked against the kind of role flexibility that the company was seeking. Webster says: 'An engineer whose job sometimes involved dealing with customers might join the consultancy community. But what happens when the role changes and that person no longer deals with customers? If he or she is still officially a member of that community, then they're disenfranchised'.

TURNING POINT

The turning point came in October 1997 – about a year after the new system was introduced – when it became clear that just 14 per cent of staff had entered a professional community and had their pay determined by CRP. Newly arrived at ICL, Webster was given the task of reforming the system. His solution involves four elements: reducing the number of communities; emphasizing development by introducing a new system of governance for the communities and focusing the training spend on competencies; making community membership compulsory; and linking pay decisions more firmly to market factors.

The first step was to reform the professional communities, giving them a proper management infrastructure and re-emphasizing the importance of development. The original 25 communities were reduced to 15, largely by combining the many small engineering communities into one.

Each community now has both a high-level sponsor and a leader who is an expert in that particular community. Most leaders have part-time responsibility, but the position of engineering leader is full-time. Key communities, such as project management, service management, sales/marketing/client management, management and business support, also have a professional development manager who is a dedicated training and development specialist. The whole system is overseen by an executive management committee of 16 people.

DEVELOPMENT AND APPRAISAL

The company's training spend of £21 million a year is now focused on a core curriculum designed to develop the competencies that individuals need to perform their roles. A new career action and learning centre has been established, with a comprehensive range of computer-based and other learning materials, and all the competency-based role profiles have been published on a company intranet.

The company's traditional, menu-driven approach to training is being replaced by targeted development options such as lateral development, coaching and mentoring, special projects and regular reviews, all focused on competencies.

ICL's Performance-Plus appraisal system is still linked to the competencies required for particular roles, and work is continuing to develop these. However, Evans explains: 'We're beginning to get to the point where we can develop a standard library of competencies, bringing together all the roles and seeing what they have in common.' The object is to encourage lateral career moves, as well as to provide a focus for training, communication, development planning and appraisal. In line with the new focus on develop-ment, the company is also putting more emphasis on self-assessment of the competencies. Finally, in August 1998, ICL began the process of allocating all 19,000 employees to both a primary and a secondary community.

MARKET PAY

The effect of all this, Webster believes, is 'to make the communities as much about development as about pay'. He says: 'Job families are a good idea if they're developmentally based. But pay has to be driven by the market; it has to be objective. With just 300 HR people, it's too time-consuming to define and measure pay for 19,000 staff in this way.'

Although employees' competencies will still be assessed at annual appraisals, and this will feed into pay decisions, the direct link between competencies, professional communities and pay will go. Webster says: 'We're now changing the nature of the employment relationship, making it more performance-focused, more market-oriented. The project people will have bonuses, for instance; the engineering people will be paid in a way that reflects what's happening in that sector.' And, overall, he believes that most staff will welcome this: 'We're trying to disentangle the link between pay and career development, and most people are relieved.'

LEARNING POINTS

In summary, therefore, ICL's experiences demonstrate both the need to relate pay to competencies, but also the dangers of too strong a focus on this linkage, and the practical difficulties of making it work.

ICL's new pay system was found to be time-consuming and did not fully support the company's new business processes. It put undue emphasis on reward, when the company wanted to focus on using competencies to develop people. With the professional communities structure, there was a danger of CRP being perceived as elitist and divisive, which contradicted the aim of encouraging people to work with others in different parts of the organization. And there was an irresistible drift back to the old concept of grading that the company had hoped to leave behind.

In the face of these problems, ICL has decided to reinforce the link between competencies and development, though competencies are being retained for use, in conjunction with other factors, to support pay decisions. The job families on which the CRP system was based are being reformed, and there is a new infrastructure to manage each one and emphasize the link to development. All training and development in the company is now being targeted at the competencies. In terms of pay decisions, competencies will still have some effect on pay but in a more tailored way, and reward is now being tied more closely to market norms.

NOTES

1. Armstrong, M and Baron, A (1995) *The Job Evaluation Handbook*, Institute of Personnel and Development, London
2. The Industrial Society (1998) *Competency Based Pay,* Managing Best Practice Report No 43
3. Hofrichter, DA and Spencer, LM (1996) Competencies: the right foundation for effective HR management, *Compensation and Benefits Review*, November/December
4. Quoted in a speech at the Institute of Personnel and Development Compensation Forum Conference, February 1997
5. O'Neal, S (1994) Work and pay in the 21st century, *ACA News*, July
6. Towers Perrin (1997) *Learning from the Past: Changing for the future*, Research Report from Towers Perrin, London, March
7. Sparrow, PA (1996) Too good to be true?, *People Management*, December
8. Lawler III, EE (1996) 'Competencies: a poor foundation for new pay, *Compensation and Benefits Review*, November/December
9. Industrial Society, op. cit.
10. Industrial Relations Services (1998) Pay prospects 1998 survey, *Pay and Benefits Bulletin* **435**, November
11. American Compensation Association (1996) *Raising the Bar: Using competencies to enhance employee performance*, ACA, Scottsdale Arizona, May
12. Collins, J and Porras, J (1992) *Built to Last*, Century, London
13. Results of a survey briefing, Is peoplism replacing capitalism?, presented by Reed Personnel Services at the 1998 IPD Conference
14. Cited in D Brown and M Armstrong (1998) Paying for competency: the UK experience, *Compensation and Benefits Review*, July/August

15. American Compensation Association, op. cit.
16. Towers Perrin, op. cit.
17. Ghoshal, S and Bartlett, S (1998) Changing the role of top management, *Harvard Business Review*, January/February
18. O'Neal, op. cit.
19. Towers Perrin, op. cit.
20. Industrial Society, op. cit.
21. American Compensation Association, op. cit.
22. Boyatzis, R (1982) *The Competent Manager*, Wiley, New York
23. Woodruffe, C (1991) Competent by any other name, *People Management*, September
24. Sparrow, op. cit.
25. Woodruffe, op. cit.
26. Emerson, SM (1991) Job evaluation: a barrier to excellence, *Compensation and Benefits Review*, January/February
27. Towers Perrin, op. cit.
28. For more examples, see D Brown (1998) *A Practical Guide to Competency-Related Pay*, Financial Times Management, London
29. Armstrong and Baron, op. cit.
30. Industrial Relations Services, op. cit.
31. Sparrow, op. cit.
32. Moloney, K (1997) Why competencies may not be enough, *Competency*, **5** (1), Autumn
33. Wallace, MJ, Making the business case for competency-based pay systems, paper presented at the ACA National Conference, Chicago, April 1998
34. Wallace, op. cit.
35. Towers Perrin, op. cit.
36. Quoted in C Brown-Humes (1998) Prudential salesforce earnings are to be less commission based, *The Financial Times*, 28 September
37. Ashton, C (1999) *Strategic Compensation*, Business Intelligence Report, London
38. Lawler III, EE (1986) What's wrong with job evaluation?, *Compensation and Benefits Review*, March/April
39. Timmins, N (1998) Top mandarin takes government to task, *The Financial Times*, 14 December
40. Moss Kanter, R (1989) *When Giant Learns to Dance,* Unwin, London
41. We are grateful to Industrial Relations Services for permission to include extracts from this article, which first appeared in *Competency*, **6** (1), Autumn, 1998

5

Improving the design of merit pay plans to reward high contribution

Managers, whose performance influenced around 2 per cent of their pay, complained of favouritism by bosses, a clustering of ratings around the middle grade and a lack of communications and feedback. Many failed to see any link between their effort and their reward… it was a big song and dance about not very much.

(Philip Lewis, Cheltenham and Gloucester College)[1]

Most grumbles were because of the size of the pot, not the mechanism.

(Scottish Amicable)[2]

As we saw in Chapter 2, poor scheme design, as well as lack of strategic direction and poor communication and management, help to explain the difficulties which organizations have been experiencing with their attempts to relate base pay increases to individual performance. In this chapter we describe common strategies and reactions to this situation in the base pay practices of UK and international organizations.

First, we briefly consider moves to abandon the link altogether and manage performance through other means, such as lump sum bonuses (considered in more detail in the next chapter). Then we look at more common responses in the United Kingdom, which are to attempt to increase the variability of pay and the line-of-sight between individual performance and reward, and to use a greater range of different pay and reward vehicles, including broadbanding. Paying for contribution is characterized by greater pay variability and an increasing diversity of tailored schemes. However here, and even in the United States, we demonstrate that putting a proportion of current pay at risk is not yet generally being adopted as a means of increasing the variability of pay.

THE LACK OF VARIABILITY

A particular difficulty with merit pay, as Scottish Amicable found in the early 1990s, has been the issue of individual differentiation over a sustained period of relatively low general inflation in the United Kingdom, the United States and most of Western Europe. Some may, like the trade union Bectu, regard performance-related pay as 'inherently unfair and discriminatory'. But for the majority of employers, the bigger crime seems to have been, as Lewis's research participants observed, a failure to actually deliver pay differentiation in practice. Thus, 8 per cent or 10 per cent salary increase budgets in the later 1980s saw people in many organizations with merit pay receiving between 0 per cent and 20 per cent, according to their individual performance. Yet current budgets of 3–4 per cent see the highest performers only receiving 3–5 per cent extra in many cases. On a proportionate, and versus cost-of-living basis, the differential is the same, but the perception and impact on employees is undoubtedly lower.

Almost three-quarters of respondents in the IPD survey[3] of over 1,000 organizations regarded their merit awards as 'too small to act as a motivator', and the median value of individual merit pay awards in that survey was 4 per cent in 1997 (see Table 5.1). To illustrate, only 10 per cent of Thames Water's employees felt that their merit pay scheme really did reward superior performance in 1996. As one employee expressed it, it also 'fails to penalize poor performers'. Indeed, in many US companies, according to Jerry Macadam of Maritz, 'merit pay is just a convoluted way of paying cost-of-living'.

Table 5.1 *Mean and median pay awards under various types of performance pay schemes*

Occupational Group	Mean values (%)			Median values (%)		
	IPeRP	Team-based pay	Profit-related pay	IPeRP	Team-based pay	Profit-related pay
Senior managers	11	11	11	5	8	6
Middle managers	9	10	11	4	5	6
Junior managers/ senior supervisors	9	7	10	4	5	7
Non-managers	9	10	10	4	7	6

Source: IPD research

The 'line of sight' between effort, performance and pay is, as we saw in the discussion of common problems in Chapter 2, further weakened by the influence of so many other issues beyond individual performance on pay: market pay rates and external market trends, internal job evaluation and relativities, company affordability, position in pay range, and so on. According to the Industrial Society's study of over 1,000 companies, on average only 40 per cent of somebody's pay increase in companies with merit pay is actually related to their individual performance.

As this situation has persisted therefore, a number of organizations appear to have concluded that they are in an untenable 'no-man's land' in which performance pay policy and practice conflict. Evidence of attempts to escape from this dilemma and bring policy and practice into alignment are evident from Income Data Services' analysis of trends in the types of pay award in UK companies (see Figure 5.1).[4] While the incidence of wholly merit-based awards has continued to increase in the UK economy, this growth has largely been at the expense of combined general and merit awards rather than wholly general cost-of-living. The message would appear to be 'do it properly or don't do it at all', and in the rest of the chapter we consider these two responses to the merit pay dilemma.

MOVES OUT OF MERIT PAY

As we saw in Chapter 2 there has been a small, if well-publicized, shift out of merit pay in the United Kingdom and a more significant move

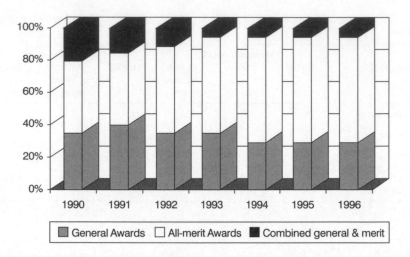

Figure 5.1 *Distribution of managerial pay awards in the UK by type of review*

away from it in the United States. In addition, there has been a continuance of general, non-merit-based pay awards, typically either on a 'zero return/impossible in practice' rationale , or more positively, on the basis of being more effective alternatives. Thus Yorkshire TV and HTV, for example, retain across-the-board increases because they regard them as the simplest and most equitable method of adjusting pay. Yorkshire TV maintain that motivation relates to a whole raft of issues and that effective development and performance management are often the key to it. General awards neutralize the danger of any negative, hygiene effects from pay.

Allied Domecq regards merit pay as divisive and believes it has never seen a scheme which actually works effectively. Staff performance is instead rewarded through a bonus scheme, which relates payments to the achievement of targets, such as profit and cash flow. Komatsu meanwhile was one of those companies who abandoned its combined general and merit approach to pay reviews in the United Kingdom in 1997, because of the small size of the total pay 'pot'. But, as it has a strong single-status ethos and reward approach, a general increase in line with inflation is seen as being fair and consistent.

Mobil, and British Gas for its Reading-based managers and staff, are two of those organizations that have dropped their wholly merit-based pay increase schemes. They both now relate base salary adjustments purely to rates of external market increase, while individual and organizational performance is rewarded through a bonus.

As we saw in the previous chapter, another alternative strategy which is becoming increasingly popular is, as at Bass, Thames Power and ICL, to relate base pay increases to growth in individual skills and competence, and reward performance in a cash bonus. Bonuses, as we describe in the next chapter, have a number of potential advantages in making effective links between performance and pay. From an organizational and cost perspective they are a non-recurring payment which reflects recent performance, that is not consolidated into future payments as is merit pay, and often does not attract pensionable on-costs. The nature of performance measures used in bonus plans also often means that they are purely driven by performance, and not diluted by other criteria such as the market or internal relativities. This tends to make them more variable from year to year and payments are often larger, at present, than under merit pay schemes. In the IPD research for example,[5] half of those with team bonus plans had made payments equivalent to 10 per cent or more of base pay in the past year (see Table 5.1).

From the employees' perspective bonuses are a discrete item received as a one-off cash lump sum, which can have a more meaningful impact than salary payments which are spread out over succeeding months. And they are not a 'zero sum' item in many cases, where in order to control the pay budget, someone's high pay increase has to be funded out of someone else's lower increase.

But for the vast majority of employees, base pay is the most substantial item in their remuneration and the company's HR spend. As Lawler puts it, 'The alternative of abandoning base pay as a motivator is always there, but it represents the abandonment of a very important potential incentive, something that most organizations cannot afford to do.'[6] And as the Towers Perrin's reward study of 300 European organizations[7] demonstrated, a majority of those organizations with collective and individual bonus schemes continue to operate merit-related base pay arrangements as well. Stephen Kerr explains how at General Electric merit pay contributes, along with individual and collective bonus schemes, to produce the level of meaningful differentials he wants to see between high and low contributors, of between 10 per cent and 20 per cent.

Indeed, competitive business pressures are, as we have seen in Chapter 2, even in Japan, forcing organizations to attempt to achieve greater variability in their pay budgets in relation to the performance of the organization. In Japan this has traditionally been achieved through the use of substantial end-of-year profit-linked bonuses, although individual performance pay schemes are now becoming more common.

In Europe this desire and necessity for a greater proportion of the pay budget to be variable are evident from the Towers Perrin data, with a continued growth in the variable proportion of total cash predicted at all job levels by the 300 participating organizations (see Table 5.2). Thus at the median level, variable pay is forecast to increase over the next three years from 20 per cent of the average senior managers' total cash, to 26 per cent by 2000. Particularly for those European organizations already paying highly against the market, and with a good benefits package, this degree of variability cannot be achieved by simply putting a new bonus scheme on top of the existing package. Greater flexibility in the base pay budget is the only alternative, and it is one that an increasing number of organizations are using.

INCREASING THE FLEXIBILITY OF BASE PAY AND PAY INCREASES

Probably the most common responses to the merit pay dilemma have been to reform the pay adjustment mechanisms and management processes, in order to attempt to achieve greater variability between individuals on the basis of their performance. Companies are thereby trying to escape the situation whereby, 'too much pay is going to too many people with too little effect'.[8]

Incremental systems of increase, which inevitably seem to degenerate into automatic progression, have been abandoned over recent

Table 5.2 *Forecast increases in the variable elements of pay*

	Now		Next 3 years	
	Base	Variable	Base	Variable
Senior Execs	80%	20%	74%	26%
Mgrs/Profs	88%	12%	83%	17%
Clerical/Support	96%	4%	93%	7%
Production/Operatives	95%	5%	92%	8%

Source: Towers Perrin (1997)

years by organizations such as Pfizer, Surrey County Council, National Grid, Midland Bank and the Foreign and Commonwealth Office, in favour of more flexible alternatives.

MORE FLEXIBLE MECHANISMS

The Foreign and Commonwealth Office (FCO) took on delegated pay responsibilities from central government in 1996. Eighty years of nationally negotiated pay arrangements may have come to an end, yet the FCO still had to cope with a government-imposed cap on public sector pay increases. It therefore replaced the system of supposedly merit-based spine points for its 5,400 staff with an equity shares system (see Figure 5.2).

Each individual's performance is rated as part of the appraisal process, and on this basis they are thereby awarded a number of shares in the total pay budget. The higher the performance and the lower in the range, the higher the number of shares and resulting pay increase. Top performers in 1996 received a 3.5 per cent payment on top of their 1.5 per cent general increase and the FCO regard the system as open, equitable and flexible while ensuring that critical cost parameters are not exceeded. As we have found, judgements of flexibility tend to be relative and even this level of variability, in our experience, can have a high impact if it represents a move out of a very structured process.

Midland Bank, meanwhile, completed the introduction of a new pay review system in the same year, which replaced the existing separation of a general award in June and a merit-based increment on the individual's appointment anniversary. The objective, according to Head of Compensation Pam Wood, was to 'focus people's attention on performance rather than just turning up and being paid', and being rewarded for service.

		Appraisal rating		
		Box 1	Box 2	Box 3
Position in range	Top third	5 shares	3 shares	2 shares
	Middle third	7 shares	5 shares	4 shares
	Bottom third	9 shares	7 shares	6 shares

Figure 5.2 *1996 equity shares matrix used at the Foreign and Commonwealth Office*

Under the old scheme, established in the 1970s, it could take nine years for a new starter to reach their competitive job rate. A new performance management system incorporating job standards, and required skills and competencies was piloted for twelve months prior to the link with pay being made. Those rated as outstanding received a 2–3 per cent market movement in 1996, plus 6 per cent for individual performance, and potentially also an 'excellence' cash bonus of £200–£400. Only those with a high or outstanding performance rating can now progress into the higher reaches of the new, wider pay scales.

The effect of these moves to increase pay variability are evident at senior management levels in the IPD research[9] (see Table 5.3). For senior management positions in 1997, 35 per cent of organizations awarded average increases of 3 per cent or less, while nearly a quarter of schemes awarded an average increase of 10 per cent or more, with ten companies awarding at least 100 per cent. Mean individual pay awards in that survey for all staff groups were also well above the median figures (see Table 5.1), demonstrating the skew caused by some very high individual payments.

Illustrating the variety of responses to the merit pay dilemma, other companies are moving to try and break down the concept of the annual pay review for all staff, which can reinforce a 'going rate' mentality. In many sectors such as the car industry and electricity sector, 'the annual pay round' has been replaced by a series of deals of different lengths, typically two or three years. A quarter of negotiated deals in the engineering sector are no longer of twelve months' duration.

Table 5.3 *Frequency distribution of individual performance-related pay awards for senior managers*

IPeRP awards as a % of base pay	Number of organizations	Percentage of those responding
0	12	3
1–3	114	32
4–6	94	26
7–10	56	16
11–20	52	14
More than 20	29	9
Total	357	100

Source: IPD

Some companies such as Scottish Power have devolved pay reviews to produce a clearer pay/performance relationship in each of their constituent businesses – Supply, Generation, Telecomms and so on, and we consider this process in more detail in Chapter 9. Others have moved to rolling reviews, such as Hewlett Packard, which operates individual pay reviews on the anniversary of joining.

Indeed, much greater variety is evident within as well as between companies as they break out of the 1980's merit pay strait-jacket. As Income Data Services[10] relate, this makes it much more difficult to summarize pay trends and averages. Johnson Matthey, for example, related pay budgets in 1998 to the performance of its different businesses. Thus the budget for a specialist subsidiary well in profit was 5.2 per cent, but staff in a less successful Midlands location received only 3 per cent.

MORE FLEXIBLE PROCESSES

Other organizations, such as insurer General Accident and the Royal Bank of Scotland, have put considerable effort into communications and training so as to better manage employee and management expectations, and also to ensure that small pay budgets are managed more effectively. General Accident invested heavily in management training, and increases for under performers and those paid highly against the external market have been reduced to zero.

National Westminster Bank, Scottish Amicable, Pearl Assurance and the BBC have all managed a stepped transition during the 1990s from HR controlled and formulaic, incremental pay systems, to much greater line management ownership and flexibility in pay increases. Again they are attempting to target the merit pay spend more effectively and directly to performance.

Pay Manager David Buchanan at Scottish Amicable led a change to the company's merit pay scheme, which had been originally introduced in 1992, after a staff attitude survey in 1995. The forced distribution of ratings and fixed matrix of increases which was controlled centrally led to 'a general lack of faith and support in the system'. Now managers have a high degree of freedom in distributing their pay budget, and the fixed matrix has become a spread-sheet model, which managers can tailor to their own departmental circumstances.

The control and allocation of pay budgets were similarly totally devolved to the local level in Lloyds/TSB during 1998 (see Case Study 9.1). At Abbey National, the implementation of the new broadbanded pay structure and contribution-based pay increase system is entirely in the hands of divisional directors. They can introduce whichever parts of the new approach they think will benefit their particular business unit, and at a speed they consider appropriate. This devolved approach matches with the overall flexibility of the new pay mechanism and is intended to increase ownership of, and accountability for, the new arrangements.

National Westminster Bank moved all staff into a single, flatter structure of eight broad, market-related pay bands in 1994, with a fixed, individual performance/position in range matrix determining the levels of increase. Under such systems staff can, relatively, move down as well as up the band if their performance no longer matches the position they have achieved in their range. But in 1995 greater variability and discretion was introduced into the matrix, and by 1997 managers were simply allocated a budgeted amount to cover both performance-related salary and bonus awards.

The BBC (see Case Study 2.1) moved progressively from over 40 to 20 grades in 1991, and then after 18 months planning into 11 grades in 1995. This change was paralleled by progressively greater variability and flexibility in pay increases. Annual increments for new staff were replaced by performance-based increases, and the top 10–15 per cent of performers in 1995 shared a merit pot of 0.5 per cent of payroll, or £3.5 million. Under the new arrangements, from 1996 onwards the pay of consistently poor performers could actually be frozen or be reduced.

At BP Exploration, managers essentially have a spot, market-related pay rate. Their pay increase in relation to this is affected by rates of market movement, but also depend on their individual performance and competence, and their contribution relative to their peers.

These examples illustrate three important pay techniques being used to support the changing pay landscape in the United Kingdom, and to effect attempts to resolve the merit pay dilemma. These relate to the increasing diversity of performance-related pay schemes in organizations, the greater use of broadbanding, and efforts to make a greater proportion of the merit pay budget variable and at risk.

PAYING FOR CONTRIBUTION WITH A VARIETY OF DIFFERENT SCHEMES

We recently reviewed the set of pay proposals which a company had developed to introduce a stronger commercial and results focus into its

sales and marketing department. The company had replaced pay increments with a merit pay scheme two years earlier, yet this was seen as
producing an insufficient stimulus to high performance. The proposals
were for a common performance bonus scheme across the department,
incorporating team and individual measures and a common on-target
and maximum bonus opportunity.

Yet when we examined the different roles in the department, we
found very different activities being carried out. Sales advisers engaged
in door-to-door selling had a very direct impact on their own
performance results, implying a high level of performance pay. Key
account managers made an equally direct but more broadly based and
long-term contribution to the company results, by negotiating and
managing contracts with the company's largest industrial clients.
Customer service advisers in the call centre, meanwhile, worked in
teams and were primarily engaged in servicing existing accounts, a
much less direct but still vital contribution to performance.

The company agreed with our analysis of these role differences and a
variety of schemes were introduced. For the sales advisers a highly
geared individual, monthly sales commission scheme was introduced.
Key account managers have a much higher base pay level, with pay
increases related to key competencies, and an objective-based annual
bonus plan now operates. And in the call centre, a small, team bonus
opportunity related to key service measures has been developed.

A similar diversity is now evident in the performance pay schemes of
an IT company's sales department. Support staff have their base pay
increase related to their broad contribution over the year, and a small
bonus opportunity based on overall sales results. Meanwhile the
common sales incentive plan for direct selling staff has been replaced
with different schemes for the different product lines (see Figure 5.3).
Staff selling high margin networked products, requiring specialist
systems knowledge and sold over a lengthy period of time to large
corporate customers, are paid a high base pay. This increases in line
with their demonstrated competence. The sales staff for high volume,
lower margin products meanwhile, have a lower base pay and an
uncapped individual commission arrangement.

The need for such variations seems obvious. Yet with traditional
concerns regarding consistency and equity, in many organizations it
has taken the experiences of applying a uniform merit pay or bonus
scheme to show them that high performance is a diverse and multi-
faceted phenomenon. It needs to be reflected by varied, contribution-
related reward schemes. Allied Dunbar even offers its new sales staff a

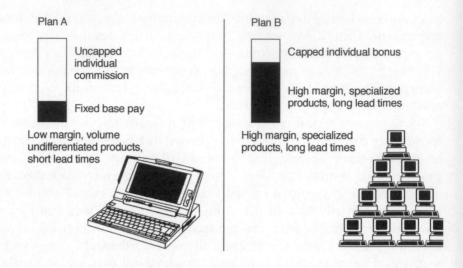

Figure 5.3 *Different performance pay schemes for different needs and audiences in an information technology company*

choice between an uncapped commission scheme with a low base pay, or a higher basic with a capped bonus, to suit their personal risk profile, perhaps the ultimate in tailored performance pay schemes

PAYING FOR CONTRIBUTION THROUGH BROADBANDING

According to Josie Pottinger of Cummins Engines, 'the full contribution of each employee is an essential feature of achieving competitive advantage ... continuous improvement has become an integral part of everyone's job'. Therefore, 'organizations are removing barriers which constrain employee's abilities to contribute fully, barriers often underpinned by multi-grade pay structures and rigid job descriptions'.[11]

Broadbanding has been championed in recent years as a method of providing greater flexibility to reward individual performance and contribution. Hofrichter describes it as 'the most effective pay tool to emerge in recent years'.[12] An example of a new broadbanded structure introduced to replace a hierarchical, 15 band structure in an insurance company is shown in Figure 5.4. Some 46 per cent of the 300 companies in the Towers Perrin European research[13] had reduced their number of pay grades in the prior three years, with 32 per cent claiming to have introduced broadbands and 49 per cent intending to do so.

THE RATIONALE

The need to provide greater flexibility for performance pay was the most common cited objective for broadbanding cited by participants in the Towers Perrin survey (see Figure 5.5). Other common objectives included:

- responding to the delayering of the organization (as at National Westminster Bank for example) and attacking the culture in which status and hierarchy rather than performance is seen to be rewarded (as at Nortel);
- providing greater scope to develop staff skills and competencies without the pressure for constant promotions (as at Unilever).

The combination of these reasons, which were used to explain to staff the move into three broad pay bands at Guinness Brewing GB, is shown in Figure 5.6.

Old grades	Band	Salary
15 14 13 12	Leaders	£50,000 – £100,000
11 10 9 12	Managers and consultants	£32,000 – £64,000
7 6 5 4	Senior professionals	£23,000 – £41,000
3 2 1	Professionals	£14,000 – £28,000

Figure 5.4 *Example of broadbanding from an insurance company*

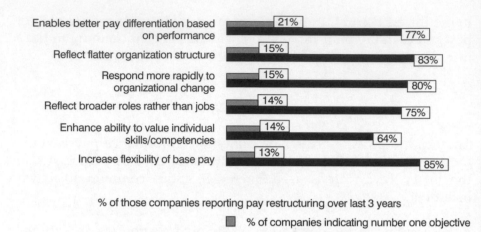

% of those companies reporting pay restructuring over last 3 years

■ % of companies indicating number one objective

■ % of companies saying objective met

Figure 5.5 *Rationale for pay restructuring and its assessed outcomes*
Source: Towers Perrin

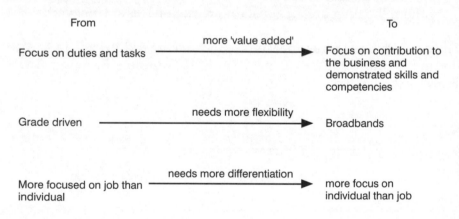

Figure 5.6 *Summary of the rationale for introducing broadbanding at Guinness Brewing GB*

Some 77 per cent of organizations in the Towers Perrin study felt that their pay structure reforms had delivered improved pay flexibility and a better relationship between performance and pay. However, in many cases the 'strait-jacket' has only been progressively loosened rather than fully removed, and in the United Kingdom at least, broader pay bands rather than broadbands is probably a better characterization of this movement. The median width of pay ranges in the Towers Perrin study were still 30–60 per cent for management staff and 15–30 per cent for non-management. Only one in every ten companies was operating ranges of 80 per cent or more, which writers such as Wilson[14] define as true broadbanding.

Movement within these broader ranges is also only rarely completely unrestricted. Three-quarters of organizations operate internal control mechanisms to limit the progression of individuals within their broader bands. The most frequently employed of these is market zoning, where the broadband is subdivided, often on the basis of job family or functions, into narrower, market-based sub-ranges. An example from the lowest two bands of an insurance company's five band structure which was introduced in 1996, is illustrated in Figure 5.7. This replaced their previous 15-grade structure.

A GRADUALIST APPROACH

More detailed research into the experiences of seven UK companies[15] indicates the reasons for this cautious and evolutionary approach to broadbanding, and to more flexible, performance-related pay

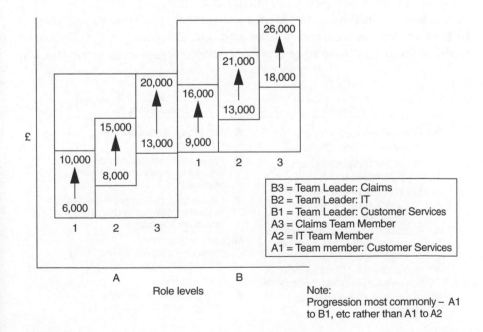

Figure 5.7 *Market zoning at an insurance company*

progression within the bands. Loss of cost control in broader pay bands was not a major concern or problem experienced by these organizations. They all said that this was an issue of pay budgeting procedures, not pay structures. After all, who has actually banged their head against a grade ceiling?

But communicating and educating managers and staff as to the potential benefits of broader bands; breaking down traditional hierarchical and status attitudes; and ensuring that the flexibility of bands is actively used in practice, these were the challenges that these organizations said were the major ones they faced (see Figure 5.8). The redesign of the pay structure into fewer bands was the easy part: the management of pay within the bands, generally on the basis of performance and contribution, was the more difficult.

Two of the seven organizations we researched had experienced industrial action as they introduced their new structures, not because of the reduction in bands and perceptions of loss of status or promotion, but because of concerns at the fairness and adequacy of the appraisal system and related pay increases. Broader bands, from the union perspective, gave greater scope for the 'blue-eyed boy' syndrome to have an effect on pay. As the case study of a UK bank in Chapter 8 illustrates (see Case Study 8.1), moving straight into very broad bands and fully performance-related pay increases, from a history of well-structured grades and incremental progression, and with no local pay management experience, was a recipe for trouble.

Advantages	Disadvantages
■ Greater flexibility: 　■ reflect market differences 　■ reflect business/functional differences 　■ encourage and reward everyone to develop their full potential ■ Reduces unhealthy emphasis on hierarchy, status, job titles and descriptions ■ Brings pay and HR issues into the business/organization mainstream ■ Reinforces culture/mindset change	■ Reliance it places on line management ■ Pressure it puts on individual pay and performance management approach ■ Lack of structure hugely increases requirement for communications openness and trust ■ Loss of traditional reward/recognition methods, eg promotions ■ Time required ■ Effort required to achieve change: status, hierarchy, etc

Figure 5.8 *Pluses and minuses of broadbanding revealed by research*

Their new scheme was withdrawn and after extensive consultation, a more intermediate balance of structure and flexibility in pay ranges and pay increases was introduced.

Performance pay flexibility *per se* is of no use if it cannot be managed, or is too far removed from the existing cultural characteristics, whatever the business and competitive rationale. Employees have to see clearly in advance which aspects of performance will produce what pay increase, and also be convinced of the quality and equity of the appraisal process, and objectivity of market pay data. One participant in our research therefore recommended the graduated approach to us, 'learning as we go, developing understanding and agreement, before we move forward again'. The 'dynamite' that another referred to as being required to destroy the gradist mentality, 'the barriers of power and hierarchy' in his company, is rarely available in pay management situations.

ACHIEVING GREATER BASE PAY VARIABILITY

As well as attempting to achieve more differentiation in the increases of individuals, within what Wilson dismissively refers to as 'piecomp' merit pay systems,[16] a number of organizations have also addressed the issue of the size of the pie. Greater variability at the level of the organization's pay budget can produce successively higher levels of variability at the levels below that: in each business, in each team, and for each individual.

Thus, 7 per cent of the 156 UK organizations in Towers Perrin's 1997 study[17] and 13 per cent of over 700 US organizations in an equivalent Towers Perrin[18] survey now relate their total pay budgets to measures of the organization's performance (see Figure 5.9). A good example in the UK is Littlewoods Home Shopping Group. They removed merit pay in 1992 for 1,400 junior managers and professionals, and in its place put in an approved Profit Related Pay scheme. The demerger of the business then provided an opportunity to review their whole reward situation. A joint working party of management and staff recommended a complete overhaul of existing arrangements, to improve individual motivation and the general perception of 'stagnation' and automaticity in pay.

The new scheme, introduced as part of a five-year agreement in 1995, now sees the size of pay increase pool related to the distributable

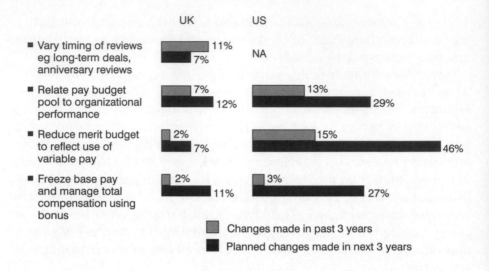

Figure 5.9 *Changes to salary increase policies in UK and US companies for management and professional staff*
Source: Towers Perrin

profits of the company. The higher the level of profit over target, the bigger the pool. A traditional matrix is then used to distribute this pool, with individual increases related to the performance ratings agreed under a new appraisal system and current range position. The 1995 profit performance of the business generated a merit pool of 2 per cent, which was distributed as shown in Figure 5.10.

From a business standpoint, the real test of the system came the following year, however, when as a result of intensive capital investment and very tough trading conditions, profitability was lower than forecast and there were no merit payments at all. The Company claims this really focused the attention of staff on improved performance, which was the only thing that funded their pay. In 1996 the profit target of £37 million was exceeded by 54 per cent, resulting in merit pay increases in 1997 of between 2.5 per cent and 9.5 per cent from the maximum size of pool.

Pearl Assurance is one of the companies that varies the size of the base pay increase 'pie' at successive levels in the organization, so that high performing individuals, in high performing teams, in high performing divisions can get very significant increases.

A similar scheme operates in a well-known travel company. Each agency location operates a traditional merit grid with increases based on position in range and individual performance. However,

Link between group profits and the pool available for merit payments	
Change in current year profits %	Distributable pool as % of paybill %
Decrease	0
0-4.9	2
5-9.9	2.5
10-14.9	3
15-19.9	3.5
20-24.9	4
25-29.9	4.5
30 or above	5

Total merit ⇩ pay pool

Performance grade	Percentage of salary to midpoint					
	89 or less	90–94	95–99	100–104	105–109	110 or above
Outstanding	3.5–4	3.25–3.5	3.0–3.25	2.75–3.0	2.5–2.75	2.5
More than effective	2.5–3.0	2.25–2.5	2.0–2.25	1.75–2.0	1.5–1.75	1.5
Effective	2.0–2.5	1.75–2.0	1.5–1.75	1.25–1.5	1.0–1.25	1.0
Less than effective	Zero	Zero	Zero	Zero	Zero	Zero
Consistently less than effective	Zero	Zero	Zero	Zero	Zero	Zero

Note: figures are % of base pay

Figure 5.10 *Littlewoods: increasing the variability of the base pay award in 1995*

the funding of the grid depends on the performance of each location, which is set annual financial, operating, and customer service performance targets. The highest performing agencies can thereby double the size of the average merit pay pool across the organization, and individual increases can range from zero to over 20 per cent.

Greater pay variability can by these means be used to reinforce collective performance and contribution, as well as achieve higher levels of individual pay differentiation within an organization.

PUTTING PAY AT RISK

Very few UK companies, however, have pushed this a stage further and introduced an element of risk and base salary sacrifice into the equation. Even in the United States, where there is no equivalent to constructive dismissal legislation, and despite the common use of the term 'at risk' pay, most schemes are actually making future increases in pay more variable and at risk, rather than putting any existing fixed pay at risk.

UK EXAMPLES

Only a handful of European companies in the Towers Perrin European survey had actually reduced fixed pay levels for any groups of staff, and these were generally in business crisis situations. Thus the electrical goods division of a UK retailer in the early 1990s, faced with a situation of mounting losses in an intensely competitive sector, undertook a radical restructuring of its working practices and pay structure. Uniform national rates and pay bargaining across all of its operations and businesses meant that base pay levels in some areas were up to 30 per cent ahead of the electrical retailing market. There was no form of performance pay in place.

The resulting restructuring saw a total paybill reduction of over 10 per cent, but an individual commission scheme was introduced to compensate for the fixed pay reduction. Staff thereby received a monthly payment dependent on the individual value of the goods they had sold. Commission rates were related to store potential, in order that staff in large out-of-town superstores did not earn more than those in smaller high street stores simply because of their location. The highest 25 per cent of individual performers in the business were actually able to earn more than their original base pay levels through this commission scheme.

Similarly, the marketing department of a privatized electricity company in the mid-1990s was faced with a major reduction in the total marketing spend permitted by the industry regulator. Their response was to introduce a £2,500 reduction in base pay for all central marketing staff. However, on the basis of their own performance against pre-set objectives, and the overall contribution of the department, staff can now earn up to an extra £5,000 in variable bonus. Achieving departmental and individual targets earns the £2,500, and over-target performance can generate the additional amount.

NPI, the mutual life insurer, has perhaps gone furthest in the United Kingdom in introducing this 'swing' principle into the pay of all of its 1,800 staff at Tunbridge Wells, from the security guard through to the Chief Executive. The latter, Alastair Lyons, explained it as a demonstration that they were, 'entirely focused on maximizing value for policyholders' and expressed the strong stakeholding philosophy behind it. He regards it as, 'a partnership between NPI, our people and our policy-holders, in which all partners share in the rewards of mutual success'.

Recognizing that higher paid staff can both afford to have more pay at risk, and generally have more scope and a more direct influence on business performance, the NPI scheme is graded into four levels. The lowest paid staff have 5 per cent of their base pay at risk, and this increases through to 10 per cent for the Chief Executive. However, the potential upside for high performance is twice these amounts, so on his 1998 salary, the Chief Executive could see a cut of £32,500 or an increase of £65,000. The position within this range depends wholly on the overall performance of the organization against three corporate targets: revenue, expenses and an index of customer service performance.

At Ryanair, the low-fare airline, the motivation stems more from their low-cost, no frills business strategy, and the vehicle is variable pay. Basic pay makes up a third of the pay of flight attendants. Another third is based on overall airline productivity, and the rest comes from commission on duty free sales.

PROBLEMS AND LIMITATIONS

Even in the United States, a recent study found that only 7 per cent of Fortune 500 companies have actually reduced base pay levels and put a proportion of pay at risk. The US research[19] suggests that:

- such actions only seem to be evident throughout a company's workforce, to any extent, in business crisis or new business start-up situations;
- that there needs to be a very clear line-of-sight between business performance and individual effort for these schemes to be effective;
- there also needs to be a realistic upside earnings potential; a Purdue University study amongst sales staff found a rapid increase in staff

turnover once the probability of exceeding the original base pay level fell below 50 per cent;

- such actions can often penalize high individual performers who if, as at NPI, the total pay budget is varied, actually stand to lose a greater amount and have a larger amount at risk than average performers.

Like any approach therefore, putting future pay increases at risk is not without its problems. Saturn Corporation, the small car subsidiary of General Motors in the United States, adopted this approach in order to build up to an 'at risk' component of 12 per cent of pay for all staff over their first six years of operation.[20]

It was an important component of a radically different, high involvement approach to HR management and working practices in the US auto industry, that initially was highly successful at Saturn. Base pay is set at below market median levels. The 'at risk' portion brings pay up to the industry average, while high performance results in cash bonuses in addition. Initially the performance measure used was profitability, but now it relates to a range of factors including quality and productivity. In 1996 staff earned the maximum bonus of $10,000. However, within GM's overall strategy, Saturn was not permitted to expand into more rapidly growing sections of the car market, such as the off-road sector, despite management and employee pressure to do so. When payments subsequently fell substantially in 1997 as a result of declining US small car sales, a 17 per cent cut in output, and reducing profitability, staff were unhappy that their pay was being reduced as a result of, in their view, incorrect decisions being taken elsewhere.

Of course, in strongly sales-focused roles and high-risk, entrepreneurial businesses in the high technology sector or financial services, a high level of pay variability and risk/reward sharing is not unusual. Even in the United States, however, for the typical worker on average earnings there are clear problems with genuinely putting people's pay and standard of living at risk. And in the United Kingdom, whatever the rhetoric underlying the introduction of approved profit-related pay schemes on a salary sacrifice basis, in the vast majority of cases there never was, and was never intended to be, any reduction in fixed pay.

The pressures of a global recession in the future may, however, encourage many more organizations to look at a more truly at risk approach. During the recession of the early 1990s, the small interior design company Atrium adopted a two-pronged strategy. First, it focused on niche markets, such as boardroom design and furnishing.

Second, it cut fixed costs, of which by far the largest was pay. Base pay was cut in half and a margin-related commission introduced, in return for a guarantee of no redundancies for their 12 employees. The strategy successfully focused everyone on margins, and pay actually rose. Atrium's pay structure is still in place and more staff have been recruited on this basis.

PUTTING THE MERIT BUDGET AT RISK

In the meantime, more limited responses are evident. Some organizations, such as Scottish Amicable, have reduced the size of their internal organizational units for pay management purposes. They have introduced pay budget variability between them, to try and replicate the sense of shared purpose and having to earn any pay award on a risk/reward basis which is often present in smaller organizations. Ellis and Haftel's research[21] demonstrated a stronger relationship between the use of performance pay schemes and both company performance and employee motivation amongst the 111 smaller US companies they studied, than in the 33 larger ones.

A more common response to increasing pay variability without cutting pay has been either to freeze base pay and introduce bonuses (as at Mobil), or more commonly put future merit budgets at risk (as 13 per cent of US companies have done), or at least to make part of the merit budget variable. The incidence of this practice can be seen in Figure 5.9.

Table 5.4 illustrates an example of how the latter approach works in a US media company. It shows for a hypothetical employee on a base pay of $50,000 how transferring part of the merit base pay budget to fund an individual bonus of up to 10 per cent each year builds up to a reasonable sum over a 10-year period. Assuming the bonus is earned, the total pay over the 10-year illustration is the same, but the level of variability in the company's cost base is much greater.

As can be seen in Figure 5.9, 15 per cent of US companies are adopting this approach, and while only 2 per cent of UK companies have followed suit, another 7 per cent have plans to do so. An example which is being piloted in a sample of the stores in a UK retailer is shown in Table 5.5.

This company wanted to introduce a stronger pay for performance relationship and was unhappy at the lack of obvious business return on the millions of pounds paid out to employees under its Approved PRP

Table 5.4 *Putting future merit pay at risk in a US media company*

	Former situation	New situation	
Year	5% Merit only	3% Merit	Incentive (10%)
1	$50,000	$50,000	$5,000
2	52,500	51,500	5,150
3	55,125	53,045	5,530
4	57,881	54,636	5,464
5	60,775	56,275	5,628
6	63,814	57,964	5,796
7	67,005	59,703	5,970
8	70,355	61,494	6,149
9	73,878	63,339	6,334
10	77,566	65,239	6,524
Total	$628,895	$573,194	$57,314

Note: Total pay is about the same

Table 5.5 *Making pay more variable in a UK retailer*

	Assumed payroll increases	Percentage removed to fund bonus	Potential savings from improved store performance	Potential rewards in highest performing stores
Y1	4%	1%	1%	4%
Y2	5%	2%	2%	8%
Y3	5%	3%	3%	12%

scheme. The base pay budget increase in 1996, on the basis of a general pay award with very limited individual differentiation, was around £12 million, while over £30 million was paid out in approved PRP. The Board questioned the effectiveness of this spend and the business return being achieved on the money.

A self-funding, store-based bonus scheme was therefore considered to provide a greater level of incentive to shop staff. However, the narrow margins in the retail sector meant that only relatively small payments could be generated on a truly self-funded basis. The company is therefore transferring part of future base pay increases to help fund and 'pump-prime' the store bonus scheme. Thus by Year 3, in the example illustrated in Table 5.5, the highest performing stores will be able to earn a bonus equivalent to 12 per cent of base pay, worth over £1,000 to each employee.

This melding of traditionally distinct base pay and bonus schemes is one of the most interesting aspects of the more holistic approach now being adopted in paying for contribution. Companies are breaking down traditional barriers and mindsets to develop tailored solutions, which can both support competitive advantage and motivate employees. Many organizations with merit pay in the UK pay any merit component for those on their pay scale ceiling as a non-consolidated lump sum, but we are now seeing a mixture of base pay and bonuses also applying within the pay range.

Thus at organizations such as National Westminster Bank, Abbey National and Pearl Assurance, there is management discretion to make individual performance payments as either a base pay increase or a bonus, with the latter being applied more heavily for those staff already high in their ranges and well paid against the market.

The way this approach is managed in a life assurance company is shown in Figure 5.11. In this hypothetical example all outstanding performers would receive a payment of 10 per cent of their base pay. Line managers would not have, however, to pass on the difficult message to high performers already high in their pay range, that because of the pay structure operated by the personnel department, they would actually only be getting a small increase despite their level contribution, as is generally the case. Here, the higher up the range employees in this life company are, then the more of the payment is made as a non-consolidated bonus. So someone high in their range gets 8 per cent as a bonus and a 2 per cent addition to their basic pay, while an outstanding individual low in their range and below their market rate would get an 8 per cent base pay increase and a 2 per cent bonus.

SUMMARY

- As the design examples in this chapter and the subsequent case studies illustrate, in its evolution from merit pay to paying for contribution performance-related pay trends are getting increasingly difficult to generalize and to characterize. Base pay and bonus, individual and team, line and HR roles, are all becoming intertwined in a rapidly changing environment. As Industrial Relations Services describes it, systems are increasingly being 'tailored to suit each particular workplace and workforce in a way that traditional, 'off-the-peg' pay systems, introduced at the turn of the decade, were not'.[22]

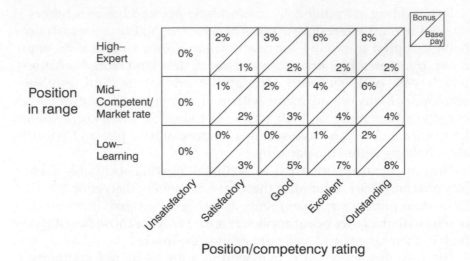

Figure 5.11 *Increasing the variability of base increases in a life assurance company*

- This tailoring also means that systems are regularly being tweaked and modified and evolving within an organization. As Pam Wood at Midland Bank observes, the moves from traditional, merit pay uniformity to the diverse, paying for contribution approach is, 'not a question of moving from right to wrong,' but rather a realization that no pay structure, 'can be set in stone; all pay systems have a limited life span and you have to review and adapt them all the time'. Pharmaceutical Company Merck describe their HR and reward approach as being like their critical research and development work: trying, testing, improving on a continuous long-term basis.
- As we have seen, for a small minority this review process has led them to move out of performance-related base pay altogether. But the majority are tweaking and tailoring schemes to produce the necessary linkage in any organization between their pay costs and their performance, and also to really motivate and recognize their highest contributors.
- We have looked at lots of individual examples and techniques in this chapter to address the merit pay dilemma, but a final conclusion on this review of merit pay trends can be illustrated by a recent study referred to by Ellis and Haftel.[23] They were researching the effects of

different motivational strategies on the patent performance of workers in research and development functions in 31 companies. They compared those companies who adopted a strong money-oriented approach to motivation through performance bonuses, royalties and equity shares, with those emphasizing non-financial forms of recognition, such as providing greater autonomy or an increase in the research budget.

- In companies using large, performance-related financial rewards they found a significant correlation with patent performance, explaining 48 per cent of the mean difference in total patent numbers. But some companies relying heavily on non-monetary recognition were equally effective.
- Their conclusion therefore was that: 'whether managers use a people-oriented or a monetary one, *the intensity of application of the reward system is tied to its effectiveness.* If they use monetary awards, the value of the reward and its method of application need to be large enough to gain the attention of staff'.
- Both conclusions: that money can be an effective lever in a company's overall HR and motivational strategy, and that significant performance-related gains need to be on offer to both the staff and the company, if it is to be effective, help to explain the move to paying for contribution in base pay. It also helps to explain the growing interest in bonus schemes, which we describe in more detail in the next chapter.

CASE STUDY 5.1

Adopting a more flexible and contribution-related pay system at Pfizer Central Research, Pfizer Inc

Pfizer Central Research's laboratories at Sandwich in Kent represent one of the most successful pharmaceutical research and development sites in the world, with an impressive pipeline of new products. They have been responsible for discovering and developing a succession of new medicines in recent years, and have given the company probably the most impressive pipeline of drugs in the industry. The company is expanding rapidly, spending over $2 billion a year on R&D, and showing double digit annual growth. They currently employ some 2,200 staff at Central Research in Sandwich. Pfizer Ltd, the UK holding company has been awarded the Queen's Award for Innovation on a number of occasions.

However, after a lengthy two years of analysis and review, the company concluded that its pay and reward systems, originally developed in the 1970s, were not compatible with the ambitious Research 2000 business goals it had set out, nor the corporate values underpinning them. In 1997 a major set of changes were implemented to pay and reward systems. These included a radical reform of the individual bonus scheme, and moving into a flatter, broader-banded pay structure, with performance-related rather than incremental progression.

With typical scientific thoroughness, they carried out a review of the changes in mid-1998, after a year's operation, and they will be taking a number of initiatives to further improve their effectiveness.

THE CHANGE DRIVERS

A 1994 attitude survey stimulated the detailed investigation of Pfizer's pay and reward systems, which had been established in the 1970s. At first sight there might not have appeared to be much wrong; 70 per cent of staff were broadly satisfied with their current package, staff turnover was low and the R&D division successful. Yet in a business in which it can take a decade to bring new products to market, from a longer-term perspective the picture was not so bright. The internal review they undertook involved director discussions, staff focus groups, a desk top analysis of current systems, and external benchmarking. Three key issues emerged from this investigation.

First, base pay management was found to be inflexible and lacking in any strong performance relationship. Essentially pay progression was service-based, and in a pay structure with 26 grades below management level, and narrow mid-point differentials, over half of staff were on their range ceiling. The pressure for real or imagined 'promotions' was therefore intense.

Correspondingly, the individual annual performance bonus and related appraisal process was found to be a highly emotive and controversial issue. Staff received an individual rating on a five-point scale each year, and then a forced ranking of individuals was made. The bulk of staff received a middle rating and a bonus in the order of 12 per cent of base pay, while the highest performers received up to 20 per cent. Staff were highly critical of the way in which performance was assessed, and of the individual focus in an increasingly team-oriented and matrix-organized environment.

Communication, and its failings in the reward area, was the third key issue. The goals of reward systems were found to be vague and unclear. The general understanding of the purpose and content of pay and reward methods was surprisingly low amongst a very well educated and professional workforce, 75 per cent of whom are scientists and technologists. As one employee put it, 'People don't understand what increments, promotions and the bonus are actually awarded for, what each is supposed to do.'

THE REWARD CHANGES

The resulting changes agreed by the Research Executive Committee and worked up in detail by a series of line and Personnel working groups were, to quote from a late 1996 communication to all staff, designed with the following issues and objectives in mind:

- We need a bonus system that fairly rewards effort and achievement. It should be simple to understand and administer and not subject to a 'force fit'.
- Consistently high performing staff should have the potential to grow their salary above that which the majority can achieve. The number of job levels/grades should be reduced to provide a simple and clearer framework for career and salary progression for all staff.
- Promotion approval should be at a more local management level, rather than always needing Divisional Committee approval. Overall, reward should be related to ability, personal contribution and achievement, and be understood by all concerned.

BASE PAY

In base pay, therefore, eleven job levels and salary bands were introduced for all jobs, across the company's four job families (see Figure 5.12). This change was designed to clarify career paths and provide greater flexibility to reward contribution. A more radical structure of three broad bands was considered, but as Personnel Director Martin Ferber explains, 'Eleven levels was felt to best reflect our overall organizational need. It is less complex than our current structure while still providing sufficient differentiation to reflect different levels of responsibility and contribution.' In a couple of years' time, he feels, the culture will be ready for a further reduction, and there are already signs of a demand for this.

Progression within the broader bands is now wholly based on appraised performance, using a matrix which relates assessed performance and current pay level to the rate of increase. The historical annual review in January and incremental review in July were combined into a single April

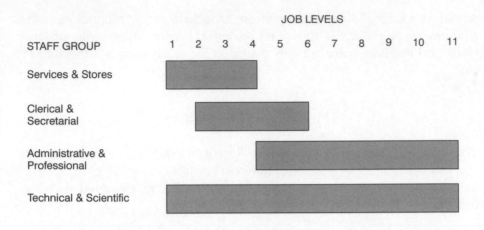

Figure 5.12   *New salary structure at Pfizer Central Research*

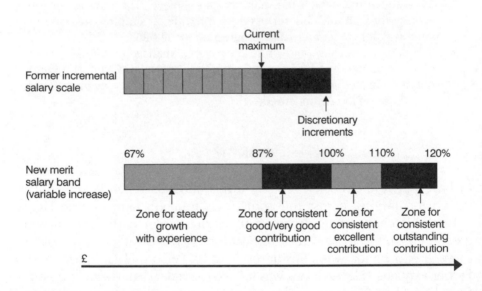

Figure 5.13   *Changes to base pay structuring and progression*

review. Consistently high contributors, and Pfizer has some world-leading experts in a number of fields, can thereby progress to a very high position versus the external market (see Figure 5.13). The individual performance review system was simplified to classify staff into three overall performance categories and focus on a broader but clearer assessment of contribution.

OTHER REWARDS

The annual performance bonus meanwhile was radically restructured. An individual bonus was retained as a reward for excellence, designed to be used to recognize the top 20 per cent to 25 per cent of individual contributors. A portion of the bonus funding was also used to boost base pay competitiveness, while a portion has been repositioned as a 'thirteenth month' payment, designed to reward the overall success and contribution of the entire operation, subject to the achievement of corporate Research goals.

A series of related changes supported this restructuring, which was implemented during 1997. The system of 'non-financial' recognition awards was totally reformed, for example, with staff nominating recipients, and a larger proportion of staff receiving the new Impact awards – a voucher-based system, more about message than money. A separate budget funds these awards, which are focused on company values such as teamwork, leadership, integrity, contribution and innovation. Special cash bonuses are also given to individuals and teams that have made a significant contribution beyond the expected level. Annual achievement awards are also open to employee nomination.

A major communications exercise was instigated to explain the new systems to staff, involving briefing meetings and a series of branded employee newsletters throughout the implementation phase.

PAY FOR CONTRIBUTION

Ferber explains how they have deliberately downplayed the use of the word performance and emphasized instead the term contribution. Assessing contribution is, 'much more complex than a decision relating to five objectives' in a Research setting, and often, 'the most measurable may not be meaningful, nor the meaningful measurable.' Contribution in his view talks to a broader series of outcomes, is easier to relate to corporate values, encompasses enthusiasm and capability, and relates to discretionary effort, rather than the sort of tightly managed, short-term results focus of merit pay which can stifle innovation in organizations.

Promotion in an R&D culture is commonly recognizing increased contribution through the acquisition of skills and ability. In Sandwich the Central Research division historically managed promotion for the scientific and technical grades through a single divisional committee. In line with other changes to reward and recognition this process has been devolved to the individual management groups with a similar process for all staff grades but with the emphasis on maintaining rigour and divisional equity.

Ferber describes the new reward and recognition approach as one that gives the line a bigger set of tools from which to draw, in order to properly balance short-term and long-term reward with career development to achieve effective people management.

LEARNING POINTS

Throughout this book we have reinforced the need to set explicit reward goals and to audit the success of reward changes, a vital requirement in our volatile environments, yet one which many companies ignore. Pfizer carried out such a review in mid-1998, with a questionnaire distributed to all staff, and around 70 staff attending group discussions.

The results of the review were 'cautiously optimistic' according to Ferber, perhaps as positive as could have been expected with a population of critical research staff and after only a year of operation. The excellence bonus received strong support, and a majority of staff fell that there was more flexibility in the new approach, to reward staff appropriately and earn more if their level of contribution warranted it. Those in receipt of the excellence bonus, and shorter-serving and younger staff in particular supported the changes. The changes to the recognition awards were very popular with all employees.

Yet while the results supported the conclusion that Pfizer now has a reward structure in place to support its Research goals, Ferber is candid in admitting that the management and processes for using this structure, whilst showing improvement, are some way short of where they need to be. Staff in the focus groups were still critical of the quality, time devoted to, and consistency of the performance appraisal process, whilst some first-level managers still felt they lacked involvement in the pay determination process. Equally important, the level of ongoing communications and staff understanding appeared to have progressed but more is needed, with one group member of the view that 'if managers don't know how it works, how can we feel confident?'

Pfizer's organization and management style are focused and highly devolved, which is probably a key reason for its success in product innovation. Yet in a performance management and communications sense, this has led to wider variations in standards than is optimal. A number of the disciplines in Discovery, for example, have clear performance and competency metrics, and regular performance review discussions. In some other departments, less attention is devoted to the process and less is expected from it.

A variety of initiatives are being considered and underway to address these process issues. They include a complete overhaul of internal communications systems. There is also continuing reform of the performance management process, involving management training and a greater emphasis on employees to maintain their own performance portfolios, as well as the development of a framework of contribution standards across the organization. There is also an ongoing project to better cascade the leadership divisional strategies and operating plans to all staff, with a direct link to individual goals and objectives. The new reward systems have provided greater opportunity to manage and leverage reward in support of business goals, but thereby have put the spotlight on existing management skills and processes.

Yet as in their business, while continuous evolutionary improvement in these processes is now being undertaken, Martin Ferber is optimistic that they have 'created a new and unified structure for all our staff that provides a much stronger link between contribution and reward... (and) is better suited to our research environment, where personal growth and teamwork are so vital to our continued success'. Evolving, testing, improving as part of a continuing process, in his mind, is the key to successful R&D and reward and recognition management.

CASE STUDY 5.2

Introducing pay for contribution at Nuclear Electric

Pay for contribution represents the latest in a series of major changes to reward management in Nuclear Electric. While the new system will not be implemented until mid-1999, their recent experiences and approach illustrates many of the trends profiled and recommended in this book.

BACKGROUND

Nuclear Electric, Britain's largest electricity generator using nuclear power, has been through a massive level of organizational change since it was formed, at the time of the privatisation of the rest of the electricity industry, in the early 1990s. Initially it was a wholly owned government corporation but since 1996, it has been in the private sector as a subsidiary of British Energy, one of the most successful of all government privatizations. These changes have involved a considerable degree of restructuring and a reduction of over 30 per cent in staffing levels.

The company has successfully pursued a two-pronged business strategy focused on delivering high levels of cost-efficiency and safety in preparation for the deregulation of the UK electricity market, along with high levels of customer service and innovation to support related diversification and expansion in the UK and overseas. It continues to restructure and is now in the process of creating a single company, combining with their Scottish counterpart – Scottish Nuclear.

REWARD CHANGES

Since the company broke out of its public sector pay structures, there has been a corresponding level of change in HR and reward policies and practices. These have included:

- moving managers onto personal contracts with market-related salaries, individual merit pay and annual bonuses;
- simplifying the complex, occupationally based pay structures inherited from the public sector and moving staff into a common structure of eight pay grades;
- introducing gainsharing bonus schemes for all grades of staff;
- operating a variety of share schemes, with a very high participation rate amongst all staff.

Two key themes have underpinned these changes and continue to drive the HR agenda, in support of a set of 'Vision 2000' goals. First, for a highly professional and well qualified workforce, as the company's annual report explains, 'the emphasis on skill enhancement and competence is essential'. The company's competency menu, used for appraisal and development purposes, has recently been simplified down to nine core behavioural competencies. Second, as Employee Relations Manager at Barnwood Bill Shirra explains, 'We want to have a flexible, highly skilled and motivated workforce with a stake in the business.' Pay and reward practices play an important role in achieving this goal and help to explain the current development of pay for contribution.

PAY FOR CONTRIBUTION

Pay for contribution is being developed as the means of base pay adjustment for the bulk of the company's employees, and will be introduced from mid-1999 onwards. It forms a key component of a package of reforms which were explained to all unionized employees, and overwhelming endorsed by a subsequent ballot, as part of the 1998 pay agreement in May of that year.

Key aspects of the changes include:

- annual RPI-plus general pay budget increases over 39 months;
- a gainsharing scheme linked to company and business unit success;
- simplifying and buying out certain cash allowances;
- harmonizing general and incremental pay review dates;
- introducing competence and contribution pay.

According to the joint management and trade union employee briefing, pay for contribution involves, 'replacing tenure-related increments with progression based on acquiring and using competencies, together with increases based on contribution to the achievement of business plan targets'.

The competence-related approach has already been applied to Operating Technicians on the power stations, which in effect have acted as the pilot for applying the concept across all work areas and functions. In their case, a series of grade-related specialist job definitions were replaced by a single broad pay range, and a much more flexible role concept. Individuals progress their pay by developing and applying the requisite technical and behavioural skills. Pay progression opportunities are much greater but only if individuals grow their skills and the value of their contribution to the business.

Across the company, all jobs have since been classified into three broad role families (see Figure 5.14) and three generic role functions: Operate, Maintain and Support. In each family the eight grades will be replaced by a single pay scale. Each scale will be divided into a number of competency platforms, defined in terms of a mix of technical or professional skill requirements and essential behavioural competencies (see Figure 5.15).

Pay progression during the 'lead-in' period of up to two years, as the individual acquires the basic role competencies, will be in fixed salary steps. Thereafter, however, progression between platforms will not be automatic but depend upon the assessed contribution of the individual. The higher the level of contribution to business and team goals, the higher the level of increase and faster pay progression. Above the top competency platform in each family, high levels of contribution will be rewarded with ex-gratia bonuses. A key factor is that each team must have a business plan and this requirement has been built into the company's business and budgetary planning system.

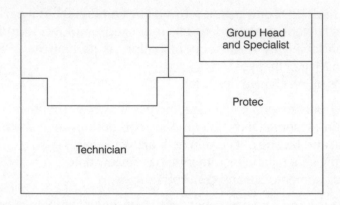

Figure 5.14 *Role families at Nuclear Electric*

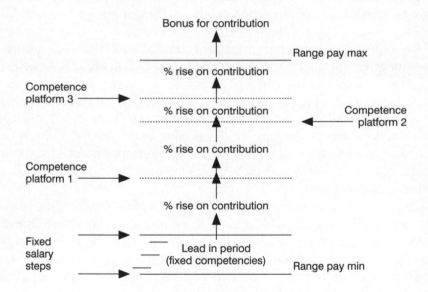

Figure 5.15 *How base pay progression will work for each role*

LEARNING POINTS

Design teams are currently working on the detail of the definition of competency platforms and on the assessment of contribution process, ready for implementation later in 1999. So it is obviously far too early to assess the success of these changes. However, the approach the company has taken so far appears to have laid on an excellent basis for successful change, with overwhelming staff and trade union support. This contrasts with attempts by some other electricity companies to rapidly introduce individual performance pay. So what characterizes Nuclear Electric's approach?

First, as Employee Relations Manager Bill Shirra explains, 'it is very much following an evolutionary approach', with sufficient time being allowed for to develop well thought-through, effectively operated, and understood and trusted arrangements: 'It's better to get it right than fast.' The outline of initial proposals was developed by a multi-functional group over the best part of a year. Then in 1998 a series of joint management/trade union groups have been working up the detail of the proposals, initially testing them on a small sample of core roles. The 1998 pay agreement runs for 39 months, giving sufficient time for these new arrangements to be developed, trialled and tested.

As Bill elaborates, this also allows time for effective support systems to be developed, such as appraisal, assessment and leadership training, and for the proposals to be understood as part of the broader, business-related HR and reward agenda, along with share incentives, more flexible working arrangements, and so on.

But the timing issue also relates to the vital importance of achieving and maintaining high levels of trade union and staff communication and involvement. As Project Facilitator Nigel Dixon explains, the company is avoiding the performance pay nomenclature very deliberately. It has strong associations of hastily introduced and imposed pay schemes, which only serve to reinforce staff fears of the 'blue-eyed boy' syndrome. When initially applied to senior staff in Nuclear Electric, the difficulties of achieving effective performance management, and particularly handling under-performance were experienced, and now a much larger population was involved. Thus the staff communication materials, jointly produced and presented by senior management and trade unions, emphasize the importance of using, 'objective criteria, applied so staff are treated fairly and consistently'. Team and business, not just individual, contribution will be assessed and rewarded.

It is this attention to joint development and building a trusted, credible system that really distinguishes this company's approach. Joint management/union groups, under the auspices of the Company's National Joint Council, have developed the detail of the proposals and worked on their implementation. There has been a regular feedback to meetings of all shop stewards and line management. The latter have been well represented on the design teams, rather than consisting entirely of members of the HR function. The joint management/union team working on the definition of competency platforms, under Nigel Dixon, is involving over a hundred employees on various sub-teams. This ensures that the platforms reflect real-life skills and experience, and can thereby be understood and operate as intended in practice. All staff are receiving regular communication updates as the project progresses.

The exercise is perhaps best summed up by George Jenkins, Operations Director, and Dougie Rooney, National Officer of the AEEU, who see pay for contribution as an important part of an 'overall package which reinforces our goal of having well rewarded, motivated and flexible staff, which will help to create a safe, successful nuclear company in an increasingly competitive marketplace'.

NOTES

1. Quoted in J Pickard (1997) Experts greet moves to collectivism, *People Management*, 24 July
2. Case in Industrial Relations Services (1997) Merit moves on, *Pay and Benefits Bulletin*, **416**, January
3. Institute of Personnel and Development (1998) *1998 Performance Pay Survey*, Quantive Summary, IPD, London
4. Incomes Data Services (1997) General awards: fact and fiction?, *Management Pay Review*, July
5. Institute of Personnel and Development, op. cit.
6. Lawler III, EE (1987) Pay for performance: future directions, in *New Perspectives on Compensation*, ed DB Balkin, Prentice-Hall, New Jersey
7. Towers Perrin (1997) *Learning from the Past: Changing for the future*, Research Report from Towers Perrin, London, March
8. Milkovich, G (1992) Strengthening the pay for performance relationship, *Compensation and Benefits Review*, November/December
9. Institute of Personnel and Development, op. cit.
10. Incomes Data Services (1998) Management pay awards', *Management Pay Review*, **208**, June
11. Pottinger J (1997) Foreword to *The IPD Guide on Broadbanding*, IPD, London
12. Hofrichter, D (1993) Broadbanding: a second generation approach, *Compensation and Benefits Review*, September/October
13. Towers Perrin (1997), op. cit.
14. Wilson, TB (1994) *Innovative Reward Systems for the Changing Workplace*, McGraw-Hill, New York
15. Brown, D (1996) Broadbanding: the UK experience, *Compensation and Benefits Review*, November/December
16. Wilson, op. cit..
17. Towers Perrin (1997), op. cit.
18. Towers Perrin (1996) *Compensation Challenges and Changes*, Towers Perrin US research study, available from Towers Perrin, London
19. Gherson, D (1996) 'When pay at risk is a risk worth taking, *ACA Journal*, Winter

20. Bohl, DL (1997) Saturn Corp: a different kind of pay, *Compensation and Benefits Review,* November/December
21. Ellis, LW and Haftel, SH (1992) 'Reward strategies for R&D, *Research and Technology Management*, March/April
22. Industrial Relations Services, op. cit.
23. Ellis and Haftel, op. cit.

6

Bonus schemes rewarding team and collective contribution

Policies which recognise collective endeavour are well suited to the economic realities and management philosophy of the late 1990s: keep costs down, concentrate on the basics, maximise the utilisation of human resources.

(IDS Focus)[1]

New Labour believes in a society where we do not simply pursue... individual interests, but where we work together to achieve our aims.

(Labour Party Election Manifesto 1997)

We worship at the altar of team working, and then destroy it with our pay system.

(Manager, UK manufacturing company)

Team-based bonus schemes appear to have a lot going for them in the new millennium. Not only the reaction against wholly individualistic and restricted merit pay plans, but the wholesale restructuring and re-organization of UK industry, a more 'caring, sharing' late 1990s' political and social milieu, and the popularity of team-based working and related HR initiatives; these have all fuelled the interest in team and collective rewards. According to the Industrial Society, two-thirds of UK companies have undertaken team working initiatives in the last two years, while almost 50 per cent are currently considering ways of using pay to reinforce team working according to the Institute of Personnel and Development.

The compensation journals have seen a spate of adulatory articles hailing this new Messiah of performance pay, and according to one author, 'whereas individual merit pay has been found to be a demotivator, team bonuses pull staff together'.[2] Thompson recommends team bonuses as a more appropriate incentive for modern industry than the individual incentives of the 1980s.[3] Kent County Council and Portsmouth NHS Trust are amongst those who have dropped individual performance pay in favour of team bonuses. Tony Strike at Portsmouth claims that the switch for managers to team PeRP 'has fostered a corporate spirit toward the achievement of the Trust's objectives.' Indeed, so high has been the level of interest in the team-based reward bandwagon, with 'teams all the rage', as *The Economist*[4] notes, that there might appear to be a danger of repeating the earlier experience with merit pay: considerable initial publicity and promotion, building exaggerated expectations, leading to over-hasty scheme borrowing and introduction, with insufficient attention to scheme tailoring and implementation, leading to disappointing results, disillusionment and rejection.

In this chapter we therefore consider in more detail the incidence and types of collective and team reward schemes. We review why they are being introduced and look at the evidence for their success in achieving these aims. Finally, we consider the factors that make for successful introduction and operation which, as with other forms of contribution-related pay, depend heavily on the relationship to the strategy and structure of the organization, and the management, operating and involvement processes. We attempt thereby to address three main questions:

1. What are the main types of team and collective bonus schemes?
2. How successful are they in creating effective links between pay and performance?
3. What differentiates the successful and the less successful schemes?

THE GROWTH IN INTEREST

There can be no doubt that, following the trend in the United States, the level of interest in team rewards has grown substantially in the United Kingdom, and latterly in Europe, in recent years. An IPD study[5] on the subject, encompassing over 100 UK organizations, found that 24 per cent rewarded team work in some way, with 19 per cent doing so in the form of a cash bonus. Other methods included rewarding an individual's competence at team working in base pay, and non-cash recognition awards for high performing teams. Towers Perrin's 1997 study of 300 organizations based in Europe[6] found that 50 per cent had company or business-based general employee bonus schemes covering large groups of staff, and 16 per cent had schemes focused on rewarding small groups (see Figure 6.1) The incidence appears to be about half of that amongst major US organizations, where an equivalent Towers Perrin's survey of 200 large companies found that 37 per cent operated profit sharing schemes, another 30 per cent combination or multi-level bonus schemes and 33 per cent small group bonus schemes. Indeed, such is the growth in these forms of variable bonus schemes, that it has presented problems to government statisticians responsible for calculating average earnings growth rates. Bonuses added 0.7 per cent to May 1998's growth rate figure of 5.2 per cent, for example.

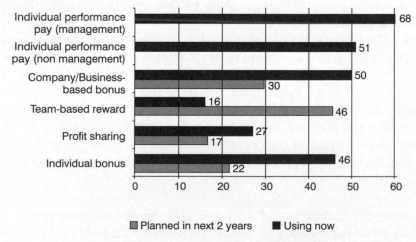

Figure 6.1 *Use and forecast growth in different types of performance pay schemes in Europe*
Source: Towers Perrin

Many of these sorts of team reward, as we go on to illustrate, have a long history. There are examples of profit sharing schemes from the last century in businesses as diverse as Proctor and Gamble in the United States, French house-painting and German farming. Gainsharing schemes originated in US heavy industry, pioneered by the designs of Rucker and Scanlon in the 1920s and 1930s.

The traditional image of collective bonus schemes in the UK is perhaps of the type of discredited, 1970s' style productivity scheme in manufacturing industry. These were often incredibly complex yet generated a fairly consistent payout, and often were simply a device to avoid government income controls. Or there were the contemporaneous schemes evident in the building industry, which gained a not underserved reputation for encouraging speedy but poor quality work.

Yet now, in the 1990s, team reward schemes are evident across the full range of traditional and newer industries. Applications range from bank administrative and branch staff at Lloyds TSB, to insurance sales staff at Norwich Union, to factory staff at Rank Xerox, offshore oil workers at BP and to call centre staff at Barclays and BT. Indeed, in telephone call centres, one of the most rapidly growing employment sectors in the UK (forecast to employ 2 per cent of the employed workforce by 2005), and often representing the leading edge in technology and work organization, a recent study[7] found that 65 per cent of centres operated profit-sharing schemes, and 14 per cent team reward schemes (although interestingly, 40 per cent operated individual performance-based schemes).

DEFINITIONS AND TYPES

Given the confusion in the definition of performance-related pay, it is important to establish what we mean by team bonus and reward schemes. Most of us probably think of a team as a small group of people, maybe up to a dozen, working together to achieve a shared goal. There is a growth in cash incentive schemes applying to such groups. However, if we take Katzenbach and Smith's definition of team working as 'two or more people intereacting (where) the combined effort and cooperation of each team member enhances the performance of the rest... (and) characterised by a deep sense of common purpose',[8] then potentially much larger groups of people might be involved.

Compensation writers have therefore often used the shorthand of team reward to cover a whole variety of collective pay and reward schemes, with Milkovich and Newman[9] defining it as 'any form of variable pay scheme which rewards employees collectively on the basis of their performance'. This definition includes organization-wide profit-sharing, site-based gainsharing schemes and small group incentives.

As we shall see, this broad definition is helpful in considering pay and reward schemes, because few small teams operate in isolation, and so the relationship between inter-and intra-team performance is often a key consideration when designing bonus schemes. Within this broad definition, reward schemes can therefore be considered in terms of:

- the level in the organization and size of the team (organization-wide, location or unit, or small group);
- the nature of the team (permanent, temporary, project);
- the form of reward (cash bonus, shares, base pay increase, non-financial recognition);
- the type of performance measure used, be it financial, operational or other types of criteria.

Figure 6.2 gives a summary picture of over 170 plans on Towers Perrin's remuneration database, categorized in terms of company-wide profit-sharing schemes, unit or team-based gainsharing, and combination plans in terms of the organization level of teams involved and/or the mix of performance measures used.

As we noted in the previous chapter, paying for contribution approaches are characterized by a broad diversity of methods of relating pay and performance, combining company, team and individual levels and a broad scorecard of criteria and measures. Over half of new collective reward schemes in the United States and Europe are now tailor made, but none the less, it is possible to illustrate the major types.

PROFIT-SHARING SCHEMES

As can be seen in Figure 6.2, in UK industry profit sharing schemes generally operate on an annual basis and pay out a flat percentage amount to all company employees. Formulas generally specify a fixed proportion of profits to be shared with employees, sometimes above a

FEATURE	1. FINANCIAL, PROFIT SHARING PLANS
Number of plans	65
Membership	All full-time employees in majority of cases: professional, managerial and clerical staff most often (80% + of cases)
Performance measure	
■ Level	60% Company 30% Business Divisions
■ Measure	1 measure, most commonly: – net profits – ROE
■ Setting standards	Typically a management target is set
■ Performance threshold	Yes, although fixed % shared in a number of cases
■ Changing set standards/targets	In approximately 50% of cases, particularly to reflect changes in: – business conditions – strategy
Payments	
Median last payment per employee PA	£1,240
Share of gains	5 – 6%
Distribution	Equal percentage of salary
Maximum cap	Yes
Timing of payments	Annual
FEATURE	2. OPERATIONAL GAINSHARING PLANS
Number of plans	58
Membership	Focus on production, supervisory and related support staff. Senior executives, corporate and sales staff generally excluded.
Performance measure	
■ Level	64% Plant/Profit Centre 22% Small Group

■ Measure	3 – 5 measures, most commonly:
	   – output – productivity
	   – waste – quality

■ Setting standards	Typically use historical performance
■ Performance threshold	Yes
■ Changing set standards/targets	Least commonly done, typically only to reflect changes in: – technology/capital – supplies
Payments	
Median last payment per employee PA	£1,300
Share of gains	50%
Distribution	Equal percentage of salary
Maximum cap	Yes
Timing of payments	Monthly
FEATURE	3. COMBINATION PLANS
Number of plans	54
Membership	All categories of employees included in over 50% of cases, except senior executives and corporate staff. Clerical, production and supervisory staff most often (70 – 80% of cases).
Performance measure	
■ Level	40% Business/Division 58% Plant/Profit Centre
■ Measure	3 – 5 measures, most commonly: – sales – quality/service – operating profits
■ Setting standards	Typically against set targets
■ Performance threshold	Yes, sometimes with a financial qualifier
■ Changing set standards/targets	Most commonly done, particularly in cases of changes in: – business strategy – business conditions
Payments	
Median last payment per employee PA	£1,475
Share of gains	N/A
Distribution	Equal percentage of salary
Maximum cap	Yes
Timing of payments	Either quarterly or annual

Figure 6.2 *Design features of team-based reward plans drawn from Towers Perrin's survey*

defined target or budgeted level. Over four million employees now participate in company profit sharing schemes, but their rapid growth in the UK has largely been the result of the tax effective treatment for Approved PRP schemes afforded them under the Conservative government's legislation. This is now being progressively removed up to the year 2000.

GAINSHARING

Gainsharing schemes, by contrast, typically relate to a specific part of a business, be it a factory, or an administrative processing centre. Gainsharing schemes are what they say: bonus schemes which directly share a proportion of the gains made above a defined target level with employees. An example of a Rucker plan (named after the scheme's original designer and the productivity measure he employed) in a US plant is shown in Figure 6.3. Here the company budgets a particular cost of goods produced at 41.7 per cent of their sales value. If the employees manage to increase their contribution, either by producing a greater amount of goods for sale at the same cost or the same quantity of goods at less cost, then they share 50 per cent of the gain. Examples in the UK include Kwikfit, BP Exploration and Blue Circle.

Unlike a profit-sharing scheme, therefore, you can actually say directly what the return on the cost of a gainsharing scheme to the company is – in the example shown, the company benefits by the same amount as it pays out to the employees. These schemes typically operate monthly or quarterly and are designed to produce a stronger incentive effect on behaviour than profit sharing. Both types, however, depend on staff being able to feel they can influence the overall performance criteria being used. If they are unaware of or don't understand the measures, or feel powerless to influence them, then the schemes are unlikely to have any motivating effect.

An additional difficulty with gainsharing can be trying to isolate the effects of new technology on the performance measured, in order to ensure that it is the performance of employees that is improving the measure, rather than simply new capital equipment. We reviewed a scheme in a food processing plant in the mid-1990s which had been introduced over 20 years previously. Payments had steadily increased over the years simply because the payment formula had never been adjusted to take account of the regular improvements in the speed and reliability of the machinery.

	£
Sales Value	1,500,000
Less materials, supplies, etc	1,000,000
Value added	500,000
Allowed employee costs (41.7%)	210,000
Actual employee costs	180,000
Bonus pool	30,000
Employee share (50 : 50)	15,000
Reserve	3,000
Employee bonus	12,000

- Formula based on the difference between selling price and employee costs: target ratio in this case is employee costs equal to 41.7% of added value (sales less other manufacturing costs).
- In this example, employee costs are £30,000 below the targeted value, and so employees share 50% of this gain.
- Plan assumes a consistent relationship between value added and payroll costs
- Payment is on quarterly basis

Figure 6.3 *A Rucker gainsharing plan*

We have also often seen the issue of controllability emerge in connection with gainsharing schemes. Thus in an Irish medical products manufacturing plant, the Gulf War created a huge demand for their products, which vastly inflated employee bonus payments. Yet the US parent company could equally rapidly divert production away from Ireland at short notice under its global sourcing policy, reducing bonuses through no fault of the employees.

SMALL TEAM SCHEMES

Team reward schemes applying to smaller groups are generally designed to have an even more direct incentive effect, either for teams to work harder, more efficiently or more effectively, to improve their results. Thus at Carborundum, a specialist brick manufacturer, there are separate schemes in each area of the factory: a scheme based on the productivity of material usage for the pairs of workers in mixing; a scheme based on the number of pieces produced in moulding; one based on the tonnage through the ovens (minus breakages) for shift teams in firing; and one based on the percentage of right first time orders in packing. The bonus is paid weekly and comprises over a quarter of total pay.

In Sun Life Assurance's processing centre the team bonus scheme is less aggressive but equally designed to be a direct incentive to high performance. Each processing team has a cost reduction target and performance against this funds a bonus pool. Payments from this pool depend on customer service performance, measured in terms of cases processed per hour, error ratios, mystery shopper ratings, and so on, and payments range from 0–10 per cent of base pay, made on a quarterly basis. Staff in areas of the company where performance cannot be so directly measured have a general profit sharing arrangement. Indeed, the vast majority of UK companies now have more than one performance bonus scheme in place, with different schemes for different parts of the company and different groups of staff.

COMBINATION PLANS

Combination or blended plans typically incorporate both a range of organizational and team levels, and also often a mix of financial, operational, service, quality and a whole range of other performance measures. As we saw in previous chapters, around one-third of collective bonus schemes now employ measures of customer service, for example at Volvo, Severn Trent Water and Prudential Direct. Figure 6.4 illustrates a combination plant and team bonus scheme in a UK engineering company. The scheme is designed to act as both a direct incentive for teams to high performance, and to reinforce the overall contribution of the plant and co-operation between the teams with it. Performance is monitored monthly and payments earned are made on a quarterly basis.

Thus if the plant achieved 100 per cent of its operating profit target, and a high performing assembly team achieved 105 per cent of its output and quality goals, then they would receive a bonus of 10 per cent of base pay over the year. A support team only achieving 90 per cent of its targets would receive 4 per cent, and a team member in a team performing below this threshold performance level no bonus at all.

Ikea in France operates a similar scheme. An overall country funding measure determines the size of the bonus pool, and each store's allocation from this pool depends on their performance against local

		Plant Performance vs. Target - Sales - Costs				
		90%	95%	100%	105%	110%
Team Performance vs Target	90%	0	2	4	6	8
	95%	2	4	6	8	10
	100%	4	6	8	10	12
- Output	105%	6	8	10	12	14
- Quality	110%	8	10	12	14	16

Payout % of base pay p.a.

Figure 6.4 *A combination bonus approach in a UK engineering company*

measures of cost control, sales volume, service levels, and breakages. In France, such schemes can qualify for tax effective treatment.

Lloyds Bank operates the same type of combination plan, according to points scored against set targets, in its branch network. Branches earn points based on both their sales and service performance, but the value of these points depends on the overall performance of all branches. Again, this is designed to encourage strong branch and inter-branch performance.

Combination plans are proving increasingly popular because they capture the 'real-life' balance of different leverage points on performance in an organization. Indeed, an increasing number (20 per cent of new collective bonus plans in the United States) are also including individual performance as a modifier, demonstrating that contribution-based approaches are not on the whole rejecting individual performance pay, but modifying and combining it in a more holistic approach. Severn Trent in the United Kingdom did introduce bonuses as a replacement for its merit pay scheme in 1998, but as we saw in Chapter 5, this is not a common response. A 1996 American Compensation Association study[10] found that 37 per cent of the 700 companies they reviewed operated both individual and team-related performance pay, compared to 2 per cent who operated just team pay.

Thames Power Station at Barking operates this type of combination scheme, with station performance, team performance and individually appraised performance all affecting the level of payment. If the station does well against its heat rate and efficiency targets, then a high performing individual on a high performing team can earn up to 20 per cent of their base pay. Similarly, in the Fabrications Division of BOC, 70 per cent of a sales representative's bonus is determined by the profits generated on their own territory, while 30 per cent depends on the profitability of the group of territories within their geographic region.

As well as providing an incentive for the teams and individuals within them, the higher level company or business unit financial measures ensure that the scheme can in fact be funded. Thus large bonus payments do not have to be justified to shareholders when the overall financial performance is poor.

A potential danger, however, is the complexity of these combination schemes which can become difficult to understand, and thereby defeat both the aims of collective reward and direct team or individual incentive. In a number of US electricity companies, for example, around 10 measures are used at two or three different levels in the organization and one wonders whether employees feel they can really influence these measures and their levels of payment. The 'salami-slicing' syndrome of a lot of criteria worth hardly anything may also come into play.

We were working recently for a telephone banking company who had introduced an individual incentive scheme for staff, with measures relating to individual productivity and service levels, but with an overall business performance modifier on payments. If the 80 per cent business performance threshold was not achieved, then the individual incentive payments were nullified, while if the 100 per cent business performance target was exceeded, staff could earn a bonus of up to 25 per cent of base pay. In the first full quarter of operation in 1998, only relatively few of the highest performers exceeded their individual performance targets, yet they and everyone else then found it totally demotivating to find the payment wiped out because the business performance threshold had not been achieved. 'We're not interested now' was the staff response in the next quarter, and the scheme has had to be re-designed as a result.

In summary, therefore, survey data shows the considerable current interest in the subject of team and collective reward schemes. Some 47 per cent of those in the IPD survey[11] and 44 per cent of UK companies in Towers Perrin's[12] are seriously considering or planning to introduce small team bonus schemes, with a somewhat slower growth forecast but considerable redesign work evident in respect of profit sharing, company and site-based bonus schemes.

Yet the actual growth in the incidence of team rewards during the 1990s has been much slower than surveys such as these have predicted. For example, Industrial Relations Services survey[13] of 240 companies in late 1997 found that 8.8 per cent were operating small team reward schemes compared to 6.6 per cent in 1996. 12 per cent were planning to introduce them in the next twelve months, but 14 per cent had been planning to do so twelve months earlier. As we have already begun to illustrate, team reward plans are no more of a panacea for truly performance-related pay arrangements than individual merit pay or bonus schemes. They are equally liable to succeed or fail, and as with individual performance pay, the key success factors relate once again to the strategic, structural and process variables which provide the context for their introduction and operation.

THE OBJECTIVES OF TEAM REWARDS

A variety of factors appear to explain the growth in interest and incidence of team reward schemes. Figure 6.5 illustrates the reasons which the companies in one survey gave for introducing or redesigning team reward plans, as well as their own self-rating of the extent to which these objectives had been achieved. Dissatisfaction with individual incentives is apparent and 20 per cent of the UK companies in Towers Perrin's executive remuneration database are planning to place a greater emphasis on team goals in the future within their management incentive plans. Business restructuring and the increasing importance of team-based working are also evident from the list of objectives shown.

But the two over-riding sets of criteria that consistently come out from this type of study, and from individual HR managers responsible for introducing team rewards, are:

- to help to improve 'hard' business performance and competitiveness;
- but also to have a 'softer' and more general impact in support of this, of reinforcing employee involvement, team work, communications and commitment.

Thus, for the salesforce at Norwich Union, a team bonus element was introduced in 1995 to support the strategic and cultural shift towards more service-oriented and long-term relationship building activity. It

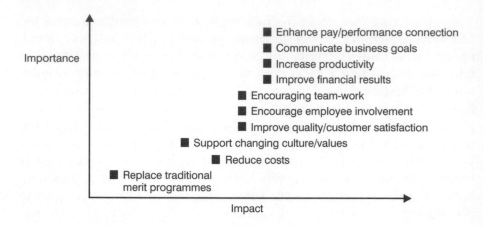

Figure 6.5   *Objectives of team reward plans from Towers Perrin's European survey*

was also designed to encourage financial consultants to share best practice and work with each other, rather than competing on an individual basis to maximize short-term sales.

At Nuclear Electric, the aim in introducing power station-based gain-sharing in the early 1990s was to reinforce everyone's commitment to the key performance goals of their station, and to change the hierarchical, status-based culture and engineering task focus which characterised the electricity industry before privatization. Just 4 per cent of companies in the IPD[14] research felt that average and poor performers were motivated to significant performance improvements by individual merit pay schemes, and this desire to mobilize and motivate everyone's performance is often a major goal of team reward plans.

THE EFFECTIVENESS OF TEAM REWARDS

So what is the evidence as to the effectiveness of team and collective bonus schemes in motivating people to achieve improved results by improved team working and greater commitment? Katzenbach and Smith[15] assert that, 'teams outperform individuals acting alone or in large organizational groupings, especially where performance requires multiple skills, judgements and experiences'. Yet Kohn[16] argues that, 'performance-related rewards rupture relationships', irrespective of their definition and team or individual focus.

We have carried out a fairly widespread review of the research literature and case studies. Accepting the problems of performance pay research noted in earlier chapters, it has to be said that there is a fairly impressive body of evidence to indicate that, in appropriate circumstances, team reward plans are effective, in terms of both their 'hard' results and their 'soft' behavioural impact. The research seems to compare particularly favourably with that on individual performance pay. However, this may relate to the fact that more research has been carried out and that particularly in the case of gainsharing, it is often easier to attribute and measure outcomes for team rather than individual performance pay schemes. We would emphasize that word 'appropriate', as team reward schemes are definitely not for everyone.

The American Compensation Association carried out a large study of 2,200 collective reward plans in 1995.[17] In plans where the performance impact was measurable, they calculated an average return on the cost of scheme payments of in excess of 200 per cent: that is performance improvements associated with such schemes generated $2 to the company for every $1 of payment to their employees. The average satisfaction levels of these companies, represented on a Likert scale from 1 not satisfied to 5 very satisfied, in terms of scheme effectiveness were as follows:

- improve business performance: 3.25;
- foster team work: 3.09;
- improve communications: 3.39.

Improved team working, greater commitment and improved employee relations were similarly the factors demonstrating the greatest improvement according to an earlier study by the American Productivity Centre,[18] with productivity, quality and absenteeism all seen to generally improve. Plans based on smaller teams, and those using operational rather than financial measures tended to score most highly in this regard. Towers Perrin's study[19] of over 150 collective reward plans revealed very similar results, with 73 per cent of participants feeling that their plans had exceeded their expectations. Combination plans scoring most highly in terms of perceived effectiveness, and profit sharing lowest.

Looking at the effectiveness of specific plans, profit-sharing schemes which generally reward the whole corporate team may not therefore provide strong individual motivation. But as one HR manager told us, 'by focusing the attention of employees and increasing their understanding of the business', they can still make a significant business contribution. Comparing the performance of over 1,000 matched UK companies,

Wallace Bell[20] found total investor returns over an eight-year period to be almost twice as large in companies with profit sharing schemes, compared with those without (474 per cent compared with 266 per cent).

Gainsharing plans demonstrate some of the most impressive results. Bullock and Lawler's[21] study of 33 plans found that 75 per cent reported a rise in productivity and or/quality, with gains ranging from 4.5 per cent to 23.7 per cent per annum. Individual case examples support these general findings.

After introducing a scheme to reward customer service and productivity in its Manchester plant, Elida Gibbs, the Unilever subsidiary, saw right-first-time delivery levels improve from 88 per cent to 99 per cent. Scottish Nuclear Electric saw productivity improvements between 1994 and 1996 of over 40 per cent, after the introduction of a station and head office gainsharing scheme. Sun Life Assurance saw controllable cost reductions of 30 per cent and improvements in turnaround times of 45 per cent after the introduction of team incentives in its processing activities. And Whitbread Inns found that rewarding staff teams with a cash bonus for excellent customer service in 100 of its pubs saw sales in those pubs rise by over £1 million compared to the remainder. Staff turnover was also 11 per cent lower in these pilot pubs.

In general, therefore, the data is fairly impressive but as we have already seen, team rewards are far from being a foolproof means of creating really effective pay-for-performance linkages. In many of these studies it is difficult to assess the extent to which the performance gains are dependent on improved team working rather than the team reward vehicle. Indeed, there is evidence to suggest that bonuses can help improve the performance of an already effective team, but simply exacerbate the problems in a poorly performing group.

Another difficulty is that many of these studies rely on management assessments of effectiveness. A very interesting exception is the study which De Matteo[22] undertook in 1997, looking at the perceptions of reward plans by 330 employees in 57 different teams. In general, these employees were somewhat dissatisfied with their team reward plans, with an average satisfaction level of 3.59 on a scale from 1 to 7. While satisfaction with team rewards increased with the size of reward in this study (the average payment was under 4 per cent of base pay), it was also strongly influenced by employee perceptions of a link between their individual performance and the reward. Indeed, the belief that team reward payments were distributed equitably in relation to each individual's contribution, rather than equally within the team, had a strong correlation with satisfaction.

THE PROBLEMS OF TEAM REWARDS

The data would therefore suggest that team rewards are well worth a serious examination as a means of reinforcing performance and contribution, but that there are clearly also potential problems with their usage. Some of the most significant to be drawn out from the research, and our experience as consultants and plan designers, are as follows:

- Individual perceptions of an inability to affect team performance, which clearly is likely to increase with the size of the collective unit. Thus in a 1988 study[23] of company profit sharing schemes, only 1 per cent of employees reported that the scheme had any affect what soever on their effort or work output. Rank Xerox's gainsharing scheme for its Gloucester operations was initially introduced on a site-wide basis, but after the first year of operation, it was found that staff in the individual units on the site felt unable to influence the overall results measured. Maggi Coil, formerly Corporate Compensation Director at Motorola, describes team pay with equal payments to team members as, 'often problematic and dysfunctional, rewarding mediocrity'.
- The effect of external and uncontrollable factors on the performance of the team. In line with expectancy theories of motivation, employees find it especially demotivating if they feel that factors outside of their control actively influence whether or not they can achieve a team bonus. Thus in Nuclear Electric's bonus scheme covering all staff at the Berkeley power station, the threat of a BR strike, and a major crane breakdown were all significant potential demotivators in the early months of the scheme's operation.
- Correspondingly, as with individual incentives, as Kohn notes, there can be undesirable side effects of the team bonus on aspects of performance not included in the scheme, and on broader relationships in the organization. One of the UK roadside service organizations introduced a team bonus scheme in conjunction with its 'Service Beyond the Call' customer service initiative. Bonuses were paid for the achievement of the advertised target of over 90 per cent of breakdowns being reached within one hour. In the first two quarters of operation, the scheme paid out to teams in the call centre. It was only then that the downsides started to become apparent. First, costs ballooned over budget as callers made much

greater use of externally contracted patrols to ensure the hour deadline was met. Secondly, services suffered for those who were 'missed' within the hour deadline. Callers would then divert patrol vans from going to them in order to service those who could still fall within the hour deadline, leaving those poor individuals abandoned for hours at the roadside!

- In addition, group norms may develop which actually impede individual or corporate performance, as demonstrated by the treatment of individual 'rate busters' in the famous Hawthorne studies in the 1920s. This is the pay equivalent of Janis's famous 'group-think' phenomenon. Or as at Pearl Assurance, employees may be encouraged to migrate from poorly performing teams to those earning higher rewards, or an internal transfer market may start to develop. In one Welsh company, a finance specialist was recently 'poached' from the Head Office function to the Investment Division, lured by the promise of a high team bonus payment, much to the annoyance of the Corporate Finance Director.

- Related to the above is the absence of effective team performance measures and performance management systems, which in our experience has prevented the introduction of small team incentives in a number of cases following feasibility studies. Having said this, around a quarter of European organizations have plans to make their performance management systems more team-oriented and organized in the future.

- One of the key problems specific to team bonus schemes is the 'social loafing' or 'free rider' phenomenon, of recalcitrant individuals earning bonus through the efforts of their higher performing and harder working colleagues, as evidenced in the work of Heneman and Von Hippel.[24] In the ACA's research,[25] staff were far more dissatisfied with team rewards where they were not distributed to reflect individual contribution and where they believed that work was not shared equally amongst team members. Indeed, perhaps not surprisingly, individuals rating themselves as high performers were less satisfied with team rewards than those who rated themselves as average contributors.

- A final issue which the research highlights with team and collective rewards (see Bullock and Lawler[26] for example) is a 'peaking out' effect, which is that performance gains achieved tend to fall significantly after the initial 2–3 years of operation. This is one of the factors leading Scottish Nuclear Electric to review the operation of its scheme after several years of success in 1998.

Team-based reward plans are therefore no more likely to be universally successful than individual schemes, but they can, in many organizations, act as an effective component of a contribution-related pay and reward strategy. What then are the factors that differentiate successful from unsuccessful team bonus schemes, and how can you maximize the chances of success in your own organization?

Figure 6.6 illustrates those factors which have been shown to correlate with the successful operation of team reward plans in a variety of research studies. Traditional advice tends to concentrate on technical design issues: keep the team small, have a few, simple measures, introduce them on a business upswing, and so on. As you can see, these studies are remarkably consistent with each other and those we have highlighted in respect of other forms of performance-related pay and an effective contribution-based approach. Rather than just being related to design details such as payment frequency, they centre on:

- using team rewards as part of a stated reward strategy, with defined and measurable objectives;
- clearly relating the scheme to the structural and team dynamics in the organization;
- adopting an implementation and operating approach which is high on employee involvement and communication.

REWARD STRATEGY AND OBJECTIVES

Successful team reward plans are not introduced as isolated pay initiatives, purely in response to what other companies are doing, nor as a knee-jerk response to admonishments from the Chief Executive that 'we need better team working'. Rather, as Schuster describes, they need to be introduced and operated, 'with clear objectives, as part of a comprehensive management strategy to engage employees in a collective effort to achieve key business goals'.[27] The ACA's research[28] led them to the conclusion that, 'the stronger the relationship between plan objectives and organizational objectives, the higher the satisfaction of staff, and the more successful the scheme'. In Schuster and in Bowey's[29] research studies, those companies without clearly stated objectives and a clear business rationale generally had unsuccessful plans.

De Matteo	Clarification of team goals Communication and understanding of schemes Team interdependence
Bullock and Tubbs	Formal plan involvement structure Staff involvement in plan design Employee favourability Participative management style Productivity rather than profit orientation
Bowey and Thorpe	Extent of consultation – Involvement in design – Amount of communication Supervisory skills/spans of control Market/sales growth* Shorter payout periods* Smaller size of membership*
Towers Perrin	Senior management commitment Employee support/involvement Emphasis on communications Related HR activities, eg training Performance measurement at levels below corporate* Shorter payout periods* Operational or blended rather than wholly financial measures*
American Productivity Centre	Management and supervisory support Amount of communications Clear and shared objectives

*Note: Weak correlations

Figure 6.6 *Summary of factors relating to the success of team-based reward plans*

Successful companies, on the other hand, operate their team reward plans as part of a total, holistic approach incorporating senior management support and endorsement, and alongside a wide range of other team-building, performance management and communication initiatives.

One recent study looked at the influence of four variables on the effectiveness of reorganizations in over 50 teams engaged in silicon chip manufacturing, which all had moved from a linear to a cell-based organization design. These variables were the physical environment, the job design, the reward structure, and the performance management and measurement systems. The study found that the reorganization of the manufacturing process on a team basis without actions in at least two of these areas actually worsened performance in terms of productivity and quality. None of the variables, on their own, had a positive effect on performance. But actions in three or more areas such as: putting team members in close proximity to one another, reskilling them and broadening their jobs, giving them regular information on the performance of the team, and reinforcing the performance of the team with cash rewards; these actions in combination led to significant performance improvements in both productivity and quality. Similarly, an ACA project[30] looking at 57 teams in 10 organizations found the following factors to correlate with successful team performance:

- clear goals and procedures;
- interdependence of tasks and actions;
- distributive justice, with rewards allocated equitably rather than equally within the team.

Clear goals for team reward plans therefore appear to be essential for four reasons:

- defining what the actual success criteria for the plan are and how they will be assessed;
- demonstrating clear links between the reward plan and the achievement of business goals;
- providing a co-ordinated direction for a range of team-building and reinforcing activities, including the pay plan;
- communicating to staff the purpose and rationale for the plan.

In respect of the goals for any team bonus plan, we often find a key issue to be the relative emphasis on 'line of sight' versus 'common fate' and success sharing objectives (see Figure 6.7). As we have seen, different forms of team rewards can be effective in addressing either of these overriding categories of goals. Profit-sharing schemes, for example, can reinforce employees' sense of collective belonging and purpose and focus attention on the importance of a simple, common business goal. Levi Strauss perhaps illustrates most clearly a scheme focused on this objective with its millennium bonus scheme. This is a 5-year scheme, with payments in 2000 depending on the achievement of a single, corporate cash flow target at the end of the period, based on ambitious compound growth goals. If it is achieved, all employees with more than three years' service will be entitled to a bonus of one year's salary. Clear, simple, common and by the later years, presumably pretty motivating as well. But what if external economic conditions render it unachievable?

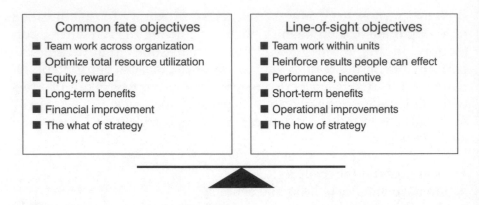

Figure 6.7 *A common balance in the objectives for team-based reward plans*

Other schemes, particularly small group schemes, are more focused on the right hand side of the balance in Figure 6.7, seeking to create an immediate and direct incentive effect by demonstrating that specific employee actions will produce performance gains, and result in bonus payments. Thus Sun Life Assurance was clearly attempting to impact on employees' day-to-day actions and behaviours with its processing team bonuses, with payments based on the productivity and quality performance of each team. In areas of the company where the line-of-sight between actions, performance targets and reward is not so clear, such as support functions, then a general profit share is employed.

Indeed, while profit sharing schemes are often rated as less effective than small team or individual schemes by managers (see Towers Perrin,[31] for example), this is typically judging them against the wrong set of line-of-sight criteria. As we have seen, they can have a significant effect in giving people a sense of common purpose and a stake in the business.

In Figure 6.8 we show a further means of categorizing team and collective reward schemes in terms of the level at which the team is defined in the organization structure on the vertical axis, as well as the focus of objectives on the horizontal. Generally speaking, the stronger the degree of incentive required, and the greater the independence of functions and teams in the organization, then the greater the focus on smaller group and individual incentives. The greater the structural fluidity and interaction between units, and the lesser the availability of detailed performance data, then the greater the probability that schemes will be to the left and in the upper half of the model. Schemes are typically positioned on an axis from top left to bottom right across the diagram.

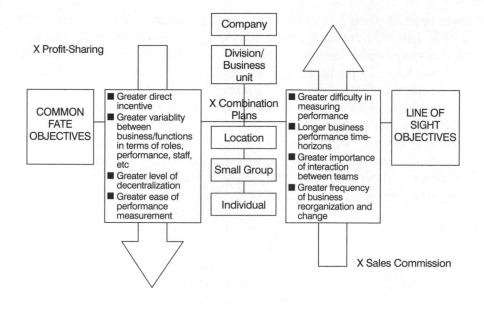

Figure 6.8 *Conflicting pressures to define teams at different levels in an organization within team reward plans*

Those seeking to deliver both sets of 'common fate' and ' line-of-sight' goals can do so in two main ways. They can either use the 'layer cake' approach to combination, using a number of different schemes. This is the case for the telecentre staff of a large UK bank which operates a company-based profit share, and local team and individual incentives. Or they can use a combination, 'cascading' scheme, which links up these different levels of team in the organization, as already described at Thames Power.

TEAM STRUCTURE AND DYNAMICS

This last point highlights another critical factor in the design of effective team reward plans, which is the definition and characteristics of teams and team working in the organization. Not just the level of team in the organization and its size, but also the nature of team and its membership, its purpose, and the way in which the work is organized, all exert a significant influence on the design and potential for success of team rewards plans. As Abosch and Reidy[32] found, the most effective team reward plans are 'customized to support the activities of specific teams'. Just as there is no one, universally successful type of collective or individual performance pay plan, so there is no single, totally effective formula for team working. Different team designs and structural variations will necessitate different reward approaches.

De Matteo,[33] for example, found that team rewards were rated much more highly by participants in teams in which there were high levels of interdependence between team members, an equal allocation of workload, and also prior experience of team working by team members. Where activities and workload varied significantly within the team, the preference was for individual incentives.

THE TEAM PAY IMPERATIVE

The nature of the teams and team working in the organization will, at an early stage, help to determine whether or not any form of team reward is appropriate. A particular concern of ours has been the over-hasty application of team working and team reward schemes in inappropriate situation in recent years. This can result from what *The Economist* referred to as, 'the follow-the-herd syndrome', or because of the assumed, simplistic strategic imperative that goes along the lines of 'team working improves performance, so we need team working, so we need team rewards'.

Team working has indeed been shown to have significant potential performance benefits, for example across whole swathes of manufacturing industry, in situations of high work interdependence and complexity, with wide employee choice and high uncertainty. Yet in situations where rapid decision-making and the application of individual expertise are the keys to high performance, then any form of team-related HR or reward initiative is liable to backfire.

Two examples demonstrate the problem. In one large public corporation a project group led by the personnel function developed a variety of detailed proposals for introducing team-based gainsharing programmes. Yet the Board did not share their views on the strategic imperative of team rewards and rejected the schemes as being inconsistent with the principle of public funding. The lack of effective team performance measurement systems would, in addition, have presented formidable barriers to implementation.

Similarly, the research division of a pharmaceuticals company in the United Kingdom sensibly resisted a corporate world-wide mandate to introduce team bonus schemes, with the purpose of reinforcing their team-based culture and values. A preliminary study demonstrated that while team working was indeed critical to their strategic success, in an R&D environment of fluid, inter-disciplinary and multiple project team memberships, any small team bonus scheme risked the creation of rigidities and barriers to the co-operation and team work it was designed to reinforce. As an Income Data Services review of reward schemes for creative staff put it: 'The difficulties in defining teams means that many innovative firms favour gestures which recognise team work, such as team achievement awards, rather than team-based pay.'[34]

In both cases, time spent on an initial feasibility study, to clarify the rationale for and practical ability to operate team rewards, would have saved the considerable effort and resources expended in an ultimately futile detailed design exercise.

TEAM DYNAMICS

This last pharmaceutical example illustrates a second key issue in respect of organization structure, which is the relative importance of team working within and between teams. In one insurance company which had been operating a small team-based bonus scheme, we found two significant problems. First, teams complained that if they lost staff members then their bonus was negatively affected, even if the reason was a promotion into a new role. Second, this also made teams reluctant to release team members for special and *ad hoc* projects, which were increasingly being used by the company to improve core business processes. Quite often, they would only make available their worst individual performers to these teams, so as not to impact on their bonus.

We have modelled the issues involved on Figure 6.9. Clearly, if tasks are largely individual, like selling personal computers for example, and you want to use money to reinforce performance, then individual performance pay would appear to make most sense. If co-operation between the individuals within teams is vital but there is little direct interaction between teams, for example between staff on different power stations in an electricity generator, then small team or location-based schemes are often the most appropriate, typically using local and operating performance measures. If co-operation between teams is vital or if teams are constantly reforming, as in the pharmaceutical example above and in many businesses which have re-engineered their core processes, then recognition awards or an overall corporate profit sharing or added value scheme often makes most sense.

Not only do you need to take account of the nature of team working in the organization, but successful bonus schemes also need to be flexible to take account of structural and technological changes. To illustrate, a telephone banking operation we worked with was set up in a greenfield location by one of the major financial institutions in the mid-1990s. Customer service and team work are core values of the subsidiary, and a bonus scheme to reinforce these values was promised to staff in their new contracts.

Initially customer service staff worked in teams of eight to ten people, carrying out a range of straightforward tasks, such as setting up standing orders. More complex tasks, such as the selling of add-on services, were referred to separate specialist teams of more highly trained staff. Cross-referrals and co-operation across teams were therefore vital, and in the first year, the bonus scheme measured productivity, service and sales performance across the entire location.

The introduction of new computer systems, however, then meant that the full range of activities and services could now be carried out by the individual teams, which customers preferred. Two alternative team structures for doing this were considered (see Figure 6.10). Under the first option one or two specialists would be placed in every team and the other team members would refer such services to them. In this case,

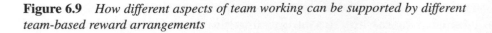

	Low	High
High	Operational Gainsharing at Small Group Level	Combination Bonus Plans at Intermediate Level
Low	Individual Bonus	Profit Sharing at Company Level

Emphasis on Team-work within Teams (vertical axis)

Emphasis on Team-work Between Teams (horizontal axis)

Figure 6.9 *How different aspects of team working can be supported by different team-based reward arrangements*

the bonus scheme would have been amended to reward the separate performance of each team, and become a genuine team bonus. Co-operation within teams, rather than between them, would have become the performance priority.

However, a second alternative (ultimately taken) was to train all staff to carry out the full range of tasks, each with their own customer population. Individual performance therefore became the key determinant of customer service, and so an individual bonus was used, with a minor team modifier.

This example also illustrates a common point which we have made regarding all types of contribution-related pay, which is the importance of changing team rewards over time, to suit the changes in environment, goals and characteristics of the team. As Abosch and Rcidy explain, 'pay approaches should evolve over time, as a team's identity, stability and role changes'. Based on their experiences, Motorola have

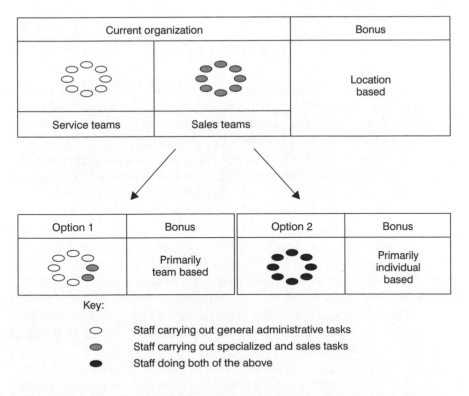

Figure 6.10 *How changes in the organization structure in a telephone banking operation implied different approaches to the team bonus design*

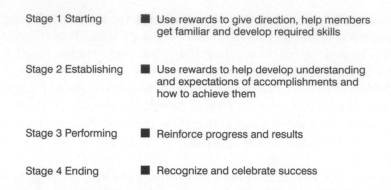

Stage 1 Starting	■ Use rewards to give direction, help members get familiar and develop required skills
Stage 2 Establishing	■ Use rewards to help develop understanding and expectations of accomplishments and how to achieve them
Stage 3 Performing	■ Reinforce progress and results
Stage 4 Ending	■ Recognize and celebrate success

Figure 6.11 *Team reward life cycle developed at Motorola*

developed a model of how a different focus to reward schemes is often appropriate at different stages of a project team's development (see Figure 6.11).

TYPES OF TEAM

Finally, as the last banking example also demonstrates, no two teams are alike, and perhaps the only thing worse than a mandate to introduce team rewards in an inappropriate situation is the requirement to introduce a specific type of scheme. Teams, even those of a similar size, vary greatly in their composition and characteristics. There are a number of well-known textbook models to help indicate the different types of team in an organization, and these can also help to suggest the type of reward scheme that is most congruent. Lawler and Cohen's[35] model is shown in Table 6.1.

Considerations of the nature of different teams and team working was vital in helping to develop effective team pay schemes in 1996 in an insurance company we worked with. Initial discussions revealed a wide variety of team types in different departments, and conflicting views on the value and feasibility of introducing team-based pay. Many thought the diversity and complexity of teams made team rewards impossible to design and operate.

However, a project group set up to investigate the matter, and representatives of all the different functions, was able to classify their various work teams into four generic categories. These were based on the directness of their impact on business results (directly measurable and

Table 6.1 *Lawler and Cohen's model of the characteristics of teams and associated reward systems*

Type of team	Work team	Parallel team	Project team
Team characteristics	Full-time Stable Multi-skilled Permanent	Part-time Stable Diverse Temporary	Full and part-time Stable core, others changing Diverse with specialized expertise Programmed duration
Nature of performance improvement	Continuous improvement	Solve particular problems, innovate	Achieve specified goals, one-off
Examples of reward plans	Team-based gainsharing	Recognition award for team success	Project completion bonuses for achieving specified goals

attributable, or more indirect) and the nature of the performance improvements they sought (one-off or continuous, see Table 6.2). Distinct incentive schemes were developed for each of these different types of team, providing a common plan framework which was simple to communicate and administer, despite the complex structure of the organization.

The 'core' plan for indirect teams pays up to 5 per cent of base pay per annum, assuming that various overall company performance targets

Table 6.2 *Different types of team and associated team reward schemes in an insurance company*

Performance improvement opportunity	Nature of performance impact	
	Direct	Indirect
One-time improvement	Dedicated, cross-functional teams that realize business results (Premium plan)	Teams that recommend changes for others to implement and realize business results (Core plan and team recognition awards)
Continuous improvement	Sales and customer service locations Other P&L organizations (Premium plan)	Staff departments Work teams with no P&L (Core Plan)

are achieved. It is based on a variety of local team goals, with both objective and subjective assessments of the results achieved. Direct teams can, however, opt for the premium plan, which pays up to 10 per cent per annum according to the achievement of specific, team financial and quality goals, without any overall company trigger.

TEAM AND INDIVIDUAL PERFORMANCE

Nor, as we have seen, can an effective contribution-based reward approach ignore the importance of individual performance. High performance in organizations is generally a contribution of individual, inter and intra-team actions and behaviours, and hence the growth in popularity of mixed, combination and contribution-based schemes.

Norwich Union Financial Services illustrates this trend. They abandoned highly geared individual commission arrangements for sales staff following regulatory criticisms in 1994. However, selling is primarily an individual activity and so commission has been replaced with a bonus which reflects a mixture of team and individual sales consultant performance. A sum of £250 per month is available as a personal activity bonus, and another £250 as a team bonus, based on the level of new business activity and customer service levels (as assessed through questionnaires) of each area team. Thus, nine of the 14 sales teams received bonuses under this scheme in November 1995.

In the car dealers of a European manufacturer in the United Kingdom this team/individual balance varies according to the role. For sales staff the emphasis is on the individual and the potential earnings opportunities are higher, while for service staff it is weighted towards the overall performance of the whole dealership team.

COMMUNICATIONS AND INVOLVEMENT

Clear business-related goals and 'line of sight', and an effective scheme design tailored to suit team structures and types, even taken together, will not create a successful team reward plan. Take the example of a European car manufacturer which developed a new gainsharing plan in one plant based on the work of external management consultants. This employed seven measures, each associated with a key strategic business goal. Senior managers were delighted at the level of business alignment and line-of-sight. Yet an employee survey one year later found that two-thirds of workers felt unable to influence the plan measures, and over half wanted a return to the old arrangements. Employees had not been involved at all in the plan's design and were not committed to its operation. Very acutely did the HR Director of an Irish manufacturing company once produce an embarrassing silence, after we had presented a detailed gainsharing plan design to him, with the simple question, 'And where are these performance gains going to come from?'

As illustrated in earlier chapters, almost all of the research demonstrates that successful performance outcomes depend to a greater extent on the way in which a reward plan is developed, implemented and operated than on the actual design of the plan itself. As Bowey[36] explains, 'the degree of involvement and communication during the design and operation was far more important than the type of plan' in explaining scheme success. Lawler in fact defines team rewards as 'reward programmes designed to involve employees in improving performance'.[37]

Scanlon's original 1930s' gainsharing schemes involved a detailed, formal communication and involvement network of plant productivity committees. While a much broader range of formal and informal communication techniques would typically be used today, the value of his original approach is still apparent. A Towers Perrin survey[38] found that combination plans, using a mix of financial and operating performance measures, were rated most highly in terms of plan success and contribution to improved team working. Yet this design of plan was also associated with the greatest investment in associated training, communications and employee involvement activities. Profit-sharing and financial schemes were rated as less effective, yet the level of employee involvement and communication associated with them was also, typically, much lower.

Involvement is at the crux of the mutually reinforcing linkages between effective team working and successful team-based pay plans, and at the heart of the pay for contribution approach. It operates through a number of channels:

- developing understanding and 'buy-in' to the goals of the plan and the team relationships and performance goals it embodies;
- generating its own Hawthorne effect; Cooper *et al.*[39] reported from their research that, 'when people work under a self-selected rule for distributing team rewards, they realise significant productivity

gains; working under the same rules imposed on them does not produce the same effect';

- improving the quality of plan design, and with employees directly generating suggestions and improvements in line with plan performance goals; we have never worked on a team reward plan where the views of employees, who know their own work better than anyone, have not improved the design and operation of a scheme;
- addressing the full range of employee motivations beyond simple monetary needs; a UK service organization, for example, operates an annual, salary-related company-wide bonus scheme, using cash payments to reinforce collective performance and team co-ordination; a second team bonus plan operates in the form of a quarterly, points-based performance competition, with teams of up to 30 employees competing to achieve the highest productivity and service levels, and rewards of publicity, vouchers and non-cash prizes for the league table winners; this second plan is designed to satisfy people's needs for achievement, recognition and reinforce co-operation within teams.

Having said this, there are very few situations in which the design and introduction of a team reward scheme is a simple, straightforward matter. Concerns at exposing these difficulties leads many UK organizations to keep the whole process secret for as long as possible: don't mention it to employees for fear of arousing concerns or expectations: better to get the compensation manager or an outside consultant to do a desk-top design job, test it out with senior managers, and only tell people immediately prior to implementation.

Yet after some unpleasant experiences, we will no longer help to design plans unless companies agree to involving employees in the process. To illustrate the benefits, at an Irish manufacturer with a reputation for a highly confrontational management style and relatively poor industrial relations, senior executives were considering a team reward plan to reinforce their recent reorganization along cell-based production lines. Yet they were fearful of the reaction of employees and trade unions to pay changes.

Group discussions at an early stage of the investigative process with employees demonstrated the suspicions: 'They'll be looking to take money from us'. But they also demonstrated a strong sense that, 'good work should get rewarded', that 'people have to get more involved in the business that keeps us all employed', and that there was, 'no incentive for good work, no recognition' in the existing situation. A joint management-employee group subsequently designed and installed a new plan, and went on to make a range of other changes, for example in shift patterns, which have all contributed to improved plant performance. The majority favoured and supported the changes, rather than fearing them as the directors had anticipated.

One of the most exciting developments at present in team rewards is the growth of employee-driven, business challenge incentives. At organizations such as Boeing in the United States and the Benefits Agency in the United Kingdom this highly empowered approach to team rewards is being put into practice. A set of central criteria for all bonus schemes is typically established. At the Benefits Agency these include that rewards must relate to 'local' measures and be made for a 'valuable, demonstrable, performance contribution', beyond normal effort or job requirements. Rewards must also be shared equally within the team. Individual line managers and work teams are then free to design their own bonus schemes, so long as they meet these criteria.

At Boeing, on the 777 project, there were dozens of these plans operating for teams of different sizes and over different time-scales, each reflecting an individual team's characteristics and performance goals, and each with a very high level of understanding and 'buy-in' amongst team members. This is perhaps the antithesis of the uniform, unthinking, mechanistic approach to performance pay scheme design which has bedevilled merit pay and led to the rejection of the whole concept in some organizations. It appears a little chaotic, yet supported a hugely successful project completion, months ahead of schedule. The level of commitment achieved was shown by the participation of employees in the initial launch demonstration of the plane to potential customers. This is really pay for contribution in action.

THE SUCCESS FACTORS AT WORK: NUCLEAR ELECTRIC

The importance of these three aspects of team-based reward plans was well illustrated at Nuclear Electric's power station at Berkeley in Gloucestershire in the early 1990s. The station was in the middle of a three-year closure programme, involving the removal of spent fuel rods, and progressive redeployment and redundancy of the remaining 400 employees. In a traditional, tight-knit community, with a long-standing reputation for difficult industrial relations, progress was understandably slow. Every week that the closure programme overran stood to cost the company over £150,000.

After a detailed feasibility study, a gainsharing plan was introduced, with workers receiving a bonus for every week saved against the planned completion time-scale. 14 months later, the job was complete, the final rod removed and transported over three months ahead of schedule. Workers with an average salary of around £12,000 earned bonuses of more than £2,000 each, and over £30 million was saved on the project. Why was the scheme so successful in an organization and for employees with no prior experience of team-based reward plans or indeed any form of performance pay? The company's management attributed it to three factors.

First, the station management ensured that the plan was designed and perceived as an integral part of a much broader operating and HR strategy at the station. The performance objective in this situation may have been unusually clear: exceed 56 fuel rods removed per week to earn a bonus. Yet it was linked to a variety of other operating goals, including most importantly the maintenance of five key safety parameters and the station's quality assurance programme.

Second, the broader human resources strategy at the site was also critical in ensuring that the plan was not perceived as a cynical attempt to buy out opposition to the loss of jobs. The company provided an extensive programme of employee counselling, redeployment and redundancy assistance throughout the closure period.

In terms of team and bonus structure, only a handful of the 400 staff on the site were directly involved in the delicate process of lifting and moving fuel rods. It would have been possible to give very large individual bonuses to these few. Yet the station's management had the clear aim of reinforcing co-operation and team working across the site. Any emerging problems, such as a crane breakdown in the first week of the scheme, depended as much on the effort of support staff in maintenance, safety and administration as on the direct operatives. This was also very much in keeping with the collective traditions and culture on the site. Thus every employee participated in the plan, with a slight payment premium for the direct operatives who most directly influenced the speed of rod removal.

Finally, a series of employee communications and involvement initiatives had been started at the station during the closure programme, including management briefings and work practice improvement teams. A sample of employees were consulted during the feasibility study and the scheme's introduction added power to these initiatives. One team came up with a means of overcoming traditional restrictive working practices, which resulted in immediate and significant productivity gains. In addition, an interim payment of £150 six months into the period reinforced employee perceptions that managers were really serious about listening to them and rewarding team success.

CONCLUSIONS

The success of the team-based reward plan at Berkeley led to the development of schemes in other parts of Nuclear Electric, although these only proved feasible on the power stations and not in support functions. Team rewards are not a universal panacea for effective links between pay and performance, although we tend to agree that the modern situation still reflects the observation that Katz and Kahn[40] made over 30 years ago, that, 'organization practice has been slow to recognise the motivating power which team rewards can provide'. Jumping on the bandwagon of the team-based reward fashion, however, is only liable to lead to a repeat of the late 1980s' roller-coaster experience with individual incentives and merit pay.

Abosch and Reidy[41] observe that, 'While some advocates of team rewards suggest abandoning the individual performance pay model, to enhance a religion of team pay, companies rated the most successful programmes as having a healthy balance between both systems.' It is a balance that we have found to be characteristic of the pay for contribution approach.

What the Nuclear Electric case does demonstrate is that even in a relatively unfavourable closure situation, group incentive plans and team working can interact in a mutually reinforcing relationship to produce impressive performance results. They have a strong performance record going back many years to demonstrate their potential effectiveness, and there is nothing to suggest that they will be any less relevant and effective in the new millennium, rather more so.

With clear goals, as part of a participative management approach, and related to the nature of team work required in the organization, such plans can be very successful. They represent a significant opportunity for many companies, facing up to the economic realities of an increasingly globally competitive world in the new millennium, and seeking to maximize the utilization of their human resources, to effectively channel the contribution of their employees to the benefit of both the organization and themselves. But as Abosch and Reidy also observe, 'the most effective team rewards are a function of management and culture, more than remuneration'.[42]

Goal clarity is essential as we have seen, to define the nature of the performance gains being sought and how reward will reinforce their achievement (by general reward and recognition, or more direct incentive). It also specifies the business alignment and success criteria for any scheme. But as a final comment on team rewards, and as we elaborate further in Chapter 8, do your external benchmarking, review your performance measures and data, define your team structures and re-engineer your processes, design and test your reward plans, but do not forget the people themselves, those on the receiving end. They are the only ones who can deliver the team work and performance improvements which team reward plans are designed to produce.

SUMMARY

- The level of interest in team reward schemes has increased rapidly in the United Kingdom and Europe during the 1990s. While these schemes have a long history, they are now evident across the full range of traditional and newer industries.
- Team reward schemes can be classified in terms of the organization level, size, and nature of the team, and in terms of the performance measures and design characteristics of the scheme. Combination plans, combining different performance measures, and sometimes measuring performance at two or three levels of team in the organization, are particularly popular at present.
- Organizations introducing team reward plans are typically aiming for them both to contribute to improved business performance, and also to leverage up employee involvement, team working and commitment.
- There is a strong body of research evidence that in the appropriate circumstances team reward plans can make an important contribution in all these areas. Profit sharing plans are associated with high levels of financial returns to shareholders and gainsharing schemes with impressive gains in productivity.
- Yet the research is far from being universally positive and as with individual performance pay, a number of potential problems with

team rewards are evident. These include demotivating high individual performers and supporting 'free riders', encouraging dysfunctional group norms, and a 'peaking-out' effect after 2–3 years of operation.

- Three factors appear to relate to the success of team reward plans. The first is to introduce and operate them as part of a defined business and HR strategy, with clearly stated aims, and a range of supporting initiatives in other HR areas. An important strategic issue is the emphasis in the plan on 'common fate' and success sharing goals versus the aim of providing direct, line-of-sight incentives.
- Second, it is important to reflect the nature and structure of teams and team-working in the organization. The relative importance of team-working within and between teams needs to be reflected in the plan design. If these dynamics change, then the team rewards scheme normally needs to be modified as well.
- Finally, high levels of involvement and communication with staff during the design and operation of a team reward plan correlate strongly with its success.
- Team rewards, as with the other components of an effective contribution-related pay approach are, therefore, generally working as part of a mixed model. They operate in conjunction with other types of pay and reward schemes and as part of a much wider HR and motivational strategy, designed to enhance the commitment and contribution of all employees.

CASE STUDY 6.1

Eli Lilly and Company's gainshare programme

The experiences of Eli Lilly, the global pharmaceutical company, at its manufacturing unit in Basingstoke, illustrates the important part which an appropriately tailored bonus scheme can play, in supporting a major culture change and business turnaround.

BACKGROUND

Eli Lilly have been in Basingstoke for over 60 years, with 500 employees manufacturing products that are exported throughout the world. But by

1993–94, the situation in an increasingly competitive and globally sourced market place looked bleak, both from a business and a HR perspective. Almost all aspects of factory performance were poor compared to the company's other plants. The factory was still managed in a fairly traditional top-down style, the appraisal system was regarded as ineffective, and morale had been affected by a major voluntary redundancy programme.

THE STIMULUS FOR CHANGE

At the end of 1993 a new General Manager was appointed and a clear, three-year turnaround strategy was established. This focused on improving base operations with key success factors and performance goals set, and with people at the core of the improvement efforts. Team work, communications and empowerment were all stated priorities, but as in all situations, these are much easier to state than to practise. None the less, the senior management team put an enormous effort into making them happen; General Manager briefings and 'any questions answered' initiatives formed part of an extensive communications effort; and team and staff goals were established in all areas, based on the key success factors of the site.

GAINSHARE

'We didn't set out to have a gainshare programme,' explains Martin Neville, Manager for European Compensation and Benefits Development. 'It was only at this point that we asked, "If we are going to be successful through the efforts of every single employee, how are they going to share in the success of the site?" Hence the idea of gainsharing emerged.

The scheme was designed in a very short space of time, based on clear agreement of the principles underpinning it:

- that it should focus on the three key success factors and challenges for the site;
- that all employees should participate;
- that it had to be self-funding.

The scheme measures have been adjusted from year to year, and those used in 1997 are illustrated in Table 6.3. There are typically three measures based on the key success factors, with three performance levels on each. The total gainshare pot is funded from efficiency savings and 5 per cent of this pot is awarded for each target achieved. A maximum ceiling on payments was set at £1,500.

Table 6.3 *Performance measures in Eli Lilly's gainshare scheme*

% improvement	Level 1	Level 2	Level 3
% improvement in service level	+1%	+2%	+3%
% improvement in lots right first time	+1%	+2%	+3%
% improvement in cycle time	+10%	+20%	+30%

The scheme operates on an annual basis, but here again an extensive communications and involvement effort surrounded the launch and ongoing operation of the scheme. Regular team progress meetings, written briefings and posters designed by teams of employees, progress reports and milestone celebrations are all employed.

THE RESULTS

The scheme did not make an auspicious start. The plant was performing at well below business plan levels. Yet the 1995 targets were set beyond plan, and were recognized early on to be unachievable. Again, management on the site openly admitted this to employees and the 1996 goals were set on a stretching but achievable basis, with the understanding that the performance stretch would be ratcheted up each year.

The progressive impact of the changes on the site, supported by the gainshare, have been spectacular. Between 1995 and 1998 service levels improved from 91per cent to 99per cent, right-first-time lots went up by 8 percentage points, cost savings and efficiencies have totalled over £5 million, and cycle times have improved significantly.

In 1996 the facility was awarded Class A manufacturing status within the company and was rated the top supplier worldwide for internal customer service to Lilly's operating and sales companies. In 1998 further gains saw it win the Golden Eagle award for the Number 1 Lilly manufacturing site worldwide, an incredible turnaround. External recognition came in the form of *Management Today* UK Best Factory awards, giving the site a high commendation. Employees have generally earned around £1000 pa as a result of these achievements, and maximum payment on one occasion.

LEARNING POINTS

Martin Neville is obviously delighted by the success of the Basingstoke plant and the gainshare scheme. While he feels the gainshare scheme has played a 'significant part' in this success, he puts this down to the communications and involvement aspects of the cultural change that has taken place, with the bonus scheme playing a reinforcing role. The example set from the top, and the consistency of performance messages from all sources were key to enabling the bonus to have an effect.

Nor does Neville see the Basingstoke scheme as perfect by any means. There have been recurring debates over membership, with only line employees included, and UK support functions at Basingstoke such as Finance and Personnel not participating. The scheme may also, he feels, be coming to the end of its useful shelf-life, and as the site progresses to its next goal of becoming the location with the shortest supply lead-times of any plant worldwide for all of its products, a more fundamental restructuring of the bonus may be required.

None the less, the evidence is clear according to Neville that the gainshare has played a 'significant part in rewarding, recognizing and reinforcing the fact that everyone's contribution has been vital to moving the plant up to world class performance standards'.

CASE STUDY: 6.2

Using a gainsharing scheme to support a business turnaround at an American steel company

The company in this case study is a leading mini-mill steel producer and fabricator based in the United States. Its experiences over the last four years, using a form of gainsharing and pay-at-risk, are an excellent example of the potential benefits of these forms of relating pay to business performance, and of the factors which cause such approaches to succeed.

A BUSINESS WITH PROBLEMS

This company was a very traditional and traditionally managed US steel producer. Employees came to work, did their jobs, and went home. The management style was top-down: employees did not see why decisions were made or what impact they had on the business. Communications and team working were generally poor. But wages were very competitive and a good benefits package was provided.

The stimulus for change was declining business performance, with 1994 representing the third year of losses. Employees neither realized nor believed the scale of the problems, but it was a serious situation with declining profits, sales and productivity. Productivity is the key to success in the manufacture of low margin steel bars, and employees had a major impact on the efficient use of the high cost capital equipment in the plants.

The new company's new business strategy, adopted as a result, focused on creating efficient, self-standing business units (each mill employed approximately 250 people). But a key component was also the need for culture change and a desire to get employees fully involved in business actions and decisions, so that they could fully contribute to the company's success. And a new gainsharing programme, emphasizing the importance of 'partnership' to improve business performance, was an important means for communicating the importance of business productivity, and of getting employees much more fully involved in the business.

GAINSHARING

The gainsharing scheme was introduced in January 1995 and as the company's Compensation Director explains, 'We adapted the generalized concept of gainsharing to the specific context in which it operates.' Given the severity of the business situation, the new plan was introduced in conjunction with a 15 per cent reduction in base pay levels, although staff's original base pay level was guaranteed for the first three months of operation.

The plan works as follows. Every 1 per cent improvement in productivity over 70 per cent of the 1994 level earns employees 0.5 per cent of their pay, so at the 1994 productivity level, base pay is 100 per cent of its former level. But for every 1 per cent improvement in productivity above this employees earn 1.5 per cent of base pay. They thereby receive 33 per cent of the financial gain resulting from their enhanced performance. And enhanced output and performance are what the scheme is focused on, as the company emphasizes, not about lowering labour costs.

The plan operates on a business unit basis, paying a common amount to all staff in each mill. Teamwork is vital to improving productivity in a process business: a few star performers will have little impact. All staff, from Chief Executive down, participate on the same basis. The plan pays out weekly, to give it maximum impact.

Yet, as previously discussed, gainsharing schemes are not just pay schemes, and securing and maximizing the contribution of all employees to the success of the business requires more than just a financial carrot. According to the Compensation Director, 'The success of gainsharing hinges on the quality and openness of communication… there needs to be mutual trust.'

The gainsharing scheme was not just a pay plan but a major communications and training programme. Obviously these were the briefings, meetings, videos and brochures about the scheme itself. But more importantly a series of open book management initiatives took place. Workers are now given 15 days training each year, covering work skills such as problem solving and team working, but also business education such as reading financial accounts. In their rest areas, they can now access a wide range of performance information by computer, including how much they are earning under the gainshare.

As well as the gainsharing plan committee, they are also a whole range of vehicles to channel employee involvement: productivity committees, process improvement teams and so on. This whole change of approach according to the Compensation Director means that 'Workers act together in ways they never did before.'

THE RESULTS

The turnaround since 1994 has been spectacular. Table 6.4 charts the improvement in steel production and financial results since then, as well as the payouts under the gainsharing scheme. In 1998 these averaged 46 per cent of base pay across the plants, as profitability more than doubled over the previous year. As the Compensation Director explains, it has become a self-reinforcing cycle with employees, 'more willing to work in teams and contribute, which in turn improves productivity and their pay.'

THE LEARNING POINTS

According to the Compensation Director, gainsharing is not a 'magic bullet', although looking at the numbers in Table 6.4, one could be excused for thinking this to be the case. It was, rather, one of a number of components of a strategy to align people with the goals of the business, including the organization of work, the management and decision-making style, the communications and involvement vehicles, the pay and reward systems.

Nor is this company's scheme perfect, and the plan committee have made a number of revisions to it since its introduction, another common theme underpinning the successful pay schemes described in this book. For example, support staff were brought into the scheme on a common

Table 6.4 *Company results since the introduction of the gainsharing scheme*

Item	Pre-gainsharing	1995	1996	1997*	1998 (projected)
Tons	100%	115%	122%	112%	133%
Profits	100%	550%	550%	400%	950%
Gainsharing payout (% of base pay)	n/a	35%	27%	27%	46%

Note: *Major capital projects at two mill locations

basis with production employees, and the original 'no show, no pay' principle has been modified, to give people their average payment over the last 12 months during their vacation for example.

Yet this gainsharing plan has made a demonstrable contribution to the company's success, both in competing in the increasingly international steel market, and in competing in their labour market. If analysts such as Stephen Roach are correct, and the balance of power is swinging back from employer to employee, then the sort of environment this organization is creating will be the key to success in the people market. As the Compensation Director explains, 'In today's market, workers are choosing where they want to work. Creating a working environment that encourages workers' participation, and provides the opportunity for linking improved performance to improved compensation is one way to create a workplace to attract the type of workers we want.'

NOTES

1. Incomes Data Services (1991) Performance Pay, *IDS Focus*
2. Smith, A (1992) Team Prize, *Personnel Today*, 10 November
3. Thompson, M (1995) *Team Working and Pay*, Institute of Employment Studies, London
4. *The Economist* (1995) The trouble with teams?, 14 January
5. Institute of Personnel and Development (1994) *The IPD Guide on Team Reward*, Institute of Personnel and Development, London
6. Towers Perrrin (1997a) *Learning from the Past: Changing for the Future*, Research Report from Towers Perrin, London, March
7. Towers Perrrin (1997b) *Survey of Remuneration and Benefits in Call Centres*, Produced by Towers Perrin, London, available to participants only.
8. Katzenbach, J and Smith, D (1993) *The Magic of Teams*, HBS Press, Boston
9. Milkovich, G and Newman, JM (1987) *Compensation*, Business Publications, Illinois
10. American Compensation Associates (1996) *Team-Based Pay*, Satellite Conference, ACA, Scottsdale, Arizona
11. Institute of Personnel and Development (1994), op. cit.

12. Towers Perrin (1997a), op. cit.
13. Industrial Relations Services (1997) Pay prospects for 1998, *Pay and Benefits Bulletin*, **435**, November
14. Institute of Personnel and Development (1998) *Performance Pay Survey*, Institute of Personnel and Development, London
15. Katzenbach and Smith, op. cit.
16. Kohn, A (1993) *Punished by Reward,* Houghton Mifflin, Boston
17. Macadams, JL and Hawk, EJ (1995) *Capitalising on Human Assets*, The Benchmark Study, ACA, Scottsdale, Arizona
18. American Productivity Centre (1987) *People Performance and Pay*, Houston, Texas
19. Towers Perrin (1990) *Achieving Results through Sharing*, Survey Report available from Towers Perrin, London
20. Wallace Bell, D and Hanson, C (1989) *Profit Sharing and Profitability*, Kogan Page, London
21. Bullock, R and Lawler, E (1984) Gainsharing: a few questions and answers, *Human Resource Management*, **23** (1)
22. De Matteo, JS *et al.* (1997) Factors relating to the successful implementation of team-based rewards, *ACA Journal*, Winter
23. Poole, M and Jenkins, G (1988) 'How employers respond to profit sharing, *Personnel Management*, July
24. Heneman, RL and Von Hippel, C (1995) Balancing group and individual rewards: rewarding individual contribution to the team, *Compensation and Benefits Review* **27** (4)
25. Macadams and Hawke, op. cit.
26. Bullock and Lawler, op. cit.
27. Schuster, J (1987) Gainsharing, do it right first time, *Sloan Management Review*, Winter
28. Macadams and Hawke, op. cit.
29. Bowey, A (1983) *The Effect of Incentive Pay Systems*, Department of Employment Research Paper, DOE, London
30. ACA (1996–97) *Team Pay Field Research Project,* American Compensation Association and the University of Tennessee
31. Towers Perrin (1990), op. cit.
32. Abosch, K and Reidy, H (1996) Supporting teams through reward systems, *ACA Journal*, Winter
33. De Matteo *et al.*, op. cit.
34. Incomes Data Services (1994) Managing creativity, *IDS Focus*, December
35. Lawler III, EE and Cohen, SG (1992) Designing pay systems for teams' *ACA Journal*, Autumn
36. Bowey, op. cit.
37. Lawler III, EE (1992) *The Ultimate Advantage,* Jossey-Bass, San Francisco
38. Towers Perrin (1990), op. cit.
39. Cooper, MD *et al.* (1992) Improving the effectiveness of gainsharing, *Administrative Science Quarterly*, **27** (3)
40. Katz, D, and Kahn, RL (1964) *The Social Psychology of Organisations*, Wiley, New York,
41. Abosch and Reidy, op. cit.
42. Abosch and Reidy, op. cit.

7

Performance management and rewarding contribution

At NewCo, the lack of formal administration, of management training, and the highly subjective nature of the assessments gave rise to difficulties in terms of employee acceptability and union conflict... the justification for some qualitative managerial judgement beyond the achievement of specified objectives was often based on the view that an 'all round' evaluation of job performance is essential.

(Kessler and Purcell)[1]

The management of performance related pay is perhaps the most difficult task HR people have to undertake.

(Vicky Wright, Hay Management Consultants)[2]

It is not performance pay that is the problem, it is the appraisals and how they have been used.

(Charles Cochrane, Secretary of the Council of Civil Service Unions)[3]

INTRODUCTION

You cannot pay for contribution unless you can measure and manage contribution. Performance management processes enable measurement to take place. But they do much more. Performance management can be defined as anything an organization does to improve its total performance and the performance of the teams and individuals who work within it. Performance management is about managing the business. It is not just performance appraisal which, as Armstrong and Murlis[4] assert, has become in many cases 'a dishonest annual ritual'. Neither is it simply a method of generating information which informs pay decisions. This may well be part of the process but it is not the whole process. Performance management is about improving and developing performance as well as paying for performance. And Armstrong and Baron[5] established in their 1997 research for the IPD that many organizations see its purpose as being primarily developmental.

There are, in fact, four primary purposes of performance management. First, it provides a basis for managing expectations. These are defined and agreed mutually, covering what managers expect the members of their teams to do and the guidance, development and support the latter expect from their managers. Performance management therefore serves as a means of clarifying the psychological contract and of building a climate of trust, issues considered in more detail in Chapter 8.

Second, as a process for managing expectations, performance management acts as an integrating force. It helps to integrate corporate and individual objectives so that what individuals and teams are expected to do flows from and supports what the organization is aiming to do. It can integrate the core competencies of the organization with the skills and behaviours teams and individuals need to display, so that, again, people understand what the organization has to be good at doing and therefore, what they have to be good at doing.

In addition, and importantly, performance management assists in the communication and integration of the organization's core values. It clarifies the values that individuals are expected to uphold and serves as a means of assessing the extent to which they are doing so. Integration is the key to successful performance management which has to be regarded holistically, as an all-embracing approach to the management of performance.

Third, performance management can motivate. It strikes at the heart of the employment relationship, not only defining expectations but also providing a means for encouraging people to meet those expectations. Performance management encourages positive feedback, reinforcement, recognition and commitment. It can identify the scope for growth and empowerment. It shows the way to improving and extending skills and competence through personal development plans. All these can act as powerful and long-lasting, non-financial motivators. It can be argued that the motivational impact of properly conducted performance management can be much deeper than those provided by purely financial rewards, and there is a strong body of research to support this contention. As we have seen, the pay for contribution approach recognizes the importance of using the full range of motivators as part of an effective reward strategy.

Finally, performance management is a developmental process. It looks ahead. It establishes learning needs and outcomes. And it indicates how these needs can be satisfied and the outcomes achieved.

In this chapter we review current trends and approaches to performance management, with a focus on the links to pay systems. We then consider, in turn, the major issues which most organization's face in the difficult task of operating effective performance management systems in practice: performance measurement, performance rating, reconciling the developmental and reward goals, process and ethical issues.

TRENDS IN PERFORMANCE MANAGEMENT

Research studies and surveys demonstrate that, as with performance pay, a majority of organizations operate some form of performance management, but that a large number of these are currently engaged in changing and improving their systems to try to make them more effective.

The IPD's research[6] found that 69 per cent of the 562 organizations surveyed used performance management. The objectives of the process were most strongly developmental (see Figure 7.1), with around 43 per cent linking the process in some way to pay. Amongst larger employers and for management staff, Towers Perrin's European Study[7] of 300 organizations demonstrated that 73 per cent linked their performance appraisal data to pay, although again the emphasis in 81 per cent of cases was on assessing training needs. 74 per cent used the process for career development, 63 per cent for determining promotions, 45 per cent for succession planning, and 10 per cent to influence downsizing decisions.

Some 75 per cent of the IPD's surveyed companies regarded their performance management process as at least partly effective, but the assessment correlated strongly with level in the organization. Thus, 85 per cent of senior managers rated their system as effective, whereas only 45 per cent of general staff did so. Other studies have been more critical. Saville and Holdsworth Ltd,[8] for example, found that not a single survey respondent thought that their process was effective in motivating employees. Other reported problems included bureaucracy, and lack of effective appraisal practice: 25 per cent of those participating in the Towers Perrin study felt that the results did not justify the effort, 57 per cent identified poor management appraisal skills or lack of training, and 29 per cent saw poor or weak links to pay as major issues.

The IPD research found competencies both to be an increasingly popular and effective component of performance management systems, but also a problem and a cause of over-complexity in modern systems. Where used and linked to pay, competencies explained around 25 per cent of the overall performance rating and resulting pay increase.

Given these problems, it is hardly surprising that significant numbers of organizations are currently changing and modifying their performance management systems. Thus, 75 per cent of the 303 companies in Towers Perrin's European survey were planning changes

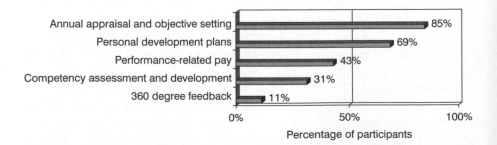

Figure 7.1 *Primary objectives of performance management in the IPD research*

in the next three years (see Figure 7.2) with the most popular including multi-rater or 360° appraisal, and integrating the individual, team and company aspects of performance more effectively in a total performance management approach.

The IPD research suggests these changes demonstrate that a fundamentally different concept of performance management is emerging, just as it is doing in respect of the move from performance to contribution-related pay. This is characterized by an emphasis on multi-directional and bottom-up involvement and performance improvement, rather than top-down performance appraisal and control (see Figure 7.3). According to Clive Fletcher,

> Companies are abandoning ever-more complex systems, and the fruitless search for perfect objectivity and measurement. Assuming both the imperfection and the necessity of appraisal, they are accepting plurality, subjectivity and focusing on achievable improvement. We can even see examples of the paperless system.[9]

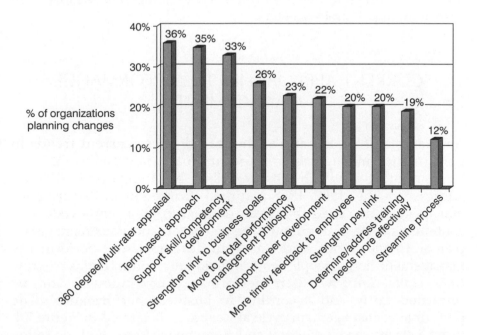

Figure 7.2 *Planned changes in performance management systems over the next three years in the Towers Perrin survey*

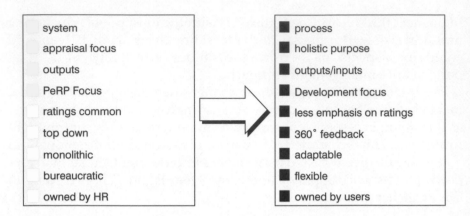

system	■ process
appraisal focus	■ holistic purpose
outputs	■ outputs/inputs
PeRP Focus	■ Development focus
ratings common	■ less emphasis on ratings
top down	■ 360° feedback
monolithic	■ adaptable
bureaucratic	■ flexible
owned by HR	■ owned by users

Figure 7.3 *The changing approach to performance management revealed by the IPD research*

Armstrong and Baron[10] summarize the changes more succinctly, defining performance management as finally moving 'out of the tick box', just as truly-effective performance pay strategies have moved out of their merit pay strait-jacket.

CURRENT APPROACHES TO PERFORMANCE MANAGEMENT

An example of a company at the lead of these current trends in performance management is the approach adopted by Zeneca Pharmaceuticals, which was described by Angela Sheard in an address to the 1997 IPD National Conference. Performance management at Zeneca has been defined to their employees as 'a continuous cycle of discussions between you and your manager, to plan and review your work and your development... performance management helps people work individually and in teams to grow their skills, improve their performance continuously and be rewarded fairly and according to business performance'. The performance management cycle at Zeneca is illustrated in Figure 7.4. It has a strong developmental and competence focus, with no rating system, but still acts as an important input into the pay determination process.

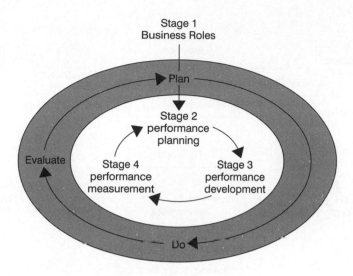

Figure 7.4 *Performance management at Zeneca*

Another good example of current trends in performance management from the public sector is provided by the Victoria and Albert Museum, as reported by Armstrong and Baron. Their process is modelled in Figure 7.5. At senior management level they have adopted a contribution-based approach, in that performance management refers both to the achievement of objectives and the application of competencies, or attributes (the latter term is preferred at the V&A). Their key attributes are defined at three interlinked levels:

- *Museum*: vision, leadership and organizational skills, awareness;
- *Team*: team/people management, decision-making, communications;
- *Self*: drive, adaptability, self-management and development, expertise.

A third good example of modern trends in managing performance is that of BP Exploration. As described by Mike Conway at the IPD National Conference in 1998 the essential elements of their approach are as follows:

- It is a holistic approach which is based on a culture of empowerment, leadership, robust targets, measures and processes.

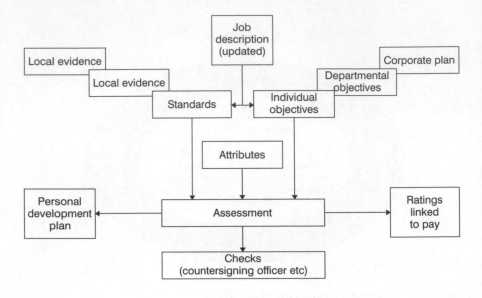

Figure 7.5 *Performance management at the V&A*

- It consists of a number of business management processes, namely: strategic targets, performance contacts, measurement and quarterly performance reviews.
- Individual performance and learning is focused on desired business outcomes and is part of 'what it takes to deliver'.
- Performance meetings are held at least quarterly, on a two-way basis.
- The reward system includes multiple methods of linking pay and performance, including gainsharing, linking reward to business performance, plus organizational, team and individual elements.

A final example is the AA. The AA uses a comprehensive objectives and competency-based approach to performance management. This is accompanied by a self-developmental, 180° feedback process for managers. The objectives used for performance management stem from the business planning process. They start with the managing director and are cascaded down through the three AA businesses. Their competencies have been developed within the organization and comprise capability, motivation, efficiency, effectiveness and presence. During the personal performance review, personal objectives, performance and competencies are assessed and integrated with forward business planning. People are also encouraged to make personal development plans.

The AA's personnel director, Peter Stemp, believes that the main benefits of the process is that it integrates objectives, focuses managers on critical success factors and encourages managers to 'think in the round' about their staff. The organization has, however, moved away from linking the entire process to pay, which was found to be overly complex. Now considerations of the market and individual results achieved drive base pay increases.

These four examples of performance management illustrate the trends and the diversity of approaches being adopted by organizations. There may be some similarities in the basic system – the plan, act, monitor and review model – but the process varies considerably.

Process is all-important in performance management and, as we have been stressing in respect of paying for contribution throughout this book, it is *how* it is done that counts, not *what* is done in terms of the review procedure or documentation. And how it is done is going to depend largely on the context and culture of the organization. In this, as in every aspect of managing and paying for contribution, best fit is more important than best practice. Moreover, performance management will not work unless all those involved (managers and the people they manage) want it to work. They have to believe in it and feel that it benefits them as well as the organization. There has to be an atmosphere of trust between those who set the agenda and review performance and those who, in a sense, are on the receiving end (although as the earlier examples indicate, it is far better to regard this as a partnership in which both parties involved give as well as receive).

Commitment, ownership and trust have to be developed by adopting a stakeholder approach in the development and operation of performance management. As Winstanley and Stuart-Smith[11] comment, 'When a stakeholder perspective is adopted in the design of performance management systems, it will offer a wider role to individuals as creators rather than victims of performance management: where consensus exists it can be built in, but where it does not, it is not silenced.' We review these issues of commitment and trust in more detail in the next chapter.

Diversity in the operation of performance management applies not only between organizations but also within organizations. The IPD research[12] established that the traditional monolithic, top-down, HR-controlled performance management 'system' is a thing of its past in an increasing number of businesses. Certain corporate principles and guidelines will be established but line managers are given freedom to apply those principles as they think fit in their part of the organization.

This was the approach adopted in the example of a new performance management system developed at a Scottish community NHS Trust. The system was designed to cover all employees and after a detailed review, including consultations with staff, a corporate framework was developed. This included common objectives, such as to enable genuine two-way communication for all staff, and common components, such as formal meetings 'at least once a year', to review past performance and set future objectives.

But in Phase 2 of the work, separate teams were set up to tailor the new system to suit the needs of their different staff groups: nurses, ancillary staff, and so on. This achieved a very high level of staff ownership and 'face validity' of the new system, which aided implementation. The paperwork of the system now looks different for the various staff groups, but the common principles and framework are adhered to. Pay is only linked to the outcomes of the process for the management group.

As Kessler and Purcell observe, performance management should be regarded as a natural process of management and, as such, it cannot be confined within a corporate strait-jacket. Yet balancing this fact-of-life with the requirement of objectivity and fairness in the management of performance is one of the major issues involved, especially when the process is linked to pay.

ISSUES IN PERFORMANCE MANAGEMENT

Performance management raises a number of practical issues, especially when it is associated with paying for contribution. The most important of these issues in our experience are:

- *Measurement*: how can performance measures be developed and applied accurately, (measuring what needs to be measured), fairly and consistently?
- *Rating*: what place does an overall rating have, if any, in performance management and how is this arrived at?
- *Reconciling* the tension between the developmental and financial reward aspects of performance management: is it possible to link

performance assessments, arrived at in performance reviews, to pay without damaging the scope for using reviews as a developmental and motivational device?

- *360° feedback*: is it possible, even desirable, to use 360° feedback data as a basis for contribution-related pay decisions?
- *Process*: what can be done about the fact that it is easy to design an elegant performance management system but much more difficult to get it work effectively in practice?
- *Ethical considerations*: what are the ethics involved in designing and operating performance management?

These issues are addressed in the next six sections of this chapter.

MEASUREMENT

The achievement of a totally accurate, fair and consistent approach to performance management is an impossible ideal. All that can be done is to work towards achieving these requirements steadily and purposefully. As with approaches to contribution-related pay, a policy of continuous improvement is necessary and as can be seen in Figure 7.2, generally being adopted. You may never win the race but it is well worth trying.

Vicky Wright, Group Managing Director of the Hay Group, emphasizes the importance of aligning performance management with business strategy. She believes that alignment matters because it reinforces clarity and direction, energizes and empowers employees and reinforces culture and values. As a method of alignment, Wright recognizes the merit of a balanced scorecard approach, considered in Chapter 3. She notes that it can be applied to teams and individuals throughout the organization. Although used as a simplifying framework to provide a clarity of direction, it involves the use of complex measures and information at all levels and requires careful introduction and rigour in its application.

Other measures of organizational performance which can be used as a focus for aligning individual and team goals and performance include economic value added (EVA), the European Foundation for Quality management (EFQM) criteria, and more traditional financial measures such as increases in shareholder value. At Boots the Chemists, for example, management objectives established during the performance management process, and the basis for subsequent pay decisions, are assessed against EVA criteria. Actions which result in a decrease in short-term performance levels for example, may be desirable as they create a longer term increase in EVA, and this should be recognized and rewarded.

At the individual level, traditional and well-established guidelines for delivering performance measures are that:

- measures should relate to results and increasingly also, as we saw in Chapter 4, to the 'hows' of observable behaviours;
- measures may be related to the achievement of targets or standards for quantity (output, sales etc) quality, productivity, timeliness and cost control;
- the results should be within the control of the individual and, so far as possible, should be agreed in the form of quantified targets;
- where targets cannot be quantified, agreement should be reached on the performance standards to be achieved, which should be expressed in terms such as: in this respect, performance is up to standard if the following things happen;
- behavioural requirements (competencies) should be defined and agreed, preferably with agreement as the evidence that will be used to assess their application, and behaviourally anchored scales used for rating purposes;
- data must be available as evidence when measuring performance.

RATING

Overall, rating is one of the more controversial aspects of performance management. It can be argued that if pay is going to be related to contribution, then there must be some way in which the level of contribution can be assessed and summarized. This implies a rating, which may then operate as part of a formula such as a pay matrix, used to indicate a particular percentage increase in pay for a particular performance or contribution rating. As we saw in Chapter 2, many of the initial movers into merit pay adopted a fairly narrow perspective, with performance management focused on the setting and appraisal of performance against specified individual objectives, with an apparently objective and simplistic final rating system. The IPD research found a five-point scale, from outstanding through effective to unsatisfactory, to be the most commonly employed.

Opposition to rating comes from practitioners such as Peter Stemp, Group HR Director of the Automobile Association who believes that 'it denigrates the whole performance management process'. And Gillian Henchley, Head of Personnel at the Victoria and Albert Museum would like to remove ratings, 'so that we can concentrate on development', and feels that, 'the performance process would be very much better if it did not feed into pay'. In the focus groups conducted by the IPD,[13] in its research with managers and staff in a wide variety of organizations, there was quite a lot of opposition to rating. A typical remark by a manager was; 'I don't like the rating. You can't sum up someone in a number.' Kessler and Purcell's research[14] demonstrated both management and staff opposition to summary ratings.

These comments highlight the fundamental problem of rating: that it is simplistic and can erode the value of the open and frank discussion that should have taken place in a performance review meeting if it becomes the sole focus of attention. Typically, ratings are made by managers as a top-down appraisal process. As a result, the concept of partnership and joint agreement – which is fundamental to effective performance management – can be damaged beyond repair.

However, managers often like to summarize their judgements, which they claim is what people do, even if there is no official rating scale. Without rating it is possible for manager and employee to retain different views on the overall level of performance, and particularly for difficult messages to be avoided for lower performers. A surprisingly common view in the IPD's employee focus groups was that managers avoided dealing with low performers, rather than that 'the blue-eyed boy' syndrome was at work in identifying high performers. And staff are not always against rating. As one member of an IPD focus group remarked: 'For me, the rating is something to work for.' Another took the following realistic view, 'I go in prepared to do battle. I always know what mark I want to get before I go in, so I go in and say exactly what I want to say.'

The most common argument for rating is the seemingly logical one that it is not possible to make performance or contribution pay decisions without it. Yet of the 43 per cent of the 562 organizations responding to the IPD survey with performance-related pay, a quarter did not use overall ratings in their performance management processes. These include Zeneca and Bristol Myers Squibb. We examine ways in which the use of ratings as part of a performance and development review process can be avoided in the next section.

RECONCILING DEVELOPMENTAL AND FINANCIAL REWARD TENSIONS

All the evidence from the extensive IPD research project[15] conducted in 1997–98 showed that, whether or not overall ratings were made, people involved in performance reviews directly linked to pay decisions focus on the financial reward rather than the developmental aspects of performance management. This was evident, for example, in many NHS Trusts in the early 1990s, once they made the decision to link performance management for senior managers to pay.

Yet the developmental aspects can make a fundamental impact on the improvement of levels of performance and competence in an organization, which is much less certain if total reliance is placed on pay as a motivator. Expectancy theory suggests that pay can only be an effective motivator if people feel they have the capability and skills to deliver the specified goals, on the basis of which performance-related payments are made. And research into goal-setting theories illustrates the powerful part which employee involvement in goal setting can play, in itself, in motivating high performance and irrespective of any link to pay.

Locke's[16] original research in a range of industries demonstrated that performance goals, accepted by the individual, seen as being under their control, and perceived as challenging but achievable, in themselves motivated higher performance than having no, or imposed goals. Numerof and Wexley[17] demonstrated that regular, participative, two-way objective setting and review correlated with high employee satisfaction and improved performance.

However, on the other hand, there is evidence that without the emphasis and discipline provided by a pay link, performance management simply may not happen at all. A US pharmaceutical company abandoned any official link between performance management and pay in 1996, in favour of market-related salaries and a totally developmentally focused performance management process. Yet in reality, on the ground, the link has been re-established in a number of functions, because high performing staff were unhappy at receiving the same size of pay increase as their colleagues and threatened to leave. In certain locations it has also been found that the incidence of performance review meetings has declined significantly since the pay link was removed.

The most common method of achieving this reconciliation is to separate the developmental and the pay review aspects of performance management, as is the case at Pfizer, Nuffield Hospitals and Bristol Myers Squibb. Saville and Holdsworth[18] found that 41 per cent of organizations now operate two schemes, compared to 22 per cent when they last surveyed the subject.

The development side of the process involves the provision of feedback on performance and competence levels with, frequently, a strong measure of self-assessment, so that the ensuing dialogue results in consensus on the key factors affecting performance which need to be addressed in a future development programme. This typically is set out in a personal development plan, in which how individuals can manage their own learning is defined, as well as the support they will receive from their manager and the organization to assist their development and improve their performance. The result of this review is an action plan which is in effect a working document owned by both the manager and the individual. This development review may take place six months away from the pay review, as in the pharmaceutical company described in Case Study 7.1. Or some organizations are emphasizing the separate and personal nature of the development review by getting managers to conduct it close to the anniversary of the individual joining the company or starting in their present job, while pay reviews take place on a common annual review date.

The pay review may involve a rating but, as at Book Club Associates (BCA), this could be an indication of the proposed size of the increase (eg above average, average, below average) rather than a rating of the individual's performance. The guidelines given to BCA managers were that:

An above average increase (say, 6 per cent to 10 per cent) could be given to people who were clearly and consistently performing at a high level and displaying more than the required level of competence. Evidence of high levels of performance and competence had to be available.

An average increase (say, 4 per cent to 5 per cent) could be given to people who were performing at an acceptable level and successfully applying the required level of competence. Evidence of performance and competence had to be provided.

A below average increase (say, up to 3 per cent) would be awarded to those for whom the evidence indicated that they were not reaching the standards required.

Managers were given an overall pay review budget which they had to work within. They were encouraged to identify high and low levels of performance and to reward or not reward items accordingly, but there was no forced distribution or quota. The other factors managers were asked to take into account were: the total rate of pay compared with those in similar jobs, any special market pressures, and the need either to accelerate pay progression for those who had fallen behind market without good reason, or to decelerate progression for those who appeared to be already well rewarded, or even over-rewarded.

Scottish & Newcastle Retail similarly specifies three different factors to managers and suggest they consider them on a 1–4 scale in respect of current performance, future potential and marketability. But there is no final rating or forced ratings distribution, but rather a fixed pay budget and suggested range between high and low performers. The Woolwich (see Case Study 4.1) has moved away from a uniform, corporate, points-based system with a fixed quota of performance ratings to a similar, more flexible approach. Staff are rated in respect of competencies and results, but the emphasis is on agreeing an appropriate rate of pay with the individual, given their performance and data on their market value. Only the total budget constrains the size of individual awards.

Two examples of companies which do not incorporate obligatory rating in their performance management and pay processes, as identified by the IPD research, are BP Exploration and Zeneca Pharmaceuticals. In another of the organizations the researchers contacted, managers propose where people should be placed in the pay range for their grade, taking into account their contribution relative to others in similar jobs and the relationship of their current pay to market rates. No ratings are made. The pay review is conducted separately from the performance and development review, which takes the form of a joint meeting.

But individuals are given the opportunity to discuss their manager's pay proposal before it is implemented. Managers explain the rationale which individuals can then question. Managers are expected to respond to and take account of the individual's comments. As Armstrong and Baron observe, based on the reactions of the managers and staff involved, 'This approach has much to commend it'.

Of course, separating performance and pay reviews does not completely solve the problem of the conflicting aspects of performance management. If pay is going to be related to performance and contribution, there is obviously a read-across between the two performance management processes. Indeed, if a broader perspective on performance is taken for pay purposes, including considerations of personal competence, the overlap is likely to be even greater (although as we saw in Chapter 4, some companies such as Scottish & Newcastle Retail avoid this by relating competence to base pay through job evaluation and grading, while linking performance results to the base pay and performance review process). Employees are not naïve. They know that this will happen and there is the danger of the separation of the processes being regarded as a sham. As Strebler[19] concludes from her research, employees may be suspicious of a pay link to competencies, but in many cases, 'it would be naïve to think that competencies will not, at some point, be linked to pay'.

There is no final solution to this problem except the drastic one, which, as we have seen, many organizations simply cannot afford, of abandoning pay for contribution. Separation will only work if the performance and development review focuses on the future rather than the past and concerns itself entirely with developmental matters. If managers can be encouraged and trusted to do this properly and if by doing so, a trusting relationship can be developed, then a separate pay review will often be accepted as such.

The other problem sometimes raised by managers concerning holding separate reviews is that it is time-consuming and bureaucratic. Computer company Digital has one common process but clearly distinct elements, resulting in employees being rated both in terms of current performance and career potential. But it does not seem to be asking too much of managers to meet their staff individually at least twice a year, and, indeed, the general trend in performance management is to hold much more regular meetings anyway.

A leading accountancy firm addresses the conundrum within its quarterly performance management process by emphasizing different aspects of the process in each meeting. All meetings involve a review of past performance and any recent development activity, the setting of future objectives, and actions to address development needs. However, the emphasis in the final quarter's review (immediately prior to the annual pay review) is on past performance and the pay link; the first quarter concentrates on objective setting; and the second and third quarters on development and career planning, and progress review and coaching. Employees are expected to play an active part in reviewing their own performance, and setting out their career aims and development needs.

360° FEEDBACK

360° feedback has been defined by Ward[20] as 'the systematic collection and feedback of performance data on an individual or group, derived from a number of stakeholders on their performance'. The stakeholders can be the individual's manager, the people that report to them, colleagues or peers and, sometimes, customers or clients. Feedback which originates solely from the individual's manager and those reporting to them is termed 180° feedback.

Towers Perrin surveyed 380 organizations across Europe in 1998[21] and this demonstrated the rapid uptake of the practice: 42 per cent of companies were already using it and 39 per cent considering its introduction. Only 17 per cent of the companies with 360° systems had been using them for longer than three years.

360° feedback can take many forms, from general opinions expressed on voicemail or e-mail, to much more structured information gathering. In large organizations, it often uses data from questionnaires that measure from different perspectives the behaviours of individuals against a list of competencies. Ratings and comments are given by the generators of the feedback against each heading, and in respect of the overall performance, strengths and weaknesses of the individual against the expected performance requirements and competence standards. We show an example of the feedback form from a large consultancy in Figure 7.6.

An important rationale for 360° feedback is that it lessens the danger of biased appraisals because reliance is not placed on one person's point of view and the prejudices that person might have. Individuals receive the feedback from people with different perspectives on their performance, which can provide them with a more rounded view of their strengths and weaknesses as perceived by others. It also encourages a two-way appraisal process, developing employee ownership and buy-in to that process. The commonest objectives reported for using a 360° system in the Towers Perrin study are shown in Figure 7.7. The emphasis is obviously very much on the developmental aspects, and in 55 per cent of these companies the process is voluntary.

Feedback form for: Feedback from:

Please circle your relationship to the individual being assessed:

Self   Manager   Peer [1]

Level: Tick/describe level displayed

Competency	Core	Contributing	Adding value	Strategic	Leading	N/A (Insufficient evidence)
Professional development						
Problem solving						
Business acumen						
Project management						
Client relationships						
Interpersonal & team skills						
Communication						
Developing new business						
Developing others						
Leadership & vision						

Comment box: provide here any comments that will help the individual to decide on development priorities. These comments will be presented verbatim[2].

Figure 7.6 *A consultancy's 360° feedback form*

Research conducted by SHL and the IPD[22] in 1997–98 showed that the most common use of 360° feedback was to help individual managers develop through various learning processes, including coaching. The least popular reason identified by SHL was to use the instrument for decision-making purposes, especially those concerned with determining pay awards.

The issue of whether or not 360° feedback should be used to inform pay decisions is one to which most employers have indicated an answer in the negative, although with greater experience of the process, the incidence of the linkage is slowly increasing (see Figure 7.7). In the

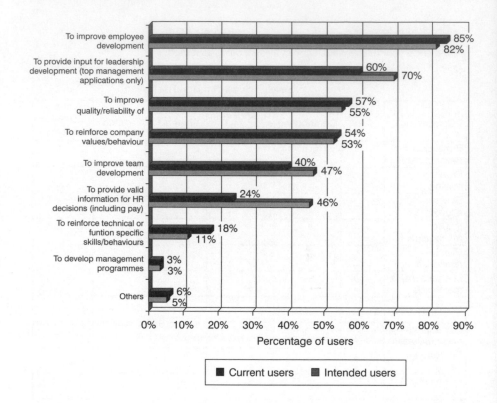

Figure 7.7 *Reasons for using 360° feedback by participants in the Tower Perrin study*

Towers Perrin study 9 per cent currently linked the process to pay and 14 per cent are intending to do so. Research conducted by Ashridge in 1996 established that a number of respondents who rejected a link with pay believed that participants would be so concerned about how their feedback would affect reward decisions that the development opportunities and the objectivity of the feedback would be lost. As one of these respondents commented: 'Direct links to pay could result in a lack of openness and honesty. This would destroy the value of the feedback.'

This belief was endorsed by respondents to a survey conducted by the Performance Management Group in 1997 (unpublished), which found that 81 per cent of the 22 organizations they contacted using 360° feedback disagreed or strongly disagreed that 'the natural use of 360° feedback is to provide a basis for reward'.

We generally support this view that 360° feedback is primarily a developmental not a pay process. However, the general principles underlying many 360° appraisal systems: that employees need to support that process, and be heavily involved in its operation; and that a fair, high quality and all-round performance discussion and summary are required, are also very relevant to the pay aspects of performance management, and are integral to the pay for contribution approach.

The key learning points drawn from Towers Perrin's research on 360° appraisal are just as relevant to the distinct, pay-linked aspects of performance management:

- tailor the design to the culture of the organization;
- be clear and open about the reasons for using the system;
- communicate and involve employees;
- test and validate the feedback instrument, and train staff in its use; and
- phase implementation and constantly review its effectiveness, making modifications as necessary on an ongoing basis.

Indeed, the irony for those companies who went down the highly mechanistic appraisal route to provide a link to pay is that it is only with the understanding and maturity of a truly two-way performance management process, with the involvement, trust and contribution of both parties, that effective linkages to pay can be achieved and supported.

PROCESS ISSUES

Whether or not performance management directly informs pay decisions, the key issue is how can it be made to work in practice. This is a process issue – what do people have to be able to do and to be willing to do, and how should they behave to gain the greatest benefit for themselves and the organization from performance management? The fundamental question about process is: how can managers and individuals become convinced that performance management is worthwhile?

Much of the research conducted by academics into performance appraisal or management, as on performance pay, has produced assertions that it cannot work. This is either because it is either fundamentally flawed as a concept, or because the people involved either do not want it to work, cannot be bothered to make it work, or are not capable of making it work.

Keith Grint of Templeton College makes a damning assessment: 'rarely in the history of management can a system have promised so much and delivered so little'.[23] Common criticisms made by academics include the points that:

- 'performance appraisal requires subtle psychological and social skills which may not be acquired by many managers'
  (Bowles and Coates)[24]
- 'appraisal is a system of bureaucratic or management control'
  (Townley)[25]
- 'appraisal enlists compliance' (Barlow)[26]
- 'appraisal is a form of control used to "police" performance'
  (Winstanley and Stuart-Smith)[27]
- 'the question is why this fundamental process (performance appraisal) is so rare and, when done at all, is frequently done badly.'
  (Furnham)[28]

These are formidable criticisms but they are mainly governed by an outdated concept of performance appraisal as a top-down, directive process which involved ratings, control, a complete pay focus and negative feedback. As we have seen, this was certainly not the practice revealed by the IPD research.[29] This established through attitude surveys and focus groups that: there was a lot of support as a concept for performance management from both managers and employees; that both parties got a lot out of the process; and that the opportunity for feedback and 'quality time' spent by managers and individuals in reviews meant that people believed that the time spent in such discussions was time well spent. In one sense the IPD research was biased, in that it was conducted in organizations with well-developed performance management processes which had spent a lot of time, money and effort in involving people, training them and communicating how they could benefit.

However, this evidence and our experience are that performance management can be effective as a means of developing and motivating people, as long as the three basic requirements of sustained and well-conceived involvement, training, and communication programmes are met. As with relating pay to performance and contribution, academics rarely offer alternative solutions, and the contention that managers and staff cannot manage or strongly influence performance in their organization; that they can afford in our increasingly competitive and cost-constrained world, not to maintain a focus on constantly improving performance, is one that senior management in most of the organizations we work in simply cannot accept.

ETHICAL CONSIDERATIONS

There are certain ethical considerations that need to be borne in mind in developing and implementing performance management, if it is successfully to meet the needs of individuals as well as the organization.

As suggested by Winstanley and Stuart-Smith,[30] there are four ethical principles which should be built into the performance management process. These are:

1. respect for the individual;
2. mutual respect;
3. transparency of decision-making; and
4. procedural fairness.

The fourth principle was defined as procedural justice by Leventhal,[31] the rules of which as applied to performance management and pay decisions are:

- *Consistency*: the allocation process should be consistent between people and over time.
- *Bias suppression*: personal (concealed) self-interest and blind adherence to narrow pre-conceptions should be excluded at all costs from the allocation process.
- *Accuracy*: it is necessary to base the allocation process on as much good information and informed opinion as possible.
- *Correctability*: opportunities must exist to modify and reverse decisions made at various points in the allocation process.
- *Representativeness*: all phases of the allocation process should reflect the basic concerns, values and outlook of important sub-groups in the population of individuals affected by the process.

- *Ethical behaviour*: procedures must be compatible with fundamental morals and values; respectful and trustworthy treatment from authorities must be seen as fair.

These rules are demanding and few organizations will be able to live up to the high standards they set out. But it is worth trying. Contribution pay as well as performance management will be more effective if the attempt is made and a climate of trust developed, as we discuss in the next chapter.

SUMMARY

- Performance management is about improving and developing performance, not just linking pay and performance.
- The four main purposes of performance management are 1) managing expectations; 2) acting as an integrating force; 3) a means of motivating; and 4) a developmental and improvement process.
- Process is all important in performance management, as it is when making the linkages between pay and contribution – it is *how* it is done that counts.
- As with other aspects of paying for contribution, the whole performance management process will not work unless those involved want it to work, and are involved and committed to making it work.
- Commitment, ownership and trust in the process have to be developed by adopting a stakeholder approach.
- The achievement of a totally accurate, far and consistent approach to performance management is an impossible ideal. As with contribution-related pay, organizations are increasingly adopting clearer, more focused and realistic aims, as well as more varied and flexible processes for performance management and any pay linkages.
- It is important to align performance management with business strategy.
- Effective performance measurement is increasingly being related to results achieved and observable behaviours, the combination at the heart of the pay for contribution approach.
- Rating can be regarded as an essential part of performance management, particularly if it is linked to pay. But many people

object to it on the grounds that it erodes the value of the full and open discussions that are an essential part of performance reviews. An open and frank, two-way performance discussion, supported by a more flexible pay linkage, managed at the local level, appears to be the best means of summarizing performance and creating an effective link to pay.

- It is increasingly common practice to separate the developmental and pay review aspects of performance management, so that the former is not dominated by concerns about pay.
- 360° feedback is an increasingly popular part of performance management, and is primarily used for developmental purposes. It is much less frequently associated with pay, although this may change as organizations become more experienced with it.
- Process issues are vitally important and revolve around the question: how can managers and individuals be convinced that performance management is worthwhile? They *can* be convinced through comprehensive involvement in designing the scheme, training and communications.
- There are four ethical considerations in developing and applying performance management systems: 1) respect for the individual; 2) mutual respect; 3) transparency of decision-making; and 4) procedural fairness.

CASE STUDY 7.1

Introducing performance management and pay review processes at a UK pharmaceutical research institute

This case study describes the experiences of the UK research operation of an international pharmaceutical company. It employs approximately 80 staff in North West England. They are engaged in a variety of product development and testing activities, with a predominance of research and technical staff, but also administrative support, warehousing and packaging employees.

Over the past three years, the Institute has reviewed and instigated a series of changes to their pay and performance management arrangements, which illustrate many of the themes described in this book: the need to replace and modify out-of-date and inflexible schemes; the design of new pay and performance management systems, within a framework of the company's worldwide business goals and HR approach, but tailored to their own specific requirements; and achieving an appropriate balance in performance management between the formal and the informal, the objective and the subjective, the pay review and the developmental aspects of the process.

THE NEED TO CHANGE

During 1996, at the behest of the Site Director, the Institute carried out an in-depth review of their existing pay and performance management arrangements, incorporating discussions with line managers, group meetings with all staff in focus groups, and a review of external industry practices and trends.

The review highlighted that a set of pay and performance management systems originally developed in the 1970s, and driven primarily by the needs of the adjacent pharmaceutical manufacturing site, were not meeting the business or employees requirements of a high quality and specialist pharmaceutical development operation. The review found the general package of pay, benefits and conditions to be good by external standards. Staff were highly motivated, enjoyed their work and respected and appreciated the company as an employer.

However, significant changes in the structure and work of the site had rendered a number of aspects of the existing approaches to pay and performance management as ineffective, even redundant. In particular:

- Job descriptions were largely out-of-date, as were the original grading descriptions which were used to place staff jobs in a particular pay range; there was a strong perception amongst staff that it was 'impossible to get an upgrade' and that cost control objectives were predominant (even though recent annual increases had been ahead of general UK industry), while separate systems for scientific, technical and manual staff encouraged perceptions of different and inconsistent standards being applied.
- Base pay review mechanisms were too inflexible to cope with external market rates of increase for key specialists; a network of pay supplements had been used, reasonably effectively, to plug the competitive shortfall but as these multiplied, they encouraged internal perceptions of inequity.
- The annual pay review and related performance appraisal process came in for particular criticism from both staff and managers.

The existing appraisal system focused on the setting and achievement of annual job objectives. It involved the award of a final rating on a five-category scale which was linked to incremental pay increases up the pay ranges, alongside of a general pay award. Criticisms voiced by staff included:

- the lack of sufficient reward for high performance;
- the 'school report', 'box ticking' nature of the appraisal which tended to 'focus on the negative' and on the pay review, ignoring personal growth and development;
- the inflexible nature of the performance and pay reviews, which 'doesn't address what you do for the rest of the year', and in which pay increases were perceived as being determined in advance, making the process 'something of a charade'.

CHANGES TO PAY AND PERFORMANCE MANAGEMENT

Aims

The annual merit review system and appraisal process had been found wanting in other parts of the company and in 1997 a new approach was launched in the United States. It was intended to be a two way, continuous performance management system, totally removed from pay reviews. But as the UK Institute's Director explained to us, while this provided useful ideas and information, and while the changes in the United Kingdom needed to support the global business objectives of productivity, growth and creating a dynamic and high performing culture, 'the approach here needed to reflect the specific work and character of the site'. As well as general updating and creating improved business alignment, the local changes were, therefore, driven by the need to do the following:

- increase the flexibility to relate rewards to personal achievement and development;
- achieve and maintain market competitiveness in all areas, so as to attract and retain high quality, committed staff;
- provide an improved framework for, and practical management of, pay and performance.

Pay bands

The first set of changes was implemented, following six months of design and preparatory work, at the start of 1998. These addressed the grading

Job/Role Title: Support Technician	Date: January 1998

Reports to: Manager, Quality Control

Main purpose of role:
To provide general laboratory support to technicians in the QA/QC department

Key accountabilities/tasks:
- To ensure all glassware for laboratories is washed and sterilised
- To dispose of all biological waste in line with safety standards
- To prepare nutrient as required
- To provide general support to laboratory staff as required

Factor	Level	Specific job components/examples
Knowledge	A Basic numeracy and literacy required. No prior experience or qualifications.	■ Awareness of basic safety requirements due to nature of materials being handled. ■ Ability to use PC to record tasks. ■ Basic knowledge of limited range of non-complex laboratory
Freedom of action	A Works within standard procedures and guidelines with work closely reviewed and with no decision-making reqirement. Works under close supervision.	■ Jobholder expected to be proactive and inform supervisior when set work has been completed.
Supervision/planning/ organisation	A Responsible for carrying out own work. No supervisory responsibilities.	■ Conducting established day to day routines in cleaning of glassware. ■ Providing ad-hoc support to laboratories as planned on a day to day basis by the Team Manager.
Job complexity and problem solving	A Generally repetitive and well-defined tasks, following clear routines/procedures.	■ Standard non-complex day to day tasks – washing of laboratory equipment.
Level of business interaction	A Work primarily requires routine contacts within immediate work unit. Few external contacts expected.	■ As work involves interacting with other laboratory staff, the job-holder is required to exchange basic information and check on understanding of requests for assistance for assistance/support.

Figure 7.8 *Example of a role profile*

and pay competitiveness issues. All staff were moved into a new, single structure of six broad pay bands. New role profiles and band descriptions were drafted, on the basis of interviews with all staff, using five criteria. These covered the essential skills and knowledge required in the Institute and a variety of role dimensions, such as business interaction and freedom of action. Figure 7.8 shows an example of a role profile.

Staff are positioned at an appropriate and regularly reviewed market point in each range, and any shortfalls revealed by market data are addressed outside of the annual pay review. Market supplements have been withdrawn and incorporated in base pay.

Performance management and pay review

During 1998, on this solid foundation, the pay and performance management of individuals were then addressed. The solution arrived at, developed by a line staff and HR working group, was two separate processes under an overall umbrella of 'Performance Partnerships' (see Figure 7.9). Both are intended to support an ongoing, continuous, non-bureaucratic and two-way process of performance management.

Performance review, which concludes its annual cycle with a November meeting between an employee and their immediate manager, focuses on

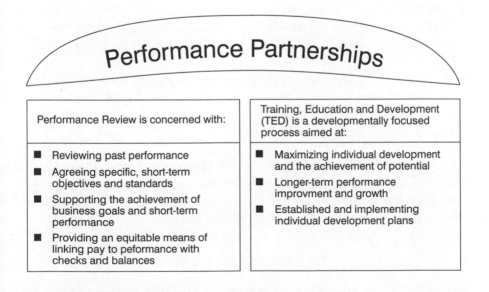

Figure 7.9 *The two components of performance management*

the short-term, annual objective setting and review of achievements, and inputs into the annual pay review decision. It also includes consideration of the level of competence displayed. The Training, Education and Development (TED) process is concerned with both short and long-term staff development required to support the achievement of business and personal goals. As the Institute's Director explained,

> In practice both processes will overlap to a degree, but we felt having two processes was vital to ensure that both the future developmental and pay review aspects of performance management are given due attention. Keeping the paperwork light and flexible makes this practically feasible.

The performance and pay review aspects of the systems are distinguished by the lack of any summary ratings 'boxes', despite the scientific liking for structure and objectivity. As the Director explained, 'Performance management is not like a scientific experiment which replicates itself every time.' The requirement instead for an open, joint discussion and summary description of the level of performance, 'ensures that we take account of the full range of a person's performance and contribution, avoids an over-simplistic "school report" approach, and emphasizes the quality of the performance discussion, rather than the size of the pay increase'. Third party input from internal and external customers, agreed in advance by the employee and their manager, is provided into these discussions.

On the basis of these performance summaries, managers recommend an appropriate rate of increase for each member of staff, taking account of:

- the individual's level of contribution, in respect of their performance against objectives and the level of competence displayed;
- the development and growth of the individual;
- the relative performance of other staff.

These increases are monitored by the HR Department for consistency and finally reviewed by a meeting in December of all department managers, who again check for consistency in the pay recommendations made and relative to the overall level of budgeted pay increase.

LEARNING POINTS

The Institute will be making a full review of the effectiveness of the new Performance Partnerships approach after a full year's operation in 2000, but the initial reactions from staff have been very positive. The absence of ratings boxes has been received particularly well, and a similar approach has been operating effectively for a longer period at another of the company's locations nearby.

A key and distinguishing feature of the Institute changes, according to its Director, has been the high level of staff involvement in the process of making changes. All staff were initially consulted and have had regular briefings on the progress of the work. Staff from different departments were involved on the design working group and, significantly, it was they who briefed their colleagues in November 1998. As he told us, 'involving them in the process has been the basis for achieving employee understanding and support'.

A second important aspect of the changes has been 'building quality up front into these processes', rather than trying to impose it, after-the-event, with rigid procedures and controls. During 1998 all staff have had a detailed briefing and practice sessions on objective setting, and those managers reviewing performance have been provided with additional support on reviewing and summarizing performance. In early 1999, sessions on identifying the full range of development opportunities, and ongoing coaching will be run. The HR Department will continue to support the process by providing this training, addressing commonly identified development needs, and will also monitor for consistency, for example in terms of the distribution of increases between males and females. But the emphasis at the Institute, as in their successful and expanding development activity, is very much on a practical and flexible, if high quality, approach to pay and performance management.

CASE STUDY 7.2

Performance management at Severn Trent Water

BACKGROUND

Severn Trent covers most of middle England and the West Country down to Bristol. It is claimed that it delivers the highest quality water in the UK. A strategy differentiator is 'to make the best use of its assets'.

The number of employees is currently 5,700, which represents a decline from 11,000 in 1980. A complete restructuring took place in 1997, changing from a regionalized to process-based organization.

THE PREVIOUS SCHEME

The Managers Performance Review and Development Scheme (PRD), described below, was introduced in 1997 for their 250 managers. It replaced a three-year-old scheme, which was based on job performance in general, the achievement of specific personal objectives, and meeting standards for common responsibilities and values. Some of the features of the former scheme have been retained.

The main drawbacks to the existing scheme were that:

- It used relatively subjective ratings as a basis for pay decisions – this led to a marked skew towards high ratings, and high performance payouts in the form of individual bonus awards;
- the developmental aspect was not as strong as it should have been, with a focus on the past performance review and pay aspect.

The new process therefore places greater emphasis on competencies and employee development.

The new scheme took nine months to develop, involving a lot of iteration. A project team consisting of a senior managers and personnel specialists was used, and focus group discussions were held with the managers involved.

THE MANAGERS PERFORMANCE REVIEW AND DEVELOPMENT SCHEME (PRD)

The Severn Trent Water guide to the scheme defines its purpose as follows:

> The PRD process is designed to provide an integrated approach to managing performance – by giving direction, targets, feedback and ensuring appropriate individual and team development. It also enables a link to be made between performance and rewards.

Aims

The aims of the scheme, defined by Paul Stephenson, Head of HR, are as follows:

- to provide a way of steering and monitoring performance;
- to focus on competency-based achievement, in order to understand how competency levels relate to business needs;
- to give us a more objective link to the bonus elements of remuneration.

The basic process

The process consists of three stages as illustrated in Figure 7.10. The three stages involve:

- performance planning – which focuses on what is to be achieved over the next twelve months;
- development review – which also supports the performance planning stage by identifying key development needs and solutions;
- performance review – which focuses on what has been achieved over the last twelve months.

Elements within the process

There are four elements within this process, against which managers are assessed. All of these are fundamental to each stage of the process:

- strategic contribution – what managers need to do in terms of achievement of targets relevant to strategic issues, listed in the ten-point business plan;
- role performance – what managers need to do in terms of maintaining and continually improving their core role;
- common responsibilities and behaviours – these apply to all employees and are a measure of behaviour in accordance with company values;
- competency assessment – what managers need to do in terms of developing their underlying skills and knowledge; this assessment is for development purposes only.

Time-scales

The PRD annual cycle operates as shown in Table 7.1.

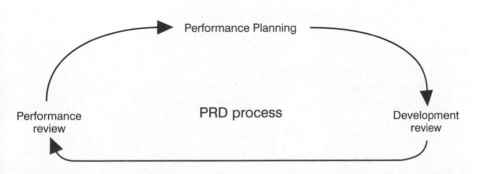

Figure 7.10   *The three stages of the PRD process*

Table 7.1 *The PRD annual cycle*

Timing	Stages	Elements
February/ March	Performance planning	• Agree performance targets for strategic contribution • Determine the priorities for role performance • Identify the key competencies which are required to fulfil strategic contribution and role performance • Agree the competency requirement for the role (role requirement)
June/ July	Development review	• Assessment of role holder against competency framework, generic to all management roles • Prioritization of development areas based on the key competencies required to fulfil strategic contribution and role performance • Review of performance against targets (strategic contribution)
February/ March	Performance review	• Review of role performance • Assessment of competence regarding Common responsibilities and behaviours • Recommendation for bonus awards

The competency framework

Competencies at Severn Trent are defined as follows:

> Competencies are not discrete activities but rather groupings of knowledge, skills and behaviours which may well be required, in whole or in part, within a variety of managerial situations. Consequently, similar behaviours may well be demonstrated within a number of competency areas.

The level of each particular competency anticipated for the year ahead is discussed, agreed at the performance planning stage and defined as low/ medium/high.

The competencies in Severn Trent's framework are:

- generates change
- ensures consistency;
- creates structure;
- ensures communication;
- commercial awareness;
- remains informed;
- motivates others;
- builds relationships;
- manages performance;

- delivers results;
- ensures quality;
- technical contribution.

Each competency is defined and illustrated by positive and negative behavioural examples.

Common responsibilities and behaviours

These define corporate values with regard to the company, customers, individual behaviour, and the environment. Common behaviours are defined under such headings as teamwork, integrity, openness, care, respect, drive, and competence.

Documentation

The PRD paperwork includes sections for:

- strategic contribution – recording, assessing and rating the role holder's achievement of targets relevant to strategic issues listed in the ten point business plan;
- role performance – an overall assessment and rating of performance against the core elements of the role;
- common responsibilities and behaviours – an overall assessment and rating of performance in these areas;
- competency assessment – comments and ratings against the specified role requirements for each competency heading – ratings are given on the following scale relative to the level of competence required: 1 (fails to achieve the required standard), 3 (achieves the required standard) and 5 (exceeds the required standard;
- personal development – a record of the outcomes of the development review meeting.
- a summary of the performance review – by the manager;
- a final assessment and rating – under three main headings (targets, role performance and common responsibilities and behaviours).

Rating scales

These are as follows:

- *Strategic contribution* – scored on a 1 to 10 rating
  10 to 9 Full/over achievement of targets
  8 to 6 Majority of targets achieved

5 to 2 Partial achievement
0 to 1 Failure to achieve
- *Role performance* – scored on a 1 to 10 rating
  10 to 9 Exceptional performance
  8 to 6 Clearly competent
  5 to 2 Partial competence
  0 to 1 Unsatisfactory performance
- *Common responsibilities and behaviours* – scored on a 1 to 10 rating scale:
  10 to 9 Exceptional performance
  8 to 6 Clearly competent
  5 to 2 Partial competence
  0 to 1 Unsatisfactory performance

Weighting

Ratings are weighted – 20 per cent for common responsibilities and 80 per cent distributed between strategic targets and role performance (eg 50/30, respectively). The weightings depend on the extent to which performance can be measured quantitatively on the basis of achievement against targets or qualitatively by reference to overall role performance (ie standards). Severn Trent allows flexibility in tailoring the balance of weighting in the determination of the final rating, which affects each manager's bonus, and provides an indicator of overall management performance.

LEARNING POINTS

Key points to be drawn out from Severn Trent's experience in reforming their performance management process are as follows:

- The changes have been evolutionary and taken time, not been rushed in as a 'quick fix'. Many features of the earlier performance management process, such as the link to pay via cash bonuses rather than restricted base pay increases, have been retained. The improvements were made after a detailed investigative and redesign process, taking nine months, and importantly, involving consultation with the managers covered.
- An important aspect of the changes has been the move to consider three aspects of performance. As well as results and the achievement of objectives, competencies and responsibilities and behaviours are also considered, to paint a broader picture of all-round contribution.

- The other significant change has been the introduction of separate development reviews. As in Case Study 7.1, without this separation the pay-linked aspect of the process became dominant, and the important developmental aspects received insufficient emphasis.
- While the process retains elements of rating and precision, there is also flexibility in the setting of standards and weighting of scores to ensure that the process does not become just a points scoring exercise, but reflects the day-to-day realities of performance in the organization.

NOTES

1. Kessler, I and Purcell, J (1992) Performance related pay: objectives and application, *Human Resource Management Journal*, 2 (3), Spring
2. V. Wright speaking at a seminar on Performance Management, IPD National Conference, Harrogate 1998.
3. Quoted in Robinson, J (1998) Government may ditch Civil Service merit pay, *Personnel Today*, 5 November
4. Armstrong, M and Murlis, H (1998) *Reward Management,* 4th edn, Kogan Page, London
5. Armstrong, M and Baron, A (1998) *Performance Management: The new realities*, IPD, London
6. Armstrong and Baron, op. cit.
7. Towers Perrin (1997) *Learning From the Past: Changing for the Future*, research report, available from Towers Perrin London, March
8. Saville and Holdsworth (1998) study referred to in Industrial Relations Services, Appraisals are failing to motivate, *Employment Trends*, **650**, February
9. Fletcher, C (1993) *Appraisal: Routes to improved performance*, Institute of Personnel and Development, London
10. Armstrong and Baron, op. cit.
11. Winstanley, D and Stuart-Smith, K (1996) Policing performance: the ethics of performance management, *Personnel Review*, 25 (6)
12. Armstrong and Baron, op. cit.
13. Armstrong and Baron, op. cit.
14. Kessler and Purcell, op. cit.
15. Armstrong and Baron, op. cit.
16. Locke, GP and Latham, G (1979) Goal setting: a motivational technique that works, *Organization Dynamic,* **8**
17. Nemerof, WF and Wexley, KN, referred to in Latham, G and Wexley, KN (1989) *Improving Productivity Through Performance Appraisal,* Addison-Wesley, Reading, Mass
18. Saville and Holdsworth, op. cit.
19. Strebler, M (1997) *Skills Competencies and Gender: Issues for pay and training*, Report No 333, Institute of Employment Studies, London
20. Ward, P (1997) *360° Feedback*, IPD, London
21. Towers Perrin (1998) *360° Feedback*, Research Report, Towers Perrin, London
22. Saville and Holdsworth, op. cit.
23. Grint, K (1993) What is wrong with performance appraisal? A critique and a suggestion, *Human Resource Management Journal*, Spring

24. Bowles ML and Coates, G (1993) Image and substance: the management of performance as rhetoric or reality?', *Personnel Review,* **22** (2)
25. Townley, B (1993) Performance appraisal and the emergence of management, *Journal of Management Studies*, March
26. Barlow, G (1989) Deficiencies and the perpetration of power: latent functions in performance appraisal, *Journal of Management Studies*, September
27. Winstanley and Stuart-Smith, op. cit.
28. Furnham, A (1996) Starved of feedback, *The Independent*, 5 December
29. Armstrong and Baron, op. cit.
30. Winstanley and Stuart-Smith, op. cit.
31. Leventhal, GS (1980) What should be done about equity theory, in *Social Exchange*, ed G K Georges, Plenum, New York

8

Communications, involvement and trust: the basis for successful pay for contribution

The only way for Britain to be at the forefront of the new, knowledge-based economies is by modern policies for employee participation and education. Employee commitment is a vital strength for companies competing in the global economy.

(Gordon Brown, Chancellor of the Exchequer)[1]

The pay for-performance era is ending: the involvement/participation era is starting'

(Marc Thompson, Templeton College)[2]

Employees aren't getting the information, don't understand or trust decisions on pay. Management goes overboard on financial and operating results, but is hesitant to discuss pay.

(Manager, UK service company)[3]

THE SIGNIFICANCE OF COMMUNICATIONS, INVOLVEMENT AND TRUST

With all the focus on performance-driven and business-aligned reward strategies in recent years, the vital importance of employee's own perceptions and motivations, the basis for their contribution to the success of the enterprise, has tended to be under-emphasized. Yet throughout this book we have seen, in the practical case material and in the research studies, that effective two-way communications regarding pay practices, and employee understanding and involvement in the design and ongoing operation of these practices are essential, if they are to succeed. The traditional, individual performance-related pay approach often failed because it was imposed in a top-down, quick-fix manner and paid only limited attention to developing employee understanding and buy-in. In essence, staff often did not trust the approach. Paying for contribution is an approach which recognizes these shortcomings.

Reward systems will only work well if a climate of trust exists in the organization. Indeed, it has been pointed out by Cox and Purcell[4] that: 'As far as trust is concerned, thwarted expectations and complaints of unfairness pervade, which results in the pay system being viewed as a source of distrust between management and employee.'

Reward policies and practices can have a negative effect on commitment and motivation unless employees trust management to act fairly, equitably and consistently in the administration of pay. Performance-related pay has had a bad press in many quarters because it is often managed and communicated badly. However, as we have seen, there seems to be a strong measure of agreement to the principle that it is right and equitable to provide higher rewards to those who make greater contributions (although some academics and trade unionists would disagree with this proposition). It is not the principle of paying for contribution that is wrong – it is the way it is often applied amidst a climate of mistrust.

The achievement of a high trust climate is an important element in the development of pay-for-contribution policies and practices. This chapter is therefore mainly concerned with the creation of trust between management and employees, and the part which pay practices and trust in them plays in supporting a positive psychological contract, the basis for employee commitment and contribution. This discussion takes place against the background of an overview of the current shortcomings in the level of employee communications and involvement in pay matters; an explanation of the meaning of trust; and the part played by the principles and perceptions of equity, fairness, and justice in creating effective reward practices and a positive employment relationship.

We then consider the broad employment relationship within which pay schemes operate, and the controversy over the current state of the psychological contract, in terms of just how committed employees are to contributing to business success. We conclude that HR and pay practices interact with a positive psychological contract in a mutually reinforcing relationship. The chapter ends with practical guidance on how to assess the employment relationship in your organization, and how to communicate with and involve employees in a genuine pay for contribution approach, to develop employee trust and commitment.

Although we concentrate in this chapter on trust in relation to pay and reward we would emphasize that trust goes much further than this. The Institute of Personnel and Development suggested in its statement *People Make the Difference*[5] that building trust is the only basis upon which commitment can be generated. The IPD commented that: 'In too many organizations inconsistency between what is said and what is done undermines trust, generates employee cynicism and provides evidence of contradictions in management thinking.'

It has also been suggested by Thompson[6] that trust should be regarded as social capital. He sees trust as a 'unique human resource capability that helps the organization fulfil its competitive advantage' – a core competency that leads to high business performance. Thus there is a business need to develop a climate of trust, as there is a business need to introduce effective pay-for-contribution processes which are built on trust, and supporting a positive psychological contract and employment relationship in the organization.

As we shall see, open, two-way communications and high employee involvement, designed to develop trust in pay, are perhaps the most critical ingredient in a successful pay for contributing approach. It is the feature which distinguishes it most clearly from the earlier and more narrowly focused attempts at performance pay.

COMMUNICATIONS AND INVOLVEMENT: THE CURRENT SITUATION

THE BUSINESS CASE

As we enter the new millennium, one might think in these enlightened times of employee empowerment, management by walking around, open book leadership, focus groups and quality circles, that we would need to spend very little time explaining and justifying the benefits and processes of employee communications and involvement in regard to pay issues. As Martin Neville at Eli Lilly told us in respect of their gain-share plan (see Case Study 6.1), 'nobody has ever told us we are over-communicating', and he emphasized the criticality of the senior management briefings, employee-designed performance updates, performance discussion groups and so on in the success of that scheme. We have referred already in this book to the research support for his views, with Bowey,[7] for example, demonstrating the correlation between the levels of employee communications and involvement, and resulting positive employee perceptions, and the success of performance pay schemes.

Indeed, there is an increasing body of evidence as to the business benefits of employee involvement more generally. A University of California study,[8] for example, rated 216 companies according to their level of staff participation. It found better financial performance in companies with high levels of employee involvement (EI). In 1996 the average return on investment was 21 per cent amongst high users of EI programmes, and 14 per cent amongst low users. The Workplace Employee Relations Survey,[9] a major study of attitudes amongst 30,000 employees in 300 UK organizations, reported a widespread belief that, 'employee involvement methods will engender employee commitment and promote high performance.' It found that, 'Workplaces with a high number of employee involvement schemes were substantially more likely to report high productivity growth'.

A government White Paper[10] cites the concrete benefits of EI, including the savings of £2 million resulting from the introduction of team working at an electrical goods factory and a 30 per cent increase in productivity as a result of setting up self-managed teams in an automotive company. In respect of pay communications and involvement, a Towers Perrin study[11] found some significant differences between the financial performance of companies over the prior three years related

to the openness of the pay communications climate. The most financially successful companies were more likely to communicate pay
information and keep employees informed on pay matters, as well as
providing training to first-line supervisors on pay communications and
performance appraisals (see Figure 8.1).

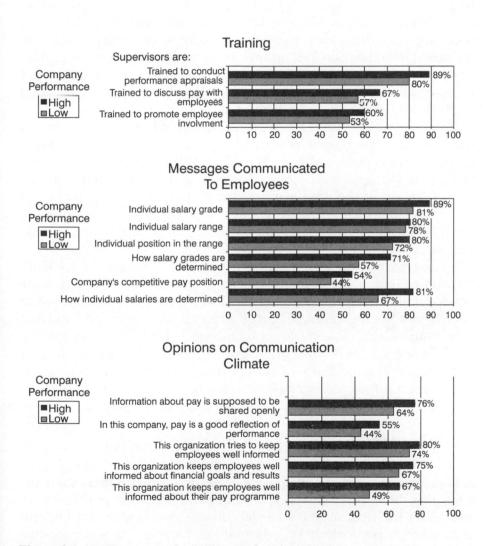

Figure 8.1 *Differences in the training and communications on pay matters
between the highest and lowest performers among 270 companies*
Source: Towers Perrin

GROWTH IN COMMUNICATIONS AND INVOLVEMENT PRACTICES

The spread of communications and employee involvement practices during the 1990s would appear to indicate that employers recognize this business case already, without the requirement for encouragement from European Union directives. The Workplace Employee Relations Survey[12] observes that, 'these clusters of new workplace practices might be construed as a new model of direct employee involvement.' According to Industry Minister Ian McCartner speaking in late 1998, 'Leading-edge firms are pursuing a culture of partnership.' An Industrial Relations Services survey[13] of 26 organizations found a widespread incidence of employee communications, participation and representation schemes (see Table 8.1), with company journals, team briefings and meetings and collective bargaining all predominant.

Marchington's research for the Department of Employment[14] found that 75 per cent of companies were using six or more methods and that 80 per cent of these had been introduced during the previous five years. The Workplace Employee Relations Survey revealed a similar rate of growth, if slightly lower incidence, in 'new' management and employee involvement schemes across a wider sample of small, medium and large enterprises (see Table 8.2), as the proportion of trade unionized workplaces had declined.

Turning specifically to pay and reward, as the plethora of booklets, bulletin boards, and benefits statements now available in any large employer illustrates, there has been a similar growth in the volume and vehicles of communications. Figure 8.2 reveals the pay information that is communicated to employees amongst the 270 organizations surveyed by Towers Perrin,[15] and Figure 8.3 shows the most frequently used media. The incidence of communications on reward issues was higher amongst service companies and in larger organizations.

ARE EMPLOYEES REALLY INVOLVED?

Yet underneath all of this impressive data, there remains more than just a nagging doubt that the widespread incidence of these practices does not reflect the real, shop-floor level of employee understanding and involvement, particularly on pay matters. During our work for this book, one senior manager told us, 'We still tend to communicate at and down to people, not with them.' Research supports the viewpoint that it tends to be 'top-down' and one-way communication vehicles that

Table 8.1 *Types of communications and employee involvement activities in 26 UK organizations*

Organization/sector (employee numbers)	Company journal	Employee reports	Team briefings	Video presentations	Attitude surveys	Team meetings	Customer care programme	Quality circles	Suggestion schemes	Total quality management	Collective bargaining	Joint consultative committee	Works council
Chemicals													
Cussons UK (340)	✓	✓	✓	✗	✓	✓	✗	✗	✗	✓	✓	✓	✓
Hampshire Chemical (68)	✗	✓	✓	✗	✗	✓	✗	✗	✗	✓	✓	✗	✗
Morton International (157)	✗	✓	✓	✗	✓	✓	✓	✗	✗	✓	✓	✗	✓
Electricity, Gas and Water													
Portsmouth Water (287)	✓	✗	✗	✗	✗	✗	✗	✗	✗	✗	✓	✓	✗
Engineering and Metals													
BICC Cables, Blackley (350)	✓	✓	✗	✗	✗	✓	✗	✗	✗	✗	✓	✓	✓
BICC Cables, Whiston (180)	✓	✓	✗	✗	✗	✗	✗	✗	✗	✗	✓	✓	✓
Continental Can (600)	✓	✓	✓	✗	✗	✗	✗	✗	✗	✗	✓	✓	✓
GEC Alsthom Large Generators (600)	✓	✗	✗	✗	✗	✓	✗	✗	✗	✗	✓	✓	✓
Finance													
DAS Legal Expenses Insurance (240)	✗	✓	✓	✓	✗	✗	✓	✗	✗	✗	✓	✗	✗
Nationwide Building Society (11,000)	✓	✓	✗	✗	✓	✓	✗	✗	✓	✗	✗	✓	✗
Royal Insurance (6,500)	✓	✓	✓	✓	✓	✓	✗	✗	✓	✗	✓	✓	✗
Food, Drink and Tobacco													
Schwans Europe (600)	✓	✗	✓	✗	✗	✓	✗	✗	✗	✗	✗	✗	✗
Tinsley Foods (1,500)	✓	✓	✓	✗	✓	✓	✗	✗	✗	✗	✓	✗	✗
General Manufacturing													
Levington Horticulture (300)	✓	✗	✓	✗	✗	✓	✗	✗	✗	✓	✓	✗	✗
Luxfer Gas Cylinders (250)	✓	✓	✓	✗	✗	✓	✓	✗	✗	✗	✓	✓	✗
Marley Building Materials (1,800)	✓	✓	✓	✗	✓	✓	✗	✗	✓	✓	✓	✓	✓
Mizuno Corporation UK (80)	✓	✓	✓	✓	✗	✓	✗	✗	✗	✗	✗	✓	✗
Rotunda (411)	✗	✓	✓	✓	✓	✓	✗	✗	✗	✓	✓	✗	✗
General Services													
Coral (4,200)	✓	✗	✓	✓	✓	✓	✓	✗	✗	✗	✓	✓	✗
Finning (850)	✓	✗	✗	✗	✓	✗	✗	✗	✓	✓	✓	✓	✗
Granada UK Rental and Retail (8,000)	✓	✓	✓	✓	✓	✓	✓	✗	✓	✗	✓	✓	✗
Public Services													
Basildon & Thurrock General Hospitals NHS Trust (2,200)	✓	✗	✓	✗	✓	✓	✓	✗	✗	✗	✓	✗	✓
E, N & W Hertfordshire Heath Authorities (280)	✓	✗	✓	✗	✓	✓	✓	✗	✓	✓	✓	✓	✓
Hinchingbrooke Health Care NHS Trust (2,184)	✓	✓	✓	✗	✓	✓	✗	✗	✓	✗	✓	✓	✓
Southend Health Care NHS Trust (2,700)	✓	✓	✓	✗	✓	✓	✗	✗	✓	✓	✗	✓	✗
Retail and Wholesale													
Littlewoods Stores (10,000)	✗	✓	✓	✗	✓	✓	✗	✗	✓	✗	✓	✗	✓

Source: IRS

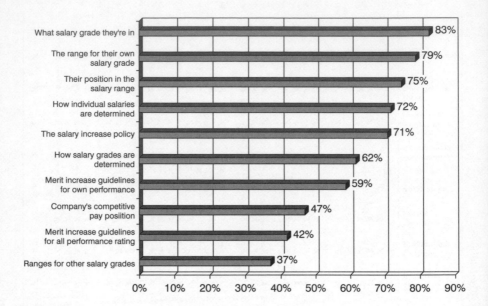

Figure 8.2 *Messages employees receive on pay issues in 270 companies*
Source: Towers Perrin

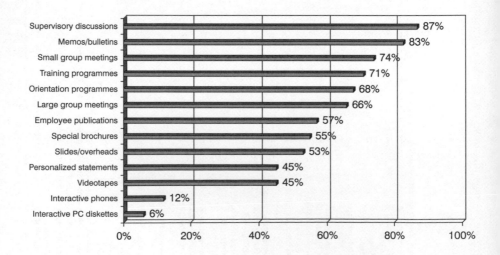

Figure 8.3 *Most frequently used media for pay communications*
Source: Towers Perrin

Table 8.2 *The use of 'new' management practices and employee involvement schemes*

Type of practice	% of workplaces
Most employees work in formally designated teams	65
Workplace operates a system of team briefing for groups of employees	61
Most non-managerial employees have performance formally appraised	56
Staff attitude survey conducted in the last 5 years	45
Problem-solving groups (e.g. quality circles)	42
'Single status' between managers and non-managerial employees	41
Regular meetings of entire workforce	37
Profit-sharing scheme operated for non-managerial employees	30
Workplace operates a just-in-time system of inventory control	29
Workplace level joint consultative committee	28
Most supervisors trained in employee relations skills	27
Attitudinal test used before making appointments	22
Employee share ownership scheme for non-managerial employees	15
Guaranteed job security or no compulsory redundancies policy	14
Most employees receive minimum of 5 days training per year	12
Individual performance-related pay scheme for non-managerial employees	11

Source: WER survey

predominate, and that employee representation and involvement mechanisms are often operating within a very restricted management brief. The Workplace Employee Relations Survey[16] found, 'discontent about the true extent of consultation and involvement in decision making', with for example, only 5 per cent of employers operating fully autonomous teams, 28 per cent workplace consultation bodies, and a low incidence of financial participation schemes. Thus, 40 per cent of employees rated their managers as poor at consulting on key issues, and the incidence increased significantly for lower level and blue-collar employees. A London Business School study[17] of 650 companies claimed that employee involvement in the United Kingdom is the worst in Europe, while Marchington's study[18] speaks of 'a haphazard, piecemeal approach', pursuing fads and fashion, and lacking the 'energy and direction to get real employee buy-in.

A possible economic downturn at the end of the 1990s may even be leading some to question the rhetoric of participation. Wajcman's research[19] in five multinational high technology companies found, 'a major gulf between the rhetoric of "soft" HRM and the "hard" reality…

with continued downsizing management is returning to a more traditional, hierarchical style'. A manager told her, 'When things are tough, people like to be in control. The culture of the organization is becoming more direct, more controlled from Head Office.' Another claimed, 'We have returned to the 1960s' model of military management.'

Commenting on Salford University's Corporate Communications Unit research, Kevin Thompson argues that:

> For the last two decades, British business has been stuck in a time-warp, struggling to make do with an outdated approach called employee communications, that managers see as a way of transmitting information, rather than getting people's commitment. Vital corporate change initiatives are failing to achieve the necessary employee buy-in.[20]

This divorce of the rhetoric and reality in communications and involvement appears most clearly and perhaps understandably, in the arena of pay. Research shows the increasing volume of pay information to be, to quote from one study,

> Mostly top-down from line and HR managers, with written back-up, focused on individual technical details of pay programmes... in other words companies provide employees with some information about the mechanics of pay programmes but don't offer a broader perspective that would provide a context for the information received.[21]

Towers Perrin's communications study[22] demonstrated significant gaps between the rhetoric and the reality of communications on pay matters. These included:

- a predominance of written and one-way media, when face-to-face communications were regarded as overwhelmingly the most effective;
- thus, in spite of the volume of information on specific pay scheme details, only 30 per cent of managers in the study believed their employees really understand how their pay is determined;
- 68 per cent of managers felt that information on pay should be shared openly, compared to 40 per cent who believed that it is actually shared openly, and 46 per cent that it is only shared on a strictly need-to-know basis;
- 58 per cent of managers regarded supervisory/immediate manager discussions as the most effective method, yet only 22 per cent felt supervisors were effective in relaying information; 80 per cent train

them in performance appraisal, yet only 21 per cent believe they provided proper performance feedback (Figure 8.4 demonstrates the general gloomy picture of the effectiveness of supervisory communication on pay and performance management).

Perhaps not surprisingly then, only 39 per cent of employees in this study regarded pay as a good reflection of their performance, and only 20 per cent that the pay system's operation makes it worthwhile for a person to work hard. This communications breakdown lies at the heart of the performance pay paradox.

THE LACK OF TRANSPARENCY IN PAY

A degree of reticence, particularly in the UK culture, on pay matters is probably not surprising, given the well-researched failures of UK managers to communicate effectively, and a generally expressed fear of arousing suspicions and jealousies if pay details were fully open. In a completely transparent reward system everything is out in the open and there are no hidden secrets. Employees know:

- the rationale underpinning the pay structure and pay progression within the structure;
- the reasons for their ratings and pay awards;
- the basis for decisions on how much money should be allocated for pay reviews;
- what other people in the organization are paid.

In the private sector many organizations shrink from total or even partial transparency along these lines. It may be believed that pay decisions are the prerogative of management, or that employees do not really want everyone else to know what they are paid (although in our experience, employees frequently exchange information on their pay increases after a pay review). There may be a fear that employees will, as in the famous General Electric studies by Mayo, manipulate performance pay schemes to their own advantage and 'fix' the scheme, if they know too much about it.

Some organizations keep information secret because, explicitly or implicitly, they feel they cannot justify their policies or their actions. Sir Stuart Hampson asks pointedly, from the perspective of a company – John Lewis – with a very open approach to business and pay communication

Most Supervisors...

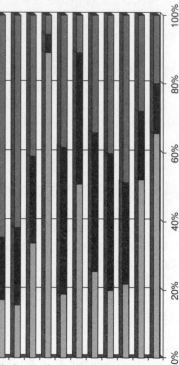

- Clearly understand their pay communication responsibilities
- Feel comfortable conducting performance appraisals
- Feel comfortable discussing pay
- Clearly understand the mechanics of the salary management system
- Know where to get answers to salary questions
- Set clear performance expectations for employees
- Are open to suggestions from employees
- Discuss the company's business goals with employees
- Provide ongoing feedback outside a formal performance appraisal
- View salary communication as a key responsibility
- View salary communication as a responsibility of HR function
- The HR function provides adequate information for supervisors to carry out communication responsibilities

■ Agree ■ Unsure ■ Disagree

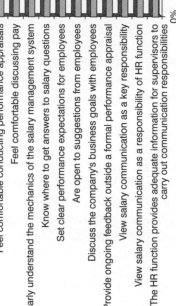

The amount of salary information most supervisors disclose to employees is:

■ Too little ■ About right ■ Too much

Figure 8.4 *Companies' assessment of the immediate manager's/supervisor's role in pay and performance communications*

and participation, 'Is it good manners, modesty or embarrassment that stops directors talking about their pay?'[23] And in the public sector the introduction of devolved and performance-related pay has often led to a reduced level of disclosure of pay information.

Given the high level of change to pay and particularly performance pay systems revealed in this book, one might assume that there has been a corresponding shift to involve employees in making and understanding these changes. Yet concerns of arousing expectations or fears amongst employees, in our experience, often lead to a complete lack of involvement, and the restriction of any communication until the changes are about to be implemented. Then a top-down avalanche of information often follows, which is usually as effective, in the long-term, as a day-long crash-course language training course. When we are reviewing the pay situation in an employer, in order to assess the requirement and direction for changes, many senior managers still oppose the involvement of employees in this process for these reasons.

Thus while Towers Perrin's European pay study[24] found over 90 per cent of 303 European organizations making and anticipating reward changes, only 12 per cent had actually consulted with employees in putting their new reward strategies in place. Amazingly, only 7 per cent had involved employees in redesigning and introducing their new performance pay and bonus schemes. To our minds this is incredibly short-sighted.

Research and our experience show that involving employees in pay redesign and change has many benefits (see Figure 8.5). As well as actually producing higher quality scheme design, because employees generally know their jobs and the factors contributing to their performance better than anyone, asking employees for their views and explaining any changes builds support for a new scheme, and makes its success more likely. It becomes something of a self-fulfilling prophecy. Most critically of all, it builds trust. A certain way to destroy trust in the reward system, indeed in management, is to take pay decisions behind closed doors, without any explanation of how or why they have been made.

TRUST

THE MEANING OF TRUST

Trust, as defined by the *Oxford English Dictionary*, is a firm belief that a person may be relied on. An alternative definition has been provided by

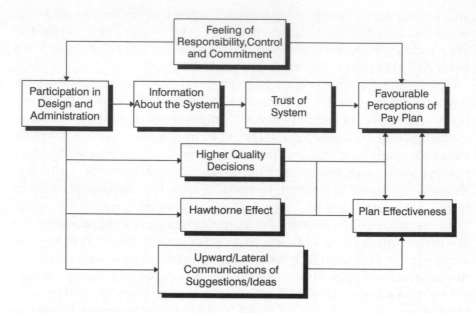

Figure 8.5 *How involvement and communications help ensure the effectiveness of new and redesigned performance pay schemes*

Shaw[25] to the effect that trust is the 'belief that those on whom we depend will meet our expectations of them'. These expectations are dependent on, 'our assessment of another's responsibility to meet our needs'.

A high trust organization has been described by Fox[26] as follows:

> Organisational participants share certain ends or values; bear towards each other a diffuse sense of long-term obligations; offer each other spontaneous support without narrowly calculating the cost or anticipating any short-term reciprocation; communicate honestly and freely; are ready to repose their fortunes in each other's hands; and give each other the benefit of any doubt that may arise with respect to goodwill or motivation.

This ideal state may seldom, if ever, be attained, but it does represent a picture of an effective organization in which, as Thompson[27] notes, trust, 'is an outcome of good management'.

There are four main aspects of trust in reward systems. First, employees need to trust and understand the pay systems that are used. Second, they need to trust their management to operate the reward processes fairly. Third, they need to understand and trust the reasons for the increasingly common changes to pay programmes that are evident. Finally, senior managers and HR specialists need to trust managers to carry out their reward duties properly, especially when more responsibility for making pay decisions is being devolved to line managers, as is increasingly the case.

WHEN DO EMPLOYEES TRUST MANAGEMENT?

Management and the pay systems they design are more likely to be trusted by employees when the latter:

- believe that the management means what it says;
- observe that management does what it says it is going to do – suiting the action to the word;
- feel they are treated fairly equitably and consistently;
- know from experience that management, in the words of David Guest,[28] 'delivers the deal – it keeps its word and fulfils its side of the bargain'.

FAIRNESS, EQUITY AND JUSTICE AS A BASIS FOR TRUST

A very common component of reward strategies in contemporary organizations is the requirement for 'fairness, equity and consistency'. Although the emphasis on these goals may have been supplanted by the contemporary stress on business alignment and a strong performance relationship, they remain as policy goals of many companies' pay systems. And the lack of perceived equity and fairness in performance pay schemes, as we saw in Chapter 3, often lies at the heart of trade union opposition to the approach. This was recently expressed for example by Doug McAvoy of the National Union of Teachers in respect of teacher's pay, describing PeRP as 'totally unfair' in principle and practice.

FAIRNESS

Fairness in relating to people, especially over rewards, is a matter of acting in accordance with the principles of distributive and procedural justice. The reward system should not only be fair in these terms, it should be seen to be fair in accordance with the 'felt-fair' principle. This was first defined by Jaques[29] and states that pay systems will be fair if they are felt to be fair. His assumptions were that:

- there is an unrecognized standard of fair payment for any level of work;
- unconscious knowledge of the standard is shared amongst the population at work;
- to be felt fair it must be believed that pay matches the level of work and the capacity of individuals to do it;
- people feel that pay is unfair when they receive less than they deserve by comparison with their fellow workers.

People are more likely to feel that they are rewarded fairly if they understand the basis upon which pay decisions affecting them are made (for example, how performance-related pay works), if they believe that these decisions have been made objectively on the basis of an analysis of factual evidence relating to performance, competence or contribution in which they have shared, and if their pay in relation to other people can be objectively justified. All these criteria are related to the principle of transparency and the processes of communication, involvement and performance management, a subject we return to later in this chapter.

The principles which need to be followed if trust through fairness is to be achieved are therefore:

- develop reward processes which meet the requirements of procedural and distributive justice;
- ensure that everyone concerned understands how and why pay decisions affecting them are made, including the standards they are expected to achieve to gain rewards;
- base pay decisions on objective evidence of performance, competence or contribution;
- provide people with the opportunity, skills, encouragement, feedback and support they need to perform well and therefore be rewarded.

EQUITY

The concept of equity meanwhile refers to the perceptions people have about how they are treated in relation to others. To be dealt with equitably is to be rewarded appropriately in comparison with another group of people (a reference group) or a relevant other person. Equity involves feelings and perceptions and it is always a comparative process. It is not synonymous with equality, which means treating everyone the same, because this would be inequitably if they deserve to be treated differently.

As formulated by Adams and expressed by Jacques,[30] equity theory states that people will be better motivated if they are treated equitably and consistently, and demotivated if they are treated inequitably and inconsistently. Adams distinguished two forms of equity: distributive equity, which is concerned with people's perceptions about how they are treated and rewarded in comparison with others; and procedural equity, which is concerned with perceptions about how organizational procedures such as performance management are being applied to them, compared with how they are being applied to others.

Equity in pay terms can refer to internal equity – comparisons between pay levels within the organization, and external equity – comparison between an individuals' rate of pay and their perceptions of their market worth. External equity may be applied to comparisons of base rates of pay but it could be extended to the belief of individuals about what they could earn elsewhere in a bonus or incentive scheme.

Trust is engendered by adopting an equitable approach to the management of contribution-related pay systems. This means:

- assessing the value of individual or team contributions as objectively as possible to minimize biased decisions, which lead to differences in rewards which cannot be justified;
- auditing the distribution of pay for individuals in similar jobs or jobs which are in the same grade as determined by job evaluation, identifying exceptions and establishing their validity;
- conducting a comparative analysis of proposed pay increases to ensure that any exceptions to the norm can be objectively justified;
- benchmarking the pay arrangements of other organizations, to determine the extent to which external equity is being achieved;
- applying analytical and transparent job evaluation processes to ensure that gradings and levels of pay are equitable.

Complete equity and total consistency in pay management is an impossible ideal. There will always be an element of subjectivity in deciding on pay increases and ratings and in this respect at least, critics of performance or competence-related pay have a point. But an attempt can be made to minimize inconsistency and develop trust in pay by such means as:

- defining the factors that should be taken into account in deciding on whether, say, an above average, average or below average increase should be awarded;
- specifying the performance dimension of jobs in terms of the competence or contribution levels which indicate the relative size of awards – this could be achieved by, for example, the identification of differentiating competencies which define the behavioural characteristics which high performers display, as distinct from those characterizing less effective people;
- defining rating scales as precisely as possible, perhaps using behaviourally anchored rating scales for this purpose;
- briefing managers thoroughly on the performance level, competence dimensions or rating scales, to explain what they mean and how they should be applied;
- holding rating workshops in which managers practise using the rating scales or case study examples to increase familiarity with them and achieve greater consistency in their application;
- coaching managers by providing them with help and advice during the decision-making process (a useful role for HR practitioners);
- providing guidelines on the distribution of awards or ratings indicating in general terms what would normally be expected (but preferably avoiding the use of forced distributions – managers should not be compelled to adopt a rigid approach, some flexibility is desirable);
- monitoring the distribution of ratings and rewards and questioning any unusual distribution (revealed by inconsistencies between departments) or any marked deviation from the guidelines;
- holding 'moderating' meetings at which peer groups of managers review each other's proposals and ask for explanations of any significant variations.

The importance of this level of training and support, and of open communications and staff involvement in changes, is a consistent theme throughout the case studies in this book.

JUSTICE

To treat people fairly, equitably and consistently and to deal with them justly. Laventhal[31] distinguished between distributive and procedural justice. Distributive justice refers to how rewards are distributed. People will feel that they have been treated justly in this respect if they believe that rewards have been distributed in accordance with their contribution, that they receive what was promised to them and that they get what they need. Procedural justice refers to the ways in which reward decisions are made and reward systems are managed.

The five factors that affect perceptions of procedural justice, as identified by Tyler and Bies[32] are:

1. Adequate consideration of an employee's viewpoint.
2. Suppression of personal bias towards an employee.
3. Applying criteria consistently across employees.
4. Providing early feedback to employees about the outcome of decisions.
5. Providing employees with an adequate explanation of decisions made.

Justice in managing reward systems and trust in the ways in which they are managed are achieved by attending to considerations of equity, fairness and consistency, and through communications and involvement.

TRUST AND THE PSYCHOLOGICAL CONTRACT

Trust, as Guest[33] points out, is 'located at the heart of the psychological contract'. This refers to the often-unwritten set of expectations that operate between employees and employers in terms of what the organization expects from employees, and what they receive in return for working there. A positive psychological contract, based on trust, can make a significant impact on job satisfaction and commitment, and its achievement is a necessary part of the process of developing effective, contribution-related reward systems.

THE PSYCHOLOGICAL CONTRACT DEFINED

The psychological contract has been defined by Herriot and Pemberton[34] as: 'The perception of both parties to the employment relationship, organizations and individuals, of the obligations implied in

297

the relationship.' The concept of the psychological contract emphasizes the fact that employee–employer expectations take the form of unarticulated assumptions as well as stated contractual terms. In Europe this employment relationship or 'deal' is often not specified but in the United States it has become more common for companies to explicitly define it. The stated 'deals' at Johnson and Johnson and Apple, which represent very different philosophies about employment and about how pay practices operate within them, are shown in Figure 8.6.

Rousseau and Wade-Benson[35] point out that:

> Psychological contracts refer to beliefs that individuals hold regarding promises made, accepted and relied upon between themselves and another... because psychological contracts represent how people interpret promises and commitments, both parties in the same employment relationship (employer and employee) can have different views regarding specific terms.

It is these inconsistencies and differences in beliefs and action that often lie at the root of opposition to, and the failure of, performance pay schemes.

The psychological contract represents the framework within which both parties act and respond, within which they interpret HR and pay practices. Perceived breaches of the contract, by either party, have serious implications. As Thompson[36] observes, 'There is a popular belief

Apple Deal	Johnson & Johnson Deal
Here's the Deal Apple will give you; here's what we want from you. We're going to give you a really neat trip while you're here. We're going to teach you stuff you couldn't learn anywhere else. In return. . . we expect you to work like hell, buy the vision as long as you're here. . . We're not interested in employing you for a lifetime, but that's not the way we are thinking about this. Its a good opportunity for both of us that is probably finite.	We are responsible to our employees, the men and the women who work with us throughout the world. Everyone must be considered as an individual. We must respect their dignity and recognise their merit. They must have a sense of security in their jobs. Compensation must be fair and adequate, and working conditions clean, orderly, and safe. Employees must feel free to make suggestions and complaints. There must be equal opportunity for employment, development and advancement for those qualified. We must provide competent management, and their actions must be just and ethical.

Figure 8.6 *The stated employment 'deal' in two US companies*

that performance pay is a powerful motivator yet a neglect of the conditions that must exist for pay to have any motivational impact.' Thus the 'unclear objectives', 'operating problems' and 'inconsistent management' of performance pay have contributed to 'undermining the psychological contract of trust, motivation and commitment', in the companies he has researched.

CHANGES IN THE PSYCHOLOGICAL CONTRACT

The unspoken psychological contract that developed post-war, in the expanding, globalizing, major industrial, western corporations is simply represented in the left column of Figure 8.7. It was an era of labour specialization and tight management control, of the spread of detailed, points factor job evaluation, rather than person and performance-based pay. But in return for loyalty and effort, employees in these companies received what looks today to be an attractive deal in return: high job security, steady and often service-linked pay increases, promotion opportunities and an excellent benefits package. Take ICI, for example, which as *The Financial Times* describes, 'for decades stood for sound training, decent wages, good fringe benefits and a job for life, embellished with social clubs and outings, a Christmas hamper and a good pension'.[37]

As Pemberton and Herriot describe, this contract came under severe pressure in the 1980s and 1990s. Increasing international competition, globalization, technological and market changes, in an era particularly in the United Kingdom of right-wing, individualistic political ideology, and with the spread of US HRM ideas, all saw business responding with downsizing, re-engineering, outsourcing and a range of other initiatives. These pressures heralded the breakdown of the traditional deal, as well as the spread of performance-related pay. Herriot and Pemberton are critical of many employers' failure to explain these changes to employees, leaving them with a sense of betrayal and injustice as increasing numbers of them were made redundant. Even for those remaining in employment, their contract and their trust had been breached.

Yet a number of companies explicitly defined a 'new deal', more in keeping with the faster-changing 1990s, which we illustrate on the right-hand side of Figure 8.7. It is a deal based on employability rather than employment for life, developing employees, rewarding them in relation to the market and their performance, and giving them the

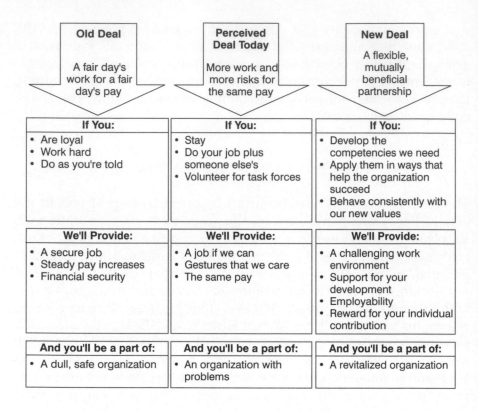

Old Deal A fair day's work for a fair day's pay	Perceived Deal Today More work and more risks for the same pay	New Deal A flexible, mutually beneficial partnership
If You: • Are loyal • Work hard • Do as you're told	**If You:** • Stay • Do your job plus someone else's • Volunteer for task forces	**If You:** • Develop the competencies we need • Apply them in ways that help the organization succeed • Behave consistently with our new values
We'll Provide: • A secure job • Steady pay increases • Financial security	**We'll Provide:** • A job if we can • Gestures that we care • The same pay	**We'll Provide:** • A challenging work environment • Support for your development • Employability • Reward for your individual contribution
And you'll be a part of: • A dull, safe organization	**And you'll be a part of:** • An organization with problems	**And you'll be a part of:** • A revitalized organization

Figure 8.7 *Changes in the psychological contract in the past two decades*

skills and experience to succeed in the company or outside of it, in return for continually growing and maximizing their contribution. *Fortune Magazine*[38] defined it as follows:

> There will never be job security. You will be employed by us for as long as you add value to the organization and you are responsible for finding ways to add value. In return you have the right to interesting and important work, the freedom and resources to perform it well, pay that reflects your contribution and the experience and training needed to be employable here or elsewhere.

Hewlett Packard, for example, explicitly put the psychological contract as a strategic priority in 1996, and their HR and pay policies are designed to support it. Its components include role competency profiling, options on flexible working, three-year self-development plans, 360° performance feedback, market and performance-related pay and employee share ownership. Professor Sumatra Ghoshal of the

London Business School, speaking at the Linkage International Competency Conference in London in 1998, spoke of the requirement for this 'new manifesto for management: while the old way offered employees security in return for loyalty and obedience, the new proffers employability in return for contribution, responsibility and continuous learning'. Yet even he noted the 'real problem' of 'lack of guts overtly to follow and explain', this change in the relationship.

THE STATE OF THE PSYCHOLOGICAL CONTRACT

The effects of the prevailing changes in employment and the psychological contract on employee motivation, morale and contribution has been a highly contested and hotly debated issue throughout the 1990s. Herriot and Pemberton[39] initially expounded the popular view that many employers broke the old deal, yet failed to provide any alternative new deal. They write that, 'the old contract was smashed... new arrangements unfairly imposed' and new HR practices such as performance pay, 'aimed at improving productivity, have severely damaged it in the long-term, stifling innovation'.

According to a report in *The Independent*, 'Employers are creating a climate of fear, with high rewards in the boardroom and dispensability for the rest.' A US manager at the Prudential Company told researchers, 'Five years ago we played softball on the company fields. The message we're getting now is the company doesn't give you anything. We're therefore cold and calculating, looking out for ourselves. If the economy picked up, I'd look for a job outside.'[40]

Some of these organizations ended up in a situation summarized in the central column of Figure 8.7. It is the Janus-faced deal in which, as Hamel and Prahalad[41] note, 'What employees hear is they are a company's most important asset: what they see is that they are its most dispensable.'

The large employee research studies we have been referring to, however, appear to present a different picture in the late 1990s. The old deal was stifling and restrictive, and has little appeal to many younger employees today. According to union official Mike Brider, at ICI, 'it was talking, sleeping ICI; you were engulfed... like wading through treacle. The whole culture of "let's not challenge" created a moribund business.'[42]

Pat Milligan suggests that there is always a difficult period of transition after a contract is broken. Now, however, 'The economy is picking up. Workers are saying to management I have a choice to work here now. Tell me what new relationship is so I can decide if I want to stay.'[43] The employment relationship has therefore become more of an employment brand, a way of retaining and motivating highly committed and high performing employees who, if they do not like the relationship, will simply move on. Keith Todd, Chief Executive of computer company ICL, believes that a key characteristic of the 'new millennium business world, the information society, is that citizens have the choice where and how they work. People will work with you because they want to, they believe in your cause and you treat them with respect.'

The Research conducted by Guest and Conway[44] on behalf of the Institute of Personnel and Development amongst 1,000 UK employees reveals a generally positive view of the state of the psychological contract in the United Kingdom; and of some of the pay and HR practices underpinning it.

- 88 per cent expressed loyalty to their organization, and 76 per cent were proud to work there;
- 80 per cent of respondents felt they were well informed on business issues and treated very or quite fairly by their employers;
- 79 per cent trusted the organization to keep its promises a lot or somewhat;
- 35 per cent felt very motivated and 46 per cent fairly motivated;
- 68 per cent felt fairly rewarded for the effort they put in and 58 per cent that there was a fair pay-for-performance relationship;
- 58 per cent felt their organization 'delivered the deal' always, or to a large extent, so far as its promises concerning pay were concerned;
- 62 per cent agreed that management and employees were 'on the same side'.

The researchers found 'conflict replaced by a shared commitment to competitiveness, and a greater emphasis on individual responsibility'.

Specifically in respect of pay practices you can find other examples to support this finding. In a recent review[45] British Waterways' new pay scheme was described by a union official as follows: 'the competency pay scheme was part of a new culture of working together, sharing information and taking joint responsibility'. Sandy Boyle describes Bank of Scotland's pay-for-contribution scheme as 'an opportunity for employees to have their pay reflect more fairly on what they are doing'[46] and infinitely preferable to merit pay. A Royal College of

Nursing official similarly described the new competency pay scheme at Ealing Hospital as 'very transparent... equitable and reasonably popular'.[47]

Similarly, the major Workforce Employer Relations Survey[48] (WERS) found a high level of employee commitment with:

- 65 per cent loyal to their employers;
- 51 per cent sharing the values of the organization;
- 56 per cent proud to work for their employer;
- 60 per cent satisfied or very satisfied in their job and work.

It concluded that 'satisfaction at work is widespread... harmonious employee relations very much the norm'.

Yet for those of us still rubbing our eyes at these figures and wondering what we are doing wrong in our own organizations, both of these major recent studies for the IPD and Department of Employment carry a significant sting in the tail. For while both find that HR and involvement practices, including performance pay, influenced a positive psychological contract and related sense of trust, fairness and commitment, as Guest and Conway[49] note, 'employees want to be trusted, treated fairly and know what is happening. They want to believe that their commitment to the organization is matched by a similar commitment by the organization to them'.

LACK OF RECIPROCITY

Both surveys indicate that significant numbers of employees do not feel this sense of reciprocity in their deal, nor are they as positive about their employers. As Guest and Conway observe 'despite the rhetoric, many firms are far from being partnership companies', with significant numbers of employees feeling excluded from the new employment relationship, especially those in blue collar occupations and at lower levels in their organizations.

The WERS[50] similarly found that 'a significant minority of employees feel that the overall deal they have is a poor one'. For example, only 35 per cent of blue collar employees were committed to their organization, compared to 75 per cent of managerial and professional staff. Some 41 per cent were dissatisfied with pay and 40 per cent with the true level of involvement and consultation. Here again we see the contradiction between the policy and the practice that we have discussed already in respect of communication and involvement.

Most worrying of all perhaps is the negative trend in some of these statistics regarding trust and commitment (see Table 8.3). Between 1996 and 1998 Guest and Conway found a declining proportion of employees feeling they were kept well informed, had interesting work and saw employee/management relations as positive. Towers Perrin's data show a similar trend.

Indeed, the conclusion of Towers Perrin's Workplace Index[51] places a somewhat ironic interpretation on the 'new' deal. Rather than pining for an old paternal relationship, this research suggested that employees have generally accepted the concept of the new deal, with the vast majority agreeing that they should be responsible for learning new skills, for their own career, and for pay to be related to their contribution. A majority were satisfied with their work and say they are coping with the work pressures they face.

But the declining levels of trust suggests that companies are not seen to be delivering on their side of this deal. Employees have less faith than two years ago that their interests are being considered, and do not feel that they are generally sharing in the success their efforts have generated. They have done as their employers said, and become more independent, motivated, business literate and performance-orientated. Yet in return, they want information on the business, genuine opportunities to contribute and be involved, appropriate training and development support, and rewards linked to their contribution, allowing them to share in business success. As we saw in Chapter 1, employees

Table 8.3 *Attitude survey data showing declining levels of perceived trust and reciprocity in the psychological contract by UK employees*

Statement	Attitude survey data on proportion of employees agreeing with statement	
	Two years previous	Data from most recent study
This company considers my interests[1]	50%	41%
Workplace policies are administered fairly[1]	59%	56%
There is a positive employee relations climate[2]	2.78[3]	2.58[3]
The company keeps me well informed[2]	81%	71%
My work is interesting[2]	59%	52%

Notes: 1 = Towers Perrin Workplace Index Figures in 1995 and 1997
2 = IPD Research in 1996 and 1998
3 = Average rating on linked scale where 1 = strongly disagree → 5 = strongly agree

who believe they share in business success, and that outstanding performance was reflected in their pay, were more committed to supporting their employers business goals. Yet fewer than 40 per cent had such a belief.

It is a failure to deliver in these areas that currently seems to be souring the employee relations climate in some companies. As Sir Stuart Hampson[52] puts it, 'companies need to take a view on fairness', and 'not enough is done to ensure that the benefits of success are shared widely throughout the workforce. Modern management thinking stresses the contribution flowing from all employees. This should be matched by a sharing of the benefits, rather than the bonuses or share issues being confined to the boardrooms.'

SIGNIFICANCE OF THE PSYCHOLOGICAL CONTRACT

The significance of the concept was noted by Sims[53] as follows: 'A balanced psychological contract is necessary for a continuing, harmonious relationship between the employee and the organization. However the violation of the psychological contract can signal to the participants that the parties no longer share (or never shared) a common set of values or goals.' Guest's research for the IPD[54] demonstrated that a positive psychological contract is based on three factors: employee perceptions of fairness, trust and delivery of the 'deal'. It is therefore influenced by the organizational climate, HR policies and practices, employee experience and expectations. Its consequences include job satisfaction, organizational commitment and citizenship, motivation and effort, and high organization performance.

Both the Workplace Employee Relations Survey and the IPD research on the psychological contract demonstrate that a positive and trusting 'deal' is associated with high levels of job satisfaction, employee commitment and business performance, and is in turn dependent on high levels of employee involvement and the type of HR practices in use (see Figure 8.8).

The significance of pay practices to the psychological contract are essentially threefold:

- First, they are a very visible and for most of us an essential and important part of 'the deal' our employer offers us.
- Second, dissatisfaction with pay schemes can help to create a negative employment relationship; 41 per cent of staff were

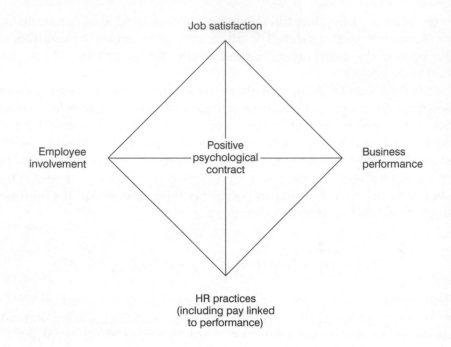

Figure 8.8 *Significant relationships revealed by the IPD and WERS research*

dissatisfied with their pay in the WERS research, and 33 per cent in Guest and Conway's IPD study, representing in both cases the highest levels of dissatisfaction with any aspect of HR management in their companies.

- Third, however, and much to the surprise of some academics, pay related in some way to performance is a component of the progressive HR practices which have been found to correlate with perceptions of a positive psychological contract.

MANAGING THE PSYCHOLOGICAL CONTRACT

Cox and Purcell[55] refer to 'the holy grail of a positive psychological contract', even though they describe it as being associated with fairness and higher levels of employee motivation, contribution and organizational commitment.

The concept of the psychological contract is complex and, as Hilltrop[56] indicates, it is unique in that it is voluntary, subjective, informed, individually orientated and evolves and flourishes over time. There may well also be many different deals in operation in different parts of the same organization.

Sparrow[57] is cautious. He identifies a number of scenarios and comments that: 'Without better knowledge of the role and contribution of causative influences on the contract and better evidence to help us decide which scenario is correct, the dynamics of the contract will be hard to predict and the agenda for the field of HRM hard to specify.'

Similarly, in respect of managing trust, Sako[58] comments that 'trust is a cultural norm, which can rarely be created intentionally, because attempts to create trust in a calculative manner could destroy the effective basis for it.'

It is safe to assume that because of its very nature – unarticulated, subjective and evolutionary – the psychological contract will be difficult to manage. Sitting in an ivory tower, away from the pressures of international competition and shifting employee expectations, it is perhaps easier to recommend that it is let alone and ill-defined.

Yet few HR managers can agree with, or afford to take, this perspective, unless they agree with the criticisms of the function we presented in the Introduction to this book. It may not be possible to 'manage' trust, or perceptions of the psychological contract which are heavily affected by it, in a simplistic, manipulative manner, just as simplistic attempts to cajole employees to higher contribution using the 'carrot' of performance-related pay have often failed. But as Thompson points out, both are an outcome of good management. Trust is created and maintained by managerial behaviour and by the development of better mutual understanding of expectations – employers of employees, and employees of employers.

Clearly, the sort of behaviour that is most likely to engender trust is when management is honest with people, keeps its word (delivers the deal) and practises what it preaches. Organizations which espouse core values ('people are our greatest asset') and then proceed to ignore them will be low-trust organizations.

More specifically and this applies particularly in the field of reward, trust will be developed if management acts fairly, equitably and consistently; if a policy of transparency is implemented; if intentions and the reasons for proposals or decisions are communicated both to employees generally and to individuals; if there is full involvement in developing reward processes, and if mutual expectations are agreed through performance management. Failure to meet these criteria, wholly or in part, is perhaps the main reason why so many performance-related pay schemes have not lived up to expectations. Moreover, there is now strong research support for those of us who believe that it is well worth trying, through our pay and HR and involvement mechanisms, to create a positive, trusting psychological contract, as the basis for high performance in our organizations.

In their major survey for the IPD, Guest and Conway[59] found that the factors leading to a positive psychological contract are:

- a culture or climate of high involvement;
- job security and low expectations of future redundancy;
- working shorter rather than longer hours;
- the use of a series of what they define to be progressive human resource practices, including making jobs as interesting and varied as possible, filling vacancies from within the organization, a statement of avoiding compulsory redundancies and 'more surprisingly, an attempt to relate pay to performance'; these practices are listed in Table 8.4, along with employee perceptions of them, and they were found to have the strongest influence of any criteria on the state of the psychological contract.

The researchers also found that when trust is high, fairness and 'delivery of the deal' are also high. This produced a positive psychological contract which leads to commitment, motivation and higher levels of performance.

Similarly, on the basis of their research at Sundridge Park, Herriot, Manning and Kid[60] recommend that employers need to attend to the basic and transactional constituents of the psychological contract, to restore mutual trust and commitment. Their research identified the following constructs held by employees about their expectations:

- provide adequate induction and training;
- ensure fairness in selection, appraisal, promotion and redundancy procedures;
- provide justice, fairness and consistency in the application of HR practices and disciplinary procedures;
- provide equitable pay in relation to market values across the organization;
- allocate benefits fairly;
- allow time off to meet family and personal needs;
- consult and communicate on matters that affect employees;
- interfere minimally with how employees do their jobs;

Table 8.4   *Progressive Human Resource practices associated with a positive psychological contract*

HR Practices	Yes %	No %	Don't know %
Your organization actively carries out equal opportunities practices in the workplace	86	10	4
Your employer provides you with sufficient opportunities for updating your skills through training or development	80	20	1
Your organization keeps you well informed about business issues and about how well it is doing	77	22	1
When new positions come up in management, your company normally tries to fill them with people from inside the organization rather than recruit them from outside	57	37	7
You receive formal performance appraisals	54	44	1
Your organization tries to get employees more involved in workplace decision-making using things like self-directed work teams, total quality management, quality circles and involvement programmes	53	43	3
There is a serious attempt in your organization to make the jobs of people like you as interesting and varied as possible	51	45	4
Your organization has a stated policy of deliberately avoiding compulsory redundancies and lay-offs	36	36	28
Your organization has established facilities to help employees deal with non-work responsibilities. These are sometimes termed family-friendly policies, such as on-site child-care facilities, counselling for non-work problems, financial planning and legal services	34	62	4
Your pay is related to your performance in some way	30	70	0

Source: IPD research

- act in a personally supportive way to employees;
- recognize or reward contribution;
- provide a safe and congenial work environment;
- provide what job security they can.

Guest and Conway found that, 'perceptions of fairness and a positive psychological contract are higher in organizations that do attempt to link pay to performance'. Their research also demonstrated that 'the number of progressive HR practices in place is the key determinant of whether employees feel treated fairly', and part of a reciprocal deal. It is not of course the existence of these practices that makes the difference. It is their operation and the perceptions of their workings by employees.

REVIEWING AND CREATING A POSITIVE PSYCHOLOGICAL CONTRACT

We are therefore left with two questions to address in the rest of this chapter:

1. How do you set about trying to create a positive psychological contract in your own organization, through pay and other HR policies?
2. How do you get employees to trust and support your pay schemes and the linkages to their contribution?

While it may be impossible to accurately define and exactly manipulate your company's psychological contract, we would argue that attempts to analyse and shape it can be an extremely beneficial process.

The steps we recommend to do this are illustrated in Figure 8.9 and basically involve:

- attempting to define the current psychological contract;
- assessing the extent to which it supports your organization's business strategy and the behaviours and workforce characteristics needed to succeed in the future;
- defining any changes to the deal that are therefore required, and then developing changes in pay, communications and HR programmes to reinforce this change.

An example of this process as undertaken by a large accountancy firm is illustrated in Figure 8.10. This company was finding it increasingly difficult to attract the best graduate recruits in a very competitive market-place. Its traditional structure of a relatively slow progression (8–10 years) up to partnership level, involving long working hours with regular 'culls' of lower performing staff, but then large rewards for all those entering the hallowed gates of partnership, appeared much less attractive to young recruits in the late 1990s. In addition, increasing international competition had slowed the firms expansion, reducing the opportunities for upward progression.

The 'new deal' the firm developed and promulgated therefore placed a much stronger emphasis on staff development, and the introduction of pay for contribution at all levels in the organization. At partnership level this involved greater individual differentiation, on the basis of the

Assessing the current Deal		Identifying Gaps	

Step I:
■ Identify types of employee groups for analysing the different versions of the current Deal and developing the New Deal
■ Basis for categorization can vary:
  – Career focus
  – Job classification
  – Relationship
  – Other
	Step II:
	■ Understand and articulate the company's current Deal
		Step III:
		■ Analyse the attributes for different employee groups in the following areas:
		  – Environment
		  – Culture
		  – Pay/rewards/ benefits
		  – Development
			Step IV:
			■ Identify current and desired states relative to the components of the attributes
			■ Assess whether gaps exist between current and future states
			■ Determine actions necessary to close gaps

Defining the New Deal		Implementing the New Deal	

Step V:
■ Develop a New Deal philosophy or a statement of the New Deal based on the business and people strategies
	Step VI:
	■ Obtain senior management buy-in
		Step VII:
		■ Implement (any or all of):
		  – Communication of the New Deal, including the implications of changing the Deal
		  – Cultural transformation
		  – Leadership communication and change
		  – Alignment of HR programmes, practices and policies to support the Deal
			Step VIII:
			■ Validate the New Deal and establish mechanism to periodically review the Deal in light of changing business and people strategies

Figure 8.9 *An eight-step approach to analysing and managing the psychological contract*

value added by each partner. Another important component was the introduction of programmes to support a better work-to-life balance.

For a major retail company, we found that the components of their reward package underpinned a somewhat different 'deal' to that predominating in the blue chip companies they regarded as their real

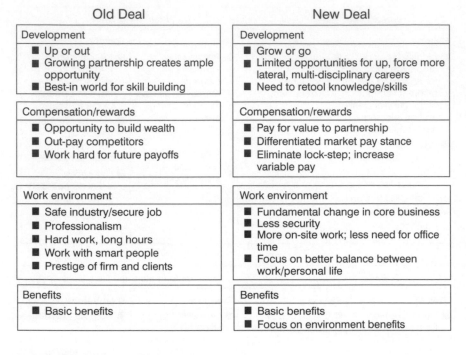

Figure 8.10 *Understanding and articulating the company's deal in a large accounting firm*

competitors in the future. Figure 8.11 shows that their traditional retail deal involved a large spend on staff benefits, but a comparatively low investment in training and development. The need for a greater commitment to staff development was one of the conclusions the company drew from this study, as well as the need to move towards more of a genuinely commitment-based employment relationship, (see Figure 8.12).

Our experience is that there is no universally successful employment relationship for the new millennium, just as there is no single, universally successful bundle of HR practices or pay scheme. The major problems arise from an inconsistency between the stated and the experienced deal, the 'say/do' gap, not from any particular relationship. A number of companies such as Marks and Spencer, for example, retain what might be defined as a fairly traditional, even old-fashioned paternalistic deal, yet they have very successfully modified it to suit today's commercial environment.

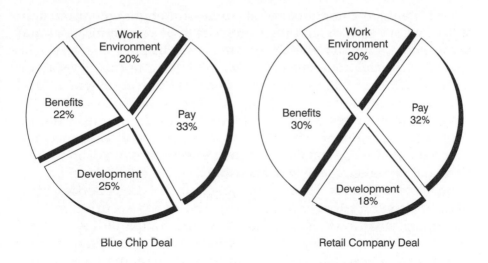

Figure 8.11 *The different balance within the total reward arrangements in different sectors*

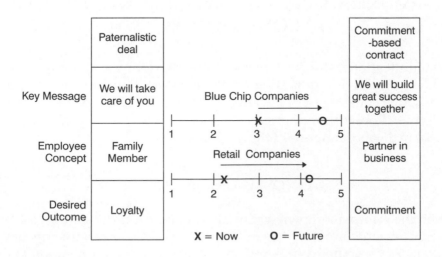

Figure 8.12 *The desired change in the employment relationship in a sample of UK companies*

Yet a common component of all successful employment relationships, and attempts to shift them, appears to be communications and involvement. Chevron, the US oil company illustrates this very well. Extreme cost and competitive pressures starting in the 1980s and a merger with Gulf Oil, saw the traditional lifetime employment deal shattered. Significant restructuring and downsizing followed, and as vice-chairman James Sullivan puts it, led 'to a B-minus score on employee commitment'.[61] Yet the company has openly discussed and communicated these changes and their effects on morale, and publicised and promoted the new relationship they are establishing.

Similarly at Reuters, Head of Training in the US Celia Berk explains that, 'we couldn't just announce the end of job security without explaining what to do in its place'.[62] So the company has invested heavily in developing employee skills and careers, and held numerous workshops to explain the new approach to employees. It has developed explicit guidelines of what is required of managers, as well as what is expected of employees, in the relationship going forward. Performance and pay management are now affected by a wide range of client and employee criteria, not just financial results achieved, including the extent to which managers 'walk the talk'.

COMMUNICATIONS AND INVOLVEMENT IN PAY FOR CONTRIBUTION

Communications and involvement are therefore a key aspect of building a positive and trusting employment relationship and are also an essential component of effective systems for relating pay to contribution. As Robert Levering puts it, 'Good two-way communication is probably the most important thing companies can do.'[63]

PAY COMMUNICATIONS

Given the information reviewed in this chapter, it is difficult to justify or explain why so many organizations remain so secretive on pay matters. At computer company CMG all aspects of remuneration and performance are open, including individual pay levels. Various forms of performance-related reward schemes are in operation, including individual bonuses and share schemes, and the company and many employees have made significant financial gains since their flotation in 1995.

The large Texas food supplier Whole Food Markets has a similar, totally open-book approach for all of its 1,100 employees, supported by performance-related base pay, gainsharing and share schemes. According to HR Vice President Jody Hatch, 'There's a risk of envy and resentment, but that is going to happen even more if you don't tell them and they try to guess.'[64] Hatch has a realistic view of the pros and cons of such an open approach, with the downsides including that, 'it takes more energy and patience, is more costly and you make more mistakes'. But she is convinced that 'in the long run, you get a better team, better ownership and commitment, and that is better for the business'. Clearly, however, many organizations in the United Kingdom may be looking for more practical guidance in how to move in this direction.

The trouble with offering any advice on communications and involvement is that it is easy to resort to 'motherhood' statements and generic lists of 'good' practice. Hopefully we have already exploded two popular myths on pay communications: that a series of memos will do the trick, and that you can't do or say anything until any changes are clear. Companies in Towers Perrin's European survey[65] saw a major need to improve their pay communications practices and communicate much more openly.

The aspects of any pay for contribution system that employees generally need to understand are:

- the policies on progressing pay within the pay structure;
- how individual, team and organization-wide schemes work in general terms;
- the factors taken into account in progressing pay – performance, competence or contribution;
- how assessments are made of the level of performance, competence or contribution (including details of the rating scheme where appropriate);
- how assessments are translated into pay increases (including details of the pay matrix or other mechanism used);
- the measures taken to ensure that pay decisions are fair, equitable and consistent; the basis upon which the budget for pay reviews is determined (and the actual budget when that has been fixed);
- the reasons for any changes to the reward system and how employees will be affected by them.

Individual employees, or teams where there is team pay, need to know and understand:

- the pay opportunities open to them – the scope in an individual's grade for pay progression or the scope for earning individual or team bonuses;
- the basis upon which their pay will be linked to their performance, competence or contribution;
- the results and/or behaviour expected of them if their pay is to progress, or if they are to earn a bonus (this can be done through performance management processes);
- how assessments of their performance, competence or contribution will be made and the opportunities they will have to take part in these assessments and comment on them;
- the reasons for particular decisions on pay increases or bonuses;
- their right to appeal against pay decisions or to take up a grievance on any aspect of their remuneration.

The responsibility for briefing individuals or teams should in our view rest with the line managers, and the Towers Perrin European[66] study noted this shift towards more open and line-led pay communications. It is a demanding agenda and managers generally need to be trained in this aspect of their duties and provided with help and guidance as required by HR specialists.

But simply firing information at employees, even face-to-face, will not involve or engage them in the process, nor achieve their trust and commitment to the organization and its pay practices. Particularly in such rapidly changing times, when corresponding changes in pay systems are being made, employees will only support pay changes if they understand the business rationale for them. They have to see 'the bigger picture' (see Figure 8.13) if they are to commit to making a contribution which supports the success of the organization. Many organizations have totally failed to make the linkages illustrated on Figure 8.13, to explain why changes are required and how a pay for contribution approach actually does relate to the performance and success of the business. Building business awareness on its own, as many employers have been doing, does not automatically create this understanding. Reward practices will similarly be less effective if employees do not understand how their contribution and the rewards for it relate to the success of the whole business.

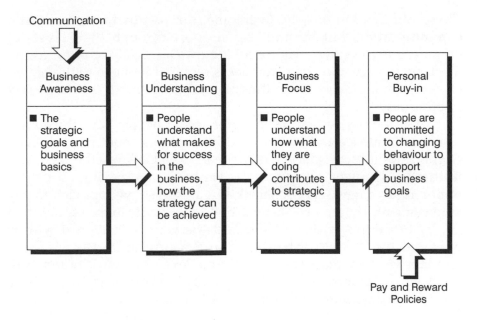

Figure 8.13 *Communications as the key to closing the gap between strategic business awareness and pay*

Some 59 per cent of employers in Towers Perrin's European survey[67] were aiming to more strongly communicate this contextual aspect of pay programmes to their employees and develop a better sense of ownership and understanding. This requires not just communications but also high levels of employee involvement.

INVOLVING EMPLOYEES IN PAY

Changing the way people are paid, as those who have experienced it or managed it will know, is a significant change management challenge. Resistance can emanate from a series of sources including:

- general suspicions and mistrust;
- conflicts of interest;
- fears of pay reductions or cost increases;
- lack of resources;
- general change overload and the influence of other priorities.

These hurdles can only be overcome, not just by being open and communicating, but by building support through high levels of employee involvement. Figure 8.14 shows a model we often use to illustrate how genuine involvement is required to move to the higher stages of employee commitment and ownership of new pay approaches.

Trust in the pay system will be enhanced if people have the opportunity to influence and be involved in decisions about pay schemes. Ownership and acceptance of such schemes will follow if they take part in the development process, for as we have said, paying for contribution is not a new set of schemes, but a process, an approach to pay management. The aim should be to build confidence in the fairness and equity of the pay scheme itself and the ways in which it will be operated by seeking, listening to and acting upon the views of employees. The time taken and the level of consultation and involvement undertaken by our case study companies when changing their pay practices are an example we all should follow.

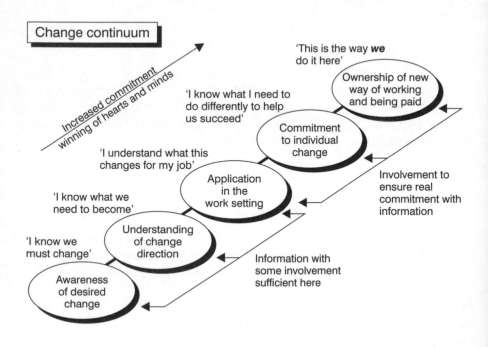

Figure 8.14 *A model of increasing levels of involvement through information and communication*

Involvement can take place through working parties, project teams or task forces. If the organization is unionized, union representatives should be included. Although it may be necessary to negotiate a formal agreement with a union or unions, and they may find any involvement compromises this negotiating role, it is still advisable to involve union representatives at an early stage in any pay change, to seek their opinions and reach agreement on the way forward. The process should be regarded as a partnership which aims to reconcile divergent views in the interest of both parties.

We would highlight ten requirements for successful involvement in respect of truly performance-related pay schemes and changes to them:

1. The objectives of involvement should be discussed, defined and agreed by all parties. A communications and involvement plan should be made.
2. Terms of reference should be discussed and agreed. These should specify the purpose of the working party, the scope of its deliberations in terms of what it is there to examine (indicating any areas excluded from the discussion), the deliverables (what the working party is there to produce and by when), the membership, the chair, and the resources available to the working party to pursue its enquiries, including support from HR and external help from consultants.
3. Management must believe in and be seen to believe in involving employees. It must listen to the outcome of discussions and be prepared to put into effect joint decisions made by the working party.
4. If unions are taking part, they must believe in participation as a genuine means of advancing the interests of their members. Representatives should show by their actions that they are prepared to support decisions which they have agreed.
5. Managers and team leaders should be included in the involvement process. They should not be allowed to feel that they have been by-passed. Tower Perrin's communications study[68] identified first-line and middle managers as a key blockage to effective communications in many companies.
6. The working party should be required to report progress regularly to management and employees generally. It is often advisable to take soundings from time to time to test reactions.
7. The working party should be expected to consider how their proposals will be communicated to employees and implemented.

8. If a good case can be made, the working party should be allowed to commission an opinion survey, conduct pilot schemes in conjunction with HR and, possibly, hold focus groups to test reactions.
9. In making its formal proposals, the working party should have direct access to top management.
10. Members of the working party can usefully take part in implementation.

Our work with companies, and the contacts made in researching this book, lend weight to all of these points, and we can think of no better way to end this chapter than to relate some of these to you.

First, we found that employee perceptions of a fair and effective relationship between their pay and their contribution depends on communications and involvement. As the HR Director of Saffrey Champness puts it, 'performance-related pay works here as it operates in an open and co-operative environment',[69] or as banking union BIFU's guide on competency pay explains, 'the transparency of any pay package is crucial; it must be absolutely clear to employees how their pay is determined'.[70] The AUT's opposition to the HERA system of competency-based role evaluation for further education colleges was on the basis that it was, 'complex and lacks transparency'. Stuart Hampson's view is that 'Transparency is key. British business can no longer ignore its responsibility to explain the rationale for executive pay... directors should start the process of winning understanding by talking to their employees.'[71]

Second and perhaps most critically, when making changes to pay systems and performance management systems, staff have to be involved, accept and support such changes. As the Compensation and Benefits Director of clothing retailer Lands End explains, 'when we are rethinking reward we go to people and listen to their views', and as the HR Director of Metropolitan Life Automotive says regarding their pay change experience, 'the key was to get buy-in, for managers to communicate continually and address any problems head-on'.[72]

Pauline Wells, Executive Director of HR at Tussauds Group, who have been implementing a whole series of pay changes, elaborates:

It is important for employees to be involved in any pay redesign exercise. Involvement creates more understanding and helps build ownership of any changes. To get commitment people must know why we want to change and what will be better for them as a result... great effort needs to be made to communicate continually, face-to-face, not just at implementation time.[73]

Such efforts and employee involvement in redesign, 'greatly increased the credibility' of the new, more performance-related pay structure at accountants Saffrey Champness, according to their HR Director. At British Gas Trading it was the key to implementing a difficult series of changes to pay practices, including pay freezes and reduced hours. According to Unison rep Dave Johnson, 'If the proposals were simply to boost profits, we would have fought them. But we were convinced by the commercial realities'[74] of fierce competition in the energy market. Opening up the accounts was an unusual and powerful mechanism to gain staff confidence. BG Trading made an enormous communications effort, including videos and road shows, to explain the changes to staff. Going forward, union representatives will be invited to reach annual pay agreements before they are presented to the board.

Finally, however, financial participation and reward for contribution help to cement employee's own sense of involvement and commitment to the business. It is a two-way process in this sense. As the Chairman of Wainwright industries put it, 'the only way to create genuine ownership is giving people full financial information and a stake in the business', or as US consultant Corey Rosen explains, 'you have to share the action, the information, the decision-making and the financial rewards.'[75]

CONCLUSIONS

According to the RSA report *Tomorrow's Company:*

> Tomorrow's Company has a purpose that is understood and shaped by its people, which inspires them in their work. In tomorrow's company the reward system and the company's open approach to communications are designed in such a way that employees feel a real purpose in wanting to achieve the stated goals.[76]

Throughout this chapter we have seen the evidence for the self-reinforcing relationships illustrated in Figure 8.8. Whatever the pay plan design, effective relationships between pay and contribution can only be established in the context of an open and trusting employment contract, founded on progressive and equitable HR and pay practices. Yet these practices in turn help to build a committed, high contribution workforce which is the basis for the business success of many of the company's who will prosper well into the new millennium.

As the Director of Compensation in one of our Case Studies explains, the success of gainsharing and any scheme which genuinely links pay and performance, 'hinges on the quality and openness of communication… there needs to be mutual trust'. Within such a self-reinforcing partnership, employees are 'more willing to contribute, which in turn improves productivity and their pay'.

SUMMARY

- High levels of communications and employee involvement are associated with successful business performance and the operation of effective pay programmes for rewarding performance and contribution.
- Employee involvement practices and communications on pay have increased significantly during the 1990s. Yet there is evidence of a significant gap between the rhetoric and the reality of involvement, particularly in respect of pay and reward. Pay communications are invariably top-down and technically focused, and employees are not involved when considering pay changes.
- This lack of openness has helped to produce a mistrust of reward systems, and particularly pay-for-performance systems. Trust is vital if pay systems are to operate effectively. Trust depends on employee perceptions of fairness and justice which themselves can only exist within an explicit and trusting employment relationship.
- The psychological contract between employers and employees should set out the basis for a mutually reinforcing, reciprocal relationship, within which trust and effective pay systems can flourish.
- The traditional job-for-life contract has been broken by economic and social forces. There is considerable debate as to the effects of this breakdown. Some see it as having a disastrous effect on employee morale, trust and commitment.
- Yet recent large-scale surveys by the IPD and DTI suggest employees have taken on the components of the 'new deal', and value the independence and responsibility it provides them. Even here, however, a significant minority of employees feel that the relationship is not reciprocal, and that they are not sharing in the success of their business.

- Certain progressive HR practices, including attempts to relate pay to performance, are associated with a positive psychological contract. So, there are benefits in trying to make explicit and influence the state of the psychological contract, to help create a fully committed, trusting and motivated workforce.
- Open, two-way communications and genuine employee involvement are at the heart of such relationships, and of truly effective relationships between employees pay and their contribution. In return, pay can be used to help develop a sense of ownership and participation among employees in the business.

CASE STUDY 8.1

The importance of involving employees to reform pay in a UK bank

This bank introduced appraisal-linked base pay increases, as well as individual performance bonuses, for approximately 6,000 staff and managers soon after it became a subsidiary of a larger international bank in 1989. However, it was a series of further pay changes proposed in 1994 which significantly increased staff and trade union dissatisfaction, and led to industrial action in connection with the January 1995 salary review. The way in which the bank subsequently reviewed and modified its proposals, with a high level of staff involvement and subsequent support provides strong justification for adopting such an open approach.

PAY CHANGES

These pay changes followed a significant reorganization and delayering exercise in the bank, as it adopted a strategy emphasizing greater business focus rather than a general banking approach, with the introduction of separate business banking and personal banking organizations. The aim was also to achieve greater efficiency and flexibility with the removal of traditional grade and status distinctions. Twelve pay grades were replaced by five broader bands, with for example, the new pay range for Customer Service Managers being from £15,000 to £26,000. Managers were also given much greater autonomy in determining pay increases.

AN IN-DEPTH REVIEW

In order to investigate and address the staff concerns raised by these changes, following resolution of the pay dispute in March 1995 at ACAS, the bank undertook a major staff consultation exercise, unprecedented in its long history, as part of a fundamental six-month long review of its pay and benefits strategy. An employee opinion survey solicited the views of all staff and a dozen employees focus groups were established to examine areas of concern, including performance management and appraisal. Video updates and regular reports were produced during this process, with for example senior executives being questioned by focus group leaders in response to issues raised by the consultation.

Key concerns expressed by staff included:

- a perception that salaries had fallen behind market rates and technical specialists in particular were not being recognized;
- a lack of recognition of changing job content and responsibilities, and of the loss of promotion opportunities within the new broadbanded structure;
- major concerns over the opaqueness, equity and quality of the appraisal process, with many staff unclear about what they needed to do to progress, and fearful of being held back in the new broader pay ranges.

REVISIONS TO THE PROPOSALS

Revised change proposals were developed as a result of the review, and the new arrangements were supported by senior management staff and unions, and implemented in November 1995. The tenor of the changes was to develop greater staff understanding and confidence in the reward system and changes to it. The original objectives of a stronger pay-for-performance orientation and less hierarchical system remained, but much greater attention was now given to developing the appropriate pay and HR infrastructure, and ensuring the appropriate balance of flexibility and consistency in the pay management process. There was, in effect, a recognition that the original changes had been something of an immediate response to the strategic and organizational restructuring that had been undertaken, and a more in-depth, evolutionary change process needed to occur.

The proposed five band structure was replaced with separate pay structures for five distinct job families, with the number of levels in each family varying from four in the Bank Service Centre to nine in Personal Banking. Jobs were placed in the appropriate band after a detailed points factor job evaluation exercise had been undertaken, with the criteria and results being made available to all staff.

An equally thorough external market benchmarking exercise was undertaken to establish the appropriate pay ranges. This found that the staff perception of being generally low against the market was not accurate and that while some staff categories were below their competitors, others were significantly above.

The new pay ranges introduced reflected this market data, which is now reviewed on a regular basis. There is a job family structure with five families which allows the bank to tailor ranges very specifically to each pay market. So, for example, the introduction of this structure saw pay for entry level Customer Service Officers in Personal Banking increase by 18 per cent, with a range of £8,000 to £11,400. In corporate banking, however, a higher level of experience and skill is required and the entry level range is from £11,000 to £15,500. It also provides a very clear basis for career and pay progression within each family, with band characteristics and promotion requirements made much clearer to staff

A series of changes were also made to the performance-related pay arrangements. A more structured pay matrix was introduced (see Table 8.5), to guide manager's pay decisions and to reassure staff that consistent levels of performance will result in fair and appropriate increases. Thus for example, satisfactory performers are now guaranteed progression to their pay range mid-point within four years of joining.

The individual performance bonus scheme was replaced with a variety of collective and individual schemes in order to recognize high performance but in a more flexible manner. These performance awards are funded from an overall budget, the size of which depends 70 per cent on

Table 8.5 *Performance pay progression matrix in a UK bank*

		Performance rating				
		5 Low	4	3	2	1 High
Position in Range	Maximum	0%	0%	40% of X	X	X + 1%
		0%	0%	60% of X	X + 1%	X + 3%
		0%	0%	80% of X	X + 2%	X + 4%
	Mid-point	0%	0%	X	X + 3%	X + 5%
		0%	40% of X	X + 2%	X + 6%	X + 8%
		0%	X	X + 4%	X + 7%	X + 9%
	Entry point	0%	X + 2%	X + 6%	X + 8%	X + 10%

Note: X = Rate of overall market movement

bank performance, 20 per cent on group performance, with a 10 per cent discretionary element. There are three types of reward:

- an individual annual performance bonus of between 2 per cent and 10 per cent;
- quarterly team performance bonuses linked to specific team objectives, such as customer service, work volume and turnaround times, worth between £25 and £150 to each team member per quarter.
- 'spot' non-cash recognition awards for exceptional sales or service performance, which can take the form of concert tickets, vouchers, meals out, and so on.

These changes were supported by trade unions and staff in late 1995 and then implemented, and a biannual attitude survey showed that the largest improvement in any area was in the satisfaction with pay and benefits arrangements. Recent changes have involved the introduction of greater flexibility in the base pay award in 1998, with the removal of the guaranteed, market related 'X'-Factor in the matrix. However, the basic philosophy and approach has been maintained.

LEARNING POINTS

Key learning points for the bank from their experiences were:

- the critical importance of staff perceptions and the need to involve and communicate on reward issues on a regular basis;
- the need whatever the business pressures, to introduce rigorous and well prepared pay and reward systems to deliver on the stated reward strategy objectives, rather than introducing rapid and under-prepared arrangements.

CASE STUDY 8.2

Implementing pay for contribution through a high involvement, partnership approach at Ericsson Telecommunications

Ericsson Telecommunications Ltd is a UK subsidiary of Ericsson, the Swedish telecomms company with a reputation for forward thinking and employee-oriented management practices. This reputation is evident in the process by which it has developed, implemented and now operates a contribution-related pay system in this rapidly growing UK subsidiary. It has done so in a manner which illustrates many of the key themes we have been emphasizing in this book.

THE MOVE TO PAY FOR CONTRIBUTION

Pay increases at Ericsson were formerly based on an annual management/ trade union, confrontation-style negotiation, which resulted in a fixed increase related to RPI for all staff. Selected staff received additional increases but this was communicated privately in an ad hoc manner. Yet in the ruthlessly competitive and rapidly changing telecomms sector, HR Director Phil Hooper explains that it is essential for the business to have a continually improving, 'customer focused and flexible workforce'. ETL needed to have, 'a more realistic way of rewarding people', using pay as, 'a major engine to drive our business priorities.' The company needed a catalyst for change and breaking the link with RPI would signal to employees:

- the need for focus on business performance;
- the requirement for individuals to understand how to make a contribution to this performance;
- the necessity to develop new skills and capabilities.

According to Hooper, aside from the necessity of a business performance linkage, there were only two immovable principles: 'Keep it simple, and keep employees involved.' A joint team of three managers, including Hooper, and three representatives from the Electrical Engineering Staff Association was set up to consider the issue. In Hooper's mind, it was essential 'to be open, to create trust', thereby, 'letting people understand how they're being paid and why'. The company's partnership approach to employee relations had to be reflected in the design and operation of the new pay system, and Hooper knew that any successful pay system 'cannot be imposed in an alien way'.

The group initially had no single solution in mind, and there were suspicions on both sides at the motives for, and methods of, relating pay to performance. In particular, there were union concerns at the operation of 'the blue-eyed boy syndrome'. Mark Benjamin of the EESA knew that, 'some schemes produced divisiveness but we preferred to be involved rather than being on the outside'. The managers feared in particular that the development and communication benefits of appraisal would be lost if the process was linked too closely to pay (a conflict we considered in Chapter 7).

The group consulted internally, and reviewed external examples of the best means of relating pay to performance, and the changes which other companies were making to their approach.

THE NEW SYSTEM

Under the new pay scheme, which was introduced in July 1997, there are two levels of pay award. A small part of any increase is a common, nego-tiated award given to all employees and is based upon company performance. But the remaining larger part of the increase is distributed according to individual performance in each business unit. Recognizing the problems which other companies experienced from too narrow a focus on individual results, the criteria used relate to a broad assessment of contri-bution, considering the competence and flexibility of the employee, as well as the results they achieve and effort they put in.

The performance management process has two parts: the assessment and pay linked component and a communications and development part. This helps to prevent an excessive pay focus. Employees can also appeal against the personal rating they receive, which is made on a five-point scale, and which influences the size of their pay increase.

This high involvement, partnership approach did not stop with imple-mentation in 1997 however. The six-person team has continued to meet, to review the scheme, and modify it to improve its effectiveness. Managers and staff views were surveyed, further reviews of external practice carried out and changes were implemented as a result as part of the 1998 agreement. An initial difficulty had been that different staff received different increases in different parts of the business at an equivalent level of performance, which was perceived as unfair. A common rating distribution was therefore introduced, according to Hooper as 'a safety net', to help develop the required trust in the system. Other changes may occur in the third year.

LEARNING POINTS

According to Phil Hooper, there are no easy, quick-fix answers to effectively relating pay to performance: 'it will take three years to get where we want to be and have the scheme embedded in our culture.' Yet through their inclusive, partnership approach, Ericsson has developed a scheme which has the understanding and support of everyone in the business, and which is recognized and accepted as a business necessity in a ruthlessly competitive market-place. In addition, both the company and employees have something to gain by the implementation of the new system:

- The company is better able to target its investment in people and secure a return on this. Also, it is now able to provide an incentive to employees to raise the level of their contribution.
- For employees the new system brings more openness – it is clear to employees what they need to do and the basis upon which decisions about pay are made. Also it seems fairer under this new approach that employees who make a superior contribution are paid more.

In passing, it is interesting the extent to which the new venture has become a joint exercise. At a meeting to review the past operation of this plan, two groups, one comprised of union representatives and the other of managers, were asked to feedback what they believed were the pluses and minuses of the exercise. Remarkably, both groups came back with very similar feedback.

According to Managing Director Nils Grimsmo, 'to compete successfully we cannot stick to the practices of yesterday. With this new pay strategy, we are ready to compete in the next millennium.'

NOTES

1. Quoted in Brown, K (1998) An economic policy with enterprise at its heart, *The Financial Times*, 4 November
2. Thompson, M (1998) Trust and reward, in *Trust, Motivation and Commitment: A Reader*, eds S Perkins and St John Sandringham, Strategic Remuneration Research Centre, Faringdon
3. Towers Perrin (1993) *Communication Management Issues: Talking Pay and Performance*, Towers Perrin Research Report, London
4. Cox, A and Purcell, J (1998) Searching for leverage: pay systems, trust, motivation and commitment in SMEs, in *Trust, Motivation and Commitment: A Reader*, eds S Perkins and St John Sandringham, Strategic Remuneration Research Centre, Faringdon
5. Institute of Personnel and Development (1994) *People Make the Difference*, IPD, London
6. Thompson, op. cit.
7. Bowey, A (1983) *The Effectiveness of Incentive Pay Systems*, Department of Employment Research Paper, DOE, London

8. Quoted in More staff involvement the route to success, *Personnel Today*, 10 August 1998
9. Cully, M *et al.* (1998) *The 1998 Workplace Employee Relations Survey: First Findings*, ESRC/ACAS/PSI, October
10. Board of Trade (1994) *Competitiveness: Helping Business Win*, HMSO, London
11. Towers Perrin (1993), op. cit.
12. Cully *et al.,* op. cit.
13. Industrial Relations Services (1996) Assessing employee involvement strategies, *Employment Trends*, **614**, August
14. Marchington, M *et al.* (1992) *New Developments in Employee Involvement*, Manchester School of Management/Employment Department, UMIST, Manchester, May
15. Towers Perrin (1993), op. cit.
16. Cully *et al.*, op. cit.
17. Voss (1994) *Made in Europe: A four nation's best practice study,* London Business School, London
18. Marchington *et al.*, op. cit.
19. Wajcman, J (1998) *Managing Like a Man*, Pennsylvania State University Press
20. Quoted to in Trapp, R (1996) Bosses should learn to listen, *The Independent on Sunday*, 9 June
21. Towers Perrin (1997) *Learning from the Past: Changing for the future*, Research Report from Towers Perrin, London, March
22. Towers Perrin (1993), op cit.
23. Hampson, S (1998) Directors' pay should be above board!, *The Financial Times*, 10 November
24. Towers Perrin (1997), op. cit.
25. Shaw, RB (1997) *Trust in the Balance*, Jossey-Bass, San Francisco
26. Fox, A (1973) *Beyond Contract*, Faber and Faber, London
27. Thompson, op. cit.
28. Guest, D (1998) The role of the psychological contract, in *Trust, Motivation and Commitment: A Reader*, eds S Perkins and St John Sandringham, Strategic Remuneration Research Centre, Faringdon
29. Jaques, E (1961) *Equitable Payment*, Wiley, New York
30. Ibid.
31. Laventhal, GS (1980) What should be done about equity theory, in *Social Exchange*, ed GK Georges, Plenum, New York
32. Tyler, TR and Bies, RJ (1990) Beyond formal procedures: the interpersonal context of procedural justice, in *Applied Social Psychology and Organizational Settings*, ed JS Carrol, Lawrence Erlbaum, Hillsdale, NJ
33. Guest, op. cit.
34. Herriot, P and Pemberton, C (1996) Contracting careers, *Human Relations*, **49**
35. Rousseau, DM and Wade-Benson, KA (1994) Linking strategy and Human Resource practices: how employee and customer contracts are created, *Human Resource Management,* **33** (3)
36. Thompson, op. cit.
37. ICI paternalism dies, *The Financial Times*, 16 November 1998
38. O'Reilley, B (1994) The new deal, *Fortune Magazine*, 13 June
39. Herriot, P and Pemberton, C (1995) *New Deals: The revolution in managerial careers*, John Wiley, US
40. O'Reilley, op. cit.
41. Hamel, G and Prahalad, CK (1994) *Competing for the Future*, HBS Press, Mass
42. *The Financial Times*, 16 November 1998, op. cit.

43. O'Reilley, op. cit.
44. Guest, D and Conway, N (1998) *Fairness at Work and the Psychological Contract*, IPD, London
45. Adams, K (1998) Union views on competency related pay, in Industrial Relations Services, *Competency*, **6** (1), Autumn
46. Ibid.
47. Ibid.
48. Cully *et al.*, op. cit.
49. Guest and Conway, op. cit.
50. Cully *et al.*, op. cit.
51. Towers Perrin (1997) *The 1997 Towers Perrin Workplace Index*, available from Towers Perrin, London
52. Hampson, op. cit.
53. Sims, RR (1994) Human Resource management's role in clarifying the new psychological contract, *Human Resource Management*, **33** (3)
54. Guest and Conway, op. cit.
55. Cox and Purcell, op. cit.
56. Hilltrop, JM (1995) The changing psychological contract: the Human Resource challenge of the 1990s, *European Management Journal*, **13**(3)
57. Sparrow, PR (1998) Can the psychological contract be managed?, in *Trust, Motivation and Commitment: A Reader*, eds S Perkins and St John Sandringham, Strategic Remuneration Research Centre, Faringdon
58. Sako, M (1994) The informational requirements of trust: evidence from the UK and USA, unpublished paper
59. Guest and Conway, op. cit.
60. Herriot, P, Manning, WEG and Kidd, JM (1997) The content of the psychological contract, *British Journal of Management*, **8** (2)
61. O'Reilley, op. cit.
62. Ibid.
63. Ibid.
64. Ashton, C (1999) *Strategic Compensation*, Business Intelligence Report, London
65. Towers Perrin (1997), op. cit.
66. Ibid.
67. Ibid.
68. Towers Perrin (1993), op. cit.
69. Ashton, op. cit.
70. Adams, op. cit.
71. Hampson, op. cit.
72. Ashton, op. cit.
73. Ibid.
74. Welch, J (1998) British Gas leaks vital information, *People Management*, 19 February
75. Ashton, op. cit.
76. *Inquiry into Tomorrow's Company*, RSA, London, 1995.

9

Managing and devolving pay for contribution

Decentralized pay determination, it is widely argued, allows pay strategy to relate to specific business strategies, enhances management control of pay costs, and tightens the links between pay and performance.

(IRS *Employment Trends*)[1]

One size doesn't fit all.

(Divisional Head, international water company)

Decentralizing pay decisions: empowerment or abdication?

(Murlis and Wright)[2]

We saw in the two preceding chapters that the process aspects of paying for contribution are key to the successful implementation and operation of new pay systems: effective performance management processes, and particularly high levels of management and staff communications and involvement. The greater variety of schemes for linking pay to performance, tailored to the particular needs of each business, division and function in large organizations has also, necessarily, involved the devolvement of reward management responsibilities from the HR function at the corporate centre to line managers in local businesses. Increasingly, organizations are giving line managers more freedom to make pay awards within a budget, with only broad guidelines.

There is, of course, nothing new in this trend. Sales staff in a majority of large companies, for example, normally have their own, distinct bonus schemes. But this decentralization process appears to have accelerated. Indeed, it has been hailed as something of a universal process solution to the problems and paradoxes of performance-related pay, the key to implementing HR and reward strategies in practice. The advocates of devolution say that managers are there to achieve results by making the best use of the resources available to them. As their most important resource is people, it would be illogical and counterproductive to remove from them the responsibility for one of the key decisions they have to make about those people – what they should be paid.

In reality, here again we shall see in this chapter a more complex and diverse picture emerging. Excessive and over-hasty devolvement and a plethora of different pay plans can create just as many problems for effective linkages between pay and performance as applying over-centralized and uniform schemes, with no business fit or local buy-in.

In this chapter, we describe the actual trends in the management and control of pay and reward and examine the advantages and practical difficulties of devolved pay management. We go on to present a framework, illustrated with examples, to help you to establish the appropriate balance in managing pay for contribution in your own organization, between common components and local diversity, and between the HR function's input and line management ownership.

DEVOLVEMENT AND DECENTRALIZATION: THE RATIONALE

In any large organization, be it the European Union, General Motors or Shell, the balance of power between central headquarters and the constituent parts is a complex and often contentious issue, and subject to the various swings and fashions in corporate organization design. Compensation and benefits managers are well used to addressing these issues. What happens if one division wants to pay a bonus to reward managers for good performance, but the company as a whole has not made any profit? Or one part needs to provide a car to recruit a key specialist who would be positioned below the corporate car policy threshold? Or secretarial staff are paid more in one part of the business than another?

Throughout the late 1980s the predominant management orthodoxy, preached in private and public sectors was 'decentralize or die', as large organizations 'unbundled' reduced central headquarters staff and devolved responsibilities to independent SBUs. Reward management ideas and practices followed the trend.

There was a substantial decline in multi-company, industry-level pay bargaining (from 40 per cent of workplaces in 1984 to 25 per cent in 1990). Private sector employers such as British Aerospace and BP, privatized companies such as Scottish Power and BAA, government departments and agencies under the 'Next Steps' initiative, and the NHS, all substantially devolved pay management responsibilities in the early 1990's. Writers such as AW Smith[3] and Sue Hutchinson[4] advocated 'wholesale decentralization' and empowerment of local managers, with the stated benefits including improved business and organizational 'fit'; better relationships between local business needs, performance and pay; and much greater local support and ownership. Sir Bryan Pitman at Lloyds (see Case Study 9.1) described the breakdown of company-wide bargaining and local control of the pay review process as 'the best decision we ever made'.

Research generally supports this rationale and agenda for pay decentralization. Purcell and Ahlstrand's[5] 10-year research project found business diversification and organizational decentralization to be the prime drivers, as profit centre managers argued for local control of a major cost item. Jackson's[6] research across five sectors similarly found the business and organizational drivers to be primary, with the need to tailor systems to local needs and strengthen pay for performance linkages, being of secondary importance.

Senior managers in a UK-based water company which we worked with supported this agenda for their own internal pay decentralization in 1997:

- 'We have to devolve to the people closest to service delivery.'
- 'Devolvement was driven by unbundling the businesses.'
- 'We weren't involved in pay decisions. They were divorced from business reality.'

Similarly, in a UK-based pharmaceutical company, consultations with staff and managers in 1997 revealed a strong perception of the lack of any pay-for-performance relationship in practice. The company operated a centralized pay matrix to control the annual pay review process, with managers rating staff, submitting their ratings to central HR, and actual increases being determined by them and communicated some weeks later. Even senior line managers in the field felt that they had little influence on the increases their staff received, and felt there was far too little differentiation for high performers. This lack of line management accountability and ownership was raised as concern by 30 per cent of companies in Towers Perrin's European reward survey.[7]

At Zeneca, this performance and pay review process has been completely reversed. Line managers drive the pay review process and have a high degree of freedom in allocating awards in relation to individual contribution, with, for example, no uniform and prescribed rating and pay matrix scale. HR's role is one of helping to share experience and facilitate the process, building quality in at the front end, rather than policing and controlling. Similarly, at NatWest, managers have considerable flexibility in awarding pay increases, and in the extent to which they are delivered as a base pay increase or as a cash lump sum.

At the Woolwich (see Case Study 4.1) Head of HR David Smith describes how devolving pay responsibilities and building up local reward management expertise has led to the implementation of a wide range of different performance pay schemes, tailored to the needs of different parts of the business: a year 2000 bonus in IT, market-aligned bonuses for treasury staff, a sales bonus in the branches, and so on. Forty line managers were trained up to help facilitate the company's movement into broad pay bands, which has provided greater flexibility for pay levels to reflect individual contribution. Tim Wilson similarly describes the considerable benefits of devolving the pay review process to the local level at Lloyds TSB (see Case Study 9.1).

Research indicates that these objectives for, and benefits from, pay devolvement can be realized. A study of 30 devolving organizations carried out by Industrial Relations Services[8] revealed the benefits of the approach to include increased local accountability and faster decision-making, as well as lower costs. It also found, interestingly, that pay was generally one of the later aspects of HR policy to be devolved.

Hutchinson[9] found similar benefits and 'little evidence of major difficulties in handing over responsibilities to line managers'. Jackson's research[10] found little difference in the actual rate of pay increase between devolved and centralized management, but that in the devolved cases, 'the overwhelming drive by managers has been to get employees to work harder and more efficiently in return for pay increases', with a shift from, 'something for nothing to "something for something" bargaining.'

DECENTRALIZATION: THE REALITY

Yet the research, and our experience, demonstrate that the devolvement of reward management responsibilities is neither an unstoppable, one-way trend, nor a problem-free approach. While the Workforce Industrial Relations Survey[11] revealed the break up of national and industry-level bargaining, it also found some evidence of a centralization of pay bargaining inside organizations, and a growth in company-level pay determination for non-manual employees (see Figure 9.1). The recession in the early 1990s focused the spotlight on cost effectiveness and duplication of resources. It encouraged companies such as BP and Philips to reduce the degree of cross-business variation and re-centralize aspects of pay management.

More recently, the developing force of European Union employment and equal value legislation has pushed the consistency issue higher up the corporate agenda. In a recent Towers Perrin study anticipating the effects of European Monetary Union,[12] 54 per cent of participants felt that it would significantly increase the pressure for pan-European pay determination, and 73 per cent referred to the problem of mobility of staff between businesses and across borders. Some 15 per cent already operated common, pan-European bonus arrangements for some staff (usually senior managers) and 7 per cent operated a common pay structure.

Staff Group	Bargaining Level		
	National	Company	Local
Non-manual workers	-7.1%	+7.5%	-3.9%
Manual workers	-4.0%	-2.0%	+3.8%

Note: Figures are Net Change in Workers Covered

Figure 9.1 *Decentralized pay management in the private sector*

Research and cases have generally demonstrated that the wholesale and rapid decentralization of reward management can result in a number of problems. These can be grouped into three categories.

COMPANY-WIDE CONCERNS

First, there are the organization-wide issues such as mobility and career development, equal pay, and the benefits of a common company culture. 'Who protects the total competencies of the company,' asks CK Prahalad, 'if each business unit does its own thing?'. At the 1995 IPD Conference, Director General Geoff Armstrong referred to similar, 'problems which arise when decentralized bargaining and performance pay are imposed' on large organizations such as the NHS. One oil company, for example, found that the emergence of different pay and bonus practices in its constituent business introduced barriers to the development of graduates and high potential managers, who needed to broaden their experience.

In the international water company referred to above, local managers were aware of these potential problems:

- 'We'll be reinventing the wheel, inventing a new package every time.'
- 'Are the issues for each business today the key ones for the whole organization to succeed tomorrow?'
- 'We need co-ordinated career management of staff.'
- 'There's a danger of chaos.'
- 'We don't want an internal market to occur.'

COST CONTROL ISSUES

A second set of issues relates to the loss of control of pay budgets and the potential for increasing costs and duplicating resources by building up pay management expertise in each business. Throughout the 1990s, average pay increases in local authorities which pulled out of national pay bargaining and introduced their own merit pay schemes have been consistently above the nationally determined increases. BAA meanwhile found that devolvement had actually increased costs, as each business developed its own expertise to operate tailored pay schemes.

MANAGEMENT COMPETENCE

Even so, concern at the competence and willingness of management to actually manage pay and reward schemes locally regularly emerges from research and experience in devolving companies. As one of the international water company's executives put it to us, 'we're light on the required expertise'. In the past, we have come across a divisional long-term bonus scheme, developed locally, which could have ended up bankrupting the entire company; a bonus scheme introduced in the sales division of a privatized electricity company, introduced alongside a 10 per cent base pay cut, designed to reduce total pay costs, which actually led to an average payment of 190 per cent of base pay in its first year; and a joint venture between a US and UK energy company which had been operating for 18 months without any form of life cover for its staff.

Moreover, the experiences of a number of companies suggests that local managers recognize the need for such expertise and can find their own reward management extremely difficult. One of the major UK retailers fully devolved the allocation of its annual pay increase budget to store level, following criticisms of the lack of flexibility to reward high performers within their centrally controlled, fixed matrix system. Yet the results in practice, when local managers really did have to 'rob Peter' to 'pay Paul' in their own area, was that there was even less differentiation in increases according to performance than in previous years.

In our water company example, a number of business heads questioned, 'Why are we going down the devolved route?', 'Isn't there enough flexibility now?', and one told us 'There is no real sense of central constraint.' Another UK utility negotiated an enabling agreement with its trade unions to allow for the devolvement and negotiation of local terms and conditions and performance pay schemes in each business area. Twelve months later nothing had changed. In an integrated utility business local management saw no strong requirement for, nor felt they had the expertise to develop, their own schemes.

DEVOLVEMENT?

Indeed, so prevalent are these fears of local chaos and 'losing the plot', as one of our water company managers put it, that some research suggests that the level of 'real' pay devolvement has been considerably exaggerated. The actual control of payroll budgets was still determined centrally in the vast majority of the 176 decentralized companies studied in a piece of research undertaken by Warwick University Business School.[13] Their conclusion was that central financial controls 'significantly limit any apparent decentralization of pay decision making'. They also found that the consequences for any business units failing to operate within their pay budgets were generally severe, including senior management removal, redundancies and closure, hardly an encouraging environment for creating schemes to really effectively link pay to local contribution at the business unit level!

The IRS study[14] of 30 devolved organizations found that pay budgeting and pay negotiations were generally the last area of HR management to be devolved. Local freedoms on recruitment, induction and redundancy practice were generally introduced much earlier.

In the public sector, the lack of any real budgetary flexibility, as well as the continuance of centralized bargaining rendered the devolution of pay management responsibilities in the NHS largely meaningless. We saw one government agency develop a team-based reward scheme to create effective pay-for-performance linkages, in an environment with a strong team culture and the lack of an effective individual appraisal system. Yet the scheme was rejected by the Treasury for not fitting with its required, individual merit pay template. So much for devolvement!

Despite the strong arguments for devolution, we often find that organizations are often reluctant to put it into practice, or at best make only a half-hearted attempt to do so. Perhaps this is because some HR specialists (supported by many academics) seem to believe that line managers are generally not to be trusted to do what is expected of them so far as their responsibilities for people are concerned. This can arise from a peculiar form of arrogance: 'We are the experts, we know best.' Line managers sense this and react by saying in effect: 'who are you to tell me about running my department? What makes you think you know more about managing people than we do?' The lack of trust is reciprocated. Mistrust breeds mistrust, as discussed in Chapter 8.

DEVOLVING PAY: FINDING THE RIGHT BALANCE

So the picture is not a simple one, and devolving responsibility for performance pay schemes is not a universal solution to the process problems of PeRP. According to Kathryn Riley at the RAC, 'Lots of organizations are starting to realize they have decentralized too much. We have to find the right balance: empowering people to run their own show but still keeping a common frame of reference and the same core values.' But how do you define and achieve the appropriate 'balance' in your own organization for policies linking pay to performance and contribution?

Research suggests that three types of variables have a significant influence on a company's prevailing levels of integration and consistency in their HR and reward policies. These are as follows:

- the business strategy and goals of the organization;
- the internal structure;
- the approach to human resource management.

These variables are represented in Table 9.1. The table shows some of the strategic, structural, and HR characteristics that are commonly associated with various compensation arrangements, at the two opposite extremes of centralized and decentralized.

The underlying theory is relatively simple. Pay systems that differ among divisions and are controlled at the local level are most commonly found in more diverse companies, operating across a wider range of businesses and activities. These organizations operate with a looser, less integrated management style and structure. Correspondingly, less diverse companies with high levels of business interaction between divisions, as in a vertically integrated business, and with a more centralized organization structure, tend to control pay and benefits centrally, and operate with a greater level of consistency in their compensation arrangements. A number of research studies provide support for this model.

Michael Goold and Andrew Campbell examined 16 major UK companies in the late 1980s[15] and classified them into two main types: diverse conglomerates that had grown through acquisition and had a 'hands-off' management approach (such as BTR), and more centralized and structurally integrated companies (such as United Biscuits). The differences in the pay and benefits arrangements were significant. The diverse conglomerates made much greater use of bonus plans linked to local subsidiary rather than common, corporate performance, and the incidence, opportunities and payments under performance pay schemes were considerably higher than in more integrated companies. These integrated companies placed much more emphasis on group performance in their bonus plans and operated

Table 9.1 *Framework for determining an appropriate degree of centralization/ decentralization*

	Compensation arrangements in large companies	
Influencing variable	Decentralized and Varied	Centralized and Common
Organization strategy		
Business relatedness	Unrelated activities and businesses, eg a diverse conglomerate	Pursuit of common goals through related businesses
Competitive edge	High value added/quality strategy	Strategy based on low-cost leadership or business synergies
Growth	Growth by acquisition	Internal growth
Performance emphasis	Short-term, financial performance emphasis	Subsidiary performance viewed from longer term and broader business perspective
Structure		
Degree of centralization	Distinct, self-standing divisions or units with own employment contracts	Centralized and integrated, with common corporate functions and common employment contracts
Head office	Small head office	Large head office
Location	Different locations of divisions	Common locations and country
Management style	'Hands off' management style	'Hands on' management style
Human resources		
Employees	Highly varied staff profiles in divisions (skills, age, etc)	Similar types of employees in divisions, with cross-divisional career moves common
Reward philosophy	Emphasis on market-driven pay, with minimum perks/ benefits	Emphasis on internal pay considerations, and high emphasis on perquisites and benefits
Industrial relations policies	Division or site-based industrial relations	Central industrial relations arrangements, supporting common corporate culture

more consistent base pay and benefits policies for large numbers of their staff.

Similarly, a Towers Perrin/Institute of Management study[16] of 30 large British companies found a significant correlation between a centralized structure and style of management and the central control and coordination of pay and benefits arrangements (see Table 9.2). Companies with centralized structures operated with a relatively large corporate head office and were twice as likely to centrally control and administer pay and benefits for all divisions in the company compared with other companies in the sample. The study also found correlations with other personnel policies, such as integrated career development and centralized graduate recruitment.

At the same time, the management structure and style in more decentralized companies led in a different direction. These firms

Table 9.2 *Relationship between head office structure and the control of reward and other HR arrangements*

HR Activity	Percentage of companies for each type of head office centrally carrying out each activity	
	Small head office 'Hands off' management style Average 17 staff 5 main activities	Large head office 'Hands on' management style Average 114 staff 11 main activities
Pay/Benefits in general	50%	100%
Payroll	0%	50%
Base pay management	50%	100%
Pensions	100%	100%
Training	50%	100%
Succession planning	50%	83%

Source: Towers Perrin

operated with a smaller staffing in their head offices and lower levels of control over HR and pay matters. Pensions was the one major exception. All companies controlled and operated their plans centrally, primarily because of the scale and administrative economies involved.

MANAGING THE BALANCE IN PRACTICE

Four important practical points emerge from these studies and from our framework for analysing the relationships between performance pay arrangement and strategic and structural variables, as presented in Table 9.1.

ALIGNING PAY WITH THE OTHER VARIABLES

First, while no position on the centralized/decentralized scale is universally 'right' or 'wrong', any significant mismatch between the positioning of pay arrangements and these other variables is liable to create major problems.

This was clearly the case in one large gas company with which we worked. The company's business strategy had emphasized diversification, and it had established a new division in an area unrelated to its core business. The division was highly successful and growing rapidly. Unlike the main business divisions, which operated in mature markets and pursued low-cost business strategies, the division operated in a high-growth sector in which companies competed on the basis of technical and service quality. Because of the distinctive nature of the division's market, the bulk of its predominantly professional employees had been recruited externally.

In this labour market high variable pay levels, based predominantly on individual contribution, were the norm. Base pay levels were largely established on the basis of personal skills and experience, rather than job specification and size. Bonuses were generally fairly unstructured, funded out of company profits but allocated in a discretionary way, with large variations between individuals. Rewards were highly skills and performance-related with a sparse benefits package.

Virtually no movement of staff occurred between this division and other divisions of the company. In terms of business relatedness, competitive edge, and employee profile, the division fell very much within the left-hand column of Table 9.1, suggesting the need for divisionally specific pay arrangements.

However, the management style, as well as the industrial relations and reward policies in the gas company had remained very much in the right-hand column – highly centralized and controlled by the powerful, Group HR department. The objectives of internal consistency and cost control drove all pay and benefits arrangements. A consistent, detailed company-wide job evaluation method, common pay ranges, bonuses restricted to senior positions and with a strong corporate component, a fairly generous grade and service-based benefits package, and common employment terms and conditions of employment reinforced this objective. The need to recognize and reward individual contribution was not reflected in any of these policies.

As a result of having to apply these policies, the new division faced increasing difficulty in recruiting and retaining staff. To cope, the division built a complex web of 'quick-fixes' such as market supplements, 'golden hellos' and boosts to job evaluation scores and discretionary bonuses. Over time, these makeshift arrangements created complexity, confusion, and jealousies on all sides, as people outside of and inside the division realized that the formally communicated policies were a sham.

The problems were finally resolved with the creation of entirely separate terms and conditions for the division to match its distinctive strategy, situation, and employee profile. These included a distinct pay structure of broad, market-related ranges, highly variable and individually based bonuses, and its own money purchase pension plan. The recent move of the division's head office to a new location, well away from the Group head office, served as a geographical symbol of its necessary distinctiveness and the need to relate its pay arrangements to the character and contribution of its own staff.

Interestingly, a number of well-known multi-divisional companies, operating in different product and labour markets, none the less operate annual bonus plans for their most senior executives based wholly on group performance. This is a case of conscious 'misfit', ensuring that the bonus scheme is the one major management tool used to ensure that the businesses do not act entirely in their own self-interests, and disregarding the needs of other businesses and the Group as a whole.

Even for distinct businesses in new markets, the case for wholly separate pay schemes is not always clear-cut. The opening up of the UK electricity and gas markets to competition has significantly increased the importance of power trading activities, requiring very different skills and staff profiles to those in the more traditional, operational parts of utility companies. Recruits have come from IT and energy consultancies and commodity trading houses. Some of the regional electricity companies established totally separate trading businesses with staff on their own terms and conditions. These included aggressive pay and annual bonus levels, more reflective of a financial services institution, and with a very light benefits package.

Others, who are less interested in trading as an independent source of profit, but emphasize more the purchase of power as an integrated activity, for their own customers' purposes, have kept trading staff within their corporate pay arrangements. They may therefore not attract the best traders in the market, but are still able to purchase power at a competitive price.

Yet some companies have fallen in-between these two approaches, making financial sector-style base and bonus payments, yet also providing trading staff with a utility-style, rich benefits package of car, pension and lengthy notice period. In addition, some of those who established totally separate pay and conditions for gas traders, have experienced problems as they have subsequently integrated their gas and electricity trading activities, to reflect the opening up of the UK power market to competition.

EVOLVING OVER TIME

The second important point about these relationships is that they are rarely stable over time. Thus, any significant shift in the business strategy or the organization structure might well necessitate a shift in compensation arrangements. A takeover or merger (as in the Lloyd's TSB case) or a change in the top executive team, will often result in such changes, as will a shift into new business areas, as in the case of our gas and electricity company examples.

A related point to this is that in the vast majority of situations, as we have seen throughout this book, these pay and process charges need to be managed in an evolutionary manner. As we saw in earlier chapters, rapid devolvement of responsibilities for performance pay can create significant problems of management capability, of cost control and of staff reactions. An evolutionary approach along the lines of Unilever (see Case Study 3.1) or National Westminster Bank generally appears to work best.

NatWest's devolvement of performance pay responsibilities involved a staged transition from a fixed corporate pay matrix to determine base pay increases; through a matrix with a much broader range of increases in each segment of the matrix, and greater scope for movement in a broader banded pay structure; finally to giving managers full discretion within their total budget, to use an appropriate mixture of base pay and bonus awards, to genuinely reinforce individual contributions. Significant investments in training and communications have underpinned this transition.

EVOLUTION IN A LOCAL AUTHORITY

This evolutionary process has been evident through the 1990s in a large UK county council. It has over 20,000 employees, across a wide variety of occupations, ranging from lawyers and accountants, through social workers and psychologists, to engineers and manual workers. The work locations also vary, from rural areas to small county towns and into large metropolitan areas. This authority had been one of the first to opt out of national pay bargaining and introduce its own, tailored pay arrangements. These included the introduction of its own management and staff pay structure, and an incremental system of performance-related base pay increases.

Since then, driven both by a management approach of greater internal freedom and empowerment (championed by the new Chief Executive), and the external pressures of central government efficiency initiatives and competitive tendering, individual departments and business units had been given much greater decision-making and budgetary authority. But this was very much based on a stated philosophy of 'freedom with a framework', and that the authority did want to relinquish a common culture and identity. This philosophy was evident in a number of its HR and employment policies, such as a common equal opportunities policy, supported by generous provisions, for example, for maternity.

An initial review in 1995 of the effectiveness of the current Council reward arrangements revealed a number of strengths (see Table 9.3), but two key weaknesses:

- First, the relatively rigid and formulaic merit pay scheme, with incremental base pay progression related to appraised ratings, (a midpoint ceiling for 'satisfactory' performers, 110 per cent of range ceiling for those rated 'more than effective', and only the 'outstanding' able to reach the range maxima) received strong criticism, summed up by one executive who said that, 'imposing one fixed system isn't the way to do it'.
- Second, there was seen to be insufficient flexibility in reward to allow terms and conditions to reflect local needs; managers in central specialist departments claimed corporate pay scales restricted their ability to recruit and retain high calibre and high contributing staff, while managers in provider units facing external competitive tenders for their services complained that the authority's total rewards package was too expensive.

A staff attitude survey supported these conclusions (see Figure 9.2) and demonstrated that the criticisms of the performance-related pay scheme were generally not directed at the principle of PeRP. They rather stemmed from the lack, in practice, of significant rewards for exceptional performance, as well as a failure to reflect the contribution of teams. Considerable emphasis had been placed on a number of the business units on team working, while in many professional areas, staff found it difficult to specify six output-based objectives as a summary of the contribution which they made in their job.

So, while the authority had taken pay management responsibility on itself and out of national pay determination, now business units were saying they needed a similar level of their own pay control and flexibility. A design team was therefore set up to look at how best to establish pay schemes more tailored to business unit needs, and it worked up a number of alternative options for developing truly performance-related pay arrangements (see Table 9.4). However,

Table 9.3 *Assessment of effectiveness of current reward arrangements in a local authority*

	Effectiveness		
Objectives	Low	Medium	High
Reinforce Council values		✓	
Recruit/retain			✓
Cost control			✓
Flexibility in relation to suiting			
Departmental aims and characteristics	✓		
Recognize and reward achievement	✓		
Further business aims		✓	
Clear and understood		✓	
Simple/low cost to operate		✓	

1. Revise performance-related pay scheme

2. Provide more training and development opportunities for staff

3. Revise job evaluation schemes

4. Give departments/units greater freedom in how they deal with pay

5. Introduce greater choice of benefits

6. Introduce new rewards for team performance

7. Make wider use of honoraria

Figure 9.2 *Staff attitudes in the local authority and priority charges*

concerns at the management, equity, and cost of many different schemes operating amongst over 40 business units soon emerged.

The solution adopted was one of 'freedom within a framework' in a reward sense. Units were initially given the freedom to set market rates of pay and all staff were moved into a common, broader-banded structure to facilitate this. Thus, staff could still be aligned across the authority, for example for career development purposes, but at an equivalent grade the market-related pay range for specialists in one area could be higher than that for staff in a less marketable function.

Meanwhile, a menu of different performance pay schemes was developed, and this was progressively implemented over a three-year period (see Figure 9.3). All units have to have some form of performance pay but they can now select from a central menu of

Table 9.4 *Pay for performance options in the local authority*

Option	Possible rationale	Change required
1. No change	<ul><li>Current problems due to poor and inconsistent implementation</li><li>Time and resources required to amend scheme cannot be justified given other pressures</li><li>Current scheme has only been in place for 2 years – hasn't had a chance to succeed</li></ul>	<ul><li>Revised guidelines for managers and staff</li><li>Enhanced training programmes</li></ul>
2. Removal of PeRP	<ul><li>Current scheme hasn't worked</li><li>To make it work too expensive in time and resources</li><li>It could never be made to work given nature of jobs and motivation of the people filling them</li></ul>	<ul><li>Changes in salary structure eg<ul><li>removal of 'shaded' area of current pay scales or</li><li>movement towards spot salary</li></ul></li></ul>
3. Adjusting current arrangements	<ul><li>Present scheme can be made to work if most obvious shortcomings addressed</li><li>Radical change not required, would be unsettling and further undermine credibility of Council Reward Scheme</li></ul>	<ul><li>Changes in pay mechanism eg. mixture of increments and non-consolidated bonuses</li></ul>
4. Radical change	<ul><li>Problems with existing systems too deep-seated to mean that adjustments would be successful</li><li>Giving present scheme sharper 'teeth' will reinforce performance culture</li></ul>	<ul><li>Changes in pay mechanism ie. merit and general increase dependent upon performance; matrix to determine whether increase is consolidated or not</li></ul>
5. Evolutionary approach	<ul><li>Only simple changes to the mechanics of pay link required</li><li>Necessity in local authority environment of appraising performance on objective/target/output basis</li></ul>	<ul><li>Move to a 3 point rating scale</li><li>Flexibility of pay ranges attached to each rating.</li><li>Match assessment criteria to jobs</li></ul>
6. Assessing competencies	<ul><li>Effective for jobs without clear, individual short term goals.</li><li>Relates pay to training and career development policies</li><li>Potential link to Career Guide scheme</li><li>Gives appraisal clear, developmental focus</li><li>In other organizations has proved attractive to professional staff</li></ul>	<ul><li>Definition of competencies either<ul><li>centrally</li><li>department/unit/job family</li></ul></li><li>Extensive training and development programme</li></ul>
7. Assessment of team performance	<ul><li>Current focus on individual can lead to uncooperative, divisive behaviour</li><li>Important that pay system supports team based working</li></ul>	<ul><li>Alternatives for introduction include:<ul><li>included as criteria for individual assessment</li><li>team bonus</li><li>gainsharing</li></ul></li><li>Needs to define team and performance to be assessed</li><li>Training and development programme eg. team-based skills</li></ul>
8. Honoraria/ Recognition Awards	<ul><li>Ensures period between performance and reward is short</li><li>Overcomes difficulty of identifying and assessing individual/team performance</li><li>Can focus on individual/team as well as results</li></ul>	<ul><li>Honoraria replace PM as main method of rewarding performance</li></ul>

around half a dozen different schemes, which were designed to suit the vast bulk of staff. One variant on the menu focuses more on team than individual contribution, another includes consideration of individual competencies displayed, as well as results achieved. Even within the same business unit, there are now different schemes in operation for different types of staff, but all are based on these common design templates. By adopting this balanced approach the degree of local tailoring and 'fit' of performance-related pay schemes has been considerably improved, while avoiding the problems of duplication of resources and poor local design which can result from total decentralization.

A BALANCED POSITION

The third important conclusion we have drawn from our work, and illustrated in this last example, is that while the two extremes of the centralization/decentralization spectrum are illustrated in Table 9.1, the appropriate position for many organizations will be somewhere in-between. A UK electronics firm provides a good example of this balance

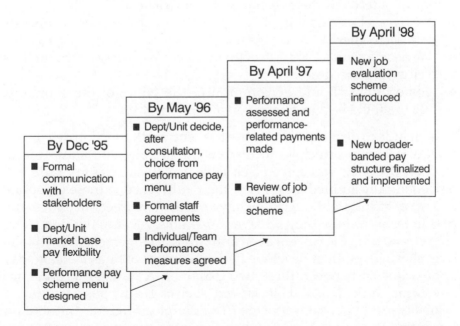

Figure 9.3 *Implementation approach for moving to a more devolved arrangement*

between centralization and decentralization – in strategy, in structure, and in compensation. Several years ago, it had established self-standing business units to respond to market fragmentation and faster rates of market change. At the same time, the company retained a single salesforce and a centralized research function, thus gaining benefits in terms of cost effectiveness and cross-fertilization of ideas.

The company's compensation approach reflects this balance. In the main, this approach involves business unit control: local divisions pay local market rates and design their own incentive plans. But these variations occur within a company-wide grading structure. This allows for the redeployment of staff between business units (considered vital for business flexibility) and provides a common, cost-effective approach to benefits and perquisites.

A similar, intermediate set of arrangements, and progressive devolution of pay management responsibilities and performance pay schemes have occurred in the international water company, which we have made reference to throughout this chapter. Discussions with managers revealed strong support for this type of balanced, intermediate approach:

- 'We need a clear HR strategy and performance framework before we can effectively develop our own approaches.'
- 'We have a business unit philosophy but we still need to co-operate with each other.'
- 'We need a common infrastructure and mechanisms to support it, as well as local freedom.'
- 'Some things should be common to the ethics of the company, others should be ours to develop and operate'.

As a prelude to devolving therefore, the central HR function developed a set of common principles for its reward strategy, and a list of local business decisions was agreed (see Table 9.5). Businesses in future will be periodically audited in terms of their adherence to these corporate reward principles, although they have much more freedom than in the past in terms of how they achieve those aims. A central design team, after considering the current overcentralized arrangements, and totally local alternatives, then developed a whole series of 'intermediate' pay approaches, in between these two extremes. A number of these are now being worked up and introduced, such as greater business-related flexibility in the pensions scheme (for example, different contribution rates), and moving to a broader-banded corporate pay structure, with different business and market-related pay ranges (see Table 9.6).

Table 9.5 *Strategic reward principles and local business responsibilities agreed in a water company*

Corporate principle	Business decision/responsibility
• Alignment with local business strategy	• Total reward/ recognition costs • Emphasis on particular strategic goals eg financial, service • Appropriate rewards systems eg bonus, recognition • Variations by type of employee • Measures of success • Definition/demonstration of cost effectiveness
• Reinforcement for performance and contribution of teams and individuals	• Levels of emphasis on performance pay • Delivery vehicle eg base pay and/or bonus • Link of reward and performance management/appraisal • Measures of performance/contribution
• Alignment with corporate values	• Appropriate reward systems eg pay, recognition
• Local business and market-related	• Market definition • Market stance • Make up of reward package • Required emphasis on various factors in setting pay levels eg performance, skills
• Common group-wide reward strategy framework	• Determine expertise/value added elsewhere • Determine potential cost savings • Experience worth sharing
• Equitable and legal compliance	• Means of ensuring equity eg job evaluation • Legal compliance
• Devolved reward management	• Developing local management expertise • Devolving accountability with relevant HR support
• Motivating employees	• Assessing/responding to employee needs • Tailoring packages to suit • Measuring success

Base pay budgeting will still be carried out centrally, but in future there will be more freedom for each business to allocate its budget according to local considerations and circumstances, such as the level of business unit performance. Bonus schemes as a principle, to reward performance and reduce the fixed cost base, are being encouraged in all parts of the business. Already, in those parts of the utility subject to the most significant, external competitive and cost pressures, base pay has been restructured and more variable pay introduced. The new pay schemes were largely designed and negotiated locally, with the Group HR function acting as a technical consultant.

Table 9.6 *A framework for devolving pay responsibilities*

	Central	Intermediate	Local
1. Job Evaluation	• Common JE system across all businesses • Retain common arrangements for senior staff	• Businesses/Units have flexibility to grade jobs and responsible for operating common JE system (with audit) • Move to a system of job families, with jobs graded on basis of local criteria • Businesses/Units responsible for grading unique jobs; common system for job families	• Businesses have own market related bands and grade jobs on basis of own criteria • Businesses/Units responsible for grading non-management staff
2. Pay Ranges	• Common pay ranges for all staff set with reference to overall market and JE scheme	• Common structure but fewer grades/broader bands and market related pay ranges vary according to job family • Businesses/Units given flexibility on recruitment position; can fix other salaries according to market movement within broad(er) pay ranges • Businesses/Units set own pay ranges for unique jobs	• Businesses/Units set own pay ranges with reference to market
3. Pay Budgeting	• Centre sets pay budget and overall increase • Centre prescribes allocation eg on basis of performance	• Centre determines overall increase in pay budget; sets guidelines for allocation, eg 2% for general increase; 2% for performance; 1% for development • Departments/Units determine basis for allocation within that criteria • Formula for varying budget increases within and between businesses eg high performing business 5%, median 3%, low 1% • Guidance matrix, used purely to plan allocation, not to enforce pay increases	• Businesses/Units set own pay budget and allocate according to local needs

Table 9.6 *continued*

	Central	Intermediate	Local
4. Rewarding Performance	• Mandate performance pay and scheme	• Businesses/Units have choice of PeRP schemes within centrally designed/audited schemes	• Businesses/Units to determine own arrangements (including rejection of PeRP)
Rewarding Individual Performance	• Centre sets individual pay adjustment mechanism and ratings distribution	• Departments/Units allowed to set pay range within matrix • Ratings variation allowed	• Allow local management complete discretion within budget limit to allocate pay increases
Rewarding Team Performance	• Design common, corporate wide schemes	• Centre sets policy and % allowed to recognize team performance. Designed and operated locally	• Businesses/Units allowed to design and operate own schemes
Rewarding Competence	• Define corporate competencies • Define link to pay	• Centre Sets corporate competency areas but lets departments/units define them • Allow flexibility in pay link	• Businesses/Units define competencies and pay link
5. Benefits	• Centred designs common flex scheme	• Centre sets flex policy • Businesses/Units can determine benefits within this min/max framework	• Businesses/Units define own schemes
6. Employee Relations	• Centre determination/ negotiation of all items following consultation with trade unions	• Central determination of some items, eg. pay increase. Local consultation for others, eg. terms and conditions	• Business/Units consult and negotiate with trade unions locally
7. Terms and Conditions	• Negotiated and controlled centrally	• Central standards/framework agreed but set at business/unit level with audit	• Businesses/Units determine own terms and conditions

On many aspects of pay, while this water company has found that a 'one size' model is too rigid and restrictive, the business units in a reasonably integrated business have found that they do share many issues, and so they are combining to develop joint solutions to these issues they face. Thus three business units have been co-operating in developing solutions to introducing more flexible working and shift arrangements, while two units have been working together to leverage off the experience of a third in introducing a gainsharing bonus plan. This evolutionary and intermediate approach to devolving pay allows the different units to proceed at different speeds to suit their own local needs and competence, increasing the chances that genuinely effective links between pay and contribution can be established and operated.

A DIFFERENT BALANCE FOR DIFFERENT POPULATIONS

A final point we would note is that even these illustrations of 'balance' in the reward management relationship over-simplify what is often the real situation in large organizations. A different degree of cross-divisional and business consistency in reward often may be appropriate for different types of employees. Generally speaking, more central control and consistency might well be appropriate for more

Table 9.7 *Variations in the management of reward arrangements for different types of employees in a multinational oil company*

Level of HR staff	Senior management	Types of employees Managers and professionals	Staff and manuals
HR at Corporate HQ	Design, operation and control of pay	Guidance via principles and advice. Agree to and audit actual systems	Guidance via principles
HR at Divisional HQ	Administer pay	Design pay systems Operate for HQ employees Advise and audit for country employees	Agree to and audit actual systems
HR at Country Operating Level		Operate and administer for local staff	Design systems, operate and administer

senior employees. This can be seen in the example of one multinational oil company, illustrated in Table 9.7. In this company, the pay systems for the top 250 senior managers are uniform across the group, and controlled by the HR department at corporate headquarters. There are common annual bonus and long-term incentive plans, operated on a worldwide basis.

For other management and senior professional employees, however, the central HR role is restricted to providing a common policy framework. Within this framework, divisional and local country HR staff can tailor their compensation systems to suit their own particular local circumstances and needs. Non-management staff have totally locally developed performance pay arrangements, subject only to corporate principles

Similarly, in an electricity company a common annual management bonus scheme operates, but the emphasis placed on the different levels of contribution in the business varies by level of management as shown in Table 9.8. Managers at lower levels in the company have greater influence on their own individual performance and that of their business unit, rather than the group as a whole, and this is reflected in the scheme weightings.

This last oil company example also illustrates that an appropriate balance in the control and management of pay and benefits and performance pay schemes, depends on a clear and shared under-standing of roles and responsibilities among compensation and HR staff at the different levels in the organization, as illustrated in Table 9.7. Even in highly decentralized companies, this will often require a common statement and understanding of reward strategy, to ensure that no confusion occurs in either the design or operation of pay arrangements. At the Woolwich, central HR has clearly set out, almost in contract form, the central and the local line responsibilities for pay management. This helps to ensure that 'abdication' of pay management responsibility does not occur.

Table 9.8 *Balanced annual bonus plan in an electricity company*

Position	Maximum payment	Corporate performance	Business performance	Individual performance
Director	50%	100%	—	—
Senior Managers	30%	50%	25%	25%
Managers/Professionals	20%	25%	25%	50%

HOW TO DEVOLVE

If an element of greater devolution is regarded as desirable in your organization, we would recommend that having assessed the appropriate level of devolvement, you follow the following six steps to implement.

1. Involve the managers in discussions on the objectives of devolution and how it will work as early as possible.
2. Proceed on the assumption that if people know what they are expected to do, know how to do it, and know that doing it will be advantageous to them and the organization, they are more likely to get on with it conscientiously and to good effect.
3. Build on this assumption by:
   – explaining what is expected of line managers;
   – pointing out why it is desirable;
   – spelling out how they are expected to do it.
4. Get these messages across by briefing, formal training and coaching. Using experienced and convinced line managers as coaches, as Zeneca did for example, when reforming its performance pay scheme, is a good idea.
5. Monitor what is being done. But this should be carried out with discretion – with a light touch. It is a matter of establishing where further guidance and help is required rather than finding fault.
6. Regularly review and evaluate the outcome of devolution, and change practices or processes as required

CONCLUSION

Professor Kets de Vries[17] of the Insead Business School believes that establishing an effective and appropriate 'balance' lies at the heart of effective management. He illustrates the damaging effects of extreme approaches and obsessions on individual and organizational well-being.

His views can be seen to have strong applicability to the management of reward arrangements in general, and to attempts to create effective linkages between pay and performance in particular. Paying for contribution involves a much greater variety and tailoring of schemes, to suit local business and staff needs. But to make this practically effective generally requires a clear corporate framework of common reward principles and values. The extremes of excessively varied and devolved pay and bonus schemes can be at least as damaging, expensive, demotivating and disruptive to organizational and individual performance as the imposition of a fixed, uniform merit pay model corporate-wide.

SUMMARY

- Heavy decentralization and devolvement of pay management have been advocated as the most effective means of establishing effective, local links between pay and contribution in large organizations. The general reward trend in the late 1980s and early 1990s in both public and private sectors was one of devolvement, reflecting this strategic and organization design orthodoxy.
- Research has demonstrated the problems that imposing fixed, uniform merit pay arrangements can create in large organizations, with a lack of local ownership and 'buy-in', and very weak linkages in practice between pay and performance. Increased local accountability, faster decision making and local tailoring of schemes can all result from devolvement.
- Yet the trend has not been all in one direction, and research also indicates the problems that excessive devolvement of responsibility for pay and pay for performance can create. These relate to:
  - organization-wide issues such as impeding mobility and career development;
  - additional costs resulting from a duplication of resources and a lack of central cost control;
  - the lack of local management competence in scheme design and operation.
  A number of organizations in the 1990s have actually re-centralized various aspects of pay management after experiencing some of these problems.
- Three types of variables influence the appropriate positioning for each organization on a scale from centralized/consistent to decentralized/varied pay arrangements. These are:
  - the business strategy of the organization;
  - the internal structure;
  - the HR approach and demographics.

- For many organizations, an intermediate approach between the extremes of one rigid scheme and the chaos of many different ones, between overly-centralist and 'hands off' management, is often appropriate. Examples of this include:
  - clearly stating common reward principles, such as linking pay and contribution, but allowing local business to design and run their own performance pay schemes to meet these criteria and suit their own local circumstances and markets;
  - designing a menu of performance pay schemes which business units can select from according to their own needs, providing flexibility but avoiding the costs of 're-inventing the wheel';
  - varying the level of diversity according to different staff populations with, for example, a common bonus plan for senior managers across the organization, but wholly local, business unit schemes for those clerical and manual staff who operate in a totally local labour market.

CASE STUDY 9.1

Defining and devolving new pay processes at Lloyds TSB

The merger of Lloyds Bank and the TSB Group in January 1996 created a major player in the financial services industry, with about 60,000 UK employees and £150 billion worth of assets. Integrating pay and reward arrangements in the new organization created major challenges, given the very different histories and cultures of the two banks. But it also presented the opportunity of removing antiquated and inconsistent policies, and developing new approaches to managing pay and its relationship to performance.

Head of Reward Tim Wilson led the process of developing and implementing a reward strategy for the new organization, which was completed in time for all staff to move into a new pay structure on 1 January 1997. The framework for the new strategy was rapidly developed (see Figure 9.4), with a focus on positively reinforcing the business strategy and the maximizing of shareholder value. The key challenge then emerging was how to pull people together into a common set of pay arrangements and approach to managing pay and performance. Both organizations, interestingly, had had fairly similar approaches to base pay management, with points factor job evaluation, 16 grades, and a merit pay scheme based on a centrally set matrix, which related individual increases to appraised performance and range position.

There was just enough difference in the application of these schemes to mean that the simple approach of slotting one into the other would have created a large number of anomalies and staff on protected salaries. More fundamentally though, as Wilson explains, looking forward to,

> Managing pay in a low inflation environment, with tremendous competitive cost pressures and the promises made of delivering major cost savings from the merger to shareholders, we realized that our existing pay methodology was simply unsustainable. For example, we calculated it would take more years than was reasonable to get from the entry level to the mid-point of our existing grades, because of the narrow differentials in pay.

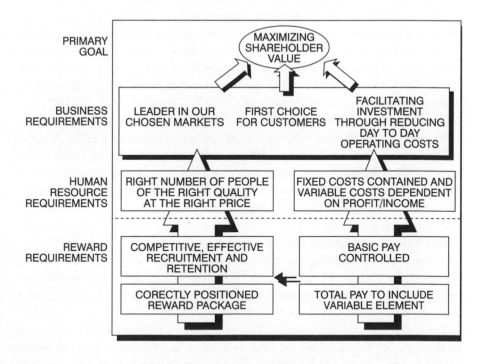

Figure 9.4 *Aligning reward to business strategy at Lloyds TSB*

Managers also described how they envisaged the content of jobs in the bank changing significantly in the future, with multi-skilling and de-skilling, and they saw existing grade structures as a major barrier to this process.

The solution Wilson and his colleagues arrived at was to move to a flatter structure of eight broad bands, to provide the necessary flexibility to reward growth in contribution and different market values. But this brought with it concerns of cost escalation and so market indicator points were introduced into each band. Each pay band is approximately 200 per cent wide but, with time, staff will gravitate towards their market point, and in future more job-and-function specific market points will be introduced.

Perhaps the key shift in philosophy within the new reward strategy, however, was as Wilson describes it, that 'line managers had to manage the pay of their staff. They had to own the process and have the information and skills to explain to each member of staff why they were getting a particular rate of increase', if the system was to be successful. Every line manager was taken off-site for training in this decision-making process, 'and to learn and practise how to determine an appropriate rate of pay increase based on the value added by the employee, their contribution relative to their peers, their current pay, the market rate, and so on.' The HR function provides supporting information, and audits the overall quality of the process, reviewing increases to ensure no discrimination is taking place for example. But the process is owned and operated locally.

According to Wilson, this has 'enabled us to manage pay in different ways to suit different parts of the business, but with an underlying, consistent philosophy', recognizing that pay for example, in call centres is a market with its own distinct characteristics. It has also provided much greater flexibility to reward high contributors appropriately.

In 1998, the approach was managed with an overall budget increase of 4 per cent. Individuals received base pay increases of 0 per cent to 8 per cent, and one-off cash lump sums were used for the first time to manage back the pay of staff who are paid relatively highly against the market.

Looking forward, though, Wilson sees difficulties for even this, more flexible form of merit pay, and sees an increasing emphasis on variable pay. In part this will result from falling inflation, although the external employment environment will play a part in shaping the pay market. If one imagines an external environment of plentiful labour, inflation of around 1–1.5 per cent, it is likely that pay for many might only change once every two or more years, something that the general population of the UK are very unused to. As part of the new strategy to focus on variable pay, incentive plans in the bank were totally redesigned. They all now link in to the concept of economic profit, which is cascaded down through the organization to ensure that individual priorities really do focus on criteria which genuinely add value to the business.

Wilson also emphasizes the importance of other aspects of the strategy in providing the appropriate motivation for the achievement of business goals throughout the organization. Rather than a total focus on individual performance, all staff benefit from company profitability through an approved profit-sharing scheme, and over 90 per cent of staff now participate in share plans that enable them to own shares in the business, giving them a direct stake in improving shareholder value. Benefits have also been reformed to remove the entitlement and status mentality that formerly prevailed, and providing well-serviced products that staff value but which do not add excessively to reward costs. The extensive communications with staff have focused on this concept of total rewards and recognizing the importance and value of the total package. Indeed, trade unions and staff groups were heavily involved throughout the change process.

Summing up Lloyds TSB's experiences, Tim Wilson sees the key components as the redefinition of performance pay and a greater focus on pay management in the business. He has two other words of advice for those pursuing a similar process. First, despite the obvious, enormous pressures to act quickly in a merger situation, take enough time to think through and develop appropriate policies and practices in your reward strategy. Second (see Figure 9.5), communicate from the outset the concept of product life cycles as applied to reward practices. Avoid the drift towards significant decay and breakdown, or 'big bang' changes by continually revisiting and modifying your reward practices within the clear direction set out by your strategy.

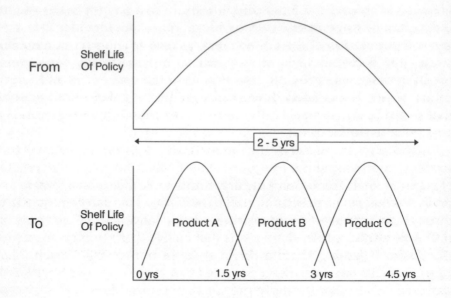

Figure 9.5   *The reward change cycle at Lloyd's TSB*

NOTES

1. Industrial Relations Services, (1995) Decentralisation in theory and practice, *Employment Trends,* **595**, November
2. Murlis, H and Wright, V (1993) Decentralising pay decisions: empowerment or abdication, *Personnel Management*, March
3. Smith AW (1992) Structureless salary management, *Compensation and Benefits Review*, July/August
4. Hutchinson, S (1998) Variations in the partnership model, *People Management*, November
5. Purcell, J and Ahlstrand, B (1994) *HRM in the Multi-Divisional Company*, Oxford University Press, Oxford
6. Jackson, MP (1993) *The Decentralisation of Collective Bargaining*, Macmillan Press, Basingstoke
7. Towers Perrin (1997) *Learning from the Past: Changing for the future*, Research Report from Towers Perrin, London, March
8. Industrial Relations Services (1994) The centre cannot hold: devolving personnel duties, *Employment Trends*, **566**
9. Hutchinson, op. cit.
10. Jackson, op. cit.
11. Millward, N (1992) *Workplace Industrial Relations in Transition*, Dartmouth Publications, Hants
12. Towers Perrin (1998) *The HR Implications of European Monetary Union*, Towers Perrin Survey Report, August

13. Marginson, P (1993) *The Control of Industrial Relations in Large Companies*, Warwick University Paper on Industrial Relations, **45**, December
14. Industrial Relations Services, op. cit.
15. Goold, M and Campbell, A (1989) *Strategies and Styles,* Basil Blackwell, Oxford
16. Towers Perrin (1989) *The Effective Head Office*, Survey Report available from Towers Perrin, London
17. Kets de Vries, M (1984) *The Neurotic Organization*, Jossey-Bass, San Francisco

10

How do you do it? A practical approach to introducing paying for contribution into your own organization

We appear to be witnessing organizations embarking on wave after wave of ambitious sounding reward programmes, as HR managers seek the magic pay formula, amidst growing anger and cynicism amongst managers and employees dissatisfied at the failure of these dazzling reward creations to deliver in practice.

(IRS Training)[1]

To assume that ordinary line managers can in anyway increase their control through this (performance pay) process, or pursue refined, strategic management objectives, is to ignore the difficulties they face in just finding the time to carry out the procedures as intended.

(Kessler and Purcell)[2]

It's not the what I'm having trouble with, it's the how.

(Winnie-the-Pooh)[3]

INTRODUCTION

So, now you have read the horror stories, like the Inland Revenue's experiences, and the academic critiques of performance pay. But what is the alternative? These academics never seem to tell you that. Some of your managers say your merit pay scheme does not work because there is not enough variability and differentiation in individual awards, yet others say they want a much stronger team and collective focus. The Operations Director says the system itself is the problem, the HR Director says it is a great system, it is just that line managers cannot use it properly. Some say pay for competence, others say never link the two.

Throughout this book, we have been reinforcing the need for a multi-faceted and contingency-based perspective on trying to create effective links between pay and performance. Contribution-related pay is not a new pay design, the merit or team pay-based scheme to suit the next millennium, but an approach that:

- while recognizing the importance of research into tested and validated pay approaches, accepts the reality that in most organizations, there has to be some element of a relationship between pay and performance, and that in many pay and reward can be used successfully to support the achievement of strategic business goals;
- stresses the importance of tailoring pay systems to suit the strategy, characteristics, people and environment of your organization, so as to produce the optimum 'fit'; each organization needs to think carefully as to why and how it introduces and operates effective pay-for-performance schemes, in relation to its own set of unique goals and circumstances; it is most unlikely you will successfully be able to 'borrow' a scheme from this sort of publication, or from a 'leading-edge' company up the road;
- sees pay for performance in its strategic context, in terms of the business strategy drivers, the nature of the employment relationship and HR philosophy in the organization, and all the other aspects of the total rewards package.

As we saw in Chapters 2 and 3, problems with performance pay are often the result of inconsistencies or difficulties in some of these other areas, which manifest themselves in pay: an unclear business strategy or an ineffective performance management system or whatever. In this sense, pay and reward is at the 'end' of the management process (see Figure 10.1), and has to be tailored to fit and reinforce these other components. We have used the model shown in Figure 10.1 successfully in a number of companies to help create a better strategic reward alignment.

But, how do you actually do this? You may not be happy with your current merit pay system, but how do you decide whether to change it, and what the best alternative is? And if as we have asserted, implementation and operating processes are key, how do you actually make it work in practice? In this chapter, we provide some guidelines, as well as examples of how other organizations have made such an assessment, and designed and implemented more effective pay-for-performance arrangements, using our paying for contribution approach.

We consider how to go about assessing whether any form of performance pay is appropriate in your organization, as well as what form has the best chance of success. We have characterized paying for contribution as a more effective and holistic approach in comparison to the 1980s' preoccupation with implementing individual merit pay. But it is also a more complex approach, involving a much wider range of choices and decisions in tailoring the pay system to suit your organization's needs and characteristics.

We therefore provide some practical frameworks to help you assess these requirements and identify and make the key decisions involved, and we illustrate these with the real experiences of organizations and managers. If paying for contribution is about strategy, design and critical process, rather than just a sole focus on design, this process of assessing and implementing the most appropriate approach is perhaps the most significant key to success.

PAYING FOR CONTRIBUTION: A THREE-PHASED APPROACH

Based on our experience, we now recommend that companies adopt a three-phased approach for moving to pay for contribution, and we would be personally unwilling to support any new reward scheme which had not progressed through all of these phases.

The first phase is diagnosing and agreeing the outline approach, understanding the organizational and business context and rationale; analysing the current reward and HR systems; examining the existing

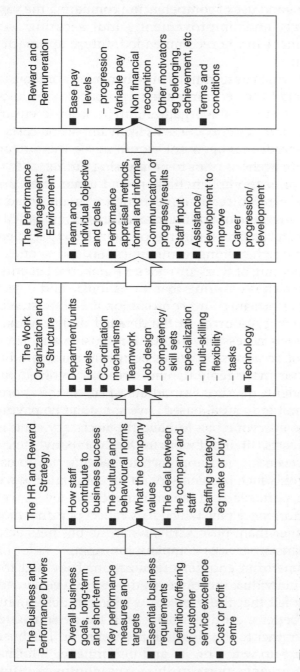

Figure 10.1 *A reward strategy framework*

The Business and Performance Drivers
- Overall business goals, long-term and short-term
- Key performance measures and targets
- Essential business requirements
- Definition/offering of customer service excellence
- Cost or profit centre

The HR and Reward Strategy
- How staff contribute to business success
- The culture and behavioural norms
- What the company values
- The deal between the company and staff
- Staffing strategy eg make or buy

The Work Organization and Structure
- Department/units
- Levels
- Co-ordination mechanisms
- Teamwork
- Job design
  - competency/ skill sets
  - specialization
  - multi-skilling
  - flexibility
  - tasks
- Technology

The Performance Management Environment
- Team and individual objective and goals
- Performance appraisal methods, formal and informal
- Communication of progress/results
- Staff input
- Assistance/ development to improve
- Career progression/ development

Reward and Remuneration
- Base pay
  - levels
  - progression
- Variable pay
- Non financial recognition
- Other motivators eg belonging, achievement, etc
- Terms and conditions

approach to performance pay; considering the current performance management systems and use of competencies; comparing the various options for change and improvement, and securing senior management agreement to the recommended, future approach and implementation plan.

The second phase, which unfortunately is where many organizations begin, is then to detail the recommended approach, often using a project team, and to test it in the organization, in order to ensure its relevance and applicability and to assess its likely impact on costs, attitudes, etc. Again, senior management would agree the outcomes, system design and implications prior to progressing further.

The third phase, prior to implementation, and again often under-emphasized and under-resourced in our experience, is concerned with the final testing of any new operating procedures or amended pay systems, and making preparations in the organization to implement and operate them, through training, communication, and so on.

This progressive phasing of work provides a number of benefits, the most important of which is ensuring that the rationale and objectives for relating pay to performance and contribution are understood and agreed, before incurring resources in the detailed design work. The second design phase is necessarily resource-intensive and we have seen on a number of occasions problems occurring fairly late in this phase because senior management, who are not involved in the detailed design, suddenly question important aspects of the approach, ('it should be team not individual based', 'we shouldn't be paying for competence because everyone has to have the necessary skills'; 'but we're trying to save costs'; 'it didn't work for XYZ company' etc).

Agreeing the rationale for, and approach to, relating pay to contribution in Phase 1 avoids such problems, or rather confronts them early in the project. Often, particularly at senior management levels, we find strong views on performance pay, which may reflect personal motives and experiences rather than, necessarily, what the business actually requires. In one financial services company for example, a lot of the senior team had come from another organization. They had tried a series of aggressive individual incentives in the last two years without much success. They felt that the problem was one of design, and so were looking for a better incentive scheme. But we demonstrated to them that it related rather to the situation they were in. The business was a greenfield start-up with new IT and performance information systems, regular re-organizations in the early months and unpredictable business volumes. The situation was clearly inappropriate for their philosophy of high levels of individual variable pay, however well or badly designed any particular incentive plan might be.

This progressive detailing and testing should also ensure that you are not applying an approach which will not actually meet your objectives, nor one which you are not able, subsequently, to implement in practice. As we saw in Chapter 2, for example in Thompson's[4] research, while everybody loves to focus on the design features of pay systems (do we use base pay or bonus?; what performance measures?; how big are the payments?; do we have a fixed formula or flexible pay linkage?), problems are often nothing to do with design. Rather, they result from unclear or lack of agreement over objectives; ('they forced me to accept it'; 'I never agreed with it anyway'), and particularly an inability to operate the systems in practice, ('it's too time-consuming'; 'I don't have the resources'; 'it's being applied unfairly', 'my manager doesn't have the skills').

The phased progression is also designed to build up the capability of the organization to operate the contribution-related pay system as planned, both in the sense of formal procedures, administrative controls, etc, but more importantly in the sense of developing the understanding and confidence of staff and management in it. This is why the communication and involvement aspects of the project are so important, and it is critically important to involve managers and staff in all phases of the project, as virtually all the companies cited in this book illustrate. We have seen already the considerable body of evidence indicating that this type of involvement has a strong correlation with the successful outcomes of pay and reward projects.

It is also vital, if you use outside consultants to assist with the project, that you, not they, 'own' the project. Their experience and learning need to be transferred into your own organization so that come implementation, you are able to effectively operate any new system on your own.

As well as regular employee consultation and communication in all three phases, we would typically recommend that your organization clarifies decision-making and work roles on such a project. Often we form both a policy or steering group, and a project or design team, at the outset.

The policy group would be formed of executives responsible for agreeing and signing off the approach, with a facilitating and overseeing role throughout the project. They would meet at the end of each phase to agree outcomes before further progress. The project design team would typically be a mixture of line and HR staff from across the organization, and they would carry out the detailed design work.

Scottish Amicable, for example, used a joint HR, management and staff working party to develop their system of competence and results-based base pay adjustment. Nuclear Electric similarly used a mixture of line management, HR and trade union staff on a number of separate design teams (one on competency platforms, one on pay adjustment etc) during Phase 2 of their project. These teams consulted with hundreds of staff during the course of their work.

Normally a dedicated manager, typically from the HR Department, would be assigned to, and might expect to work 2–3 days per week, on such a project. The length of each phase and the total project obviously vary considerably depending on the size and circumstances of your organization. However, to give you some idea, Phase 1 might typically take between one and two months to complete, Phase 2 between two and four months, and Phase 3 between three and six months. There are no 'quick fixes' in our experience, we are afraid, and over-hasty design and implementation have been a key reason for the failure of many traditional merit pay plans.

Figure 10.2 illustrates the major steps in each of the three phases, and in the rest of the chapter we comment in more detail on some of the most important aspects of each phase.

PHASE 1: DIAGNOSIS

This phase needs to provide researched and well-founded answers to a number of questions for your organization:

- Do we/why do we want to link performance and contribution directly to rewards?
- What does performance mean in the organization? What are our strategic goals? How and how well do we measure it and manage it? What is the relative importance of results compared to how these results are achieved, and of short-term versus long-term performance? Where are the main performance leverage points in the organization?
- What is the basis of our HR strategy? How do employees contribute to the strategic success of our business? Does competitive success depend on customer service quality and innovation, or low-cost leadership? What is our HR philosophy: value, commitment or cost-based? What is the nature of our employment relationship?

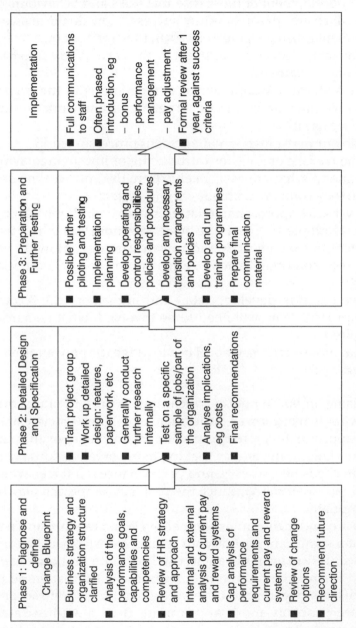

Phase 1: Diagnose and define Change Blueprint	Phase 2: Detailed Design and Specification	Phase 3: Preparation and Further Testing	Implementation
■ Business strategy and organization structure clarified	■ Train project group	■ Possible further piloting and testing	■ Full communications to staff
■ Analysis of the performance goals, capabilities and competencies	■ Work up detailed design: features, paperwork, etc	■ Implementation planning	■ Often phased introduction, eg
■ Review of HR strategy and approach	■ Generally conduct further research internally	■ Develop operating and control responsibilities, policies and procedures	– bonus
■ Internal and external analysis of current pay and reward systems	■ Test on a specific sample of jobs/part of the organization	■ Develop any necessary transition arrangements and policies	– performance management
■ Gap analysis of performance requirements and current pay and reward systems	■ Analyse implications, eg costs	■ Develop and run training programmes	– pay adjustment
■ Review of change options	■ Final recommendations	■ Prepare final communication material	■ Formal review after 1 year, against success criteria
■ Recommend future direction			

Figure 10.2 *Typical project phases in a contribution-related pay project*

- How well do our current pay and reward systems encourage and reinforce the achievement of essential business results, and the display and development of those essential skills and behaviours of our people which are critical for future success? How do the answers vary for different functions/groups/levels in the organization?
- What do line managers and staff think of the current pay situation and any changes required?
- What is the state of development of competencies in the organization? Do we have an existing competency framework and do we/how do we use it?
- How well do our performance management processes work?
- What are the realistic options for introducing or improving paying for contribution? What are their likely strengths and weaknesses, and how do they compare with our current systems?
- What, if any, future approach to relating pay to contribution do we recommend is adopted? What is the business rationale and how will it complement our broader HR and reward strategy? How do we maximize the potential benefits and minimize the potential problems?
- How are we going to develop, detail and implement the recommended approach? Who will need to be involved, what resources will be required?
- What are the success criteria we will use to judge the new/improved approach against?

There is no shame, in our minds, in concluding at the end of this first phase that any particular form of performance or competency-related pay is not an appropriate approach in your organization, or that the time is not right. Thompson[5] argues that too many organizations try to use pay as a direct business strategy and performance reinforcer, when in some situations a 'neutralize/reduce the problems' approach may be the most appropriate.

Perhaps you are under enormous competitive cost pressures and pay costs represent a significant part of your total costs. Michael O'Leary, Chief Executive of Ryanair has been accused of 'tooth and claw capitalism' by Irish Premier Bertie Aherne.[6] Yet in the cut-throat world of low cost airlines, his pay policies of low basic and high bonuses and commission are probably more appropriate than a sophisticated competency pay scheme.

Perhaps your organization is undergoing major structural changes and redundancies. Perhaps you do not yet have a competency framework and want to establish one and apply it initially for development purposes, and incorporate it in your performance management system before linking it to pay. Perhaps you have no team component in that system yet, and perhaps the performance management approach needs redesigning and testing before any new pay links are established. Far better that this is raised and clarified now, before you incur significant resources in developing a pay-related approach which is not suitable and will not work.

As external consultants, you definitely think seriously before recommending not to proceed or make any changes at this point, but it is a far more uncomfortable situation to be helping to implement an approach which you know will not achieve its objectives. And some benefits and usually some level of change invariably occurs as a result of the investigative work you undertake in Phase 1. Earlier in this book we have referred to organizations who did just this.

For example, there was the research division unit that was under a directive from their US parent to use bonuses to reinforce team working. We concluded that in the fluid, multiple and shifting team environment in this unit that this might actually damage the type of team work they needed. Various training initiatives were the appropriate way forward to improve team working, along with some small, team-based recognition awards, rather than cash team bonuses.

In Figure 10.3 we give a much more detailed breakdown of the steps which would normally be included in Phase 1, drawn from an actual company situation. Rather than laboriously describing each of these stages, which are hopefully fairly self-explanatory, we will concentrate on illustrating some of the most important and describing a few of our personal experiences of this phase and its outcomes.

A DIRECT BANKING EXAMPLE

In the direct banking subsidiary of a UK organization the primary issues leading to the Phase 1 investigation taking place were the opening of a new location, in conjunction with the adoption of a more service-driven business strategy. There was also apparent dissatisfaction with the bonus schemes which operated for sales and customer service staff in their existing call centre location. Individual interviews and a structured group discussion with senior managers and directors revealed a wide range of views on both the current performance pay situation and the approach required in the future (see Figure 10.4).

Phase 1: Diagnosis and Define Change Blueprint

1. Planning
   ■ Agree objectives, content and scope of the project
   ■ Plan stages and logistics
   ■ Form and brief policy group and project team
   ■ Develop communications strategy

2. Investigate Business Case
   ■ Interview senior executives covering:
     – business drivers
     – essential requirements and competencies of staff
     – views on current pay and reward systems, especially links between pay and performance/competence
   ■ Review strategic plans and performance reports

3. Analyse current pay and reward, and related HR systems
   ■ Any written HR and reward strategy
   ■ Work and job definitions
   ■ Job evaluation method(s)
   ■ Pay structures and actual pay levels
   ■ Pay review and adjustment process
   ■ Bonus schemes
   ■ Recognition awards
   ■ Performance management system
   ■ Training and development plans and provisions
   ■ Existing competency frameworks and usage

4. Solicit Staff Views
   ■ Group discussions with samples of employees:
     – current experience of work
     – incentives to develop and support strategic goals
     – views on current reward and HR methods
   ■ Possible attitude survey

5. External Analysis
   ■ Analyse desired and actual pay position vis-à-vis comparable external companies
   ■ Review reward trends and practices in comparable companies
   ■ Review approaches to competency and performance-related pay in external companies
     – main types
     – learning points
     – strengths/weaknesses
     – relevance

6. Project Team Workshop: Option analysis
   ■ Review/agree main findings and implications
   ■ Analyse potential change options and agree most appropriate
   ■ Draft recommended outline contribution pay approach
   ■ Develop detailing and implementation plan

7. Report/Presentation to Policy Group
   ■ Rationale for paying for contribution:
     – business needs
     – current pay and reward situation
     – future requirements
   ■ Recommended approach and rationale
   ■ Detailing and implementation plan
   ■ Debate/agreement

8. Communicate to staff regarding Phase 1 Findings and agreed changes

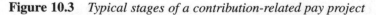

Figure 10.3 *Typical stages of a contribution-related pay project*

However, they all agreed that a business strategy based on long-term relationships with customers, depended on establishing an HR strategy and employment relationship, based on high levels of staff commitment (see Figure 10.5). They favoured moving to an 'employee ownership' commitment type of deal to support their business strategy.

Discussions with a cross-section of staff revealed a high consistency of views, in terms of the enjoyment of the work environment in the organization – their job, the friendly, non-hierarchical atmosphere, the regular recognition schemes, the emphasis on staff development. But strong dissatisfaction was expressed with the current bonus schemes which were based largely on business unit rather than personal performance.

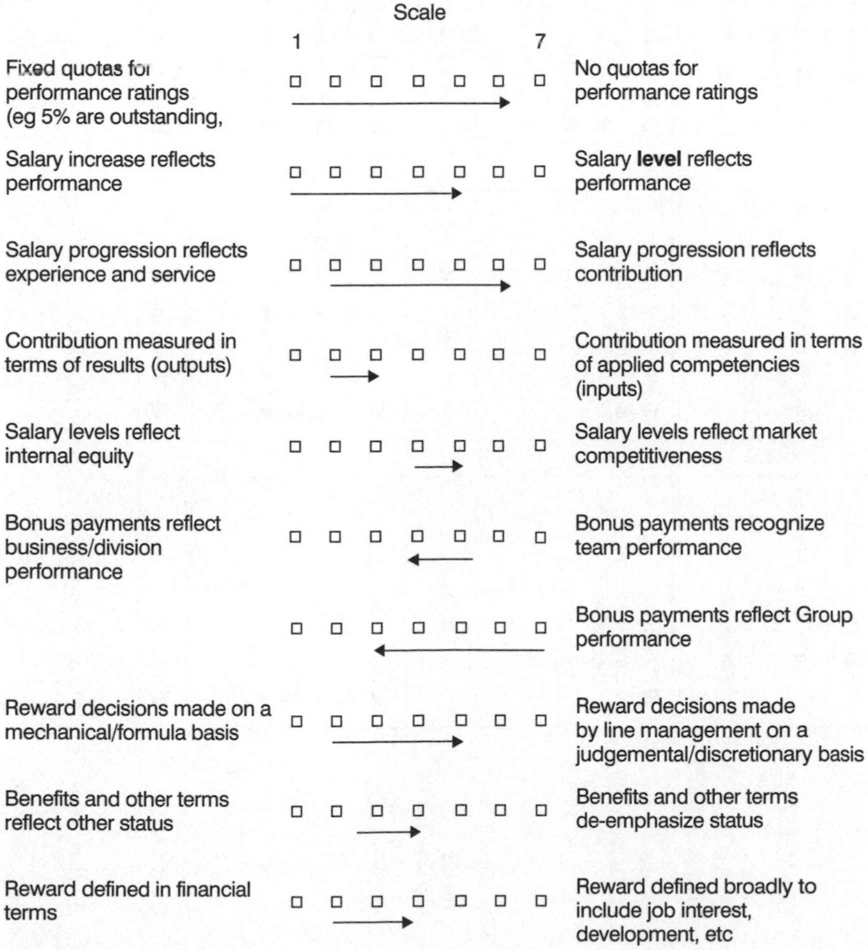

Figure 10.4 *Results of a gap analysis conducted with directors*

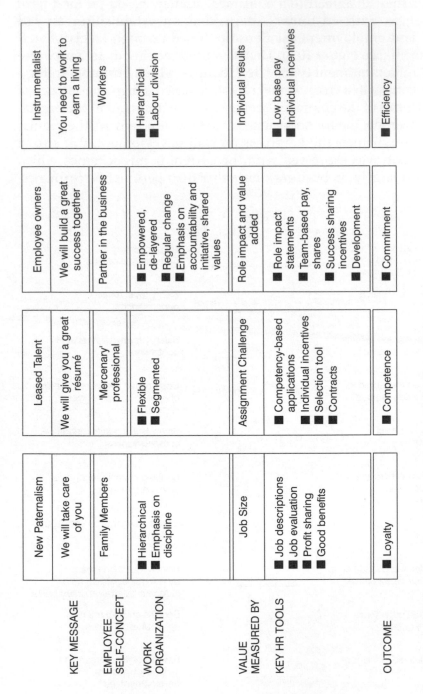

	New Paternalism	Leased Talent	Employee owners	Instrumentalist
KEY MESSAGE	We will take care of you	We will give you a great résumé	We will build a great success together	You need to work to earn a living
EMPLOYEE SELF-CONCEPT	Family Members	'Mercenary' professional	Partner in the business	Workers
WORK ORGANIZATION	■ Hierarchical ■ Emphasis on discipline	■ Flexible ■ Segmented	■ Empowered, de-layered ■ Regular change ■ Emphasis on accountability and initiative, shared values	■ Hierarchical ■ Labour division
VALUE MEASURED BY	Job Size	Assignment Challenge	Role impact and value added	Individual results
KEY HR TOOLS	■ Job descriptions ■ Job evaluation ■ Profit sharing ■ Good benefits	■ Competency-based applications ■ Individual incentives ■ Selection tool ■ Contracts	■ Role impact statements ■ Team-based pay, shares ■ Success sharing incentives ■ Development	■ Low base pay ■ Individual incentives
OUTCOME	■ Loyalty	■ Competence	■ Commitment	■ Efficiency

Figure 10.5 *Choice of employment deals for the bank in the future*

Staff felt these incentives were not focused on the new strategic goals, and that they were unable to influence them. A summary of their responses to a questionnaire used in the investigation is shown in Figure 10.6.

The project group worked up a number of change options shown in Table 10.1, in respect of both base pay progression and bonus scheme design, and considered the strengths and weaknesses of each. A summary of the rationale for, and nature of, the changes within a redirected reward strategy, that was used to recommend the approach to the directors, is shown in Figure 10.7.

The agreed changes included:

- relating base pay increases with much more flexibility to key competencies such as customer service and communications, instead of using incremental steps;

Table 10.1 *Change options and recommendations*

Bonus	Purpose/issues addressed	Issues raised

• Option 1: operate two/three distinct bonus schemes
  • as at present, a business bonus, driven wholly/largely by strategic goals for indirect staff
  • a personal bonus, driven wholly by individual performance for processing and sales staff, varying in each part of the business, but within a common framework
	• Gives some bonus opportunity to 'indirect' associates
	
	• Gives meaningful incentive to sales/direct associates
	
	• Reflect different characteristics of sales and processing work
		• No incentive effect
		
		• Cost/funding control

• Option 2: operate linked schemes based on overall business and individual performance, but with emphasis on levels and measures varying by function/activity	• Ensures funding of bonus • Provides flexibility within a common framework	• Complexity of design and operation • Novelty of performance measures in many areas • Not a viable option in short-term

• Changes under either option:
  • top half of performers get something
  • maximum 25% of bonus for best performers
  • focus is on fewer, individual, primary measures: rest as thresholds and/or affect basic pay
	• Provides motivation
	• Ensures cost control
	• Provides focus
		• Possibly cost
		• Any expectation of no cap
		• Need to manage overall performance

• (–), something for each target achieved	• Enhances motivation	• Effects on other measures

• Common principles for bonus management and changes
  • business case/rationale
  • published standards
  • 25% maximum unless demonstrable returns to bottom line
  • review/audit standards and timing
	• Ensures cost control and equity	• Should not limit flexibility

• Discontinue team bonus at year end	• Teamwork appears effective anyway • Use more effectively in other bonus schemes	• No apparent expectations

Question	Mean	Median	Mode	
This is a pleasant environment to work in	1.71	2.0	1	
We need to make changes to our current pay and reward scheme	1.71	2.0	1	
We are all working as hard as we can here	1.82	2.0	1	
I enjoy working for XYZ Banking	1.93	2.0	2	
I would welcome an element of choice in the make up of my rewards package	1.96	2.0	2	
I have regular performance discussions with my immediate manager/team leader	2.00	2.0	2	
I am motivated to help this company be successful	2.04	2.0	2	
The company gives me the opportunity to learn new skills	2.04	2.0	2	
I believe the company provides me with career development opportunities	2.21	2.0	2	
Morale is generally good here	2.43	2.0	2	
Effective team behaviours are recognized and rewarded here	2.71	3.0	2	
The overall package of pay and conditions here is a good one	2.75	3.0	2	Agree
High levels of customer service are rewarded and recognized here	2.79	3.0	2	↑
There is a strong link between my earnings and my individual performance	2.85	3.0	2	
I will get the opportunity to share in the future success of this business	2.86	3.0	3	
I am clear about the performance goals of the business and my unit	3.00	3.0	2	
There is a strong link between my earnings and the business's performance	3.00	3.0	4	
Pay is fairly adjusted here to reflect growth in my skills and job size	3.11	3.0	4	↓
We are paid competitively compared to similar jobs in other companies	3.14	3.0	3	Disagree
My pay is fair compared to other jobs inside the company	3.21	3.0	2	
Pay and reward matters are communicated well here	3.36	4.0	4	
Outstanding performance is appropriately rewarded and recognized here	3.39	4.0	4	
The bonus scheme uses appropriate performance measures	4.07	4.0	4	
The bonus scheme motivates me to perform highly	4.18	4.5	5	
The bonus scheme is fairly and objectively determined	4.26	4.0	5	
The bonus scheme is realistic and achievable	4.32	4.5	5	

Figure 10.6 *Staff views on current bonus and reward arrangements in a UK bank*

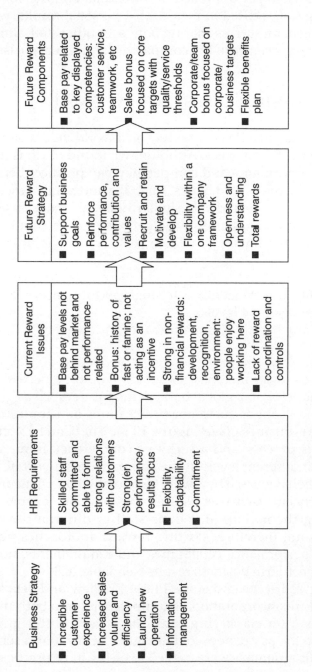

Business Strategy	HR Requirements	Current Reward Issues	Future Reward Strategy	Future Reward Components
■ Incredible customer experience ■ Increased sales volume and efficiency ■ Launch new operation ■ Information management	■ Skilled staff committed and able to form strong relations with customers ■ Strong(er) performance/results focus ■ Flexibility, adaptability ■ Commitment	■ Base pay levels not behind market and not performance-related ■ Bonus: history of fast or famine; not acting as an incentive ■ Strong in non-financial rewards: development, recognition, environment: people enjoy working here ■ Lack of reward co-ordination and controls	■ Support business goals ■ Reinforce performance, contribution and values ■ Recruit and retain ■ Motivate and develop ■ Flexibility within a one company framework ■ Openness and understanding ■ Total rewards	■ Base pay related to key displayed competencies: customer service, teamwork, etc ■ Sales bonus focused on core targets with quality/service thresholds ■ Corporate/team bonus focused on corporate/business targets ■ Flexible benefits plan

Figure 10.7 *Recommended reward strategy and changes in a UK bank*

- moving to a variable pay approach of individual bonuses for sales and processing staff, related to measurable personal results, with a lower-geared, general success sharing bonus for other staff, aimed at reinforcing the importance of the company's key annual goals.

AN INDUSTRIAL GASES COMPANY EXAMPLE

This company carried out a Phase 1 review on a worldwide basis for its top 1,500 management employees. Although we found obvious differences in market, performance and competency pay practices between the United Kingdom, the United States, Australia and South Africa (see Figure 10.8), there was a remarkable similarity in the issues raised by the project team's interviews and investigations in each country. We summarize the internal findings in Table 10.2. The key issues raised were:

- the lack of strong, direct incentives for high performance, below the most senior management levels;
- the absence of any strong reinforcement for the company's values.

The company had over the past two years developed a clear set of values, designed to foster the changes which would be necessary to succeed in that industry on a global basis in the future, such as greater innovation, and a stronger customer-orientation, in a traditionally production-driven business (see Figure 10.9). The Chief Executive himself drove this process, and a series of competency frameworks were developed at different levels in the company in support of these new values and behaviours. They were not totally consistent frameworks but the concept itself was well established, and people were used to assessing themselves and their staff at different levels of competence. In sum, therefore, existing reward approaches neither rewarded future performance capabilities and requirements, nor the achievement of short-term business results (see Table 10.3).

The changes agreed at the end of the Phase 1 review, and detailed in Phase 2, included the incorporation of competencies into both the job evaluation process, for classifying jobs into a new, flatter grading structure, and into the pay reviews of managers. Below that, a series of new recognition programmes were agreed to be the most practical and cost-effective way of initially reinforcing the values among employees as a whole. Management bonus plans were redeveloped to better

Table 10.2 *Internal consultation: key findings*

	Current strengths	Current weaknesses	Indicated changes
Reward strategy	• Generally delivers appropriate internal relativities and external competitiveness • Effective cost control	• Regions varied in their level of criticisms of existing arrangements eg Region 1 least critical. Lack of effective relationships between pay and performance was the major weakness highlighted, as well as the failure to respond to business changes	• Confirmed requirement for change, although some significant variations in views on the extent and direction of change required
Base pay: evaluation and grading	• Cost control, order • Common language • Structure for worldwide career development • Promotion used as an important motivator	• Restrictive focus on the job rather than the role/person • Overly bureaucratic systems and 'points playing' • Over-emphasis on promotion rather than personal performance or development • Reinforces hierarchy not teamwork • Failure to reflect delayering/organizational change	• Support for simplification and greater flexibility, so long as cost control not compromised
Base pay reviews	• Focus on rewarding objectives/ results • Relatively easy to administer	• Lack of differentiation in increases according to performance • Compa ratio driven • Lack of management freedom/flexibility • Progression too automatic and COL based • Does not focus on behaviours, the 'hows'	• Support for idea of more upside variability, but less so if 'Robs Peter to pay Paul' • Concern at paying for competencies, without a link to outcomes/results • Changes must tie in to performance management system
Variable pay	• Clear goals in bonus plan, communicated early • Like principle of variations in schemes for other managers • Variety of all employee schemes in US	• Over-emphasis in bonus on performance criteria which individuals have limited influence on • Bonuses do not take account of market differences • Rewarding under-achievement • Not sufficiently differentiating over-achievement • Poor communication and understanding below Senior manager • Personal rating too subjective • Lack of schemes generally lower down the organization	• Need to extend schemes down, and focus more on measures which individuals can really influence
Recognition	• A few examples of schemes but little positive comment	• Critical management style, not a recognition culture • Failure to celebrate successes	• Strong need to encourage and support it • It doesn't happen naturally
Teamwork		• Overwhelming lack of rewards/recognition for teamwork	• Some concerns at team bonus schemes being inflexible and divisive, but desire to reward/ recognize teams in some way

Reward Strategy	<ul><li>Many large companies are making significant changes to their reward recognition systems</li><li>Reward generally a follower rather than a leader of major changes eg after performance management</li><li>Changing systems often straightforward: changing attitudes/culture takes time. Heavy emphasis on communication and training required</li><li>Line management role key: need to give them more authority/freedom but at a rate which matches their capabilities. Training vital</li></ul>
Base Pay Evaluation and Grading	<ul><li>Broadbanding now relatively common. 3 main drivers a) pay administration: to give more pay flexibility, b) structural/cultural: to reduce hierarchy, reflect delayering and empowerment, c) developmental: to emphasize personal development rather than job size</li><li>Evaluation systems being simplified/streamlined and computerized, and stronger emphasis placed on the market</li></ul>
Base Pay Reviews	<ul><li>All 'merit pay' adjustment philosophy increasing prevalent worldwide</li><li>Linking pay adjustment directly and wholly to cometencies relatively rare: usually in addition to consideration of objective/results</li></ul>
Variable Pay	<ul><li>Little fundamental questioning of executive incentive plans, but regular 'tweaking' of schemes</li><li>Current trends<ul><li>– use of broader range of performance measures, along balanced scorecard lines eg customer service</li><li>– use of longer term elements eg deferrals, sometimes using shares</li><li>– growth of gainsharing type plans below executive levels</li></ul></li></ul>
Team Rewards	<ul><li>Specific team bonus plans for small teams still relatively uncommon. Teamworking often rewarded via competency in base pay, through spot/ad hoc project bonuses and particularly through recognition schemes</li></ul>
Recognition	<ul><li>Lot of activity in this area, at many different levels in organizations, particularly in companies heavily focusing on customer service and/or innovation</li><li>Relatively low risk, and potentially high return for low cost</li><li>A number of companies are making specific budgetary provision for non-pay recognition</li><li>Use of shares in recognition schemes</li></ul>

Figure 10.8 *Key learning points from external benchmarking for a gases company*

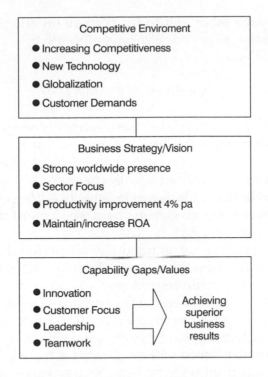

Figure 10.9 *The strategic drivers for the new pay approach*

Table 10.3 *Summary of the lack of pay for contribution in the gases company*

Business requirement	Current reward and recognition policies
• Performance: achieving superior business results	• Little differentiation in base pay levels within a grade • Limited differentiation in base pay increases according to performance • Hierarchical pay and benefits structure, recognizing position not performance • Limited variability in management bonus schemes
• Productivity improvements, increased RoA	• Cost of living pay mentality prevails in some areas • Lack of variable pay and gainshare-type programmes below management levels • Little reward/recognition for bulk of employees for substantial 1995 improvements
• Behaviours consistent with our core values to close the capability gaps: – innovation – customer focus – leadership – teamwork	• Lack of reward for such behaviours and teamwork • Evaluation and grading focuses on job content and size, not development/display of such behaviours • Very weak on non-pay recognition of valued behaviours

integrate with each other and to focus more on criteria within each individual's control, to provide a stronger incentive.

A RETAILING EXAMPLE

A similar, significant misalignment between the strategic performance goals and requirements of the business, and existing reward policy was highlighted by a Phase 1 review in a major retailer (see Figure 10.10). A summary of the situation drawn from the presentation to the policy group at the end of Phase 1 is shown in Table 10.4. The company had an excellent employee relations climate, paid well against the market and had a low staff turnover rate.

Major issues, however, surrounded pay for performance. Merit pay operated in all stores but was seen as too limited to have any effect. The company's approved profit-related pay scheme meanwhile had just paid out three times the total cost of the annual pay review, with no real effect on staff perceptions or behaviour. We considered the possible change option in terms of base pay progression methods (see Figure 10.11) and alternative bonus scheme designs. Changes recommended for Phase 2 included introducing broader pay bands with more pay differentiation on the basis of displayed competencies (including retailing NVQs) and performance, and the replacement of PRP with more focused, store-based bonuses.

PHASE 2: DETAILED DESIGN

In this phase the approach and change outline agreed in Phase 1 for moving to pay for contribution are developed in detail, normally using a part of the organization or a cross-section of jobs within it for the development and initial testing work. The stages in this phase vary considerably, depending on the approach and the changes agreed at the end of the first phase .

We have selected two examples of Phase 2 plans to illustrate typical work stages. One is from a company introducing a competency-related evaluation approach and modifying its base pay adjustment scheme to focus more clearly on contribution (see Figure 10.12). The other one is from a water company moving on a wide variety of fronts to introduce new relationships between pay and contribution (see Figure 10.13).

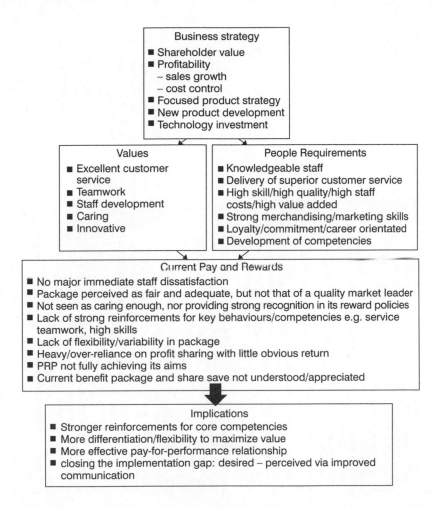

Figure 10.10 *The significant level of reward strategy misalignment at a major retailer*

Again, rather than going through each stage, relating the experiences of three organizations in this phase may be more useful.

A UK BREWING COMPANY EXAMPLE

This company had a long-standing and strong commitment to training and development, and had already operated a skills-pay system using NVQs for some of its bar staff, with considerable success. Performance

Aspect of Pay & Reward	Change Option	Strengths	Weaknesses	Recommendations & Rationale
Pay progression	i Introduce harmonized systems of base pay adjustment for all employees based on individually appraised performance, using new appraisal system: this will relate the level of pay increase to: – level of skill/competencies displayed; – a number of generic personal criteria eg. motivation, reliability; – achievement of personal objectives. – Increases for high performers will be x2 existing increments	• Clearly demonstrates to staff extra reward for increasing skills which add value to the company and sustained high performance • Consistent approach • Probably some scale economies in development and implementation • Removes automatic cost escalation in increments • Make use of define competency databank	• Again complexity of development and implementation for existing situation • Time/cost of development • Mistrust of existing appraisal system • Requires single table bargaining • Management capability issue in appraisal skills • Competency databank new, untested, and not defined in terms of levels, or generic competencies	• Again, the Rolls-Royce approach which is probably beyond the capability of the company to manage in the short term
	ii Same approach as above but separate performance appraisal and pay systems for staff and process/craft employees	• Slightly less complex • May be more positively received and owned by an employee	• Equally time-consuming • Also similar problems in terms of management capability	• Similar to above
	iii Maintain separate systems of performance appraisal and pay adjustment: – for staff update criteria judged, introduce management matrix-type pay flexibility and retrain managers and staff; – for process/craft: develop 2–3 skill steps within each pay band related to acquisition of defined competency blocks	• Still strengthens link between performance, 'added value' and pay and removes service increments • Clearly gives staff something for required skill development • Rewards process and craft for skills development, without arousing fears of individual PRP • Using existing competency work in simple manner • Still a change to address staff concerns at unfairness and lack of differentiation	• May not address staff concerns • Still doesn't 'bite' the individual performance pay 'bullet' for process/craft employees	• Recommended. Even this simpler option will be the most resource-intensive of all the pay changes to develop and take the longest to implement. None the less, the removal of service increments and addressing staff concerns on appraisal are two of the most important issues to address

Figure 10.11 *Analysis of alternative pay changes and recommendations in a large retailer*

Table 10.4 *Summary of the advantages and disadvantages of different bonus plans in the retailer*

Profit sharing	Gainsharing at company level	Gainsharing at store level
Advantages		
• Ease and cost of design/ operation • Simple to understand • Rewards overall co-operation • Creates sense of corporate identity • No profit, no payout • Reinforces a primary business goal • Can be tax-effective	• Can incorporate specific aspects of performance driving company success eg quality • Generally self-funding with measurable gains relative to payments • Promotes co-operation between teams • Can generate high levels of employee involvement	• Provides direct incentive to employees to perform • Can incorporate wide range of measures of performance • Clear gains relative to cost of plan • Promotes co-operation within stores
Disadvantages		
• No way of demonstrating impact on profits • Comes to be taken for granted • Influenced by factors outside of employee control • 'Free rider' problem	• May require heavy investment to establish and operate • May still be distant from employee behaviour • 'Free rider' problem	• Can be complex to administer and understand • Can create friction between stores • Difficult to develop for indirect support staff • Susceptible to changes in business environment/ organization

pay was well established at management levels. For its Headquarters' managers and staff, however, competencies were a relatively recent initiative, introduced by a new HR director. Her objective was very much to 'raise the bar' of competence and contribution in the organization. They had therefore decided in Phase 1 to link competencies to pay through job evaluation in order to reinforce their importance, but not through base pay increases, which might prejudice the developmental aspects of their use in the performance management system. Also, the existing objectives and results-based pay review system was found to be working very well.

They initially tested their existing competency framework as a means of evaluating a benchmark, representative sample of around 30 jobs. The existing positive and negative descriptions of the competencies had to be detailed and converted into three levels. The team found that some of the competencies, such as customer service, were so important to all jobs that they did not actually differentiate between them and so were of no use for evaluation purposes. Others such as self-development were regarded as being irrelevant for pay purposes.

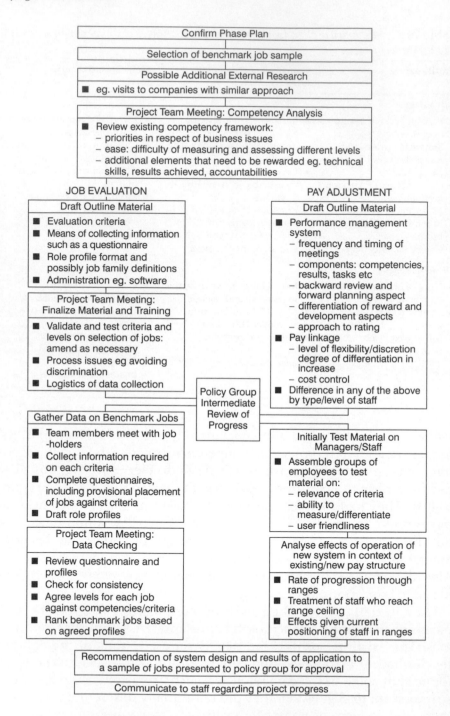

Figure 10.12   *Outline Plan of Phase 2*

Year 1

January – March	March – September	October – December

■ Reward strategy discussed and agreed by Executive
■ Consultation and communication of principles and change direction
■ Overall reward policy group set up:
  – plan and oversee process phase 2
  – set goals
  – co-ordinate/integrate changes
■ Individual project teams set up for each aspect of reward, to detail proposals
	■ Project teams develop detailed proposals in each area:
	  – job evaluation and grading (March – July)
	  – pay review and adjustments (June – October)
	  – bonuses/variable pay (April – August)
	  – allowances, terms, conditions and benefits (April – October)
	  – communication (April – onwards)
	■ Initial modelling and testing carried out
	■ Policy group/executive approval
	■ Interim consultation/communication
		■ Detailed implementation planning
		■ Establishment of operating, admin and control policies and procedures
		■ Address training requirements
		■ Finalized modelling and costing
		■ Model and establish policies for transition from old to new
		■ Further communication

Year 2

January – March	April
■ Possibly pilot changes in some areas ■ Consult/negotiate details of changes and obtain employee acceptance ■ Communicate ■ Continue training and administrative preparation	■ Implementation commences, probably on a phased basis

Figure 10.13 *Outline plan of Phases 2 and 3 in a water company*

With these amendments, and without having to add any additional criteria to a very comprehensive competency framework, the design team found it relatively straightforward to collect data from job holders using a questionnaire and then to compare the jobs against the eleven competency criteria defined at three levels. The grade structure was at the same time flattened somewhat, with broader pay bands introduced. Brief summary descriptions of each grade in terms of the competency levels required were produced and jobs slotted into the appropriate bands. Pay progression within the bands remains wholly based on results achieved. Little change in pay levels or relativities has occurred as a result of the introduction of the new system, but the company feels that the reasons for grading decisions and the reward for appropriate behaviours and contribution is now much more apparent to staff.

AN NHS EXAMPLE

For an organization in the NHS, the outcome of Phase 1 had been to agree to incorporate a more well-established competency framework into the pay review system for managers and senior professionals. For a year now managers' pay increases had been varied on the basis of individual results achieved, and this was found to have created discontent and reinforced a very individualistic perspective amongst the managers. Constrained pay funding had also prevented it having any significant differential effect on pay.

The design team initially developed some core components of the new approach to performance management and linking the appraisal outcomes to pay: principles such as an equal emphasis on the forward development and past review aspects, and practices such as review meetings at least twice a year in all areas.

Sub-teams formed of managers and staff in the different units of the organization then took this template and developed it to suit their own needs. The appraisal paperwork and the degree of flexibility and discretion in the pay linkages now vary quite considerably in the different parts of the organization, which concerned the directors on the steering group at the end of this phase. However, consistent principles were adhered to and the resulting participative approach achieved incredible buy-in amongst the managers covered, leading to rapid implementation.

A WATER COMPANY EXAMPLE

Figure 10.13 is the actual Phase 2 and 3 plan from a water company. This organization was created from a number of local authority organizations and inherited a hugely complex set of pay arrangements, characterized by no relationship whatsoever between pay and performance, and a weak infrastructure in respect of performance information and performance management.

Phase 1's outcomes were an agreement to build the basis for establishing effective pay for performance relationships, as well as harmonizing and simplifying the incredibly complex set of pay and benefits arrangements and terms and conditions which they had inherited. The recommended performance and reward management model set out at the end of phase 1 is shown in Figure 10.14.

The agenda agreed was a major change exercise and the structuring of the work in Phase 2 is shown on Figure 10.15. Five design teams were set up, working over a six-month period, on the redesign of the four main aspects of pay and reward, with a separate communications team to handle the obvious level of internal interest in the project.

The teams were all given a detailed one-day briefing at the outset at which common work components and plans were agreed, such as:

- to develop a full understanding of Phase 1 principles and outline changes;
- to review possible change options which may involve further internal and external research;
- to detail recommended changes in terms of features and content;
- to test the changes by applying them to a sample of jobs, and then to initially model the effects of implementation and costs;
- to provide regular feedback to the policy group and make the recommended deliverables to them by October.

They also agreed and set out certain principles for their work at that meeting, including:

- sticking to the brief and principles set out;
- working to plan and meeting realistic deadlines;
- openness/honesty;
- acting as teams, not a collection of sectional interests;
- confidentiality within the team.

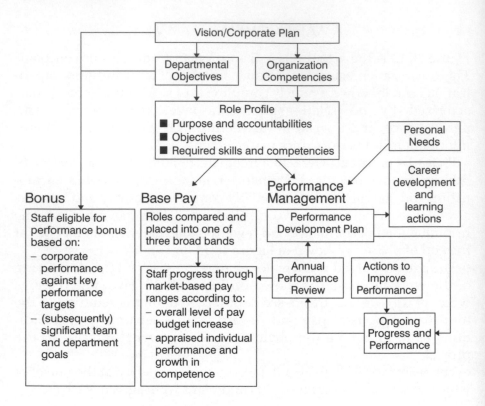

Figure 10.14 *Model of performance management and reward in the future*

Each group then developed a more detailed work plan (see Figure 10.16 for some examples) and set to work. The detailed design and preparation to implement took twelve months in all. The outcomes, which were implemented from mid-1998 onwards, included:

- moving employees from over 90 separate grades into three broad pay bands, defined in terms of responsibility and competency requirements (see Figure 10.17);
- removing many of the variable elements of pay not related to performance, with over 70 separate allowances consolidated, amalgamated or removed;
- introducing a new competency and objective-based performance management system; from 2000 onwards base pay reviews will be linked to this;

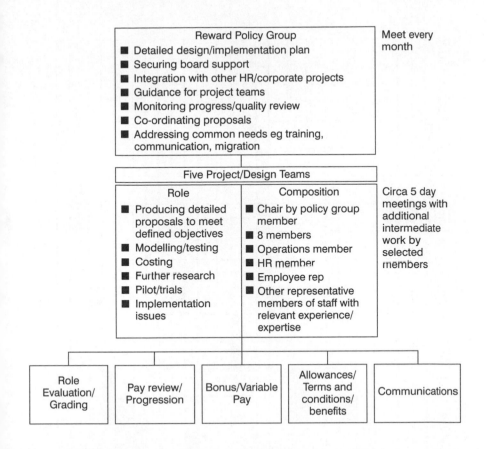

Figure 10.15 *Roles and responsibilities in Phase 2*

- introducing a new corporate bonus to reinforce key strategic goals; in 1999 a business/function and possible team component will be added to this.

PHASE 3: PREPARING TO IMPLEMENT

Figure 10.18 outlines the typical stages in this phase of a project. The reluctance of many UK organizations to include two important stages in this phase never ceases to amaze us. The first is piloting.

PAY REVIEW AND ADJUSTMENT

Task	AUG	SEP	OCT	NOV	DEC	JAN	FEB	MAR	APR	MAY	JUN	3rd QTR	4th QTR	1st QTR	2nd QTR	RESPONSIBILITY
		1997					1998							1999		
■ Analyse internal and external pay data		▓														
■ Finalize six pay ranges for each family, taking account of allowances/bonus consolidation, and any regional variations		▓	▓													
■ Model costs of transition into new structure and consider procedures for under/over graded jobs				▓	▓											
■ Finalize transition modelling and procedures on all roles placed in bands			▓	▓												
■ Finalize method of pay progression through ranges						▓										
■ Agree progression implementation requirements and necessary infrastructure development eg skill steps			▓													
■ Draft operating policies eg recruitment/promotion, payroll etc						▓										
■ Carry out April review on basis of existing system, but addressing immediate anomalies									▓							
■ Pilot link of appraisal/progression vehicle and pay														▓		
■ Carry out April review on basis of new system															▓	
■ Further improve market data gathering process								▓								

BONUS

Task	AUG	SEP	OCT	NOV	DEC	JAN	FEB	MAR	APR	MAY	JUN	3rd QTR	4th QTR	1st QTR	2nd QTR	RESPONSIBILITY
■ Finalize bonus consolidation method in relation to market rates			▓													
■ Model/cost consolidation				▓												
■ Consolidate manual workers' bonus									▓							
■ Agree design of new corporate bonus		▓														
■ Test employee views, reactions and external visits		▓	▓													
■ Detail operation and mechanics of new bonus				▓	▓											
■ Develop necessary infrastructure; measures, reports etc				▓												
■ Model using historic data						▓										
■ Introduce new bonus for 1998/9									▓							
■ Review and consider extension to measure team performance at lower levels												▓	▓			
■ Introduce any changes in 1999/2000 bonus															▓	

Figure 10.16 *Detailed Phase 2 reward project plan*

Band A	Band B	Band C
Post holders in Band A are typically experienced practitioners providing authoritative specialist advice They organize, prioritize and delegate work, deciding on the most efficient use of resources (human, budgetary and capital) and typically have an input to budgetary control or management. They develop and apply good working practices, implementing alternatives to increase effectiveness. Solutions to problems are not readily indentifiable and issues are solved by investigating, gathering and analysing information and determining actions accordingly. Decisions and actions impact on XYZ performance. They create and maintain relationships with colleagues, customers and other external contacts and guide and motivate team members. Whilst they operate within the context of their own area/department they do have an awareness of how their performance impacts on wider functional/XYZ objectives.	Post holders in Band B are typically operational, technical or support specialists and may supervise a small team. They carry out routine and non-routine activities, suggesting improvements to practices and procedures. They prioritize their own work within agreed parameters and operate with minimal supervision. Resources used will be defined by others although the role influences their efficient use to some degree. Problems are solved by choosing between a limited range of alternative actions. Decisions taken impact on the performance of the role's section. Roles develop and maintain relationships with colleagues, customers and other external contacts, interpreting information as requested. Where appropriate, the role sets an example to other team members providing advice, support and encouragement. They need to be aware of how the team's performance impacts on broader section objectives.	Post holders in Band C are typically craftsmen, operatives, technical or support assistants requiring basic technical skills and experience and may oversee a small team. They typically carry out routine tasks following standard procedures. Non-standard or complex tasks are referred to their supervisor. Resources used are defined and managed by others. Problems are easily identified and are solved on the basis of past experience. Decisions and actions impact on the operational efficiency and service delivery of the role and its team. Roles generally maintain relationships with colleagues, customers and any other external contacts, providing and obtaining information as required. They are required to be cooperative and helpful team members, with an awareness of how their role contributes to their team's objectives.

Figure 10.17   *Water company band descriptions*

```
┌─────────────────────────────────────────────────────────────────┐
│  Finalize preparation and implementation plan: steps, timing      │
│  resources                                                        │
└─────────────────────────────────────────────────────────────────┘
                                   │
┌─────────────────────────────────────────────────────────────────┐
│  Test application of new system for entire population to be covered│
│  ■ Paper test on the basis of historic and planned performance    │
│  ■ Sensitivity analysis: cost effects under different scenarios    │
│  ■ Effect on individuals: winners and losers                      │
└─────────────────────────────────────────────────────────────────┘
                                   │
┌─────────────────────────────────────────────────────────────────┐
│  Possible Pilot Testing of new approach on larger sample/unit of  │
│  the organization                                                 │
└─────────────────────────────────────────────────────────────────┘
                                   │
┌─────────────────────────────────────────────────────────────────┐
│  Development of administration and control procedures             │
│  ■ Policy manual                                                  │
│  ■ Authorizations                                                 │
│  ■ Individual responsibilities for future operations             │
│  ■ Implications for payroll management                            │
│  ■ Administration eg. computers                                   │
└─────────────────────────────────────────────────────────────────┘
                                   │
┌─────────────────────────────────────────────────────────────────┐
│  Agreement of transition procedures from old to new eg. red       │
│  circling                                                         │
└─────────────────────────────────────────────────────────────────┘
                                   │
┌─────────────────────────────────────────────────────────────────┐
│  Development and delivery of Appropriate training                 │
│  ■ Training for HR and staff who will advise on new systems        │
│  ■ Training for line managers regarding detail of new system and   │
│    building skills to operate eg in appraisal, competency          │
│    assessment etc                                                 │
│  ■ Possible training for staff eg in self-development techniques   │
└─────────────────────────────────────────────────────────────────┘
                                   │
┌─────────────────────────────────────────────────────────────────┐
│  Establishing Review Mechanisms                                   │
│  ■ Success criteria and measures for new arrangements             │
│  ■ Formal six monthly review of arrangements                      │
└─────────────────────────────────────────────────────────────────┘
                                   │
┌─────────────────────────────────────────────────────────────────┐
│  Development of Communications Materials                          │
└─────────────────────────────────────────────────────────────────┘
                                   │
┌─────────────────────────────────────────────────────────────────┐
│  Implementation (which may also be phased)                        │
└─────────────────────────────────────────────────────────────────┘
```

Figure 10.18 *Phase 3: Final testing and preparing to implement*

PILOTING

Partly we think this reluctance to pilot test stems from a black-and-white view of management, that we expect you to be confident that the solution will work perfectly, without further testing. Yet further testing of your approach on a sample beyond the initial benchmark jobs invariably has many benefits. As well as confirming on a more reliable and representative basis that your system will work in practice and achieve its objectives, it invariably provides ideas for slight modifications to the approach to improve its operation, and particularly its appearance and how best to 'sell' the scheme to those covered by it. Indeed, the communication benefits can be enormous across the organization.

In one case with a telephone company, we ran a trial incentive plan for sales staff in one region of the country. It went very well, and beyond a few minor 'tweaks' to the operation and communication details of the scheme (providing more regular performance reports, for example) the full implementation plan was confirmed. A group of senior managers subsequently spent a day learning about the new scheme and practising their presentations to their sales staff. Yet on the appointed announcement day, they found staff all knew about the scheme anyway, from colleagues and the 'grapevine', and just wanted to hear when it was going to start!

Rather than running a 'scientific' trial, we usually like to select the area where the new approach has the most favourable conditions in which to operate as the pilot site. The staff there feel good, having been selected for the trial, so you achieve some Hawthorne effect. The rest of the organization soon hears about this new system, that is hopefully working well. Sometimes, as in the IT department of a financial services company we worked with, it actually just acts as an early implementation and they carry on applying the system, which is then rolled out across the rest of the organization.

REVIEW PROCEDURES

The second common omission in this phase is setting up review criteria and procedures. Mike Langley once did an analysis of changes to pay schemes for salesmen in UK companies.[7] He found that virtually none of them made any attempt to evaluate the success of the pay changes they had made, and so none could produce any evidence as to their effectiveness. Typically, the project team disbands and line and HR managers are left to struggle with the reality of trying to operate the system as planned.

As well as clearly listing the measures and criteria for success, we typically recommend a formal review after 6–12 months, to assess how well the new systems are working. Invariably this results in some minor changes, but if these are not addressed early on, then some major problems can develop.

Table 10.5 illustrates some of the standards of effectiveness for reward practices developed in a water company. Reward practices are highly devolved and designed and operated at the local level. However, these common reward standards and criteria are applied throughout, and businesses have to report annually on their level of performance against them.

Training relevant managers and staff is also generally a key aspect of making reward changes effective. The training plan we have just agreed with a pharmaceutical company in Phase 3 is illustrated in Figure 10.19. All staff have been briefed on objective setting, with additional, detailed practice sessions running for reviewing managers. A

Table 10.5 *Corporate reward strategy standards in a UK water company*

Principle	Process Standard	Policy/Practice Standard
• Alignment with corporate and local business strategy	• Demonstrated links between strategic characteristics, requirements and goals, and reward/recognition policies • Definition and demonstration of cost effectiveness • Success criteria for reward/recognition policies established and monitored	• Key business goals evident in reward/recognition practices • Able to recruit/retain employees of the required calibre in support of resourcing goals • Necessary variations in reward/recognition practices evident between businesses
• Relationships between performance, contribution and reward	• Employees perceive a link between their own individual performance and their rewards • Employees feel that high performance is recognized/rewarded	• Performance/contribution-related pay schemes of some type in operation • Some flexibility in total pay costs in relation to business performance
• Flexibility and responsiveness	• Demonstration of flexibility to respond to local market pressures • Business managers do not feel constrained by central policies	• Evidence of changes, when required, in reward/recognition policies • Evidence that legacy issues have been addressed

subsequent workshop for them will focus on the pay review decisions, while later sessions will cover the developmental aspects of the new performance management approach, such as identifying and addressing the training needs of their staff.

Costing and financial modelling are often an important part of this phase, and some financial expertise would typically be brought into the project team. This can be critical both to assess the ultimate cost/return relationship of the pay changes, and to gauge the impact of them on staff. In one division of an electricity company, business pressures forced a reduction of over 10 per cent in total payroll costs, and base pay levels were necessarily reduced. But they developed and modelled a new incentive plan, which ensured that in whichever of the more than 90 locations that employees were based, high levels of performance would result in bonus payments which would exceed their previous base pay levels.

The costs of moving staff into any new pay schemes is also an important item and the costs and net present value of decisions such as

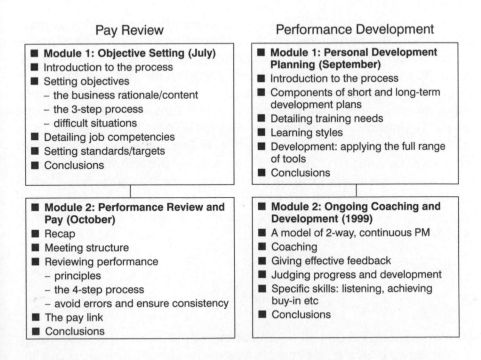

Figure 10.19 *Training workshops to support the new contribution-based performance management and reward approach in a pharmaceutical company*

red-circling or guaranteeing future increments are important items to calculate. Bonus plans need to be tested under best, expected and worst case scenarios. On one recent case we worked on the finance member of the project team defined the 'worst case' scenario as the one in which the bonus plan cost the largest amount, that is paid out the most to staff!

COMMUNICATIONS

A final complaint is that organizations typically devote too few resources to communications, as well as training, in this phase. As already shown in earlier chapters, management competence and staff perceptions are the two factors which correlate most strongly with the successful introduction of performance and contribution-related pay, and indeed any new pay system. New technologies such as e-mail make the process of soliciting staff views and communicating the general and specific effects of pay changes to them much easier and cheaper.

In a pharmaceutical company we communicated at various stages throughout the project and particularly during Phase 3, regarding the introduction of a new, broader-banded pay structure, contribution-related rather than incremental pay adjustment, and a reduction in the wholly individual and results-based bonus scheme payments. After an initial senior management briefing and overview, a branded monthly publication was produced over the next three months prior to implementation. This in turn covered each aspect of the changes: the new banding structure, the pay review process and the bonus scheme. A high level of response to the publication was received on e-mail and through this subsequent issues, and the questions and answers they contained, were tailored to address genuine staff queries and concerns.

SUMMARY

- We recommend that all organizations adopt a three-phased process for investigating, developing and implementing appropriate approaches to relating pay and reward to contribution and performance.

- This process helps to ensure that the rationale and objectives for the approach are understood and agreed, before incurring resources in detailed design work. It also progressively builds the knowledge and competence in the organization to implement and operate the new approach effectively.
- Typically, project responsibilities would be divided between a policy group, who agree the outcomes of each phase and provide general guidance and facilitation, and a design team comprised of HR and line staff, who carry out the detailed work.
- Phase 1 involves the diagnosis of the current business, HR and reward situation, identifying key issues and problems. The project team then work up a series of change options to address these issues and recommends the most appropriate future approach. Workshops with directors and staff, as well as benchmarking of external practice, provide important information for this purpose.
- Phase 2 involves the detailed design of the components of the agreed approach, be it new bonus schemes, pay structures, evaluation methods, pay progression arrangements or performance management systems. The steps will vary considerably according to the change approach that has been agreed, but it is vital to agree clear guidelines and responsibilities for those engaged in the various aspects of design.
- Phase 3 involves preparing to implement the new approach, setting up appropriate operating procedures and responsibilities, planning and costing the transition from existing to new arrangements, training relevant managers and staff, and preparing for the final communications of the changes to staff. Training and communication are two vital considerations, which are often under-resourced at this stage. Two important components often missing from this phase are running additional pilot tests, and establishing appropriate review criteria and mechanisms. The former can greatly assist in building credibility for the changes, while the latter ensures that their level of success can subsequently be assessed.

CASE STUDY 10.1

Steps in introducing pay for contribution in a Canadian telecomms company

BACKGROUND

This large North American Telecoms company was establishing a new, greenfield customer service division in Canada. The staff in the location were all telephone-based customer care executives (CCEs). They were categorized into three groups:

- sales and service executives, handling a range of inbound service and sales enquiry calls;
- technical support and repair staff, providing 'hot line' telephone support to customers;
- account service executives, concerned with resolving billing and payment queries.

The overall business strategy was to build customer retention and revenues by creating an incredible level of customer service, creating and taking cross-sales opportunities and running efficient supporting processes.

PROJECT APPROACH

The work process we used on this project, to build pay programmes to support staff's contribution to the realization of this strategy, is illustrated in Figure 10.20. After reviewing the corporate and location business strategy, the project team mapped out how each of the three main roles in the centre could affect the delivery of this strategy, producing a value tree analysis. This showed the connections between individual actions and corporate results (see Figure 10.21). Any incentive bonus schemes would clearly need to relate to the aspects of their work that staff felt they could influence, as well as creating added value for the business.

The group then examined performance information and management systems in the company, and specified the feasible measures which could be used, in each unit and for each role, to assess the performance results achieved (see Figure 10.22).

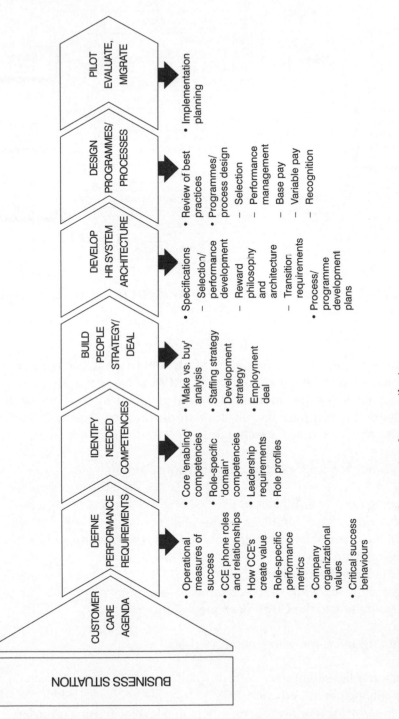

Figure 10.20 *The project approach to paying for contribution*

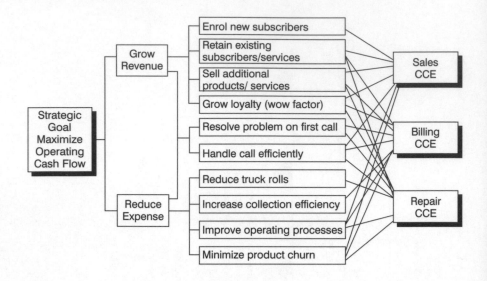

Figure 10.21 *The Group's analysis of how the three CCE roles create value for the business*

Employee competence was also clearly key to establishing the type of customer relationships that were required to achieve the long-term cash flow objectives of the business. Through detailed internal research, we identified 13 competency clusters underpinning business and role performance, including for example:

- Customer Service Orientation, which consisted of:

    - being positive and pleasant;
    - showing respect for the customer at all times;
    - taking ownership and initiative to address the customer's need;
    - being patient;
    - educating the customer;
    - going the extra mile to create a 'wow' experience;
    - committing to the Customer Care vision.

- Listening and responding, comprised of:

    - actively listening;
    - clarifying needs and concerns;
    - empathizing, connecting on a personal level with the customer;

Category	Systems Unit	Care Centre Unit	Sales CCE	Repair CCE	Billing CCE
Customer Loyalty	■ Customer satisfaction survey score ■ Customer retention/lifespan (beyond x days)	■ Customer satisfaction survey (call-related questions) ■ Customer retention (number of saves) □ Average speed of answer	■ Customer call-back score	■ Customer call-back score	■ Customer call-back score
Revenue Growth	■ Revenue/subscriber ■ Number subscribers (or market share)	■ Revenue/install ■ Revenue/subscriber ■ Transfers	■ Revenue/install ■ Revenue/call ■ Products/customer □ Controllable disconnects	□ 'Transition' effectiveness □ Controllable disconnects	■ 'Transition' effectiveness (monitoring score) ■ New revenue booked □ Controllable disconnects
Expense Reduction	■ Operating expense/subscriber ■ OCF/employee	■ Operating expense/subscriber ■ OCF/care centre employee ■ Percentage of calls cleared ■ Percentage no problem found	■ Revenue/unit of time ■ Work order accuracy	■ Percentage of calls cleared ■ Percentage no problem found	■ Availability percentage ■ Calls handled per hour ■ Safety compliance
		□ Availability percentage □ Calls handled per hour □ Workers Comp claims	□ Availability percentage □ Calls handled per hour □ Workers Comp claims	□ Availability percentage □ Calls handled per hour □ Workers Comp claims	□ Availability percentage □ Calls handled per hour □ Workers Comp claims

■ Performance measure
□ Minimum performance standards

Figure 10.22 *Measures of unit and individual performance in each business unit*

- communicating clearly and concisely;
- constructively channelling anger;
- dealing with personal stress;
- being resilient.

- Selling, which broke down into:

  - enjoying the challenge of selling;
  - matching products and services with needs;
  - identifying and overcoming objections;
  - demonstrating enthusiasm for the product;
  - communicating persuasively a course of action.

Each role was then analysed in terms of the criticality of each competency cluster to it. For example, the Sales CCE role scored highly on the three competencies shown above, as well as insight into Self and Others, Product Knowledge and Achievement Drive.

After further work on the HR strategy and desired employment relationship in the division, the overall reward strategy agreed is shown in Figure 10.23. Base salary is now related to market worth and adjusted according to the display of critical competencies, with a fairly aggressive level of differentiation between individuals. Performance management meetings are held quarterly, at which skill levels and training needs are discussed and reviewed, as well as the performance results being achieved.

Bonuses are focused on rewarding financial results and customer satisfaction levels, with an overall six monthly location bonus. In addition, specific incentives related to the key performance goals for each of the three roles also operate on a monthly basis. Thus the technical support staff can earn up to $900 per month based on a mix of team and individual performance. Threshold performance levels are for a customer satisfaction score of 75 per cent rating service as very good, for individual productivity, and for individual work quality. These all have to be achieved. Thereafter, the bonus is based on a matrix of team productivity and individual customer satisfaction scores. The sales bonus is shown on Figure 10.23 and is wholly based on individual results. Finally, non-cash recognition schemes are used to reinforce high performance and the display of core competencies, particularly customer service, in an immediate manner.

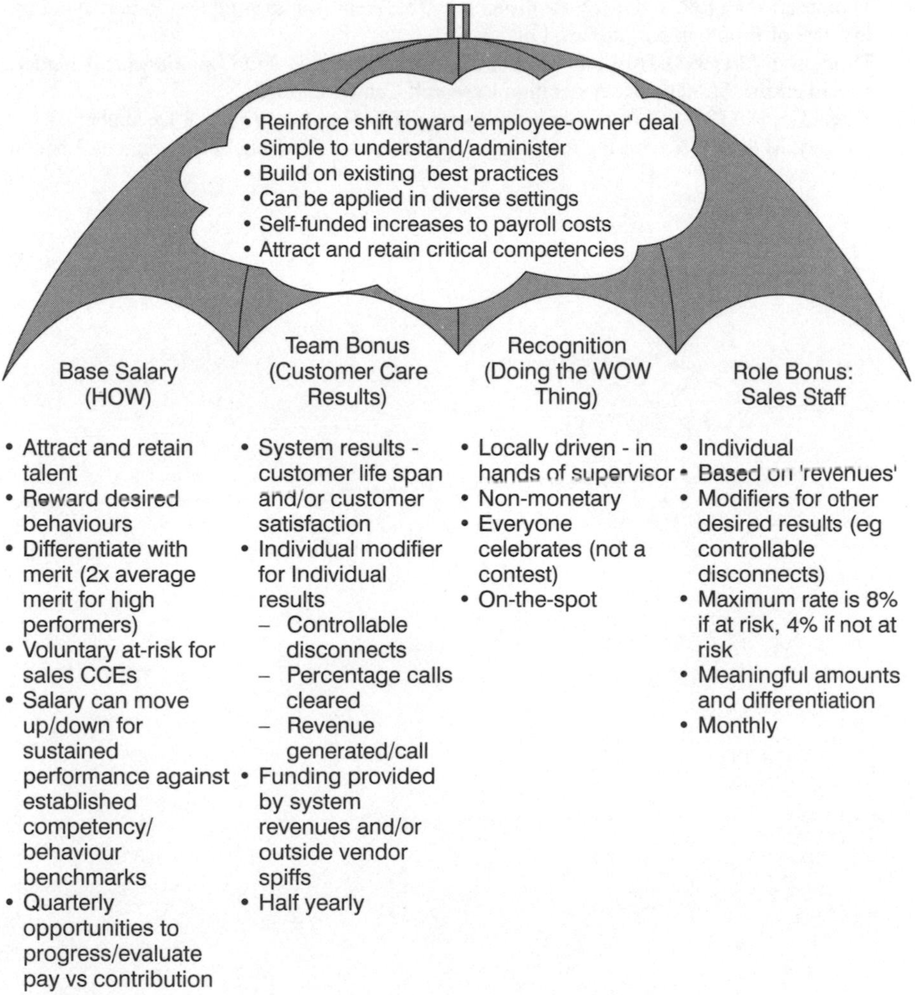

Figure 10.23 *The total rewards architecture*

NOTES

1. Industrial Relations Services (1998) Paying for performance, conference introduction, 9/10 November
2. Kessler, I and Purcell, J (1992) Performance related pay: objectives and application, *Human Resource Management Journal*, **2** (3), Spring
3. Allen, RE (1997) *Winnie-the-Pooh on Management*, Methuen, London

4. Thompson, M (1992) *Pay for Performance: The employer experience*, Report No 218, Institute of Employment Studies, London
5. Thompson, M (1998) Trust and reward, in *Trust, Motivation and Commitment: A reader*, ed SJ Perkins, Strategic Remuneration Research Centre, Oxford
6. Skapinker, M (1998) Carrying the no-frills flag, *The Financial Times*, 8 December
7. Langley, M (1987) *Rewarding the Salesforce*, Institute of Personnel Management, London

11

Conclusions on paying for contribution in the new millennium

While the distinguishing feature of the last 80 years was the increase in mobility, the next century will be marked by the widening range of choice.

(Sir John Browne, BP)[1]

The strategy of installing multiple pay systems that reward different facets of performance represents a powerful approach to improving organizational effectiveness.

(EE Lawler III)[2]

When people have the opportunity to act on their own initiative, to shape their own work and feel they are rewarded for making a difference, they can do great things. That has been true throughout the ages.

(R. Moss Kanter)[3]

THE ENVIRONMENT FOR PAY AND REWARD

As we enter the new millennium, the world of work is changing more rapidly than ever before. As Diana Coyle[4] explains, 'We are entering the next industrial revolution, distinguished by the importance of services and the revolution in IT. It is the weightless but all powerful world... a modern Nintendo games machine contains more computing power than the main processor of Apollo 13.'

Any number of statistics and examples bear this out, as virtually every economy, society and organization is buffeted by the effects of the information and communications revolution. Current trends will intensify into the next century with:

- the forecast share of the services sector in a total GDP and employment in the West increasing from around 70 per cent at present to over 90 per cent by 2005;
- knowledge-based industries and employees becoming increasingly significant; in the United Kingdom these sectors already account for nearly a quarter of national output, and their share of total employment is expanding rapidly (see Figure 11.1).
- the continuing globalization of the world economy in our ever more global 'village', as information and communications costs continue to decline and trade barriers continue to fall; the cost of a three-minute phone call from New York to London, for example, fell from $31 in 1970 to $3.32 in 1990, and computing costs by over 95 per cent during the same period;
- an intensification of the current trend for mergers and acquisitions evident within and across industry sectors as diverse as airlines and accountancy, pharmaceuticals and management consulting.

It is an ever more rapidly changing and increasingly volatile environment for those of us in work, affected and shaped by these macro changes. It took 38 years for 50 million people to have radios, it took television 13 years to acquire the same audience, while it has taken just four years for that number to become Internet users. Our fathers often had a single career. In the new millennium, forecasters predict, we will have three or more.

In our review of pay developments in this book we have touched on many of the employment trends which seem set to shape the next decade in response to these changes, including:

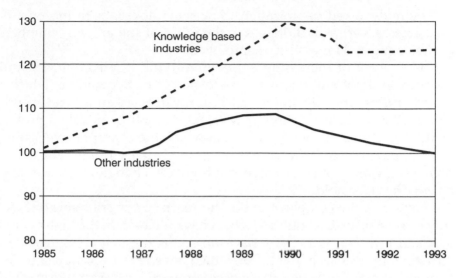

Figure 11.1 *Knowledge-based industries' share of UK employment*
Source: *Financial Times*

- organizational restructuring and the emergence of the flatter, more flexible and boundary-less organization with its shamrock, web and orchestra structures, and complicated mixture of work and home-based, full-time, part-time and contracted employees and suppliers;
- the increasingly international and multinational nature of the work-force, as localization policies develop further and companies increasingly focus on locations of excellence, wherever in the world they may be;
- the ageing of the population in the west (in 1957 300 people got a telegram from the Queen on their 100th birthday, in 1997 it was 3,000 and by 2030 it will be 10,000); but also the rise into senior management positions at a much younger age of Generation 'X', a cosmopolitan generation with a very different profile of needs and motivations to their predecessors, operating as John Browne describes in much more of a 'sellers', rather than a 'buyers' employment market;
- the increasing feminization of the workforce, with women outnumbering employed males in the UK workforce by 2002, and already doing so in traditional industrial towns such as Middlesborough and Telford.

None of these points, however, captures the real complexity of the employment picture that is emerging, with its combination of larger but more devolved organizations, fewer employees with more work and stress, severe skill shortages in the midst of still growing numbers of the young and long-term unemployed.

It is a world of increasing employment and pay complexity and paradox, and not just in terms of performance pay. A world in which a man running and kicking a ball around dressed in a lurid multi-coloured strip earns far more in a week than a fully qualified professional nurse does in a year; a world in which the concept of the 'going rate' of pay or pay increase has become virtually redundant, as an increasing variety of tailor-made and regularly changing practices and approaches take hold.

To illustrate the complexity, take the recent press criticisms of executive pay in privatized utilities, which have focused on the high overall levels of increase. What they have missed is the major strategic and structural upheavals in the sector, which have led to a complete transformation of pay and reward practices compared to their uniform, rigid and lower paid public sector past. Even in respect of executive base pay increases, there is much greater diversity evident in the sector, with the difference between the lower and upper quartile level of increases having more than quadrupled for electricity company board directors since privatization in the early 1990s. The gap between the haves and have-nots, and they would argue, the high and low performers, is widening.

Whatever happens, it seems likely that people really are, and will continue to become, increasingly important to achieving sustained competitive advantage in organizations, as technological, product and financial innovations become increasingly easy to copy. Some might argue that this has always been the case, but it is only now, with the increasing importance of service, quality and innovation-based business strategies, and as corporate downsizing has given way to the HR strategies focused on maximizing the contribution of all employees, that this is being truly and generally recognized. As Keith Todd,[5] Chief Executive of ICL explains: 'Ultimately success is only through people. This is not a cliché, it is the golden key in this new millennium business world. Consumers and citizens will have choice... people will work with you because they want to, because they believe in your cause.'

The core of this argument is that knowledge is becoming a much more important factor in economic growth because of four factors: the rapid developments in information and communications technology; the increased speed of technical and scientific progress; growing competition; and more sophisticated consumer demand patterns caused by growing prosperity. These factors increase the importance of innovation, and increase the returns on products with a large knowledge component. And knowledge is in people's heads.

A model of the change in HR approach based on research in 14 privatized utilities[6] is shown in Figure 11.2. Participants recognized the need in future for long-term and more developmentally oriented HR strategies, in order to develop and utilize employees' knowledge and to obtain the voluntary and discretionary aspects of their contribution, rather than using individual performance pay as a crude driver to push up results.

Professor Keith Bradley envisages that more and more sectors are becoming in an employment sense like professional sport, where the skills and competencies of relatively few individuals are having an increasingly disproportionate effect on the results of the entire organization. The £40,000 a week professional footballer (who incidentally earns only a tiny proportion of that as a performance payment – usually as a team win bonus), has a very major impact on club revenues and shareholder returns; the merchant banker; the corporate chief executive; this pattern of what Ruth Lea[7] terms the 'winner-takes-all society' is emerging in more and more industries.

The increasing globalization of services and cross-border transfer of technology, creating what Diana Coyle calls 'virtual immigration', is supporting this trend, with the wages of people with the same skills starting to converge across borders in Europe, while the wages of those with different skills and competencies is diverging within them.

FROM PERFORMANCE TO CONTRIBUTION

With this change in HR approach, the word 'contribution' is becoming increasingly popular in our organizations, to reflect the way in which employees will make strategy happen in the future: by growing their skills, taking new opportunities, flexing their roles, and so on.

Pharmaceutical Company Novartis explained its new reward system to staff in terms of, 'making reward reflect your contribution. It means you'll have the scope to expand your role within Novartis and develop your career and your earnings potential, all at the same time.'[8] In the public sector, Health Minister Alan Milburn[9] explained the move to performance-related contracts for consultants and nurses as 'creating a culture of success... encouraging staff to maximize their contribution',

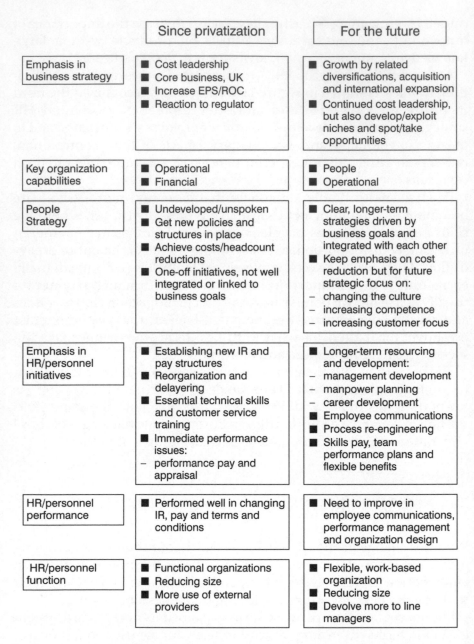

	Since privatization	For the future
Emphasis in business strategy	■ Cost leadership ■ Core business, UK ■ Increase EPS/ROC ■ Reaction to regulator	■ Growth by related diversifications, acquisition and international expansion ■ Continued cost leadership, but also develop/exploit niches and spot/take opportunities
Key organization capabilities	■ Operational ■ Financial	■ People ■ Operational
People Strategy	■ Undeveloped/unspoken ■ Get new policies and structures in place ■ Achieve costs/headcount reductions ■ One-off initiatives, not well integrated or linked to business goals	■ Clear, longer-term strategies driven by business goals and integrated with each other ■ Keep emphasis on cost reduction but for future strategic focus on: – changing the culture – increasing competence – increasing customer focus
Emphasis in HR/personnel initiatives	■ Establishing new IR and pay structures ■ Reorganization and delayering ■ Essential technical skills and customer service training ■ Immediate performance issues: – performance pay and appraisal	■ Longer-term resourcing and development: – management development – manpower planning – career development ■ Employee communications ■ Process re-engineering ■ Skills pay, team performance plans and flexible benefits
HR/personnel performance	■ Performed well in changing IR, pay and terms and conditions	■ Need to improve in employee communications, performance management and organization design
HR/personnel function	■ Functional organizations ■ Reducing size ■ More use of external providers	■ Flexible, work-based organization ■ Reducing size ■ Devolve more to line managers

Figure 11.2   *Model of changes in people strategies in the privatized utility companies*

in support of 'the high quality services NHS patients need', and replacing an, 'arcane system that paid irrespective of skill, responsibilities or performance'.

As Martin Ferber at Pfizer Research told us, assessing the contribution of his knowledge workers, who are developing products which might take ten years to get to market, is much more complex than a simple decision relating to five concrete objectives. Contribution rather than just performance is what they are looking for. In his view, contribution talks to a broader series of outcomes, is easier to relate to corporate values, encompasses enthusiasm and capability, and relates to discretionary commitment and effort, rather than just talking about individual performance and results achieved. It is about asking people to voluntarily commit and contribute to the success of the business, rather than driving them to perform.

In addition, the word used in relation to pay systems can also avoid some of the negative connotations which have come to be associated with the terminology of performance-related pay. Hence organizations such as Nuclear Electric deliberately avoided the performance-related pay nomenclature, and talked about paying for contribution instead.

PAYING FOR CONTRIBUTION: THREE MAIN CHARACTERISTICS

If you were looking for the simple answer, the off-the-shelf solution to the performance pay paradox and the failure of traditional approaches to it, then you will probably have given up on this book before now. In this context of increasing volatility, diversity and complexity it just is not there, if it ever was, which we doubt.

As we have illustrated, there is a correspondingly complex and diverse set of responses to the performance pay dilemma, which we have, with difficulty, tried to summarize and classify in this book. Traditional categorizations such as paying for the job or paying for the person; paying in fixed base pay or paying in variable bonus; paying for the team or paying for the individual's performance; and paying for results or how those results are achieved: these categories are increasingly being broken down as companies develop a series of tailored and hybrid approaches, which themselves are subject to regular modification and change. Changing a pay or bonus plan after a year of operation used to be seen as an admission of failure when we started out in consulting; now it is increasingly regarded as obvious and essential.

We have hopefully skirted the traditional, pantomime-style, 'performance-related pay is brilliant/oh no it's not, it is useless' debate that has bedevilled this subject area; as well as the deeper 'money is the key to motivation it's not, it's just a hygiene factor' academic controversy, so as to focus on what organizations and employers are actually doing, why, and with what effects.

The last of these, the account of the effects and successes of pay changes is frustratingly incomplete. This is partly due to the recent nature of many of the new pay programmes we have profiled; partly because of the shifting context and environment for them; and, unfortunately, also often because of the lack of any effective review criteria and mechanisms to accompany the changes. As the HR Director of accountancy firm Saffrey Champness[10] made clear, 'establish and rigorously measure your intended outcomes' for pay changes.

Yet as the research and our experience have illustrated, there is no universal set of success criteria, just as there are no 'right' or 'wrong' types of scheme. Success is totally dependent on your pay and reward scheme objectives, and on the environment and circumstances in which you introduce and operate it. The same scheme can work brilliantly in one setting, and fail disastrously in another.

Paying for contribution is therefore not a magical new system or scheme , the merit pay for 2000 and beyond. It is rather an approach, a process, even an attitude to reward management which we have tried to summarize in Table 11.1. It contrasts with the more restricted, uniform, design-focused and instrumentalist methodologies of many earlier performance-related pay schemes. We would summarize its main features as follows.

ACTIVE

First, while understanding Thompson's[11] point that in some situations a neutralizing, 'hassle-minimization' reward strategy approach may well be the most appropriate, generally the trends we have just been considering mean that as Lawler says, *pay is potentially a highly powerful management tool*. It is difficult to ignore it, and perhaps even an abdication of management responsibility to do so, if you are trying to build or sustain a successful, high performing organization in this increasingly global, ruthlessly competitive and resource-limited world.

Table 11.1 *Model comparing 1980s style pay for performance approaches with pay for contribution*

	Pay for performance	Paying for contribution
Organizing philosophy	Formulas, systems	Processes
HR approach	Instrumentalist, people as costs	Commitment, people as assets
Measurement	Pay for results, the 'what's, achieving individual objectives	Multi-dimensional, pay for results and 'how' results are achieved
Measures	Financial goals	Broad variety of strategic goals: Financial, service, operating etc
	Cost efficiency	Added value
Focus of measurement	Individual	Multi-level: business team, individual
Design	Uniform merit pay and/or individual bonus approach throughout the organization	Diverse approaches using wide variety of reward methods, to suit the needs of different areas/staff groups
Time-scales	Immediate past performance	Past performance, and contribution to future strategic goals
Performance appraisal	Past review and ratings focus	Mix of past review and future development
	Top down	360°
	Quantitative	Quantitative and qualitative
Pay linkage	Fixed formula, matrix	Looser, more flexible linkages, pay 'pots'
Administration	Controlled by HR	Owned/operated by line/users
Communication and involvement	Top down, written	Face-to-face, open, high involvement
Evaluation of effectiveness	Act of faith	Regular review and monitoring against clearly defined success criteria
Change over time	Regarded as failure; all or nothing	Regular incremental modification

As the CEO of Xerox, Paul Allaire, puts it, 'If you are trying to change a company to succeed in the future, one of the most sensible things you can do is change the way you reward and recognize people'.[12] Links between performance and reward, to some extent, at some level, by some means, are therefore an essential rather than a 'nice to have' component in our economies and organizations today, and increasingly tomorrow, 'not a threat but a fact of life' as Yorkshire Water Services put it. John Monks of the TUC and Adair Turner of the CBI may have different views on the means and solutions, but on this they agree.

The research may be contradictory but as the Vice President of Human Resources at Whirlpool Europe expresses it, 'While it is difficult to prove, compensation can drive business strategy, it focuses the organization on what is important and is a key factor in achieving behavioural change.'[13] Indeed, the conclusion of three respected economists and financiers is that, 'Pay for performance systems are such powerful motivators of human actions that they can induce counterproductive effects, and the substitution of less effective motivational devices in organizations, such as promotion and merit-based pay.'[14] Strong relationships between individual pay and performance are not a necessity in every organization, but the growth in variable pay and 'at-risk' approaches would suggest that more and more organizations are recognizing the applicability in this area of the old aphorism 'do it properly, or don't do it at all'. Traditional merit pay systems often did not differentiate sufficiently to satisfy either the supporters or the critics of the concept.

TAILORED

What you do not need therefore, second, is an *off-the-shelf, merit pay system* (although as we have seen, in a number of cases UK companies are still successfully introducing merit pay and very few are withdrawing from it). Contribution-related pay is all about tailoring your approach to suit the business strategy, the characteristics, HR strategy, the people and the environment of your organization. Do you have an innovation, a service or a cost-based business strategy, or bits of all three? Are you a multinational bureaucracy or do you have a local, networked structure? Do you need fewer, higher skilled people or does competitive success depend on raising the competence and performance 'bar' of everyone? Does your employment deal revolve around an instrumentalist or a commitment-based model? What do your staff think and want? What are the different approaches used by your competitors? Which succeed and why? How well do you measure and manage performance and are you focusing on this week's sales figures in the shops, or the outputs of the new product pipeline in ten years' time? What is the communications and involvement environment?

Answers to these questions and the ways in which company, team and individual performance results, and how staff contribute to achieving those results, interact and leverage on each other, in each case, will determine the most appropriate methods for relating pay-to-performance in your own organization.

STRATEGIC

Third, pay for contribution is, in that familiar but often overused phrase, *a strategic approach to reward*. Milkovich *et al.*[15] describe the key components of the definition of strategy, all of which seem to apply with great force to paying for contribution, in terms of:

- linking into and impacting on the strategic business goals of the organization, and the competences and capabilities of employees that will support their achievement; inappropriate pay schemes, as demonstrated in the experience of pensions mis-selling in the United Kingdom in the 1990s, can destroy the achievement of business goals, or as in the case of privatized electricity company retail divisions, help put them out of business altogether;
- linking in with other aspects of the HR approach to ensure, for example, that there is no conflict between the developmental and the pay aspects of competencies;
- looking at all aspects of the 'total rewards' package, ensuring they are all appropriately aligned with each other and the business strategy; that each aspect of reward has a clear rationale and ultimate linkage to business requirements or employee needs; and that the communications and involvement climate supports your pay and reward approach; your new employee bonus scheme is unlikely to work if an employee suggests a performance improvement and gets told by his boss to shut up and get on with his job.

Ed Lawler, as we have seen, defined an effective reward approach as having three elements: a clear set of shared objectives and goals; an appropriate technical design; and effective, practical operating processes. As Thompson demonstrated so well for 1980s-style performance pay, failure typically resulted from lack of attention to, or problems in, the first and third areas, not the second. Purpose and process are critical.

Effective strategies for paying for contribution recognize the validity of this perspective. They have a clear business-related rationale and serve a stated HR and reward purpose; progress towards these objectives is monitored; they have well-designed pay methods which really do differentiate between individuals if that is the goal, or reinforce team work if that is the key to high performance; and crucially, they pay considerable attention to implementation and operation, in an increasingly devolved corporate world.

The diversity of actual reward techniques and methods resulting from this process may look complex and make our jobs as reward managers and advisors difficult, yet surely it is a healthy sign. Theories of natural selection and evolution abound in management writing at present. If one believes them, then diversity reflects natural adaptation to different environments, rather than a single route of upward progress, and so encourages the long-term survival of the fittest, as these environments change.[16]

As we have seen, a key driver of contribution-related pay, alongside the emphasis on competence-based business and HR strategies, has been the failure of traditional performance pay. This has often resulted from the application of a single, rigid model to highly diverse organizations, operating in very different circumstances. As Ledford and Moss Kanter have emphasized, many traditional pay methods are simply 'too rigid, too cumbersome, cannot keep pace with current business needs.'[17] The 'cages' of traditional pay approaches have really been severely rattled, and hence the 90 per cent of European organizations making major changes to their pay systems in the last two years, a rate of change that is forecast to continue into the millennium.

So amidst all this complexity and diversity of tailor-made and evolving reward approaches which we have illustrated in this book, within and between different organizations, is there anything else we can summarize, any other overall learning points to draw attention to, which seem to support successful outcomes and can help you on your own journey? As we have said, many of these examples of pay for contribution are too new to fully evaluate their effectiveness. More systematic research of them is an urgent priority. But some additional points we would make for those considering this path of pay for contribution are as follows.

FIVE PRACTICAL POINTERS

1. Paying for contribution, with its emphasis on how results are achieved and the future success of the business, as well as short-term results delivery, does appear *to be particularly appropriate in sectors where it is recognized that employee skills and behaviours are the key to competitive success*, such as in pharmaceutical research, computer software, management consulting companies and voluntary and care-based organizations. Applications are particularly evident for

the knowledge workers and professional staff who predominate in these sectors, and for whom conventional performance-related pay schemes have often not worked effectively. These organizations are also generally characterized by flat and flexible organization designs, reflected in broadbanded pay structures. They are 'learning organizations' with lateral and continuous employee development, characterized by an HR approach which is highly involving and devolved, focused on dialogue and HR outcomes rather than systems, techniques and 'best' market practice.

If your organization is engaged in a highly structured activity with a rigid division of labour, and the basis for its competitive success still rests on low cost leadership; or if rating-less performance management and pay scares the hell out of you, then contribution-related pay may well not be appropriate for you. A simple results-focused or collective performance reward may be best.

2. *Pay generally supports the move towards a more competence and contribution-focused organization, rather than leading the change.* All of our case studies have illustrated, except in real crisis situations, the lengthy time-scales that implementing contribution-based pay strategies takes, and the importance of supportive HR mechanisms. As we saw David Norton express it, pay is a vital supporter of business strategy, but 'serves as a reinforcer, not a leader'.

In the vast majority of US and UK examples, pay has followed on from the use of competencies for recruitment and development purposes, has followed the development of more comprehensive, balanced scorecard and value added performance metrics, and more multi-directional performance management approaches. This helps to ensure that the pay linkage does not conflict with or restrict other HR and developmental objectives, and also ensures that sufficient infrastructure is in place to support the pay system, such as that any competencies used have been well-researched, designed, tested and understood. As Mike Westcott at Guinness told us, not having this detailed preparation and experience in competencies and performance management would have been a 'recipe for disaster' in introducing pay linked to competence.

3. *All aspects of pay and reward need to be integrated* within a truly effective, contribution-related reward strategy. Not only does this enable you to leverage across the full range of employee motivations, it also ensures that there is a consistency in reward messages throughout the organization, in alignment with performance goals. We have seen that even with performance-pay incentives, effectiveness is

typically dependent on other reward and HR variables, such as a co-operative and supportive, trusting environment. This 'bundle' of rewards is critical to creating the type of employment relationship in which employees voluntarily commit to high levels of discretionary contribution, the basis for competitive success in the future.

4. *In the majority of organizations, there is still the need to consider job content and results achieved as well as competencies, base pay as well as bonus, individuals as well as teams, when paying for contribution.* Contribution-related pay is in the main not replacing traditional pay approaches but fusing with them. *Contribution relation pay, in a single phrase, is paying for the what and the how, the results and the competencies.* Such combinations can help to address both the measurement concerns of academics and trade unionists with competencies, and an excessively results-focused orientation and inherent discomfort of line managers with 'softish' competencies. How results are achieved may be a vital factor in getting better results in the future. The Birmingham and Midshires Building Society, for example, used such a combination approach, with the emphasis initially on the objectives and results aspects of performance in determining pay increases. But with greater experience and confidence in their competency framework and its assessment, the weighting is now reversed.

In terms of competencies, as Bass Brewers argues, the use of results as well means that the competency measurement need not be as rigorous as it would need to be if it were the only factor determining pay. Indeed, in a number of cases, such as the Woolwich and Scottish & Newcastle Retail, planning for the pay linkage has forced organizations to much more crisply define and delineate their existing competency frameworks. In this sense, therefore, the criticisms of competency-related pay made by Sparrow and Lawler are being turned on their head in practice, with the pay link being the driver to address inexact competency definition and measurement, rather than being the victim of it.

Correspondingly, the use of broader performance criteria and competencies can help to address the traditional failings of performance-related pay systems, particularly when applied to professional staff, as has been evident for example in the National Health Service, voluntary organizations, and local government in the United Kingdom. Paying for contribution can ensure that the organization is looking at what will bring future success, rather than just rewarding past results. As we have seen, companies such as Bass and ICL have concluded that to give base pay increases wholly for past results achieved locks a company into paying in future years for a level of performance which may not be sustained. Hence they relate base pay progression to the development and application of competencies, and reward results achieved with cash bonuses, which vary from year to year. Others use different methods, but the intention is the same.

5. Finally, one traditional management mantra which seems to maintain and enhance its relevance in these turbulent times, and applies with particular force in this area of contribution-related pay and reward, is to *keep it simple*. A number of the combination bonus schemes we saw in Chapter 6 and competency pay schemes in Chapter 4 must be bafflingly complex to the employees whom they are supposed to motivate. As Lawler says, multiple reward schemes, each with a clear purpose, may be a more effective and less risky approach.

And in terms of competencies, one UK financial services organization initially introduced competencies into its existing performance-related pay review system by asking managers to rate staff against nine competency headings and levels, which they had to select from a dictionary of over 50 competencies. The reaction was understandably negative, and the system subsequently modified. Now they are provided with pre-prepared role profiles using six competencies, selected from a list of nine core competencies. Up to a maximum of six personal objectives are also set.

Job families are one way of structuring and simplifying the process of linking competencies and pay, giving flexibility and local ownership in the competencies used, their description, and the nature of the pay link, while keeping this variety within a clear and common framework, and supporting the overall business direction. Even then, however, as at ICL, too many families and too much variation can create major management problems.

South West Electricity recently introduced a six-monthly customer service bonus, paying all staff a common cash lump sum if an index of the businesses' regulatory service standards improves. Broadbrush certainly, but probably a faster and more effective reinforcer of customer service in their circumstances than trying to assess and pay every individual according to their own customer service competence.

Heavy involvement of line managers and staff throughout the development of the system; clear and unambiguous objectives related to business and staff needs; simplification and tailoring of designs; and

423

heavy devolvement, communications and involvement in operation; these appear to be the main methods by which companies are ensuring that their contribution-related reward systems can actually work as intended. As Moss Kanter says, these seem to be fairly timeless principles of effective HR and reward management. For example, most companies appear to use between five and ten competencies for the purposes of linking to pay, which is often only a sub-set of the much broader competency frameworks that are used for a wider variety of other HR purposes in the organization. Balanced scorecards are another common method being used to structure and simplify a complex mix of performance goals. Focus and usability are keys to making the pay link effective.

Of course, the strength of competitive and environmental pressures may also determine the approach you take. We generally favour evolutionary rather than 'big bang' reward changes. The extreme wholly personal competency-related pay examples, or very high 'pay-at-risk' bonus plans we have seen, have generally been in crisis situations, or in small, highly entrepreneurial organizations. In most larger, more complex companies a balanced, longer-term and evolutionary approach, weighing up a broader range of factors which need to influence pay – affordability, relativities, performance, external market rates, and so on – is generally most appropriate. As Yorkshire Water Services told us, even in a situation or rapid change and regulatory pressure, paying for contribution was a 'business' necessity, not a threat, and represented a balance between the business need for efficiency, and 'individual needs for recognition, development and fairness'.

FOUR RESEARCH STUDIES

Academic researchers have generally not been strong supporters of performance pay, yet they make few alternative suggestions. HR managers meanwhile have often fallen prey to the siren call of competitive best practice, and implemented off-the-shelf systems with unclear goals and a lack of clear success criteria or evaluation. We would draw your attention once again to four research studies mentioned in this book that we believe have relevant findings on this subject, which will stand the test of time.

First, we saw in Chapter 2 that Ryan, Mims and Koestner[18] found that individual performance-related pay decreased motivation in a low communications culture, yet increased both extrinsic and intrinsic motivation in a high communications culture. *Remember therefore the vital role of staff communication and involvement, in creating a positive psychological contract, within which reward systems can operate effectively.*

Second, while Angela Bowey's[19] studies for the Department of Employment similarly demonstrated the importance of communications and involvement, the key message here was of the essential requirement of *tailoring your pay schemes to suit your particular organization and environment*. It was the tailoring of schemes to the strategy and culture of each organization that correlated with successful operation, not any particular type of scheme design.

Third, Bowey's research and more recently that of Milkovich and Bloom,[20] which we looked at in Chapter 3, demonstrated the importance of a strategic approach to reward, with clear reward goals, and *incorporating all aspects of the total rewards package*. The latter's research showed that the success of incentive plans depended on broader aspects of 'total rewards', particularly the culture and climate of trust, openness and communication in the organization.

And, finally, remember Ellis and Haftel's study,[21] in which matched samples of companies relying on a strong use of monetary incentives, and a heavy emphasis on non-financial motivators were compared. Success in motivating staff related not to either of the two approaches, but to the intensity with which the approach was applied. *Whatever you decide to do, do it clearly, simply and properly.*

A FINAL CONCLUSION

In conclusion, what we have described in this book may have concerned and worried you (particularly given the poor history of performance and pay management in many of our organizations): how complex an approach contribution-related pay can be; how demanding on manager's time and skills and financial resources; how loosely controlled and potentially inflationary; how disruptive to your current HR and pay administration controls and procedures. How will the unions react? What if we get an equal value claim? How do we keep the lid on costs? These are all valid questions and concerns, and hopefully we have illustrated a few answers.

But ask yourself this. Even if you are currently the world champions in your industry, in a world of seismic business shifts, in which the skills and contribution of your staff are increasingly becoming the single most important, sustainable source of competitive advantage; and in which key skill shortages are increasingly evident in many technical and professional areas, what should you be paying for? Are you in danger of losing your most competent, star players, or as has happened in parts of the financial services sector, the bulk of a very successful team by adhering to traditional pay nostrums and procedures: pay for the job, pay for results, pay control. Do you have any choice in the future but to pay for contribution? Or, as Michael Bichard[22] recently accused government departments of doing, do your organizations' current HR and reward practices, 'seek to control the brain power of their organization, not to maximize it'. Hopefully we have provided some tools, ideas, and examples to assess if this is the right path for you to be following, and how best to proceed.

As Lawler says, the key to contribution-related pay is to find the most appropriate balance 'between a focus on the overall performance of the organization and the teams and individuals within it',[23] and between the 'whats' and the 'hows' of performance. And if you agree with us, then while recognizing the supporting and reinforcing role that pay generally plays, you will also agree with the leisure company executive who told writer Chris Ashton, that 'this organization does not recognize the potential power of rewards, incentives, even benefits: they are the sleeping giants of change management levers'.[24]

Good luck!

NOTES

1. Sir John Browne, quoted in Corzine, R (1998) The knight with vision, *The Financial Times* 12 August
2. EE Lawler III in Balkin, DB (ed) (1987) *New Perspectives on Compensation*, Prentice-Hall, New Jersey
3. Quoted in Donkin, R (1998) Fighting the talent war, *The Financial Times*, 25 November
4. Coyle, D (1997) *The Weightless World: Strategies for managing the digital economy*, Capstone, Oxford
5. Todd, K (1998) A strong sense of direction, *The Financial Times*, 27 October
6. Towers Perrin (1994) *The Power of People*, Towers Perrin Research Study, October, available from Towers Perrin, London
7. Ruth Lea (1998) No level playing field for the 'Winner Takes All' culture, Letters to the Editor, *The Financial Times*, 11 August
8. Internal staff communication, in *Reward and Recognition, the Novartis Way*.
9. Timmins, N (1998) NHS set for radical overhaul, *The Financial Times*, 18 December
10. Ashton, C (1999) *Strategic Compensation*, Business Intelligence Report, London

11. Thompson, M (1998) Trust and reward, in *Trust, Motivation and Commitment: A reader*, ed SJ Perkins, Strategic Reward Research Centre, Oxford
12. P Allaire, quoted in Wilson, TB (1994) *Innovative Rewards in the Changing Workplace*, McGraw-Hill, New York
13. Ashton, op. cit.
14. Baker, G, Jensen, M and Murphy, K (1993) Compensation and incentives: practice and theory, *The Journal of Finance*, July
15. Milkovich, G and Gerhart, B (19xx) Employee compensation: research and practice, in *A Handbook of Industrial and Organisational Psychology*, eds M Dunnette and L Hough, Consulting Psychologist Press, California
16. These ideas on evolution are described in more detail in D Brown (1993/4) Lessons from the Zoo, *Human Resources*, Winter
17. Ledford, G (1996) Designing nimble reward systems, *Compensation and Benefits Review*, March/April
18. Ryan, RM, Mims, V and Koestner, R (1983) The relation of reward contingency and interpersonal context to intrinsic motivation: a review and test using cognitive evaluation theory, *Journal of Personality and Social Psychology*, **45** (4)
19. Bowey, A *et al.* (1982) *The Effects of Incentive Payment Systems*, Department of Employment Research Paper, No 36, DOE, London
20. Milkovich, G and Bloom, M (1995) Managerial compensation and social contracts, *Trends in Organisational Behaviour*, **3**
21. Ellis, LW and Hmig-Haftel, E (1992) Reward strategies for R&D, *Research and Technology Management*, March/April
22. Timmins, N (1998) Top mandarin takes government to task, *The Financial Times*, 14 December
23. Lawler III, EE (1995) Team-based pay, ACA satellite seminar programme 1 December
24. Ashton, op. cit.

Index

Triplex Safety Glass 114
trust
  basis of 293
  and contribution pay 264
  and equity 294–96
  as a factor in the success of PeRP 44
  fairness and 293–94
  justice and 296–97
  managing trust 307
  meaning of 291–92
  negative trends in 304–05
  and the psychological contract 297–99, 308
  and reciprocity 303–04
  in reward systems 292–93
  significance of 280–81
Turner, A 4, 417
Tussauds Group 320–21

Unilever 92–95

variability in base pay 175–77
Victoria & Albert Museum 246

Wade-Benson, K A 298
Waitrose 24
Watchman, J 287–88
Ward, P 258
Whole Food Markets 315
Winstanley, D 249, 262, 263
Woodruffe, C 110
Woolwich 119, 139–45, 335, 422
Workplace Employee Relations Survey (1998) 29, 287

Xerox 417

Yorkshire Water Services 24, 50–54, 417

Zeneca Pharmaceuticals 125, 246, 335

Visit Kogan Page on-line

Comprehensive information on
Kogan Page titles

Features include

- complete catalogue listings,
  including book reviews and
  descriptions

- special monthly promotions

- information on NEW titles and
  BESTSELLING titles

- a secure shopping basket facility
  for on-line ordering

PLUS everything you need to know about
KOGAN PAGE

http://www.kogan-page.co.uk